SEXUAL IDENTITIES, QUEER POLITICS

SEXUAL IDENTITIES, QUEER POLITICS

Edited by Mark Blasius

PRINCETON UNIVERSITY PRESS

PRINCETON AND OXFORD

PUBLISHED BY PRINCETON UNIVERSITY PRESS,

41 WILLIAM STREET, PRINCETON, NEW JERSEY 08540

IN THE UNITED KINGDOM: PRINCETON UNIVERSITY PRESS, 3 MARKET PLACE,

WOODSTOCK, OXFORDSHIRE OX20 1SY

LIBRARY OF CONGRESS CATALOGING-IN-PUBLICATION DATA

SEXUAL IDENTITIES, QUEER POLITICS / EDITED BY MARK BLASIUS.

P. CM.

INCLUDES BIBLIOGRAPHICAL REFERENCES.

ISBN 0-691-05866-0 (ALK. PAPER) — ISBN 0-691-05867-9 (PBK. : ALK. PAPER)

1. GAY RIGHTS. 2. GAY LIBERATION MOVEMENT. 3. GAYS—POLITICAL ACTIVITY. I. BLASIUS,

MARK.

HQ76.5 .S49 2001

306.76'6—DC21

00-056507

THIS BOOK HAS BEEN COMPOSED IN BERKELEY BOOK

WWW.PUP.PRINCETON.EDU

PRINTED IN THE UNITED STATES OF AMERICA

1 3 5 7 9 10 8 6 4 2

1 3 5 7 9 10 8 6 4 2

(PBK.)

CONTENTS

ACKNOWLEDGMENTS

MANY PEOPLE have contributed toward transforming a set of conference papers into a special issue of a journal and thence, into making this book a reality. The Center for Lesbian and Gay Studies (CLAGS) of the City University of New York first invited me to organize a conference for which some of the papers in the book were written. I would like to thank in particular, Martin Duberman, Executive Director of CLAGS when the conference took place in 1996, and also all the people, too numerous to name here, who have contributed over the years to making CLAGS the preeminent research, teaching, and public education institution that it has become.

The early work of choosing a publisher and beginning to edit this book was done during my sabbatical in 1996–97, spent at a treasured, although now defunded, residential lesbian/gay/bisexual/transgender/queer (LGBTQ) "think tank," The Center for Scholars in Residence at the University of Southern California, under the leadership of Professor Walter Williams; he now leads the ONE Institute and International Gay and Lesbian Archives at USC. Each day as I wrote, I would stop for discussion with undergraduate and graduate students who lived in the complex, scholars-in-residence from different parts of the world, and activists—including a gay leader from Los Angeles who was then in his eighties. The contribution made to my work by the intellectual stimulation, individual diversity, and beauty of surroundings there cannot be emphasized enough. The possibility for doing research on LGBTQ issues depends upon such institutions that may be community or academically funded, or both, because the many years of lack of formal support of such research (especially financial) has resulted in its disallowance. I hope that Center may be started anew, and that other such efforts, particularly *residential* research centers, may become established and flourish. In this context, I also acknowledge the institutional and personal support during this period at USC, made by Professors Judith Grant of the Program for the Study of Women and Men in Society (now the Gender Studies Program), Sheila Briggs of the Center for Feminist Research, and Eric Schockman and Michael Preston of the Center for Multiethnic and Transnational Studies, all of whom, through their affiliations, sponsored my presence there. The friendship of Martin Dupuis, then a USC graduate student and now an Assistant Professor of Political Science at Western Illinois University, has also contributed to my own intellectual development from that year and onward; I acknowledge his support and his development of the field of LGBTQ studies. Close by, at Claremont Graduate University, I am grateful for friendship and discussions with Gordon Babst, Delores Griffie, and Jean Reith Schoedel.

Back at home, I received support from several PSC-CUNY Research Awards of the Research Foundation of the City University of New York, and by release from a course at CUNY-LaGuardia through the efforts of Professor Ming Yan and the sponsorship of its former President Raymond C. Bowen.

I want to express profound gratitude to Carolyn Dinshaw and David Halperin, editors, and Jody Greene, managing editor, of *GLQ: A Journal of Lesbian and Gay Studies*. David originally gave the support for commissioning me, and then strong continuing nurturance, as editor of a special issue of that pathbreaking journal in which several of these papers originally appeared in print. Carolyn was both meticulous and wise in her final editing of the issue; in doing that, she served as my mentor in becoming an editor. I am thankful to Jody for graciously putting up with my last-minute obsessiveness, and to all three, Jody, David, and Carolyn, for helping me learn how to navigate the treacherous shoals surrounding academic egos, including my own, and thereby to allow collegiality to emerge.

Readers of all or parts of the manuscript contributed insights that helped me shape the composition of and strengthen the analyses in the book. I thank, in particular, Kathy Ferguson, Ronald Hunt, Joan Tronto, and Maxine Wolfe for their support in these areas.

I would also like to express gratitude to those with whom I worked at Princeton University Press. Malcolm Litchfield's enthusiasm in acquiring the project carried through until review of the final manuscript, when he left Princeton for Ohio State University Press's directorship. Ian Malcolm was infected by Malcolm's enthusiasm and shepherded me and the manuscript through editorial board approval. With the arrival of Chuck Myers as political science editor at Princeton, the project was adopted by another caring editor who has gently but persistently guided the manuscript to fruition as a book. Although the discontinuity in editorship happened only during the final stages, it was very anxiety-provoking for me. Each of these editors superbly managed the book's progress and gave me the confidence I needed to get through to the end. Thanks guys!

I acknowledge Rebecca Myers and Brigitte Pelner at Princeton University Press for seeing that the manuscript went through production in a smooth and timely manner, and Jennifer Backer for her patience and competence in copyediting.

Finally, I want to express my deep respect for the authors whose work is represented here. They are contributing to a new field of research, an act which may be courageous when considered in the perspective (at least) of what's happening in the United States with respect to the treatment of LGBTs by some sectors of society, including governments at the local, state, and federal level. For authors writing from a perspective outside the United States, the relationship between the (LGBT/queer) writer and societal opinion as reflected in institutional life can be equally problematic. Each of the authors, further, was accommodating with my suggestions for revision, and did not take offense when I had to badger them about deadlines. I am thankful for the dedication all authors showed over a four-year period. I surmise that editing a book single-handedly with this many authors may be as challenging as chairing a small academic department. I had to make some very difficult choices about what to include and on what terms. I learned a great deal from the process, and now that it is finished, I humbly express my gratitude to all the writers who contributed their thoughts, reevaluating them every step of the way, resulting in this volume becoming what it is.

Kudos to Brian Wolbaum, who lived with me for most of the period during which this book was being produced.

Mark Blasius
April 2000

SEXUAL IDENTITIES, QUEER POLITICS

INTRODUCTION

SEXUAL IDENTITIES, QUEER POLITICS, AND THE STATUS OF KNOWLEDGE

Mark Blasius

THE PAPERS collected here are a cross-section of contemporary political science devoted to the study of lesbian, gay, bisexual, and transgender (hereafter LGBT) political phenomena. Most of the papers were first delivered at an international conference of academic and community intellectuals, elected officials, policymakers, and community-based activists organized by the Center for Lesbian and Gay Studies (CLAGS) of the City of University of New York, February 8–9, 1996. Some of these were subsequently published as a special issue of *GLQ: A Journal of Lesbian and Gay Studies* in 1997, for which I served as guest editor. Other papers were added to the preexisting collection to round it out by subdiscipline of political science and region of the world represented. Although it is by no means exhaustive of the theoretical and methodological breadth of LGBT studies or in political science (nor of regions of the world—scholarly political studies of the Islamic world, China, Eastern Europe, and the Indian subcontinent could not be found, and one commissioned on South Africa was, unfortunately, never completed), this collection will, I hope, provide a starting point for students, researchers, policymakers, and activists to participate in this emergent discourse. LGBT political studies have already had an effect in refocusing the perennial concerns of the discipline and suggesting new ones, in creating a bridge between political science and other social science and humanities disciplines, and in providing intellectual resources for the making of public policy while originating in the social movement's critique of existing public policy and the social relations that undergird it.

In this brief introduction I would like to orient the reader in two ways. First, I will present an interpretation of the development of studies of LGBT phenomena and their effects on the discipline of political science in its theoretical, conceptual, and methodological substance, in its pedagogy and curriculum, and in the social relations that make up the discipline. These latter relations are often termed "collegiality" but they also include access to employment and consequent exercise of professional authority, reflecting the broader social problem of homophobic prejudice and discrimination. As such, any discussion of the emergence of LGBT studies in political science involves analysis of the politics of knowledge and expertise. Second, I will provide a schematic guide to how each of the papers exemplifies a focus that can inform our understanding of politics and the relationship between knowledge and politics, regardless of subdiscipline or methodological predilection. I mention as a caveat that I will base my interpretation primarily on the development of LGBT studies within North American political science; its development in other regional and national contexts, though it can be inferred somewhat from the writings included here, awaits future anthologizing.

Political science has been a bit of a latecomer to studies of LGBT phenomena, especially as compared with the humanities, but also as compared with other social sciences. Outside the academy, LGBT-oriented studies have flourished for at least a century, in an effort to influence the professionally organized production, transmission, and use of knowledge to authorize the exercise of governmental, as well as nongovernmental, power through expertise.[1] However, these studies began to enter the academy more assertively from the 1960s onward in correlation with the emergence of contemporary lesbian and gay movements and a public discourse about them, and about sexuality more generally. (Some of the work here uses the more expansive rubric "sexual minorities" to refer to collective political actors, and other work uses the more recent appellations "lesbigay" (lesbian, bisexual, and gay), or "queer" as an umbrella term—inclusive of bisexual, transgender, and heterosexually identified supporters—or to signify methodological refinement within lesbian and gay studies, or even to emphasize liberationist over assimilationist political ideology. (See the discussion of ideology especially in chapters 8 and 11.) Indeed, the title of this book is meant to indicate the coalescence of sexual identity- (and in a different but related way, gender identity-) based activism around an analytical framework suited to the politics of sexuality. The concept of queer politics is used here with qualification to avoid homogenizing the differences and specificity of the political goals of each of these identity-derived movements, hence *Sexual Identities, Queer Politics*. This introduction highlights the role of a politics of knowledge in the relationship between LGBT (now sometimes written a LGBTST, the TS indicating "two-spirit" gender and sexual identities that exist in indigenous and non-Western cultures) and queer theory and politics. Since there is still controversy surrounding this relationship, following the usage of the CLAGS conference, community-based organizations, and a number of the authors in this volume, in this introduction I will use the nomenclature "LGBT" and from here onward, LGBT/queer where it seems appropriate, even in the absence of work devoted, in particular, to bisexual specificity. One projected paper on the role bisexuals played in the politics of AIDS did not, in the end, materialize, and the absence of such work in political science generally suggests that which knowledge is getting produced, and which knowledge is not, is itself an issue for further political analysis.[2] The growth of contemporary academic lesbian and gay studies has been faster in literary and cultural studies, and although it was spearheaded in the social sciences with psychology's effort to "depathologize" homosexuality,[3] this progress was far from continuous or universal across institutional contexts even in literary and cultural studies, not to mention most other social and natural science disciplines.[4] The relationship between the production of knowledge about lesbians and gays and this knowledge's proximity to the exercise of power through expertise needs much more research. In such research, a comparison with the reception of feminist scholarship in the academy, as well as its relation to feminist activism, should be central.

During the 1970s through the middle of the 1980s, published studies of lesbian and gay politics residing within the disciplinary tradition of political science, or even those presented at professional conferences, were few and far between.[5] These latter contributions appear to have occurred first with the founding of the Gay Academic Union in New York City during the early 1970s by academicians rooted in the political organizations that burgeoned after the Stonewall riots of 1969. Paper presentations appeared sporadically at annual meetings of the American Political Science Association (APSA) as singular papers subsumed on panels devoted to such topics as "interest groups," "feminist theory," or "civil rights and liberties." (Even at the time of this writing, only one LGBT-specific piece, a review essay about some recent empirical research, has been published in the *American Political Science Review*—reflecting the degree of institutionalized knowledge after almost thirty years of academic engagement.) Corresponding to the paper presentations, there were occasional and usually fairly secretive meetings of lesbian and gay political scientists at these APSA meetings, primarily to socialize and provide shelter within an otherwise "chilly climate" at the meetings—reflecting attitudes about homosexuality within the profession as a whole, and consequent fear among lesbian and gay political scientists. It appears in retrospect that the political urgency of the AIDS epidemic and the more public homophobia it occasioned paved the way for a small group at the APSA meeting of 1988 to organize the Gay and Lesbian Caucus for Political Science. This was noteworthy not only because it was an "aboveground" meeting (at an assigned room, widely publicized in advance, at the conference site) but also because it was committed both to the creation of an "affiliated group" of the APSA led by "cochairs" (beginning with Professor Sarah Slavin and myself) who would organize panels devoted to lesbian and gay political studies for the following annual meeting and on a continuing annual basis, and to addressing other professional concerns of lesbian and gay political scientists. Since that time, the LGBT presence has increased to include a standing Committee on the

Status of Lesbians and Gays in the Profession of the APSA (established in 1992), active recruitment of LGBT research into preexisting topical sections of the association, debates about discrimination, inclusion with equal status into professional life, and curricular reform at APSA governing council meetings, (albeit slight) publication in its professional journals, and "out" lesbian and gay members on many of the other APSA standing committees as well as on the council and among the officers and administration of the association.

All of these gains are in direct parallel with (perhaps as a consequence of) LGBT struggles in "the real world of politics," in addition to professional consciousness-raising about homophobia in the context of the AIDS epidemic, mentioned above. *Bowers v. Hardwick*, the 1986 U.S. Supreme Court decision upholding the constitutionality of sodomy laws targeting homosexuals, motivated lesbian and gay political scientists in a successful effort to make the legal status of lesbians and gays in a particular municipality a consideration in the siting of APSA annual meetings. The struggle to pass federal, state, and local nondiscrimination statutes had its professional parallel in efforts of political scientists to fight discrimination in their workplaces through authoritative APSA-sponsored research and publication on the status of lesbians and gays within them. There has also been a parallel between struggles to include lesbian and gay issues in elementary and secondary school curricula with inclusion of the same in political science curricula and textbooks. The occupational and legal recognition of same-sex relationships within society was reflected in the recognition of domestic partnerships in APSA benefits programs and recommendation of the same to all employers of political scientists. In all of these cases, sociopolitical struggles were reflected in professional life through APSA-sponsored research, which then led to adoption of policies not only to *counter* homophobic prejudice and discrimination but also to include policies of *affirmative action* toward sexual minorities within the political science profession that could then be refracted back to the knowledge produced and decisions made by and effecting political scientists. Finally, and significantly for the relation between knowledge and practical politics, each annual meeting has come to sponsor a panel where local LGBT/queer activists could discuss issues and strategies—and the need for new knowledge produced by political scientists—and has provided an opportunity for the (U.S.) National Gay and Lesbian Task Force Policy Institute to recruit political scientists to work with it "think-tank style." This has become increasingly important for LGBT/queer activists as well as for elected officials, policymakers, and jurists.

One of the results of the discourse on the political that LGBT/queer studies has instigated is a refocusing of the sights of political science more generally. LGBT scholarship in political science, perhaps as distinct from that in other social sciences, has been treated suspiciously from its beginnings as not being disinterested and as being political advocacy, not scholarship or "science." Yet, it has not mattered "who" is doing research on lesbian and gay politics, as long as it is informed by the methodology of lesbian and gay studies (which in turn is a refinement of extant methodologies in empirical, comparative, historical, and normative political research); this is attested by the contributions of heterosexually identified political scientists to this volume, recalling the example of psychologist Evelyn Hooker's renowned 1960s study of healthy gay men that helped removal of the illness nomenclature within mental health professions in the United States. In addition to methodological advances, there are important theoretical advances when sexuality is made an object of political analysis.

Viewed through the lens of liberalism, sexuality has usually been conceived beyond the purview of state action in a domain of "privacy." However, LGBT/queer studies' focus on the "politics of sexuality" has demonstrated how sexual relations are one dimension through which power relations operate—power being political science's subject matter—and, as such, a dimension that implicates both practical concerns of the public interest supposedly embodied in "the state" and the analytical concerns vested in political science, which has traditionally also focused on power relations in "civil society." (See chapter 14, Badgett's essay, for studies on how power relations constitutive of heterosexism operate within "the economy.") This situation is in some respects parallel to how feminism earlier had to explicate *gender* as an object for political analysis—that is, as a construct of power relations that instantiate inequality in societies, both present and past. Indeed, other concepts from feminist analysis, such as *care* and the distinction between formal "role equity" and substantive *role change* have already and will continually reshape the boundaries between public and private that can advance analysis of lesbian and gay deprivation of status.[6] Through this challenge to the limits of liberal conceptions of the political, LGBT/queer political studies have expanded what politics is conceived to be both for liberal theory and for the discipline of political science.

At the very least, for example, this expansion may include critique of how the liberal tradition itself has reflected majoritarian tyranny that, through violence or more subtle coercion, constructs "the closet" for homosexuals and bisexuals, or a life of "passing" that has led not only to the social invisibility, but to the obliteration of minorities—sexual and otherwise—thereby disallowing entire domains of human aspiration and their cultural manifestation. On the other hand, politicization of the kind of which "coming out" is exemplary—in a sense, speaking truth to power—can render a historically specific "hard shell" of the liberal self, fundamental values (e.g., what is "family"—as relationships of care—and how should its forms be socially recognized and supported by public policies?), and individual and collective political interest that derives from such values, unstable and amenable to transformation. Further, LGBT/queer studies helps us in reconceiving the public and the private as not intrinsically fixed but as historically constructed in forms of regulation that do not simply "repress" sexuality (whether in legal prohibition or in the U.S. Congress's de-funding of a massive survey about sexuality so that scientific knowledge about sexual practices could not even be produced, much less disseminated) but regulative techniques that also "shape" sexual practices (as in the battle over the content of AIDS education and those invoking recognition of sexual health generally as a public good). Viewing the public and the private as constructed this way, rather than either essentializing or obliterating the distinction between them, can render their distinction—and liberal theory—more reflective of contemporary political realities, and thus enable more informed discussion about the desirability and limits of governmental power. Finally, students of LGBT/queer politics, assisted by the feminist tradition of theorizing the limitations of individual rights in structural economic and social oppression,[7] have conceptualized (nonprocreative) sexuality as a source of personal identity—for the intelligibility of the self (its specificity, its freedom, its subjection), with implications for individual and even group-based conceptions of "rights"—that informs participation in politics. This must thus be included in any formulation of social justice, as has already been recognized in the right to sexuality or sexual self-determination as "sexual rights" in international human rights discourse (see chapter 5).

Although I am focusing here on the dominant intellectual tradition in U.S. political science—liberalism—other intellectual traditions are equally if not more open to criticism. Conservative natural law tradition, especially as it informs right-wing religious movements to suppress homosexuals and nonprocreative sexual expression, must obviously be pushed much further by critical LGBT/queer activists and those working to change the doctrines of religion and heterosexist, patriarchal political ideologies around the world.[8] For example, British commentator on U.S. politics Andrew Sullivan, in countering knowledge about homosexuality grounded in natural and religious law (but regrounding it in natural science) proposes toleration through equal rights to assimilate into traditional social institutions such as military organizations, the Catholic Church (albeit as a sinner according to its doctrine), and the monogamous family.[9] On the other side, many perspectives on radical social change or revolution focus on a hierarchy of oppressions, with sexuality near the bottom, or the "transcendence" of homosexuality in the postrevolutionary state of affairs. Even some multiculturalist and postcolonial thought has done this (where homosexuality is seen as a disease white Western males have transmitted to colonized males), as have some Marxist perspectives on the primacy of economic exploitation, and some radical feminist perspectives that view homosexuality as epiphenomenal to gender (pointing toward the disappearance of exclusive homosexuality as a consequence of the abolition of gender).[10] Theoretical reconsideration of dominant formulations of the political, conceptual clarification reflecting the politics of sexuality, and methodological refinement resulting from this that questions both a studied "neutrality" in political science and the ethics of the intellectual within an ongoing political controversy together challenge political scientists to rethink and retool in the light of studies on LGBT/queer politics.

Nevertheless, it is still possible for opponents of LGBT/queer studies to deny not only those arguments, but the legitimacy of raising these questions at all. Thus, while LGBT/queer studies are viewed as partisanship by its opponents, these same opponents claim as a matter of academic freedom what to pursue research upon and "profess" in the sanctity of one's classroom. This position argues as though a teacher's professional development (or a student's education) excludes openness to new knowledge about human sexuality in order to protect their preconceived opinions about it; the position was taken to its absurd inverse extreme in the proposition—actually put forth at an APSA council meeting in opposition to the establishment of a committee on the status of lesbians and gays in the profession—that *such a committee would itself* "out" all LGBT political scientists and force them to do research on LGBT/queer politics![11] In the face of views such as this, LGBT political scientists have made the delicate balance between their professional commitments and personal identities exemplary for their pedagogy, and have—through the vehicles of professional organizations and their meetings—cataloged how research on LGBT/queer politics can supplement the existing research interests of political scientists and contribute to the political science curriculum.

This effort of curricular reform needs to be contextualized. A 1995 survey conducted by the APSA Committee on the Status of Lesbians and Gays in the Profession on the content of introductory U.S. government textbooks found that, after twenty-six years of institutional and extra-institutional activism (counting only that which was post-Stonewall and within established institutions of higher education), lesbian and gay politics was given no treatment in almost all of these textbooks except for an occasional passing reference. A 1994 anonymous survey of political science department chairs by the same committee found that fewer than one-third of them thought being lesbian or gay-identified was acceptable at their institutions, even though (only) slightly more than half of this cohort thought including gay/lesbian topics in a course was acceptable there.[12] In the face of these findings (and even more unsettling ones on collegiality, as we shall see), and the fact that there are likely LGBT/queer students in most political science classrooms (even though their presence there may not be as obvious as a student's racial or cultural ancestry, gender, or other social categories already recognized as relevant for political analysis), lesbian and gay political scientists have worked within their own academic, professional, and research institutions to infuse the politics of sexuality into the curriculum and expand the research horizons of the professors of this curriculum.[13] The contributions to this volume are exemplary of political scientists focusing perennial research topics through the prism of LGBT/queer politics, staking out new ground for political research, and, through curricular reform, opening up new avenues for the relationship among personal experience, social movements, and students' understanding of how social change takes place. In any case, these studies create innovative dimensions for the teaching and learning of political science.

The phrase "we are everywhere" has been a slogan, albeit one grounded in cultural and historical reality, for contemporary lesbian and gay politics. The papers collected here that represent a comparative approach to political analysis attest to this as well. In general, such analysis can compare how the various ways that cultures structure sexuality will condition whether and how sexuality will become a political issue, and who the principal actors articulating a politics of sexuality within the context of its political culture will be. The emergence of a distinctive lesbian and gay politics happened first and is the most developed in the countries of North America and Europe. David Rayside, comparing Canada, the United States, and Britain, refracts their respective governmental institutions, the dynamics and efforts of political parties—as well as those of interest groups—to control or influence such institutions, and electoral and other forms of political leadership through the prism of what he terms "sexual minority" activism. In doing so, Rayside weaves together the many threads of his published book-length study on this topic.[14] Jan-Willem Duyvendak, in comparing France and the Netherlands (that has one of the most established—defined historically and through access to the government—European lesbian and gay movements) on the conditions for homosexual issues to become political ones, concludes with striking insights about how to interpret political culture, generally, derived from these two case studies. Rayside's and Duyvendak's essays—one structural, one cultural—are exemplary of the kind of political knowledge that needs to be produced both to develop comparative political science and to enable LGBT/queer activists to work together across borders as well as to understand their own national situations better through comparison. (To be sure, both essays rely on the role of activists and on "community discourses" to develop their insights in the first place.) In the work of Juanita Díaz-Cotto we see how lesbian issues coalesced, conflictually and collaboratively within feminist movements in Latin America and the Caribbean, and their relationship both to the (only sometimes, sexually) progressive movements of the left and in the context of right-wing and state-sponsored terrorism. As distinct from the civic ideologies of Europe and North America, these lesbian-feminist movements have to rely much more on religious and national liberationist traditions for constructing their own identities to engage in a politics of sexuality—in formulating issues as well as in turning them into demands on the political systems of their respective countries. From the perspective of the politics of knowledge, something very interesting happened where the level of knowledge was very low with people denying that lesbians could even exist but where, through a series of famous feminist conferences or *encuentros*, huge curious and well-intentioned audiences learned, and the status of lesbians began to change.

An analytical bridge between the comparative study of politics and international relations can be, for example, the ways in which local cultures maintain or cede their autonomous formations through a state that acts in a world of other states, and through the interaction between cosmopolitan and national cultural values that occurs in the context of contemporary forces toward "globalization." Australian political scientist Dennis Altman writes from the interface between political sociology and personal experience to show how the identities of being "gay" and "lesbian," though inventions of modern Western cultures, have had great usefulness for organizing politically around the interrelationship of gender and sexuality in the western Pacific rim. Such organizing draws upon rich indigenous traditions of homoerotic love, is inspired by and inspires transnational networks that inform local, regional, and international politics, and is producing a significant postcolonial perspective on the relation between the personal and the political in its simultaneous resistance and co-optation of globalization. The battle between cosmopolitan gay identities and local critiques and adaptations of them that Altman chronicles (he has been a principal commentator on the relation between the local and global politics of AIDS) has also been reflected in international forums such as the UN Conferences on Population and Development at Cairo in 1994 and on Women at Beijing in 1995. Rosalind Pollack Petchesky, a MacArthur Fellow recognized for her leadership in cross-cultural scholarship on reproductive freedom, analyzes here the interaction between a universalist and cultural relativist politics of sexuality through her pathbreaking genealogy of "sexual rights" as it has emerged in international human rights discourse. Both she and Altman demonstrate how the politics of sexuality, crystallized in LGBT (but notably not "queer" in this context) organizing (but also around AIDS), raises important issues for the study of international collaboration, international political economy, international law and jurisprudence, and transnational activism in the future.

Despite the empirical orientation of much of political science, political theory has provided a fertile medium for considering conceptual, historical, and methodological issues that arise out of LGBT/queer politics. My own contribution to this volume is an attempt to consider what is at stake in politically theorizing homosexuality today. Writing at the moment some participants in LGBT and AIDS activist movements were turning "queer" into a positive, not pejorative, term of political discourse, I analyzed the historical emergence of lesbian and gay political identity, how this results in an ethical stance toward politics in contemporary liberal democracies (what I term an "ethos"), and what the broader implications of lesbian and gay politics are for what we conceive politics to be. This paper inspired a critical exchange in *Political Theory* after its publication (as that journal's first article on the subject), a portion of which, directly addressing the relationship between the politics of sexuality and the politics of knowledge, I have added to the conclusion of my chapter here. The original paper was subsequently translated into and published in Dutch and Japanese and contains a portion of the argument in my book (Blasius 1994, note 10). Paisley Currah's contribution revises the rubric that I (and other "lesbian and gay" theorists) have employed by working through the practice of gender transitivity; her analysis draws on the political experience of the transgendered and the epistemological insights of recent "queer theory." At the frontier of contemporary feminist political theory, she demonstrates the absurdities, but also the forms of oppression, that arise when judicial and legislative bodies attempt to codify the unstable relationship among sex, gender, and sexuality.

Queer theory arose in the academy in the early 1990s as a response to the post-AIDS politics of sexuality of an offshoot of the AIDS-activist group, ACT-UP, that called itself Queer Nation. It was influenced intellectually primarily by the postmodern philosopher Michel Foucault and was motivated to move beyond the immediate goal of ACT-UP to "get (anti-AIDS) drugs into bodies." Queer Nation and queer theorists took every society's structuring of sexuality as a starting point to criticize the binary opposition and consequent inequality between homosexuality and heterosexuality undergirding the economic, political, and cultural functions this social structuring of sexuality by "heteronormativity" performs. In this sense, queer theory is akin to the feminist imperative to move from analysis of male-female relationships in terms of role equity to role change I have already mentioned. But by tending toward a "single-variable" understanding of social change (even to the extent of viewing the fluidity of the distinctions among sex, gender, and sexuality through erotic desire as an independent variable) queer theory became immediately subjected to constructive but well-deserved criticism of which Cathy J. Cohen's is one of the most significant examples. Her critique of the erasure of the dimensions of race and class in queer politics and the theorizing that arose from it also articulates a framework for conceiving social justice that draws on critical race theory, but has applications beyond the U.S. context. Social justice inclusive of sexuality can only be conceptualized or enacted from explicit recognition of the relationships between sexual oppression and the oppression of other disenfranchised groups and coalition with them on the basis of our intersecting identities of class, gender, age, sexual orientation, "able"- (and desirable-) bodiedness, race, and ethnicity, among others. Any single-issue politics is not only elusive, but counterproductive in Cohen's analysis—informed as it is by her published work on the politics of AIDS within communities of color in the United States. Cohen's essay offers a clear example of the relationship between knowledge and politics, and how a politics *of* knowledge may be conceived within this relationship.

If queer theory's emphasis on the fluidity of sex-, gender-, and sexuality-based identities is qualified by a caveat against "queer-specific" in the place of intersectional analysis and coalitional politics, politically theorizing homosexuality can lead us into a methodological muddle. For example, is there a "lesbian and gay community" as is often touted in political analysis and rhetoric, not to mention an "LGBT/queer movement"? How could the political phenomena we use these concepts to describe constitute a collective actor? A research population? A hypothetical voting bloc? Further, when the relationship between objective observer and research subject is problematized—as is particularly evident when research involves acknowledging one's own "multiple identities," how does this transformed relationship affect basic issues of epistemology in political analysis? Robert W. Bailey's work addresses some of these issues on the borderlines among LGBT/queer studies, urban politics, political methodology and social theory, and U.S. political processes and government. His writing over the past ten years, of which the contribution here is a distillation, breaks new ground for our understanding of how to conceive "LGBT" or "queer" (or again, as Rayside puts it, sexual minority) identification as a variable in political research, how sexual identity informs political attitudes, whether and how these coalesce to effect public policy, and, on this basis, why we need to revise standard formulations of the relationship among economic, social, demographic, and ideological variables in understanding urban politics in the United States.

One of the most obvious (because it has been strategically central) but nonetheless scarcely analyzed (by traditional political science) domains of U.S. politics is the relationship among courts, legislatures, and LGBT movements. A number of such public policy issues as civil rights laws, criminal justice, domestic partnership and other laws relating to marriage and family construction, funding for sexual health-related research, disease prevention, and care, and censorship have been or are, all on the political agenda at various stages in jurisdictions with very diverse political geographies. Rebecca Mae Salokar stakes out this terrain in a comprehensive and theoretically rich essay that contributes to our understanding of federalism and intergovernmental relations, constitutional law and jurisprudence, and state and local politics, implying greater understanding, as well, of practical strategies for LGBT populations and their advocates. Her analytical distinction between a social movement and interest groups can inform current debates about the extent to which a progressive social movement can be "privatized" and its consequences. Future empirical research, theory, and strategy might take up the question toward which she points in the closing pages of her paper. This concerns what the relative significance is of (1) shopping around among the states for the best legal forums as compared with the relationship between public and private law (resulting in the "hole in the bottom of the bucket" in states with sodomy statutes), and even family law; and (2) discovering other arenas for progressive political change from an LGBT and queer perspective, recognizing both the promise but also the limits of the logic of the law in "litigating" social change.

In a more cultural interpretation of U.S. politics, Timothy E. Cook and Bevin Hartnett revise conventional wisdom about the relationship between the media and social movements and expand upon Cook's prior contribution to political science—conceiving the news media as a "fourth branch of government." Their analysis of the news coverage of lesbian and gay issues in the United States during the 1970s opens up the field of political communication with new understandings—not only about stereotypical depictions of a minority group in the mass media and popular culture, but also about how these images reflect the degree and form of access *to* the media and other forms of political communication by gays and lesbians, and the consequences of differential access for any minority group's political goals. Their approach—textual interpretation of the news media, analyzing presentation of the social debate about the status of gays and lesbians and relating this to intramovement debate about strategy and goals—is also a convincing example of political science's role in analyzing what has come to be called the "culture wars" in the United States. These are, at least in part, wars over how the "soul" of U.S. democracy is more and more being specified through the production of knowledge about identity and diversity in the context of increasing cultural pluralism, how this knowledge is institutionalized in curricula, writing, and popular culture (including the news media), and the relationship of this to expertise in the making of public policy and the exercise of culturally inflected power in society.

Mention of the U.S. culture wars leads to a final group of essays, those directly concerned with the politics of knowledge from the perspective of sexual identity. Leonard Harris's paper, written for this volume, analyzes the "politics of" both the historical cover-up of Harlem Renaissance philosopher Alain Locke's homosexuality and contemporary efforts of LGBTs and queers to reclaim his biography and his social and political philosophy. Harris's "outing" of Locke will undoubtedly be found controversial, is long overdue, but is ultimately about the politics of knowledge. This includes the conditions under which knowledge gets produced (both by Locke himself and by others invoking his knowledge and life), how knowledge gets used, and how the production and use of knowledge is dependent on changing, but distinctively *political*, circumstances, here arising from the growth of LGBT movements in coalition with those among African Americans.

Alan S. Yang's essay considers whether the changing views of experts change the views of the public at large. He refutes some of our "received wisdom" about the top-down relationship between elites and masses in political opinion formation through his study of the American Psychiatric Association's 1973 decision to declassify homosexuality as a mental illness as compared with the U.S. federal government's 1993 decision to retain its ban against service by gays and lesbians in the military. While his conclusions may be interpreted ambivalently (what happens when there are dueling experts, a point raised in the next essay about the scientific claims of rightwing so-called experts on homosexuality), Yang points out that analyzing the politics of what counts as knowledge and how this comes about is indispensable if we are to understand how public policy "happens" and how LGBTs or other movements can change policies.

Following from this, a final area of political analysis that bridges all subfields of political science is what *kind* of knowledge is relevant to politics, who can supply it, and why knowledge of a particular phenomenon is claimed to be able to improve the social order. In other words, what *is* expertise and *why* has a politics of sexuality come to rely on it? While every author in this volume would probably have different answers to these questions, M. V. Lee Badgett, a professor of public policy as well as founder and executive director of a lesbian and gay "think tank," addresses these issues in a historical and comparative ideological context. This type of discussion is crucial for LGBT and queer politics because "the truth" has perennially been constructed about sexuality (through natural law, scriptural interpretation, sociobiological science, etc.) and used to deny people basic human rights and dignity; indeed, a politics of knowledge is about the status of truth in relation to how power is exercised. With Badgett's synoptic approach to this relationship between knowledge and politics, we come full circle, returning to the last of the questions posed at the outset of this introduction.

How do the social relations constituted by the discipline of political science reflect both what we conceive political knowledge to be, and how to get it, and what the relationship is between political science and the society in which we live? Recall that APSA survey on the status of lesbians and gays in the profession of political science. More than 80 percent of department chairs surveyed did not know of any lesbian or gay applicants for jobs in their departments (identified by research, advocacy, or self-identification) and an equal number did not know whether such identification would be considered an asset, liability, or neither. (Indeed, there was a seeming filtering-out process, a striking decrease in the percentage of people who anonymously identified themselves on the general surveys of political scientist students and faculty as gay, lesbian, or bisexual from among undergraduates, to an almost statistically insignificant number self-identifying in the political science professoriate.) What are we to make of these findings for our collegial relations, our professed liberal equality, and our own role as "guardians"—at least on the intellectual and pedagogical levels—of such pluralist, egalitarian ideals?

Is this collegial situation solely a reflection of LGBT political scientists' being closeted, or does it also reflect how interpersonal expectations coded as "professional" standards—of conduct, pedagogy, and research interest—not only coerce LGBT people into invisibility, but disallow research into the politics of sexuality, both of which have consequences for sexual choice and its implications for human happiness more generally in our society? For example, those same surveys also indicated a substantial number of gay and lesbian (as well as some heterosexual) political scientists who either have been discouraged from taking up research questions related to the politics of sexual orientation or refrain from such research for fear of not being taken seriously as scholars. A perspective from the sociology of knowledge would suggest that the tendency to subsume lesbian theory under "feminist theory" and the existence of more writing about LGBT politics by (white) gay men indicate the more precarious professional status of lesbians as both women and gay and that both lesbians and gay men of color must cope, as Leonard Harris's analysis here suggests, with invisibilization within LGBT movements as well as by the discipline of political science to the extent the latter is dominated through prejudices exemplifying gender, sexual, and racial stratification.

Perhaps another angle from which to view an interconnection between the social relations of the discipline of political science and social relations in the larger society is through a comparison with the discipline of psychology. While the professional organization of U.S. political scientists (APSA) has maintained a position of neutrality with respect to public policy issues, the American Psychological Association (APA) has sanctioned the use of its name and has allocated association resources to employ psychological expertise for *direct* intervention into the political arena to ameliorate the status of lesbians and gays in U.S. society in order to counterbalance the many years psychology was used as a means of oppressing gays and lesbians, as the APA has articulated the reason for this policy. Ultimately, it is at least a matter of professional ethics[15] with appropriate institutional support at levels of collegial relations, conditions of employment, and the norms articulated by national and international professional organizations to create a different climate for research and teaching about the politics of sexuality. And the climate within political science (although obviously reflecting) can then serve as a *condition* for more general social tolerance, and even egalitarian social justice, as is suggested by the writers in this collection. To be sure, the papers in this volume can be conceived only as keys to open the gate to this new ethos of professional life; it will only be through their use—in political science discourse and professional recognition, in advancing LGBT- and nonLGBT-specific research and methodology in the discipline, and in teaching—that the gate may be opened and we can bridge the gap between political knowledge and the better society we often profess to be the value of our pursuit of knowledge.

If, as I suggested earlier, we take some of our cues from the relationships among the feminist movement, feminist scholarship, its degree of its acceptance within the academy, and feminist knowledge's infusion back into general social relations, we might gain insight into the relationship between the politics of sexuality and the politics of knowledge. Rather than conclude this introduction with a list of avenues for future research in LGBT political science, I will suggest that the "paradigm shift" in feminist political science from "women and politics" to "gender politics" has its parallel in what is happening now in the shift from the study of lesbian and gay (or LGBT) politics to studying the politics of sexuality, that "queer" evokes.[16] Sexuality—indeed, the distinction among sex, gender, and sexuality, as well as the emergence of a new sexual ethic that has implications for morality and law—has become a part of our political universe, even if some of us want to disguise this fact with a historically misconceived and arbitrary distinction between public and private. This is attested to by social movements that force reconsideration of the knowledge we use in order to govern ourselves. So the essays in this book, while written in the genre of political science and philosophy, could only have been written but for the movements that enabled the knowledge to be produced, and that motivate the writer to engage in a dialogic relationship with movement participants. These LGBT/queers not only enabled the knowledge, but will use it, criticizing and reformulating it again, in order to affirm sexuality as a central component of the lives of individuals, of the relationships in which they are engaged, and of the collectivities through which they govern themselves as individual members and as a polity.

Notes

1. See the chronicle of this in *We Are Everywhere: A Historical Sourcebook of Gay and Lesbian Politics*, ed. Mark Blasius and Shane Phelan (New York: Routledge, 1997).

2. For an example of bisexual specificity in another discipline, sociology, see Paula Rust, *Bisexuality and the Challenge to Lesbian Politics* (New York: New York University Press, 1995). There have been no studies, to my knowledge of the political science literature, of bisexual politics except the selection by Stacy Young, "Dichotomies and Displacement: Bisexuality in Queer Theory and Politics" in *Playing With Fire: Queer Theories, Queer Politics*, ed. Shane Phelan (New York: Routledge, 1997), 51–74.

3. The classic study of the politics of homosexuality in the mental health professions is Ronald Bayer's *Homosexuality and American Psychiatry: The Politics of Diagnosis* (Princeton: Princeton University Press, 1987, orig. pub. NY: Basic Books, 1981); for, specifically, how psychology developed, there is a documentary film (available in VHS), *Changing Our Mind: The Story of Dr. Evelyn Hooker*, by Richard Schmeichen, released in 1991 by Frameline, 346 9th Street, San Francisco, CA 94103 (phone 415-703-8650). No single work has traced the development of lesbian and gay (or queer) studies across the academic disciplines; however, some representative collections include the following. For literary and cultural studies: *The Lesbian and Gay Studies Reader*, ed. Henry Abelove, Michele Aina Barale, and David M. Halperin (New York: Routledge, 1993), and issues of the *Lesbian and Gay Studies Newsletter* of the Gay and Lesbian Caucus of the Modern Language Association, published by Duke University Press, Durham, NC, can serve to trace this development historically. In

history: *Hidden from History: Reclaiming the Gay and Lesbian Past*, ed. Martin Bauml Duberman, Martha Vicinus, and George Chauncey (New York: New American Library, 1989). In economics: *Homo Economics: Capitalism, Community, and Lesbian and Gay Life*, ed. Amy Gluckman and Betsy Reed (New York: Routledge, 1997) has several essays that deal with the development of lesbian and gay studies in that discipline. In anthropology: *Out in the Field: Reflections of Lesbian and Gay Anthropologists*, ed. Ellen Lewin and William L. Leap (Urbana: University of Illinois Press, 1996). In sociology: *Queer Theory/Sociology*, ed. Steven Seidman (Cambridge, MA: Blackwell, 1996); and *Gay and Lesbian Studies*, ed. Henry L. Minton (Binghamton, NY: Haworth, 1992) provides an overview across disciplines on pedagogy and methodology, institutional reform, and cross-national analysis of the development of lesbian and gay studies. See also Blasius and Phelan and the citations of Lee Badgett's essay in this volume for the earlier "homophile studies" and their predecessors in the nineteenth and early twentieth centuries.

4. See Toni A. H. McNaron, *Poisoned Ivy: Lesbian and Gay Academics Confronting Homophobia* (Philadelphia: Temple University Press, 1997) for a study of lesbian and gay academics with at least fifteen years of experience in their profession. Progress has been uneven and slow, despite the star system of relatively few contemporary "out" academics.

5. At the risk of exclusion through inclusion, based solely on my own knowledge I will list as exemplary Dennis Altman's *Homosexual: Oppression and Liberation* (New York: Avon, 1973) and papers presented at American Political Science Association meetings by Kenneth Sherrill (1973), David Thomas (1984), and a presentation by Altman in the mid-1980s enabled by a protest by lesbian and gay political scientists because a gay male's perspective had been denied from representation on a panel on the politics of AIDS. Lesbian political scientists, to the extent they felt "safe" in a very chilly professional climate even for women, engaged in scholarly exchange through the Women's Caucus of the APSA during this period.

6. See Joan C. Tronto, *Moral Boundaries: A Political Argument for an Ethic of Care* (New York: Routledge, 1993), especially her analysis of the political implications of care in the context of AIDS at pp. 106–7, for a suggestive extension of this concept specifically to gay male politics; further extension to transgender, lesbian, and bisexual issues awaits analysis. See Joyce Gelb and Marian Lief Palley, *Women and Public Policies: Reassessing Gender*, rev. and expanded ed. (Charlottesville: University Press of Virginia, 1996) for the latter reconceptualization of role; the timeworn sociological concept of "the homosexual role" first theorized by Mary McIntosh (see McIntosh, "The Homosexual Role" and "Postscript: 'The Homosexual Role' Revisited," in *The Making of the Modern Homosexual*, ed. Kenneth Plummer [London: Hutchinson, 1981]) might be a starting point for extension of this concept, for example from equity (assimilation) to change (what is called gay liberation).

7. See, for example, Iris Marion Young, *Justice and the Politics of Difference* (Princeton: Princeton University Press, 1990).

8. Principal examples of this are Margaret Thatcher's advisor Roger Scruton's *Sexual Desire: A Moral Philosophy of the Erotic* (New York: Free Press, 1986), and more recently Oxford professor John Finnis, "Law, Morality, and 'Sexual Orientation,'" *Notre Dame Law Review* 69 (1994): 1049–76, who wrote a brief in support of the judicial voiding of Colorado's law prohibiting discrimination against homosexuals.

9. See Andrew Sullivan, *Virtually Normal: An Argument about Homosexuality* (New York: Knopf, 1995), although his thoughts on living as a gay Catholic are scattered across many of his other writings. Within the spectrum of activism, efforts to transform doctrine on homosexuality are many within the Protestant denominations, Roman Catholicism, and Islamic and Hindu thought.

10. A critique of postcolonial thought on this basis may be found in Leela Gandhi, *Postcolonial Theory: A Critical Introduction* (New York: Columbia University Press, 1998); contemporary critique of homophobia in the Marxist tradition is legion ranging from Marcuse to Foucault, but see the selections in Blasius and Phelan, *We Are Everywhere* in response to Cuba's anti-homosexual revolutionary policy (406–12) and those by Hocquenghem (412–19) and Mieli (438–43); for critiques of heterosexism in feminism, see the analyses by Morgan, Nestle, Califia, and the transgendered Lesbians for Justice in *We Are Everywhere* as well as my critique of Catherine MacKinnon in Blasius, *Gay and Lesbian Politics: Sexuality and the Emergence of a New Ethic* (Philadelphia: Temple University Press, 1994), chapter 2.

11. The author witnessed this at an APSA Council meeting in 1991, but the comment does not appear in the published minutes of that meeting.

12. Presentation and analysis of the data of surveys both of department chairs and individual political scientists has been published as APSA Committee on the Status of Lesbians and Gays in the Profession, "Report on the Status of Lesbians and Gays in the Political Science Profession," *P.S.: Political Science and Politics* 28 (September 1995): 561–74. Kenneth Sherrill of Hunter College/CUNY possesses the raw data from the survey.

13. For example, the APSA committee has made regular presentations to the program committee for the APSA annual meeting to "raise consciousness" about the relevance of research on lesbian and gay politics to the established sections (subfields) of the discipline and has an ongoing project creating curricular guides for infusing LGBT issues into teaching a wide number of topics in political science. Similar intitiatives, including the holding of conferences for a multidisciplinary professional and activist audience (such as the one this reader represents), have been undertaken at my own university and many others, as well as through both general and LGBT-specific research institutions (see Badgett's contribution to this volume).

14. I am not citing the related work of each author in this introduction. Readers might consult the bibliography of each essay, the author's biography, or more general tools of bibliographic research to find them.

15. For a perspective on what professional ethics might entail, see the program of action drawn up by the APSA Committee on the Status of Lesbians and Gays in the Profession based on its survey findings, and adopted by the APSA Council in 1995: "Working Towards an Inclusive Political Science: Recommendations for the American Political Science Association," available from APSA, 1527 New Hampshire Avenue N.W., Washington, D.C. 20036.

16. An example of this is the recent change in the Western Political Science Association's (in the United States) renaming of its section on lesbian and gay politics to "Politics and Sexuality." I view this not as merely becoming more inclusive, but as reflecting a transformation in epistemology for understanding what is political.

PART ONE

COMPARATIVE AND INTERNATIONAL

PERSPECTIVES

ONE

THE STRUCTURING OF SEXUAL MINORITY ACTIVIST

OPPORTUNITIES IN THE POLITICAL MAINSTREAM:

BRITAIN, CANADA, AND THE UNITED STATES

David Rayside

THERE ARE SIGNS of political access, uneven and inconsistent, across the landscape of mainstream institutions. Gays, lesbians, and bisexuals contest elections, and sometimes win; they meet openly with presidents and prime ministers, with cabinet members and senior officials. Activists operating both inside such networks and outside have also pushed their issues onto the political agenda. HIV and AIDS constituted a policy wedge in some jurisdictions, but activist pressure in other issue areas—policing, criminal law, censorship, family law, and more general issues of discrimination—built up through the 1980s.[1]

Since the early 1990s especially, there have been gains in public policy and the courts. Even right wings of governments have had to come to terms with the distinctive features of AIDS in ways that have increased governmental attention to sexual diversity.[2] Legislative and judicial prohibitions of discrimination on the grounds of sexual orientation have proliferated, and a number of the most obviously oppressive patterns of policing have been successfully challenged. The first steps toward statutory and administrative recognition of same-sex relationships have been taken by some governments and many private institutions.

But if the late 1980s began a period in which the political access of lesbian, gay, and bisexual activists was most noticeably improving, it was during that same period that the limits of their influence were also most apparent. Legislation was far more often pondered than delivered, even when promising only the simplest right to equal treatment. When statutory measures were suggested or introduced, they were greeted with orchestrated protests of virtually unprecedented scale, and with expressions of raw hate normally thought beyond the limits of political acceptability. Political parties claiming allegiance to principles of equality would find themselves more riven by angry division on this issue than any other.

As U.S. activist Urvashi Vaid has argued, "[G]ay and lesbian people are at once insiders, involved openly in government and public affairs to a degree never before achieved, and outsiders, shunned by our elected officials unless they need our money or votes in close elections."[3] As she and others have pointed out, access to political processes, and benefits from whatever favorable decisions emerge from courts, administrative agencies, and legislatures, are not evenly spread across lines of class, race, gender, and region. Only some places, and within them only some strata, have experienced the extraordinary progress that seems to have been effected since the late 1960s surge of gay and lesbian activism.[4]

Elected politicians and their parties are reluctant to take unequivocal stands on sexual orientation even when they are favorably disposed to do so. In most countries, they are still prone to view gay-positive measures as vote losers, or at the very least as likely to provide opponents with effective weapons for negative campaigning. They tend to see pro-gay sentiments as strong only for gays and lesbians themselves, largely outweighed by those who are strongly antipathetic.

Understanding the extent to which gains have been made in and through the political process and the factors behind such gains requires acknowledgment of the distinctive characteristics of lesbian and gay activism, and of the highly variable balance of factors favoring and impeding progress on sexual orientation issues. It needs sensitivity to some of the broader debates over inequality and political influence, but also detailed inquiry into what happens when gays, lesbians, and their issues enter mainstream political processes.

It also requires attention to the ways in which political and social contexts shape opportunities for social movements to make gains. This is a point that can be addressed through comparative analysis. Britain, Canada, and the United States have important common roots in cultural and political heritage, and continuing similarities in legal frameworks and government structures. In popular attitudes and institutional practices related to both gender and sexuality, there are still traits that distinguish the Anglo-American world from other industrialized countries. Understanding each of these countries helps illuminate the difference that geography, demographics, political structure, and party system can make in comparison within and beyond the "North Atlantic triangle."

Activist Engagement with the State

In the 1990s, more activists than ever recognized the inevitability of engagement with state institutions, even if many were still wary of assimilation or cooptation. From its very beginnings, the modern lesbian/gay movement has contained divergent organizational and strategic orientations, as well as contrasting views on the scope of the political agenda.[5] Strategic debates have centered on the merits of direct action and confrontational strategies on the one hand, and tactics that work with and, if possible, inside existing political and legal structures on the other. There have also been more specific strategic debates over the questions of working across party lines, participating in elections, endorsing particular candidates, and organizing grassroots networks.

There are somewhat distinct debates that have pitted those who prioritize democratic processes and representivity over those less preoccupied by such matters. Differences of view exist over whether or how far groups should move in the direction of specialized and hierarchical roles. Debates and conflicts recur over how to counter the tendency of movement organizations to be unrepresentative on gender, race, class, and other lines.

And again there are debates distinguishable from these over the ultimate objectives being sought by activist mobilization, pitting those who seek a radical transformation of social constructions of sexuality and gender, and of patterns of oppression in general, against those who seek entry to and acceptance in the existing political and economic order. Closely associated with this is the issue of whether the movement should focus exclusively on issues explicitly taking up sexual orientation, or broaden the agenda to take in other dimensions of political and economic marginality. There are also differences of view between those who believe that gays and lesbians are as "normal" as heterosexuals and deserve acceptance precisely because they are like everyone else—taxpayers, loyal citizens, parents, spouses—and those who assert that they are different, perhaps subversive of dominant social codes and gendered "normality," and that they have a right to be so. And then there are those who reject or wish to undermine the boundaries that distinguish gay or queer from straight.[6]

There is a tendency for the strongest adherents of narrow reformist objectives sought through cautious nonconfrontational means to be those who already have a modicum of standing in and access to existing political institutions. These circles, more than other parts of the activist movement, tend to be dominated by white men, so that debates over strategy and goals are inevitably infused with considerations of gender and race, and at least implicitly of class.[7]

The modern history of lesbian, gay, bisexual, and transgendered activism, as of political mobilizing on other issue fronts, can be written in terms of the tension between and ambivalence over "liberation" and "legitimation."[8] In this dichotomous view, the province of "mainstream" politics is that of activists who seek only incremental reform to ease the integration of sexual minorities into established systems, and who do so through hierarchical and bureaucratic structures and traditional lobbying. Some activists would see the development of the movement since the late 1960s as a shift in the balance away from those with a broad and transformative vision to those more tied to the pursuit of narrow objectives within the political mainstream. They would see the outburst of groups like ACT-UP and Queer Nation as rooted in the radical and confrontational oppositionism of the early 1970s, impatient with the accommodation and assimilation of the movement's mainstream.

From the beginning, though, the debaters over strategic and ideological orientations did not always fall into two neat camps. There were those who sought quite conventional ends by unconventional means, and those who used tactics that fit very comfortably with existing political norms but with radical end goals that envisaged undermining those norms. Even the most radical of gay political agendas included as many calls for legislative reform as for transformative change. The totality of exclusion of sexual minorities from full political citizenship gave prominence to demands for civic rights that were couched in the traditional language of liberal democracy. What was characteristic of the time is that most activists, from a wide range of ideological perspectives, believed that focusing on mainstream political processes was unproductive. The complexity of ideological and strategic drives that motivated early gay and lesbian liberation politics did not undercut the confrontational impulse of a movement that arose in the midst of the large-scale wave of protest politics in the late 1960s and early 1970s. Even after the passing of that wave, the ferocity of attacks by police authorities and the impermeability of mainstream politics to gay and lesbian pressure retained the strength of an oppositionist relationship to the state within most activist networks.

In a number of liberal democratic countries, major public policy openings and judicial opportunities became visible only in the mid-1980s, in part a function of strengthened lesbian, gay, and bisexual communities, in part a result of the policy wedge provided by AIDS, and in part because of the inroads established by other rights-seeking groups. During this period, a number of centrist and left parties took their first steps or developed more expansive views on sexual diversity. However, the shift toward the mainstream for sexual minority activists is not simply a function of new openings. It also reflects an activist agenda that has moved from simply wanting state institutions to "keep out" toward a politics that seeks more positive state policy engagement with gay-related issues. Activists of the 1960s and 1970s were more likely to see legislatures, the courts, and the police as oppressive of sexual minorities and therefore to be kept at bay.

With the spread of the AIDS epidemic in the 1980s, activists recognized the indispensability of government intervention and public funding, without necessarily abandoning their wariness of state regulation of sexuality. At the same time, the ongoing institutional and cultural development of gay and lesbian communities produced a more assertive sense of entitlement, as well as political disquiet at the absence of the most basic of the civil rights accorded other citizens in liberal democratic regimes. Lesbian involvement in AIDS work, and the expansion of the gay agenda to include relationship recognition, were among the factors that increased the numbers of women active in those parts of the movement working inside the political system. Within the political structures being targeted, of course, male dominance has been and remains the norm, as it is among those activist groups closest to them, but recent campaigns in Canada, Britain, and the United States illustrate important shifts in gender balance. Much less change is evident along racial lines, not least because of the correlation of race and class in all three systems and the tendency for political access to be highly structured along social class lines.

Finally, the preparedness of the radical right to target gay issues, particularly in the United States, added to the urgency of activist work in mainstream political institutions. Its declaration of "cultural war" on those few gains that had been won in the previous decade, and on those few legislative allies who talked in pro-gay terms, removed what little choice there was to stay removed from the legislative and partisan fray.

Lesbian and gay entry into mainstream political processes has occurred along a number of fronts. One is the pursuit of legal cases through the courts, long a prominent feature of social movement activism in the United States but increasingly common in other countries. Another is the establishment of a lobby presence to pursue objectives within legislative and administrative channels. Another is the creation of networks and institutions within political parties. And finally, there is direct intervention in election campaigns, with a view toward bolstering individual candidacies or thrusting particular issues into the light of public debate.

From the end of the 1980s on, in the three countries being examined here, enormous activist resources have been poured into legislative battles where gay and lesbian rights were at stake. By the mid-1990s, activists working for change on this front were starting to be seen as legitimate players inside party and government arenas to which they had had only partial and sporadic access before. In a number of countries, there were gay and lesbian groups operating within parties across a large portion of the political spectrum, as well as autonomous groups devoted exclusively to influencing governments. Some such developments were more advanced in the United States than elsewhere, but they were evident in countries with very different political systems. In a few instances, gay men and lesbians themselves had become legislators or appointed officials, or had come out as such having entered the political arena without being open. Mass media reports increasingly talked of gays and lesbians being able to exercise political muscle.

Social Movements, Parties, and Governments

The prominence of the roles played by the "new" social movements that have emerged or reemerged in the last quarter century has attracted a considerable analytical literature. Some movements within this amorphous category attract adherents to particular issues—environmentalism, peace, alternative health. Others are framed by the rights of an identifiable group—women, racial and ethnic minorities, Aboriginals, people with disabilities, sexual minorities.

For many observers, the term "social movement" itself suggests the mounting of disruptive challenges as part of sustained collective action on the part of people tied by feelings of deep-seated solidarity or identity.[9] A strong current in the analysis of such movements is the belief that they represent challenges to existing political patterns, largely excluded from the political mainstream.

Some writers have seen in them a revival of the sort of radicalism that was once characteristic of the labor movement (the militancy of which was also reviving as part of the larger wave of protest in which new social movements arose). But there was also a widespread belief in these new movements' acting as conduits for new kinds of belief systems that broke with earlier waves of mobilization—centered on the quality of life and new forms of community rather than on issues related to the distribution of material gain. The fact that some new social movements rejected hierarchical and bureaucratic organization is seen as a sign of renewed interest in democratic participation and a rejection of ossified and indirect representational systems. Closely allied to these views is the argument that the rise of these movements is part of a large-scale shift away from "fordism"—the industrial and political structures characteristic of modernism, based on mass production and delivery of uniform goods and services to an undifferentiated population.[10] Some writers influenced by one or another variant of postmodernism see in the development of such movements an attempt to radically undermine the universalism underlying the entire historical period stretching from the Enlightenment to the twentieth century.

The development of gay/lesbian activism includes characteristics that may be more widespread among newer than older movements. Certainly a number of the issues gay activists raise are themselves new as politically contested issues (sexual orientation is an obvious example). Like some other new movements, their agendas also cut across class lines to some extent, even if most of their recruits and advocates come from those whose class positions give them a modicum of status and privilege. Born too, as they were, in a period in which there was growing cynicism about legislative and partisan politics, and in particular about the utility of relying on left parties to effect major change, movements such as this tended to organize autonomously of state institutions in general, and political parties in particular. The American political arena has always had autonomous groups competing with parties as representative of public opinion and as brokers in the policymaking networks. But even in European systems more fully dominated by party opposition, the period beginning in the 1960s witnessed a growing challenge to party dominance—and certainly to the established patterns of party opposition.[11]

However, the evolution and present character of lesbian and gay movements, like those mobilizing around other relatively new causes, suggests that the analytical literature on new movements overgeneralizes. Those writers who claim that such movements represent challenges to dominant political ideas and established processes understate the ideological variety within them and the preparedness of significant numbers of activists to work within the systems of elections, parties, legislatures, and bureaucracies should opportunities present themselves.

Some observers of new social movements argue that all social movements go through a cycle that often begins with radicalism and unstructuredness and proceeds toward institutionalization. Some of these believe that such shifts undermine activist potential for effecting significant change.[12] Institutionalization, and increased insinuation to state policy networks, are regarded as dislodging social movements from their grassroots base and as inevitably co-optive. There is also a growing legal literature questioning the costs and the worth of depending on a system of laws and judicial institutions framed by narrow liberal conceptions of equality.[13] Feminist adherents to this view point to the extent of accommodation to prevailing (and inegalitarian) legal structures in the drafting of ostensibly reformist statutes.

These writers, along with those who once claimed that new social movements represented radically different forms of political action, have paid insufficient attention to the sheer inevitability of engagement with the political mainstream for any movement that is provided with openings to parties, legislatures, or government departments. The story of the first decade of the AIDS epidemic, no matter how frustrating, illustrates the indispensability of engaging with state authorities when opportunities present themselves.[14] Connections to partisan and legislative politics are as critical as those to other parts of the political system. However much the established patterns of legislative and electoral politics have fallen into disrepute, political parties will continue to be the principal means by which elections are organized, legislative business managed, and governments sustained.

In a number of countries, including the three used here as illustrations, lesbians and gays have gained unprecedented access to these political domains. But exercising influence is a quite different matter and subject to special circumstances. Often enough, movement activists are minor players in a game still shaped overwhelmingly by considerations of party advantage and personal prejudice. Lobbyists are expected to play by preexistent rules of the game that can separate them from their own constituencies, and yet those same activists are expected to be able to mobilize support from that constituency in sufficient numbers to register with political decision makers.

Determinants of Activist Influence

There are major theoretical differences over the susceptibility of liberal democratic regimes to organized social movement pressure. Liberal or pluralist analysis will tend toward a view of the political decision-making arena as a relatively level playing field, with success or failure largely dependent on the resources available to a group or movement and the skill applied to mobilizing them.

A variety of socialist and radical analyses, on the other hand, see the state as an interlocking array of governments, courts, parties, and administrative structures firmly enmeshed in, and defensive of, dominant interests and ideas. The socialist view sees free-market entrepreneurs, and particularly large-scale capital, as the most clearly dominant; some feminist analysis sees the maintenance of a free-market system as intertwined with the retention of highly gendered family structure. A number of theorists see the regulation of sexuality as equally embedded, some tying such regulation to the needs of capitalism. Much of contemporary "queer" theory is informed by Foucauldian ideas of heterosexual dominance being enforced by a wide range of institutional and discursive practices, with the state very much implicated in marginalizing difference.[15] A number of writers acknowledge contradictory patterns in the needs of capital and in state regulation—recognizing that the urbanization and consumerism of the late nineteenth and early twentieth centuries created openings for the development of gay and lesbian identities even while repressive regimes were at their height.[16] But they are still largely pessimistic about the possibility of effecting significant change, and in particular through existing political institutions.

I attach credence to critiques of liberal democratic regimes that see the state as upholding deeply structured patterns of inequality, but that also see contradictory roles in the functioning of state institutions that create openings for challenge within those institutions. In any event, I would argue the issues raised by gay and lesbian activists are not as central to the interests of the powerful in the political and economic arenas as those raised by social movements that challenge the distribution of material advantage (movements based on gender, race, labor, and third-world development) or those that confront disfunctions in the system of production itself (movements based on environmental concerns). They encounter an elaborate legal and administrative web reflecting traditional conceptions of gender, sexuality, and family, but change even on that front is possible.[17]

To accept the view that a number of the social movements that emerged or resurged in the last quarter century can become players inside liberal democratic systems, and that they do, at least on occasion, exercise influence over governmental and legal outcomes, is to lead naturally to the question of what factors make a difference. Other writers have talked of two clusters of factors that make sense—resource mobilization and opportunity structure. Though some analysts consider these as embodying competitive explanations, both categories refer to movement characteristics or circumstances that are essential to consider in evaluating the reasons for success or failure.

Resource mobilization includes not just the number of movement adherents, financial resources, technical networks, and media facilities, but also the skills required to deploy them. Groups must not only be able to marshall resources on a scale sufficient to be noticed, but must build a certain policymaking capacity of their own. This they must do in part to gain credibility with their own constituency and the media, but also to gain entry into the "policy communities" in fields relevant to their mandates. This may well require a degree of institutionalization—the development of specialization, experience, and clear lines of responsibility.

These are resources that few groups can marshall in significant amounts. Even on a level playing field, a single large corporation in Britain or the United States can easily spend more on a single advertising campaign than all lesbian and gay groups combined, over several years. Business groups and individual corporations benefit additionally in a climate in which the interests of private investors are thought to be coterminous with the national interest. Many social movements, representing the already marginalized, face the disadvantage of a playing field tilted against them. In addition, they face difficulties establishing resourceful centers at the national or regional levels, when the grassroots from which they spring are so localized.

The lesbian and gay movement, particularly in the United States, has moved substantially toward the creation of political institutions armed with resources targeting the political mainstream at the national level. The Human Rights Campaign is largely preoccupied with maneuvering inside national institutions, as are national organizations focusing on AIDS/HIV. (The National Gay and Lesbian Task Force devotes significant resources to the mainstream, but has a wider strategic ambit.) All have grown considerably in size and expertise since the late 1980s. In Britain, the Stonewall Group has acquired visibility and to some extent legitimacy, marshalling not as many resources (budgets, members, staff) as its American counterparts, but with more success in establishing linkages to a cross-country constituency.

The internal cohesion that is conducive to movement success is often difficult for new social movements to attain, and gay and lesbian groups provide illustrations. Social movements are often divided over the scope or radicalness of the political agenda, and over the utility of pouring substantial resources into working within political institutions. And then the very process of engaging in that work will sometimes exacerbate the divisiveness of that very project. For example, legislatures are highly ritualized and demand substantial conformity from their members and those seeking to lobby those members. The buildup of financial bases, specialized skill, and war-ready structures are all critical to work within the mainstream, but may make more difficult the retention of the critical distance or wariness that is so much a part of social movement history.

Increased access to established political processes almost inevitably highlights the contradictory impulses toward the mainstream characteristic of social movements. The greater the access, the greater the potential divide between those who are inclined toward and knowledgeable about politics on the inside, and those who are not, even when there is little to choose between their ideological outlooks. In the aftermath of defeat of the 1993 attempt to lift the U.S. military's ban on lesbians and gays, and the 1994 effort in Britain to equalize the age of consent for homosexual and heterosexual activity, acrimonious conflict arose between activists over the way in which pressure was mobilized and in some cases on the value of focusing on mainstream processes. This was to some extent a conflict between insiders and outsiders, though the boundaries between the two are quite different in these two countries. There are often class, ethnic/race, and gender dimensions to such divides, though the 1990s have seen a substantial increase in the number of lesbians visible in mainstream activism.

Resources, including the capacity for policymaking, are not countable in absolute terms, of course, since their weight must obviously be calculated in relation or comparison to the resources mobilized by opponents, each side weighed in light of whatever biases are entrenched in the existing legal and political system, and reproduced by incumbent policymakers. The resources that can be marshalled by the American gay and lesbian movement are hugely more impressive than those mobilizable by virtually any other such movement in the industrialized world, even on a per capita basis. Any analysis of the political significance of such resources, though, must take into account the extraordinary resources of the American religious right and anti-gay segments of the secular right.

Some interests (corporate, for example) are so powerful in liberal democratic systems that they can shape the policy process in a wide variety of political circumstances, with governments of diverse political stripes. Social movements representing the marginalized operate on an entirely different level, generally able to exercise significant influence only when the circumstances are right. The range of allies is important for social movement success, although account must be taken of the strength and legitimacy of the particular allies on each side and the effect their support may have on engendering mobilization among opponents. The notion of "opportunity structure" takes in such factors as the openness or permeability of the political system, the extent of centralization or decentralization of the regime, the relationship between executive and legislature, patterns of political oppositions and party cohesion, the nature of the electoral system, and the capacity of courts to challenge governmental action, the support for rights claims available in the existing legal environment, and the array of media voices.[18]

Lesbian and gay groups in a centralized parliamentary system face a much more impenetrable state system than do their U.S. counterparts, but can benefit greatly in the unlikely event of an unequivocally gay-positive government. A gay movement with few resources devoted to traditional lobbying can exercise influence in the equally unlikely event that there is no party ready to play on anti-gay sentiment. In decentralized regimes, gay and lesbian groups locked out of one level of government may have opportunities to develop inroads in others. In regimes with strong courts and constitutional protections against discrimination, such groups can circumvent the avoidance patterns of elected politicians. A strong right-wing media can undermine even the most resourceful of movements; pro-gay media can propel even a weakly organized movement onto the political agenda. In a general way, the proliferation of power centers increases access but reduces the opportunities for effecting major change at a single go.

These are not simply fixed elements of the institutional structure with which social movements interact. They certainly include stable aspects of the constitutional order that can ease access or create leverage. But they also include variable factors in the political process—shifts in party composition and leadership, changes in judicial interpretation—some of which of course are subject to influence from the longer-term activity of social movements themselves. Particular characteristics of the political structure within which a movement mobilizes can sometimes work favorably and at other times unfavorably. A centralized regime with power highly concentrated in the leadership of the governing party can be enormously advantageous when allies are in power and disadvantageous when they are not.

Social movements will often benefit from the political support of a particular party, but even that kind of opportunity can have a double edge. The unequivocal support of a small party might do little except provide occasional visibility for the group's demands inside the legislative arena. (The pro-gay stands of the federal New Democratic Party in Canada and the Liberal Democrats in Britain illustrate the point.) Similar support from a larger party may well be more useful, but can also induce its principal opposition to exploit that issue in the electorate and, if successful, to create substantial nervousness about proceeding with the issue.

A legal apparatus or statutory system that enshrines discrimination against sexual minorities may stymie social movement success in effecting change within the political system. (In most countries, for example, the privileging of heterosexual relationships over same-sex relationships is reflected in dozens and sometimes hundreds of laws.) On the other hand, the obviousness of the ill-treatment by governments ostensibly wedded to liberal democratic norms of civic equality can help in mobilizing constituencies that might otherwise be complacent. (The activism motivated in Britain by a 1994 challenge to starkly unequal ages of consent is an illustration.)

Favorable public opinion is an obvious asset for any movement seeking political change, but it is elusive. On a range of equity issues, a population may well be very favorably disposed to general prohibitions on discrimination, but more than prepared to agree with specific discriminatory acts when they are sustained by prevailing prejudice or stereotype.[19] Public opinion is also filtered through the media and often substantially shaped by the way in which protagonists shape debate. In any event, overall public opinion will often matter less than those currents of belief that are actually translated into letters, phone calls, and visits to politicians.

For reasons tied to public opinion, the availability of allies, the legal system, and the pattern of party oppositions, some issues are "easier" than others. Leaving aside AIDS-related matters, gay and lesbian activists have generally not faced the barriers that women and some racial minorities have confronted in trying to increase social spending and modify the play of the free market. The issues have often been starkly simple and almost costless, entailing the removal of discriminatory statutes or the addition of provisions in existing laws to prohibit discrimination or combat anti-gay violence. (Relationship recognition has provoked concerns over costs in the U.S. system, but largely as a result of the unusual American health-care system. In Canada, Britain, and most of continental Europe, the costs of extending "spousal" benefits to same-sex couples are extremely modest.) Some of these issues focus on formal discrimination—taken up and resolved in relation to other social groups long ago. But all sexual orientation issues run up against formidable disapproval of homosexuality itself, still vocalized in raw hateful terms that are widely used outside and within the political class. In broader circles, they also face enormous resistance to even talking about gay issues. The antipathy and fear at the root of such resistance is particularly pronounced among men, making most political institutions particularly unreceptive.

The dramatically increased capacity of highly educated, professional gay activists working in lobbying organizations like the Stonewall Group in London and the Human Rights Campaign in Washington risks opening up a divide between those lobbying within the political mainstream, locally based grassroots activists, and the larger constituency both claim to represent.[20] Both groups have made important steps to secure the involvement and leadership of lesbians as well as gay men, and both are more likely than traditional interest groups to work toward inclusiveness on racial terms. But the skills and resources required for the work they do inevitably shapes their organizational cultures in class and cultural ways. The very preoccupation with legislative and governmental lobbying can also lead to an exaggerated faith in the power of law to effect genuine equality. This risk may be especially acute in sexual minority movements, given the absence in many jurisdictions of even the most elementary civil rights protections.

All of these factors come into play when gays and lesbians set out to influence policy processes. Particular factors will operate more forcibly in some circumstances than others. Even within a single political system, the factors influencing success or failure in one case will vary from those at play in another.

Political Contexts

The institutional and partisan settings in which lesbian and gay activists operate profoundly shape the social movement itself and the opportunities for progress. The commonalities of legal and political tradition in Britain, Canada, and the United States, and the activist contact among the three countries, might suggest that sexual orientation issues play out in similar ways. In fact, activists work inside very different institutional settings, with quite different political party and media forces to contend with. The particular structure of opportunity provided to the U.S. movement is very different from that facing the British and Canadian movements.

Britain

Britain has long provided lesbians and gays with enormous impediments to change within the party system, more so in the legislative and governmental system. In the course of the 1990s, openings to reform increased the incentives to engage in mainstream work, with only modest returns through to the end of 1999 but with the prospect of additional movement under the Labour government of Tony Blair.

Political power in Britain has long been highly centralized, though Scotland and Wales now have their own assemblies. The powers wielded independently by county and local government are modest, and their exercise is entirely at the whim of the central government. The extent of control from the government at Westminster was illustrated by the 1988 Local Government Act, passed at the height of Thatcherism. It required local authorities to submit a number of services traditionally offered by local administrations to competitive bidding and limited the criteria that could be stipulated for successful contractors. That legislation also contained Section 28, which forbade local authorities from engaging in activity or providing funding to schools that "promoted" homosexuality.[21]

Power is also highly concentrated in the hands of the political executive. The British parliamentary system seats almost all legislative authority in the House of Commons, relegating only minor power of adjustment and postponement to the House of Lords. The fact that the government of the day emerges from the lower house and must retain majority support in it helps ensure the discipline of both the governing party and those that oppose it. The cabinet derives considerable leverage over the legislature as a whole, and governing party members in particular, by its dependence on majority support for survival, although its power derives as well from the prerogatives it has inherited over time from the Crown. Cabinet control over the administrative system can never be as complete as the formal relationship would suggest, but civil servants have less room for policy entrepreneurship than in the more fragmented and politicized U.S. system.

The prime minister is overwhelmingly the most powerful member of the cabinet, not least because of strong norms of cabinet solidarity that constrain dissent. Recent prime ministers (including Conservatives John Major and William Hague and Labour's Tony Blair) have had to endure periods of sniping from backbenchers and even from within the cabinet, particularly when the party itself is suffering at the polls, but open dissent generally arises on only a narrow band of issues (most recently related to the European Union) and diminishes only modestly the first minister's dominance. Factoring out the vast differences in the power of the United States and Britain internationally, the U.S. president has far less policy leverage than the prime minister.

Power within all three of the most important parties is highly concentrated in the hands of the leader, though to some extent in the hands of other members of the "front bench." The pressures for solidarity in the legislature are crucial in sustaining this power, but so is the conduct of elections. Campaigns are focused almost entirely on party programs, with the leaders' campaigns dominating media coverage and determining the vast majority of constituency outcomes. The virtues or failings of local candidates have only a modest impact on electoral outcomes. Individual M.P.'s will often express themselves freely within the party caucus, but will then be forced to toe the party line in public debate and legislative voting. What dissent there is remains largely behind closed doors and has little opportunity to translate advocacy for social movement interests into legislative initiative.

The leaders of parties other than the government party have very little influence over the legislative agenda, except through their capacity to hold the government to account in Parliament and through the media. Government bills take up the vast majority of the House of Commons timetable and are virtually guaranteed of passage intact. Committees exercise influence over such bills only around the fringes, and almost invariably only at times when the government is prepared to concede amendments.

This is a constitutional order, then, with relatively few points of access for social movement activists. Major change through either legislation or administrative action requires the government to side with the activists, and there are few opportunities for dissenters among government ranks to assist them in creating pressure for change internally. The partial decriminalization of male homosexual activity in 1967 was made possible only by the Labour government's agreeing to the allocation of parliamentary time for a "Private Member's Bill." An almost-successful 1994 attempt to equalize the ages of consent for homosexual and heterosexual activity depended on the Conservative government's being open to a parliamentary amendment on the subject and prepared to allow a "free" vote (without the application of party discipline). The late 1990's election of a Labour government expanded opportunities for change, but still within a system that is tightly controlled by the prime minister. This system creates few incentives for the development of very large organizations devoted primarily to political lobbying. Prior to the 1990s, gay and lesbian activists had engaged in some lobbying, but it was only at the turn of the decade that a permanently staffed national organization was created to focus on the legislature and government at London. The Stonewall Group expanded through the 1990s and increased its visibility in the press and government. But limits on its access points and on its leverage in an institutional framework such as the British means that it is still small by comparison to its U.S. counterparts.

British legal institutions and jurisprudence provide few incentives for gays and lesbians to attach the importance to litigation that their Canadian and especially their American counterparts do. There is not the same protection for individual or group rights as in North America, and the deeply entrenched tradition of parliamentary sovereignty makes British judges reluctant to challenge statutes or question political decisions. Gays and lesbians have resorted to European law, for example to challenge the military's ban on homosexuals and the inequality in age of consent for sexual activity, but the institutions are cumbersome and the jurisprudence not yet clearly on the side of rights-seeking groups.

In Britain, too, ideas of tradition and continuity have considerable hold, accentuating anxiety about social change. It is easy to overstate the peaceability of British political history, but there is a good deal of continuity in comparison to other countries in the industrialized world. This is an environment in which dissident political movements and cultural expressions can survive and even prosper, but are generally contained within a larger set of norms and institutions that avoid radical social and moral breaks with the past.

The British system is dominated by centralized political parties, creating major incentives for lesbians and gays to organize within them. The Conservative Party became a more unequivocally neoliberal party under the leadership of Margaret Thatcher than it had been until the 1970s. Though not as much as the Republican Party in the United States, it has retained some currents of social conservatism and some preparedness to use the instruments of state authority to regulate morality, as was evident in Section 28. Under the leadership of John Major in the 1990s and more recently William Hague, the Conservative Party has been somewhat less restrictive in its views on sexual orientation. This, along with greatly increased lesbian and gay community visibility in Britain as a whole, has created room for high-profile activism by the Tory Campaign for Homosexual Equality (TORCHE), though this has hardly transformed the party's stance.

The Labour Party was based on an industrial working-class core, but from the mid-1980s on, under the leadership first of Neil Kinnock and then Tony Blair, it has shifted its emphasis away from that constituency and toward the political center. Both its traditional constituency and its current centrism create caution around questions of gender, race, and sexuality, although in the 1980s and 1990s its party policy became officially supportive of a number of equity claims, including those demanding an equal age of consent, a repeal of Section 28, a prohibition of discrimination based on sexual orientation, and other positions advanced by lesbians and gays within the party. Gains in official policy were in large measure the result of work by the Labour Campaign for Lesbian and Gay Rights, especially in the early and mid-1980s, and by Stonewall activists in more recent years. But such activism had only modest impact on the parliamentary party until the 1990s.

The Liberal Democratic Party was formed in 1988 as a result of alliance between the Liberal Party, Britain's third party for much of the twentieth century, and a social democratic breakaway from the Labour Party. It may well have the strongest record of supporting gay and lesbians causes, the product of activist pressure applied within the Liberal and then the Liberal Democratic apparatus. But its electoral strength, and in particular its small legislative contingent, substantially weaken its voice in the British system as a whole.

The prominence of party-based activism in Britain has only recently translated into electoral work. The centralization and relative impermeability of the party system limited opportunities for lesbians and gays to create their own candidacies, or to extract policy commitments from local candidates independently of their central parties. The Stonewall Group now prepares election guides evaluating parties and suggesting questions to ask in candidate meetings. But this is modest engagement in comparison to the vast resources and energy poured by U.S. national groups into their more permeable, and expensive, electoral system.

Labour M.P. and now cabinet minister Chris Smith was one of the world's first openly gay national legislators when he came out in 1984. Since first elected, he has played an invaluable role in speaking forthrightly on sexual orientation issues, this in a legislative arena traditionally unfriendly to such voices. But his influence was long hemmed in by the Conservative Party's hold on government and control of the legislative agenda, and by wariness of "controversy" in his own party's leadership. He had virtually no capacity for the sort of legislative entrepreneurship that is part of the role of American legislators. As a minister in the Blair government elected in 1997, he has an influential voice on the inside, but is subject to even more stringent requirements of party discipline than apply to M.P.'s.

The importance of parties in the British system and the historical legacy of ideological divisions in British politics more generally create significant divisions within the gay and lesbian movement. Since the last century, Britain has had a strong socialist current represented to some extent within the Labour Party, but more prominently in some of the unions, and in a good deal of extraparliamentary social movement activism. A number of activist groups during the 1970s and 1980s were heavily influenced by left socialism. In the 1990s, ideological radicalism became less prominent, but the direct action politics of the group OutRage includes elements of it, along with widespread suspicion of mainstream political processes.[22]

The period since 1990 has seen periodic reduction in the tendency toward polarization in British activism. The campaign mobilized on behalf of an equal age of consent in late 1993 and early 1994 demonstrated unusual cooperation between lobbyists and street activists, and between gays and lesbians in different parties. But fissiparousness was evident almost immediately after the defeat of equality, with activists in each party blaming other parties, and those in mainstream and confrontational groups each claiming that their strategic course was now the only logical route.

The size and centrality of London in British social, economic, and political life make the formation of activist groups easier than in many capital cities. But the maintenance of groups engaged in mainstream political processes is more difficult, in part because of ideological and partisan disputatiousness, and in part because of the difficulties of access presented by the cohesive and impermeable institutional order. The Thatcher government's determination to weaken both labor unions and local government reduced even further the opportunities available for social movements to gain access to policymaking networks.

In the aftermath of the repressiveness of the Thatcher years, the British lesbian and gay movement has increased its political visibility in parts of the political mainstream that had previously been closed to it. Once sporadic lobbying from the outside became more continuous in the 1990s, evident in well-organized campaigning over the age of consent, highly publicized court cases challenging the military ban and other forms of discrimination, and regular statements made to politicians and the press about the need for equality. The Conservatives' hold on government from 1979 to 1997 did not provide many opportunities for change, but even the cautions and centrist Labour government has created some openings for reform. The prospects for lesbian and gay influence are augmented by the relative weakness of their opponents.

There are religious fundamentalists among Protestants, Roman Catholics, Jews, and adherents to the Church of England. But they operate on nothing of the scale of their American counterparts, and their political rhetoric is widely condemned as extremist. The Roman Catholic Church was effectively subdued as a political force during the sixteenth and seventeenth centuries, and its numerical size is not great enough to act as a counterweight to political marginality. In such circumstances, the leading representatives of the Church have few incentives to be outspoken and confrontational. The Church of England is characterized more by internal division than by assertive intervention in political debate, and is especially divided over homosexuality. Its voice is in any event weakened by low levels of religious practice.

One of the largest impediments to progress remains a tabloid press that plays on the sorts of sexual and racial anxieties fed by the religious and political right in other countries. There may be no other country in the industrialized world with as powerful a right-wing sex-and-scandal-driven press as there is in Britain, and none in which anti-gay sentiment has played such an important role. There are highly respectable media outlets that include gay and lesbian content to a considerable degree, and more positively than any counterparts in North America, but they do not yet counteract the dampening effect of the anti-gay sentiments still evident in the gutter press, the power of which rests partly on massive circulation dwarfing that of the quality press.[23]

Sexual minority activism certainly has access to important allies outside of parliamentary politics, and to some extent inside, but until now it has faced a political order heavily slanted against change with few windows of opportunity for favorable legal or legislative decisions. Activist engagement with state institutions has been recently sustained in the face of considerable challenges and made more difficult still by the deep divisions of party and ideology among movement activists.

The mainstream political work of a group like Stonewall is under enormous pressure to accommodate to the norms and rituals of a highly tradition-bound legislative system. It is therefore easily separated from more confrontational extraparliamentary forms of activism embodied in OutRage. The separation between these different courses of political action is often exacerbated by social-class differences between those who move comfortably within the halls and committee rooms of Westminster and those who do not.

In such a setting, the formation and endurance of these two groups is itself remarkable. The fact that they have attained enormous visibility within their own constituencies and in the mass media is a testament to the skillful marshalling of limited resources by each. They have placed sexual orientation issues firmly on the national policy agenda even while a Conservative government was in office. Both Stonewall and OutRage are distinctive products of the British context, but have exploited to the maximum the limited political space available to them.

Canada

The Canadian political context provides gay and lesbian activists few opportunities and motivations for institutionalized engagement with mainstream legislative and partisan processes (outside of AIDS), but it provides other supports for effecting change in state policy toward sexual minorities. There have been important opportunities, affording groups armed with small-scale resources a modicum of influence over outcomes.

Canda's decentralization is the institutional characteristic most starkly contrasted with that of to the U.K., from which "British North America" inherited so many institutional characteristics in the nineteenth century. The Canadian federation is almost unrivaled in the extent of jurisdictional devolution to regional governments and continues to move in the direction of even greater decentralization. The ten provinces have almost complete control over education, health policy, and social welfare, and their regulatory control is at least as extensive as that of the government in Ottawa.

The criminal law is entirely within Ottawa's jurisdiction, including a variety of statutes regulating sexuality. The federal government appoints most judges. In contrast to that of the United States, Canada's court system is a unified one, culminating in the Supreme Court of Canada. On the other hand, the provinces are responsible for the administration of justice and for most prosecutorial decisions. Family law and a variety of other matters affecting relationship recognition are also under provincial jurisdiction.

Governmental decentralization reduces the incentives for and the capacities of gays and lesbians to maintain large national organizations, except as in the case of AIDS, where government funding for such organization has been available. The difficulty is reinforced by very strong regional attachments, intensified by the vastness of the distances. Linguistic duality also separates the French-dominated province of Quebec from the other provinces, all but one of which (New Brunswick) are overwhelmingly English speaking.

Within each level of government, the parliamentary system leads to a concentration of authority in executive hands similar to that in Britain, creating the same disincentives for large-scale commitment to ongoing political lobbying. The dependence of governments on legislative majorities leads to firm executive control over the parliamentary agenda and very high levels of party discipline. As in Britain, backbench legislators (not in the cabinet or the front ranks of the opposition parties) have only modest power and little independence. As much as in Britain, and for at least as long a time, election campaigns have focused on the party leader, with even local media attention concentrating overwhelmingly on the national or the provincial campaigns organized by the central parties. Within each level of government, the prime minister or premier may well have political leverage inside both the government and the governing party unrivaled by chief executives in any other industrialized country.

This creates a complex institutional framework for gay and lesbian activists. A multifaceted policy area like AIDS might well sustain long-term engagement with government institutions, but in other issue areas there are few openings and rationales for large-scale lobbying organizations. The maintenance of any national activist presence is difficult, the federal government having as constrained a jurisdictional field as it has, located in a medium-sized city dominated by government. National organization is made that much more difficult by the thinness of population spread across great distance and by the expense and difficulty of operating in two official languages. In recent years, Equality for Lesbians and Gays Everywhere (EGALE) has grown in visibility not only within federal government circles in Ottawa, but also in activist networks across large parts of Canada. It has shown considerable skill in applying pressure, offering advice, and attracting media coverage, but with very modest resources and a paid staff made up of only the executive director.

On the other hand, decentralization and regional differentiation create opportunities in some jurisdictions even when they may be unavailable in others. Advances in AIDS policy were made possible, to some extent, by political openings created in one or two provinces and in the local governments in a couple of the country's largest cities, even at a time when the federal government was irresponsibly inactive. Civil rights protections for gays and lesbians in Canada as a whole were advanced by openings at the provincial level first in Quebec (1977), then Ontario (1986). The addition of sexual orientation to provincial human rights codes in those two jurisdictions helped spur activists and policymakers elsewhere to similar action.

Canada's party systems are more volatile and discontinuous from one level of government to another, reducing the attractiveness of intraparty work to gay and lesbian activists. Voters can be faced with a set of parties that is different at a provincial election from that which faces them at a federal election, or equally likely with a party standing for a platform entirely different from that presented by its federal counterpart. Electors will often vote for different parties in federal and provincial ballots, and in any event Canadian voting patterns within any level of government have long been as volatile as in any industrialized democracy. Most local elections in Canada are not fought on party lines, limiting the continuous visibility and prominence of parties.

Until recently, most of the federal and provincial party systems in Canada have not included an aggressively anti-gay party—this, too, reducing the incentives for gays and lesbians to participate in partisan politics. Up to 1993, the Canadian political landscape at the federal level was dominated by two centrist parties, the Liberals and Progressive Conservatives (or Conservatives), with little to nothing that differentiated them consistently over the postwar period. In the 1980s, the Conservatives shifted toward the neoliberal right, though with somewhat less right-wing moralism than their British counterparts and much less than American Republicans. They did nothing to advance equality for gays and lesbians while in power from 1984 to 1993, but did little to undermine it. The Liberals have at times represented a center-left reformist alternative, but they have always brokered a wide range of regional and ideological interests, and on balance in recent years have shifted toward the neoliberal positioning of their Conservative predecessors in government. On questions of gender, race, and sexuality, the party's contingent representing moral conservatism is significantly smaller than that of the Conservatives. From 1993 to 1996, the federal liberals enacted two gay-related bills—a hate crimes bill and legislation adding sexual orientation to the Canadian Human Rights Act—though each was a step of modest proportions. In 2000, they enacted legislation granting widespread recognition to same-sex couples, but only after being forced to by the courts, and only with a provision securing the heterosexual definition of marriage.

The social democratic New Democratic Party was for decades Canada's "third" party. It has at times occupied power in three of the western provinces and, during the first half of the 1990s, in the province of Ontario, but has never risen above minor party status in Ottawa. Of the three traditional parties at the federal level, it has had the longest-standing and relatively speaking the most solid commitment to the rights of lesbians and gays.

The 1994 and 1997 federal elections left the NDP and Conservative Parties with much reduced parliamentary contingents. They also elevated two new parties to the status of official parties in the House of Commons. The Bloc Québécois campaigned on platforms centered on Quebec sovereignty, with a majority also favoring a number of moderately social democratic stands on social issues, including homosexuality. The Reform Party, heavily concentrated in western Canada and nonmetropolitan Ontario, represented a neoconservative mixture of free-enterprise economics and morally conservative social policy. (It has recently changed its name to the Canadian Alliance.)

Like their British counterparts, Canadian parties are less permeable than American parties. In any event, the practical benefit of links to a party vary so completely as a function of its being a government party or not that long-term connection is risky. Of the long established parties, the New Democrats would be attractive to many gay and lesbian activists, but it has had a chance at governing in only a few provinces. The fact that the centrist Liberal Party includes some politicians with a degree of sympathy to the causes represented by new social movements also means that activists have an interest in avoiding too strong an affiliation to the NDP.[24] And since local politics in Canada is generally not structured on partisan lines, there is less draw of local activists into party folds.

To the extent that Canadian activists have become involved in electoral politics, it has been more often at the local level, in candidacies within areas of Vancouver, Toronto, and Montreal with residential and commercial concentrations of gays and lesbians. There have been openly gay politicians like the federal NDP's Svend Robinson who have attracted sexual minority support, but not on the scale of their American counterparts.

Svend Robinson's preparedness to champion sexual minority causes from his first election in 1979, and even more after his coming out in 1988, did build for him an enormous following among gays and lesbians across the country. His standing was partly based on the energy with which he defended these and other causes, but also on his readiness to break the norms of party discipline in publicizing his views. Respect for him in the activist movement crosses party lines more than would be true of his counterparts in Britain and the United States. But except for a brief time in 1995 when Robinson ran for the leadership of his party, his high standing in the activist movement has not been accompanied by particularly strong engagement with partisan or electoral politics within the movement.

Where gay and lesbian entry into the political mainstream has become markedly more pronounced in recent years has been in the courts. The legal framework within which political groups operate in Canada has shifted dramatically since 1985, in ways that create substantial incentives to engage in the sort of litigation that has characterized American social movements. The 1982 Charter of Rights and Freedoms, and in particular the equality rights section that came into force three years later, entrenched rights in a constitutional document that stood over the enactments of all legislatures. The Charter's prohibitions on discrimination (mainly contained in Section 15) are wider-ranging and more flexible than those in the U.S. Bill of Rights and more open for use by groups other than those most watchfully protected by U.S. courts. Equity-seeking groups (and their opponents) that previously had only modest reason to go to court now have very strong reasons to consider litigation among their options. Although it did not name sexual orientation specifically among its designated groups, the wording of the section was almost immediately being interpreted by courts as implicitly including protections for gays and lesbians.[25] Recently, the Supreme Court of Canada has made clear that the Charter prohibits discrimination against same-sex relationships, and has forced sweeping legislative change.

Pro-gay forces in Canada face opposition of course. Religious groups are more prominent and influential in Canadian politics than they are in Britain, but less than those in the United States. The Roman Catholic Church has the largest number of adherents, but is not a unified force. The hierarchy in Quebec has been relatively liberal since the 1960s and is in any event politically weakened by the religious abstinence of the vast majority of French Canadians and the considerable suspicion of church intervention in political life. The church hierarchy in the rest of Canada has very right-wing elements (for example in Toronto), but is itself highly variegated, with a highly diverse population of adherents.

Most of the mainline Protestant denominations are moderate in their political leanings, the largest of them—the United Church—relatively progressive on gay-related and other social issues. Protestant fundamentalism has been growing in English Canada and is able to feed off American televangelic broadcasting so readily available to most Canadians. Like the U.S. fundamentalists, they have targeted pro-gay initiatives in recent years and are able to mobilize letters and phone calls in numbers that have few precedents in Canadian politics.

The strength of regional and linguistic divisions, though, makes the organizing of a cohesive religious right as difficult as the maintenance of coherent national organizations for other social movements. In Canada, too, the discriminatory judgmentalism in much of the right's rhetoric, and the American influence so transparent in much of it, exposes it to charges of extremism in at least some political circumstances.

Overall, the Canadian political system has somewhat more opportunities than that of the British for mainstream political entry, and more opportunities to make gains. Although within each political order there are strong British elements that prevent easy access for all but the largest and most privileged, gay and lesbian rights groups have gained an entry point, and in some respects a degree of legitimacy, since the enactment of the Charter. Governmental decentralization creates alternatives for groups locked out of one level, in those issue areas in which more than one level of government has jurisdiction, particularly in regions with stronger than average progressive political traditions at provincial or local levels.

The energies of Canadian groups are spread over three important levels of government and vast distances, of course. Compensating to some extent is the fact that they are less divided over either strategy or ideological vision than are their British counterparts, and less riven by differences in strategy or party allegiance than are Americans.[26] Division there certainly has been, over gender and race, for example. As in other social movements, gay and lesbian groups also include activists influenced by socialist or other frameworks oriented to radical transformation alongside liberals who believe in the attainability of equality within existing institutions. The contrast with Britain lies partly in the fact that the ideological range is not as great, not as likely to coincide with social-class differences, and not as regularly translated into particular strategic preferences.

In Toronto, for example, the relationship between AIDS Action Now and AIDS service organizations has little of the explosiveness that has recurred in the relationship between ACT-UP and AIDS service organizations in the United States. When human rights work has been mobilized in Canada, there have been only modest versions of the divisiveness that has occurred in Britain (and institutionalized in the often antagonistic relationship between Stonewall and OutRage).

Relatively small population size reduces the potential for activist groups to divide infinitely on ideological fissure lines. There is also less resistance to entering into mainstream political processes. State authority has been more often marshalled for progressive policy ends in Canada than in the United States, and in the Canadian socialist left there is a stronger tradition of conceiving of important gains within the existing institutional fabric than in either Britain or perhaps even the United States. In grassroots gay and lesbian networks, there is less of an antistatist current than in the United States, with its much more powerful individualistic culture.

United States

The American political system has provided the most sustained incentives for lesbian and gay groups to participate in mainstream partisan, electoral, legislative, and judicial processes. For that reason it has encouraged institutionalization at the national level, and in some places state and local levels. But it is also the system in which progress is most challenged. The American polity is the most fragmented of the three and creates the strongest incentives for even the most skeptical of social movements to participate in mainstream institutions. In contrast to Britain, incremental gains are easier at one level of government or another. But large-scale changes are as difficult as those cautious founding fathers intended when they institutionalized complexity.

In all branches of government, and at three jurisdiction levels, opportunities abound for rights-seeking groups to make at least modest gains, and abandoning such fields risks leaving the way clear for opponents. Federalism creates a degree of state-level autonomy that proliferates openings to the political mainstream. Even if state governments have less tax room or jurisdictional breadth than Canadian provinces, they do have more fully autonomous legal systems. Municipal government also has greater autonomy in the United States than virtually any other system in the industrialized world, creating both opportunities and barriers for such groups, depending on the political climate of the locality.

Washington is still a significant site of political intervention. The federal government is a much more substantial player in domestic politics than its Canadian counterpart, and the superpower status of the United States provides the national capital with an aura of power and drama unattainable by almost any other capital city. But the enormous power concentrated in Washington is not concentrated in the hands of the president or in any other single institution. The constitutional separation of powers may well contribute to the ceremonial aura surrounding the presidency, but it also weakens it in relation to the other branches, particularly the legislature. The proliferation of administrative agencies outside the established departments has fragmented political control even within the executive branch, creating the capacity for a degree of policy entrepreneurship among administrators that is rare in other political systems.

The president would be properly jealous of the capacity of the prime minister in either Britain or Canada to enact an almost completely unaltered budget proposal or to move on a statutory agenda with only modest concern for blockage or alteration at the legislative stage. Instead, he must contend with not just one but two powerful legislative chambers, within which party discipline on both sides of the aisle is weaker than in any other liberal democratic system. No more dramatic illustration can be provided of the relative weakness of executive control than the fate of President Clinton's proposal to lift the ban on homosexuals in the military.

The fragmentation of power in Washington provides enormous lures for social movements to institutionalize their lobbying presence. The lack of administration control over the legislative arena proliferates opportunities for gay and lesbian rights proponents to increase the number of supporters among legislators and officials. It also does so for their opponents, making sexual minority vigilance that much more important. The complexity of the system requires expertise in legislative and legal process, and a degree of comfort in maneuvering within Washington networks, furthering the tendency toward institutionalization. This is evident in the growth in size of the annual budget and staff complement of the national group most committed to lobbying and to other forms of participation in mainstream political processes, the Human Rights Campaign.

Since the U.S. party system is a highly decentralized one, it creates ample opportunities for grassroots activist entry. U.S. parties are permeable at local and regional levels, with few restrictions on the formation of Democratic and Republican clubs that are distinctive from party norms in their ideological direction or their demographic makeup. In that sense, the parties may be more impermanent than their counterparts elsewhere, particularly in Europe, but at the local and regional levels their memberships connect them to a wide range of social movements.

Elections are party affairs, of course, as in other countries, but less than elsewhere. Every four years, the presidential campaign towers over others and accentuates the party coloration of all other contests. But even then, campaigns of individual candidates are more separable from the party and from the campaign of the leader. The sheer number of elections being conducted at the same time—for national legislative houses and executive office, for state and local offices, and in most areas for a number of initiatives—requires that individual candidates rise above the fray with personalized campaigns. The demand for resources, especially money, and the electoral finance rules of state and federal governments, weaken candidates' dependence on their parties and increase their need to work with local and regional political networks to sustain campaigns.

The party and electoral systems, then, create openings for gay and lesbian involvement at all levels, doubly so with the spread of anti-gay initiatives at the local and state levels since the 1970s. The permeability of the party system, the relative independence of legislators, and the sheer proliferation of electoral contests has also increased the number of openly gay and lesbian candidacies. By the late 1990s, there were more than 125 such candidates who had won elected office, a number of them having acquired high profiles in the movement. The prominence of such candidacies in American lesbian and gay politics is reflected in the fact that one of the three largest national groups—the Gay and Lesbian Victory Fund—is focused entirely on encouraging lesbians and gays to run for office, providing them with financial support. The Human Rights Campaign is also heavily involved in financially supporting the candidacies of pro-gay legislators.

The importance of openly gay and lesbian legislators in the American activist movement is illustrated by the roles assumed by many of them, including members of Congress Barney Frank and (until his retirement) Gerry Studds. Both have been crucial in sponsoring pro-gay legislative measures and, just as important, in mobilizing congressional allies to block anti-gay measures. Despite his having alienated some activists by offering a compromise on the issue of the military ban, Frank has always been particularly important as a source of strategic advice for lobbyists on Capitol Hill, being such a skilled operator within that arena. Similar points could be made of such legislators as Deborah Glick in the New York state assembly, Allan Spear in the Minnesota state senate, and many others in high-profile state and local offices.

The pull of gays and lesbians into partisan and electoral politics is uneven across gender, race, and class categories, particularly because money is so important in U.S. elections. Women have begun overcoming some of the impediments to entry, but American electoral politics is still overwhelmingly male, white, and upper middle class. The networks of funders and fundraisers who provide the money required by the Human Rights Campaign, the Victory Fund, and individual campaigns for office are heavily slanted toward white male professionals.

Gay and lesbian attraction to party politics has been intensified by the starkness of choice facing them in most parts of the country. Both the Republicans and Democrats are highly decentralized and variegated formations, with especially strong regional variations in strength and ideological centerpoints. Like members of left and center-left parties in other countries, the Democrats have moved toward the ideological center since the 1970s, especially under the leadership of Bill Clinton. Nevertheless, the national party includes a number of firm supporters of gay and lesbian equality, backed on occasion by two-thirds of their congressional colleagues.

The Republicans moved pronouncedly right under the leadership of Ronald Reagan and have maintained that positioning under subsequent leadership. The rightist politics of the Republicans has free-market neoliberalism at its core, but has always included a very prominent element of conservative authoritarianism. This latter element is much stronger than in the British or Canadian right-wing parties, or in most of the European parties that have adopted neoliberal positions. At the national level, 90 percent of congressional Republicans can be counted on to oppose gay and lesbian equality, and many can be assumed ready to campaign aggressively on anti-gay themes. The willingness of the Republicans to play on the themes that in most other systems would characterize the party as extreme speaks loudly to the power of the religious right within its ranks, and in the wider political system.

The power of religious fundamentalism in U.S. politics can be overestimated, but it is enormous. Religious belief and church-going practice in general are significantly higher in the United States than in Canada and Britain, and indeed higher than almost anywhere else in the industrialized world.[27] Some estimates indicate that close to 40 percent of the American population adheres to one or another fundamentalist interpretation of the Bible, with 25 percent of the total population identifying politically with the Christian right.[28] The figures for fundamentalist adherents in Canada and Britain would likely not exceed 12 percent.

More significant still is the extent to which the Christian right has marshalled its enormous resources to oppose equality. Churches with devoted adherents constitute ideal instruments for political mobilizing—they have strong local roots, have clear and sometimes charismatic leadership, and meet regularly in a way that matters greatly for those in attendance. Churches belonging to a number of fundamentalist and evangelical denominations also have access to huge media systems. When such institutions turn their attention to political objects, they are ideally situated to communicate messages to their constituencies, to make the content matter in a spiritual way, and to train adherents in transmitting opinions to political offices. The powerful religious right is reinforced on sexual orientation issues by elements of the secular right, with its own media voices in talk-show radio—an equivalent of Britain's tabloid press. These forces are prepared not only to resist gay-positive measures, but to mobilize voters to roll back modest gains already made. In such a context gays and lesbians have no alternative but to apply large-scale resources to the development of visibility in political decision-making arenas.

The legal context accentuates the draw to the mainstream so evident in other aspects of the political system. The separation of powers, the Bill of Rights, and the assertiveness of early courts all provided the judiciary with the grounds to challenge legislative decisions, creating an incentive from the nineteenth century onward for groups to use the courts to further political ends. The strategic and successful use of civil rights litigation in the second half of the twentieth century intensified the attraction of this mechanism to gays and lesbians particularly, in light of the difficulty of effecting change through legislative channels.

The Bill of Rights' long standing has strengthened rights claims and entrenched them more deeply in political discourse than in any other political system. Some groups are particularly well protected by such claims, even if not always by the economic system. African Americans are one example of a group that has made successful claims on the basis of the Fourteenth Amendment's equal protection clause. Women's groups have made a number of gains through the courts, using "privacy" claims along with "equal protection" arguments, some of them sanctioning affirmative action.

U.S. sexual minorities are not as favorably positioned in law as are their Canadian counterparts. The 1986 Supreme Court judgment in *Bowers v. Hardwick* sustained the most blatantly discriminatory statutes then in existence—the sodomy laws that criminalized same-sex activity in, at the time, about half of the states. (Both Britain and Canada decriminalized most homosexual activity in the late 1960s.) Still, there have been courtroom victories on the basis of both privacy and equal protection arguments. A favorable 1996 Supreme Court judgment in the challenge to the constitutionality of an anti-gay Colorado referendum is one example. Many lower court judgments have also been won on other fronts.

Further increasing the attraction of litigation as an activist strategy is a peculiarly American optimism about the power of law to effect change. Even in a country so marked by unruliness and distrust of government, there is widespread belief that a change in law can and will change minds and lives. This optimism about the possibility of individual and institutional change translates into extraordinary political energy, even in the face of disillusion about ordinary politics. De Tocqueville was hardly the last outside observer to comment on the organizing drive that gets channeled into all manner of groups and movements.

The U.S. political and legal arena attracts groups and activists as no other system, in large measure as a result of the openings for influence created by a highly fragmented system built upon a social and cultural foundation that is almost entirely based on liberal individualism, and on an accompanying belief in the possibility of change even in the most adverse of circumstances. The sheer complexity of the system, and the multiplicity of fronts on which activist visibility must be maintained, sometimes in the midst of lobbying din, requires the mobilizing of substantial activist resources, doubly so because of the scale of operation that can be mounted by the religious right. Gay and lesbian presence in Washington reflects this, with large permanent organizations established to lobby politicians and support the electoral candidacies of sexual minority legislative candidates and their allies.

It is not just that the American system fosters group formation, but also that is draws them into the Washington vortex. A great many of the causes that in other countries are evident primarily in local associations have national organizational presence in the United States in addition to their local presence, and locate themselves in Washington. They establish themselves because of the importance of U.S. national politics and to take advantage of openings within the capital's institutional networks.

And yet for the lesbian and gay movement along with other social movements drawn to the political mainstream, the very strength of individualism and the antistate sentiments that have been so prominent in American political history generate distrust of the institutions of that mainstream, and of the activists and politicos who get too absorbed by them. The national government's headquartering in a purely government town simply accentuates distrust, particularly of that level of government furthest away and most inaccessibly large. It is therefore precisely in that political system in which the inducements to mainstream engagement are greatest that conflicts over strategy are most intense. Thus the gay and lesbian movement, like many others in the United States, is not as divided as British movements over long-term ideological goals as over the appropriate strategic means to achieve them. The differences tend not to divide Washington activists from one another (although there is often bitterness across party lines) but to separate all of the major national organizations in the capital from many of the activists in localities across the country. Sometimes the differences that separate them do not arise out of sharp disagreements over either strategy or ideology, but out of the simple absorption of activists working in the national capital in the preoccupations and language of life inside the beltway.

Conclusion

Public policy and law matter to sexual minorities. Statutory reform will not on its own transform the everyday lives of lesbians, gays, and bisexuals. But it is an essential part of longer-term transformation, and one with critical significance in legitimizing diversity. Even small and largely symbolic gestures adopted by politicians wanting to cede only minor concessions to sexual diversity can end up contributing to the empowerment of communities seeking much more.

Gays and lesbians have entered the political mainstream in all three political systems—Britain, Canada, and the United States—though on different scales and with different levels of institutionalization. The relationship between resources devoted to established political processes and favorable outcomes has varied significantly across the three, in large measure, reflecting the differences in the scale of opposition to equality, the alignment of partisan forces, and other more enduring features of the institutional context.

But despite their dramatically increased visibility, the gay and lesbian movements in various countries are minor players at the fringes of mainstream political processes, only occasionally given access to exercising power through political institutions. These movements have played indispensable roles in raising public and media awareness of sexual orientation issues, without which no progress inside governmental institutions would be imaginable. But those instances in which specific sexual diversity issues have been brought to the legislative table demonstrate that social movement activists are entirely dependent on a complex array of favorable circumstances, even when parties ostensibly committed to their rights are in power.

Demands for sexual equality run up against legal systems that still presume and enforce heterosexuality, in many cases explicitly discriminating against homosexuality and in some criminalizing it (though Canada has seen important shifts in this regard). Such demands also encounter stiff opposition within and beyond the legislative arena. Within parties formally committed to equality, activists still routinely encounter significant dissension and a widespread desire to avoid the subject. American activists may well face the most serious challenges. The system they work in contains innumerable checks against wholesale change, but requires constant intervention and vigilance. By so drawing activist resources to the mainstream, however, the American system inevitably generates debate over their allocation, about the appropriateness of compromise, and about the meaning of victory.

As a result, engagement with the mainstream has provoked tension and sometimes conflict within groups and movements. This is no longer—if it ever was—a conflict simply between the accommodating and the transformational, between narrow agendas and coalitional politics, between middle-class professionals and others who are doubly or triply marginalized. There are elements of all of these, compounded by a tension between local and national activism especially evident in the United States.

The inevitable gaps and tensions between activist networks oriented toward mainstream politics and those that are not is heightened by the inexorable pressures toward institutionalization in the former, and the strong tendency for those who acquire roles within them to reflect the unrepresentivity of the overall party and governmental milieus in which they operate. This necessarily evokes issues of class, gender, and race. These tendencies and forces can be tempered, to be sure, but only with great difficulty.

Though this is not simply a question of mainstreaming versus grassroots politics, there is a tendency for those closest to the political inside to disdain the confrontational styles of direct action and outrageous acts that have recurrent prominence in locally based activism. There is an equally strong tendency for those most engaged in the politics of the street or alternative cultural networks to condemn insider politics. There sometimes seems only a minority prepared to assert that change necessarily entails both the accommodative and the confrontational, the respectable and the outrageous.

Notes

1. For a useful comparative overview of legislative progress, see Barry D. Adam, *The Rise of a Gay and Lesbian Movement*, rev. ed. (New York: Twayne, 1995), chapter 7.

2. I use the terms "sexual diversity" and "sexual minorities" to refer to variation in sexual orientation, and in general synonymously with the phrase "lesbian, gay, bisexual, and transgendered." I often use the phrase "lesbian and gay" or the reverse, and occasionally the word "gay" in adjectival or adverbial form, for reasons of simplicity and flow, though without wishing to downgrade the social or political significance of bisexual or transgendered identities.

3. Urvashi Vaid, *Virtual Equality: The Mainstreaming of Gay and Lesbian Liberation* (New York: Doubleday, 1995), 4.

4. Ibid., 6–7.

5. An overview of divisions and debates in the American movement is provided in Margaret Cruikshank, *The Gay and Lesbian Liberation Movement* (New York: Routledge, 1992), chapter 7.

6. There have been recurrent activist currents, but more pronounced academic ones that see sexual orientation as a social construct or that see sexual boundaries as more fluid and changeable than is suggested by the forms of identity politics that imply clear and unchanging boundaries between groups defined by sexual orientation.

7. In North American gay and lesbian politics especially, class issues have not had the same prominence as either gender or race issues, even if the movements are as unrepresentative in class terms as they are on other dimensions.

8. Vaid, *Virtual Equality*, chapter 2.

9. This is based in part on Sidney Tarrow, *Power in Movement: Social Movements, Collective Action and Politics* (Cambridge: Cambridge University Press, 1994), 3–6. Tarrow is also useful for an overview of the new social movement literature, in addition to Russell J. Dalton and Manfred Kuechler, eds., *Challenging the Political Order: New Social and Political Movements in Western Democracies* (Cambridge: Polity, 1990);

and Hanspeter Kriesi, Ruud Koopmans, Jan-Willem Duyvendak, and Marco G. Giugni, *New Social Movements in Western Europe: A Comparative Analysis* (Minneapolis: University of Minnesota Press, 1995).

10. See Robin Murray, "Fordism and Post-Fordism," 38–53, along with other contributions in *New Times: The Changing Face of Politics in the 1990s*, ed. Stuart Hall and Martin Jacques (London: Lawrence and Wishart, 1989).

11. On the relationship of party decline to social movement emergence, see Sidney Tarrow, "Political Parties and Italian Movements of the 1960s and 1970s," in *Challenging the Political Order*, ed. Dalton and Kuechler, as well as his own book *Power in Movement*.

12. This view is to be found to some extent in Vaid, *Virtual Equality*; and Gary Kinsman, *The Regulation of Desire: Homo and Hetero Sexualities*, 2nd ed. (Montreal: Black Rose, 1996).

13. Representative of this view are the contributors to Didi Herman and Carl Stychin, eds., *Legal Inversions: Lesbians, Gay Men, and the Politics of Law* (Philadelphia: Temple University Press, 1995), and in feminist analysis such as Gillian Walker, *Family Violence and the Women's Movement: The Conceptual Politics of Struggle* (Toronto: University of Toronto Press, 1990).

14. The epidemic required state funding for public education programs, community group programs, and research, as well as shifts in state policy on epidemiological controls, drug testing, and other fronts. By the end of the first decade, activists in most industrialized countries were at least partially successful in persuading or forcing governments to change. On this see David L. Kirp and Ronald Bayer, eds., *AIDS in the Industrialized Democracies: Passions, Politics, and Policies* (New Brunswick, NJ: Rutgers University Press, 1992).

15. See Michel Foucault, *The History of Sexuality*, vol. 1: *An Introduction* (New York: Random House, 1978), and among those influenced by him, David Halperin, *Saint Foucault: Towards a Gay Hagiography* (New York: Routledge, 1990); Mark Blasius, *Gay and Lesbian Politics: Sexuality and the Emergence of a New Ethic* (Philadelphia: Temple University Press, 1994).

16. An articulate and sweeping account of contradictory tendencies can be found in John D'Emilio and Estelle B. Freedman, *Intimate Matters: A History of Sexuality in America* (New York: Harper & Row, 1988).

17. I recognize that in making such claims I differ from many who argue that sexual regulation is more deeply embedded or structured into existing political and economic frameworks, in the same way as are class, race, and gender.

18. The political opportunity structure is discussed in Tarrow, *Power in Movement*, chapter 5; and Kriesi et al., *New Social Movements in Western Europe*.

19. For a general discussion of attitudes toward civil liberties, see Herbert McCloskey and Alida Brill, *Dimensions of Tolerance: What Americans Believe about Civil Liberties* (New York: Russell Sage Foundation, 1983); and Paul M. Sniderman, Joseph F. Fletcher, Peter H. Russell, Philip E. Tetlock, *The Clash of Rights: Liberty, Equality, and Legitimacy in Pluralist Democracy* (New Haven: Yale University Press, 1996). For more specific treatment of sexual orientation, see Kenneth Sherrill, "The Political Power of Lesbians, Gays, and Bisexuals," *PS: Political Science and Politics* 29 (September 1996): 469–73; Clyde Wilcox and Robin M. Wolpert, "President Clinton, Public Opinion,

and Gays in the Military," in *Gay Rights, Military Wrongs: Political Perspectives on Lesbians and Gays in the Military*, ed. Craig A. Rimmerman (New York: Garland, 1996), 127–46; Alan Yang, "Mass Opinion Change with and without Elites: Examining a 'Top-Down' Approach to Public Opinion about Homosexuality," paper presented to the Annual Meeting of the American Political Science Association, 1996; and David Rayside and Scott Bowler, "Public Opinion and Gay Rights," *Canadian Review of Sociology and Anthropology* 25 (November 1988): 649–60.

20. To be sure, engagement with mainstream processes does not necessarily produce unrepresentative leadership and co-optation, any more than grassroots activism naturally leads to greater radicalism and representivity. There are, however, serious risks of assimilation to institutionalized political cultures when groups are preoccupied with lobbying, and those cultures have biases along class, gender, and cultural lines.

21. According to Section 28, "A local authority shall not (a) intentionally promote homosexuality or publish material with the intention of promoting homosexuality; (b) promote the teaching in any maintained school of the acceptability of homosexuality as a pretended family relationship."

22. OutRage, formed in 1990, was influenced by U.S. ACT-UP groups and bore some similarity to Queer Nation in its use of media-savvy theatrical tactics and its preparedness to be confrontational. See Chris Woods, *State of the Queer Nation: A Critique of Gay and Lesbian Politics in 1990s Britain* (London: Cassell, 1995); and Cherry Smyth, *Lesbians Talk Queer Notions* (London: Scarlet Press, 1992).

23. There have been occasions in recent years when the anti-gay side of the tabloids has been softened, in part as a response to activist complaints. But they are still prone to treating sexual diversity exclusively under the rubric of scandal and impropriety.

24. This is a point, made among many other useful points, by J. Lisa Young in *Can Feminists Transform Party Politics? Women's Movements and Political Parties in Canada and the United States, 1970–1993* (Ph.D. thesis, University of Toronto, 1996).

25. On the profound impact of the Charter, see Miriam Smith, *Lesbian and Gay Rights in Canada, Social Movements and Equality-Seeking* (Toronto: University of Toronto Press, 1999), as well as the earlier and wide-ranging book by Didi Herman, *Rights of Passage: Struggles for Lesbian and Gay Legal Equality* (Toronto: University of Toronto Press, 1994).

26. Jill Vickers has made this point in relation to the women's movement in "The Intellectual Origins of the Women's Movements in Canada," in *Challenging Times: The Women's Movement in Canada and the United States*, ed. Constance Backhouse and David H. Flaherty (Montreal: McGill-Queen's University Press, 1992), 39–60.

27. On Canadian–U.S. comparisons, see Seymour Martin Lipset, *Continental Divide: The Values and Institutions of the United States and Canada* (New York: Routledge, 1990), chapter 5.

28. The latter figure comes from W. Craig Bledsoe, "Post Moral Majority Politics: The Fundamentalist Impulse in 1988," paper presented to the Annual Meeting of the American Political Science Association, San Francisco, September 1990, p. 13.

TWO

IDENTITY POLITICS IN FRANCE AND THE NETHERLANDS: THE CASE OF GAY AND LESBIAN LIBERATION

Jan-Willem Duyvendak

Introduction

SOCIAL MOVEMENTS based on the collective identity of a specific group do not have equal opportunities to develop in their respective countries. France is especially interesting in this regard, because its prevailing republican tradition of egalitarianism and universalism conflicts with the pursuit of a specific group identity and the representation of particular desires and interests (Ambler 1971; Hazaseeringh 1994; Hoffmann 1963). In this article, I will discuss how this tradition affected the development of emerging identity-based movements, especially that of the French gay and lesbian movement. My analysis starts with the following question: To what extent and in what way did the broader political context in France affect the manner in which the French gay and lesbian movement voiced its collective interests and desires? In answering this question, the circumstances in the Netherlands will serve as a basis for comparison, wherever relevant. The situation in the Netherlands is of interest in this respect because of the country's longstanding policy on groups: until the late 1970s "pillarization" existed throughout the country. This system provided an organizational framework for politics and social life (parties, school, sports associations, the media, and social interaction) within carefully delineated groups (usually by religious denomination). Although the Netherlands has recently been "depillarized," it certainly does more to accommodate group manifestations and policy than does France. I will start with a broad overview of political protest in France and the Netherlands, focusing on the specific nature of the gay and lesbian movements that have emerged in both countries.

Political Protest in France and the Netherlands

Most people have come to take vehement social conflict in France for granted.[1] Mass demonstrations and teetering governments seem to be part of an age-old tradition. Passion has been a characteristic feature of French politics since the Revolution of 1789. Politics in France has therefore always had a dramatic and emotional ring to it, as exemplified by the events of 1830 and 1848, the Commune de Paris of 1871, the Dreyfus Affair, the prewar Popular Front, May 1968. More often than not, heads must roll, either literally or metaphorically, to appease the citizenry.

This representation of French politics as a battlefield, where citizens and their elected representatives are locked into a state of ongoing conflict, is contrasted by another cliché, which holds that the French are politically passive. De Tocqueville was among those who vehemently criticized the lack of political commitment among his compatriots. He urged them to follow the lead of their American counterparts, whose commitment to the civil cause was exemplary. He pointed out that civic commitment was flourishing in the United States, while France was characterized by an almost total lack of civic bodies dedicated to a cause. France lacked intermediary organizations between individuals and the state; in other words, France was missing a civil society (Tocqueville 1968, 1988).

At first glance these views seem contradictory, but closer scrutiny reveals that they are perfectly compatible. Out of fear of near-revolutionary political upheavals, which seem to occur every other decade, citizens are denied access to the political arena. Professional politicians are in control and generally ignore "interference" from lobbies or social movements. Whether originating in the left or right wing, French politicians are inclined to turn a deaf ear to the populace. In contrast to the Netherlands, access to political debate and decision making is very limited.

Although the regular recurrence of political unrest may suggest otherwise, French trade unions and most other organizations are in disarray, particularly compared with other Western European countries. In the Netherlands, Sweden, Germany, and Austria, workers benefit from their membership in trade unions, which engage in regular consultation and negotiation with employers—often under the watchful eye of the state. In France, however, it seems pointless to join a trade union, because employers and the state largely ignore such organizations. Therefore, the low levels of organization in France go hand in hand with an increased tendency to strike—certainly in comparison with the previously mentioned countries. If employers refuse to take a seat at the negotiating table, workers must find other ways to vent their dissatisfaction. Other organizations, such as those involved in the environmental movement, face a similar predicament. Unlike those in many other European countries, environmental organizations in France are usually not represented in state advisory bodies. Here, too, the state's reluctance to accord legitimacy to intermediary groups reduces the incentive to become a member. It is hardly surprising that the French state is even less tolerant of radical groups. The sabotage of the Greenpeace ship *Rainbow Warrior* during

Mitterrand's first term as president was certainly no coincidence. It was yet another grim reminder that members of the French political class have maintained their traditional stance and will not tolerate interference from citizens—let alone noncitizens—in matters of the state.

Presented as part of a deliberate strategy to protect democracy, these efforts to exclude movements from politics and small political parties from parliaments actually undermine democracy. In the first place, political stability is repeatedly endangered when the arrogance of the political establishment sparks a spiral of events leading to a head-on confrontation: groups of citizens become frustrated, they organize demonstrations, the state refuses to negotiate with the protestors, the demonstrations grow and become more radical, the political opposition senses an opportunity to bring down the government, police action becomes more and more repressive, and eventually the left- and right-wing blocs engage in open confrontation. At this point, the parties have lost sight of the concrete demands, and only one question remains: will the government and the president survive the conflict? Though France is fairly similar to other Western European countries in terms of the quantitative aspects of political protest (i.e., the sheer number of movements and activists, Duyvendak 1995a; Kriesi et al. 1992, 1995), it differs greatly with respect to the qualitative *dynamics of protest*. In France, demonstrations are not organized by specific large groups that systematically take to the streets for a cause. Instead, political action is the domain of individual citizens, most of whom are not members of an organization. For a brief period they are induced to participate in mass mobilization, formulating ever more general goals as they move through the spiral of protest toward head-on confrontation.

The system's inaccessibility leads not only to the crippling political dynamics sketched above but also to a stagnation of political innovation. In contrast to the Netherlands, where a multitude of new issues (e.g., the environment and liberation for women and homosexuals) have been added to the political agenda over the past decades, contemporary France remains trapped in age-old political *cleavages* (Kriesi and Duyvendak 1995). These include the divide between urban and rural areas, the struggle between centralist Paris and areas striving for autonomy (Corsica, Brittany), the relationship between church and state (the struggle surrounding the Catholic *école privée*), and last but certainly not least, the ongoing class struggle. Whereas 75 percent of all political action in Germany, Switzerland, and the Netherlands is related to new issues (e.g., the environment, the third world, women, and gays), this holds true for only one-third of all popular action in France (Kriesi et al. 1995). The mobilization capacity of so-called new social movements (women's movement, gay and lesbian movement, ecological movement, peace movement) in France is extremely weak. Apart from the demonstrations organized by the antiracism movement (Blatt 1995), nearly all other major demonstrations held in France during the past twenty-five years have dealt with traditional political issues. For example, Catholics and right-wing parties have demonstrated against the Socialist government, unions and left-wing parties have demonstrated against the right-wing government, and farmers have launched protests against Paris (Duyvendak 1995a).

The political stagnation in France may be attributed to the dominance of the traditional political parties, especially the ones left of the center, which are hardly threatened by political newcomers. No other Western European country had a communist party as powerful as the Parti Communiste Français, which constituted a serious threat to the Socialist Party for many decades. Nor did any other European country have such prominent Trotskyite and Maoist groups. As a result, attracting political attention in France requires that issues are framed in orthodox class terms. Hardly any latitude was granted to the independent, noncommunist peace movement, which dared to criticize the French nuclear arsenal, la force de frappe. Similarly, the broader protest movement against nuclear energy was unable to gain momentum because it failed to garner any real support among the traditional parties in Parliament.[2] Only very recently have ecological issues reemerged in the political arena, especially now that the Green Party supplies a minister to the Jospin cabinet.

The gay and lesbian movement in France has also been deeply influenced by these limited opportunities for new social movements. Until the late 1980s many members subscribed to the neo-Marxist line, presumably because the radical leftist parties were the only ones somewhat receptive to the homosexual struggle for emancipation in 1970s. Even they demanded that the effort figure within the class struggle.

In the Netherlands the leftist political parties had a similar impact on the ideology of the gay and lesbian movement during the 1970s. At no point, however, did the movement submit its interests to those of these parties: it managed to establish itself independently, rather than purely as part of a "political family" (Duyvendak 1995a). Moreover, the Dutch movement's emergence proceeded far more smoothly than that of its French counterpart, which became entangled in the ups and downs of the French left because of its dependency. How can we understand these differences? What kind of political culture exists in the Netherlands, providing opportunities to social movements for autonomous development?

In the Netherlands the authorities take political protest seriously and are quick to accommodate demonstrators, even if their demands deviate from the prevailing opinion. Operating within a pluralist democracy, traditionally based on agreements between religious minorities, political authorities cannot afford to disregard "new" minorities such as homosexuals (Schuyf and

Krouwel 1999). When the Netherlands was still "pillarized" (1950–70), this arrangement involved contacts behind the scenes between the heads of the political and religious groups and the leadership of the incipient homosexual emancipation movement (Tielman 1982). In subsequent decades, interaction became far more open between the main organization of Dutch homosexuals (the COC) and numerous political parties, including right-wing and Christian parties. The early interest in homosexual issues in politics resulted from efforts by other emancipation movements that preceded them (especially the women's movement). This cannot explain, however, the willing ear homosexual issues found in Dutch politics, since the women's movement cleared the way for gay and lesbian liberation in many other countries as well. What, then, gave the Dutch gay and lesbian movement its surprising strength and success in politics, at least compared to that in France?

French and Dutch Political Culture/Political Structure

The rather limited specific opportunities for (new) social movements in France can best be explained in terms of both the informal cultural and the formal structural characteristics of the country's political system. The *political culture* in France is overwhelmingly republican. Since the French Revolution of 1789, intermediary bodies are distrusted as representatives of specific interests, which are believed to harm the common interest. There is a republican distrust of separate identities, which manifests itself not only among politicians but also among the population. This deeply rooted antipathy toward groups and intermediary organizations between the state and the citizenry is both characteristic of French politics and of a selective nature. The republican logic has greatly impeded the rise of the homosexual movement, which through its public manifestation elicited a vehement response not only as a sexual minority but also through its quest for acknowledgment as a minority and its effort to avoid becoming caught up in a universalist discourse.

Here, the central slogan of the French 1970s gay and lesbian movement (the FHAR, or the Homosexual Front for Revolutionary Action) merits consideration: *le droit à la différence*. It added an entirely new element to French politics. After all, groups demanding "the right to be different" were something of a novelty within the political culture of egalitarian France, and such demands had certainly never been made in combination with an attack on dominant, heterosexual normality.[3] The FHAR clearly refused to bow to the republican logic, which held that minorities should merely pursue the same rights as the majority. Instead, the FHAR turned this logic upside down: as a minority, it not only demanded the right to be different, but also argued that the majority should change. This countercultural trend, which also emerged in many other Western European countries during that time (Adam 1995; Duyvendak 1995b), was not likely to last very long in France. In the first place, the political establishment interpreted the emphasis on collective identity as an appeal for equality, because variety or multiformity has never been seen as a legitimate political objective in its own right. Therefore, in contrast to the gay minority in the Netherlands, which demanded to be recognized as a minority (Seidman 1997), the dominant political culture in France forced the gay and lesbian movement to restrict itself to the language of egalitarianism. So, in order to achieve its political goals, the French gay and lesbian movement had to join the majority, instead of turning against the dominant "normality." In the Netherlands, it was, given its political culture, normal to claim a space for being different (on the basis of equal rights), whereas in France no such claim is imaginable: equality is the best you may hope for as gays and lesbians.

In practice, the French gay and lesbian movement therefore had to join the left-wing family. This brings us to the second reason underlying the transience of the French gay and lesbian movement's bid to be "different." The coercive solidarity within the left-wing bloc forced the FHAR to generalize its demand for *le droit à la différence*, thus expanding the bid beyond gays and lesbians to include all minorities. Paradoxically, the generalization of *le droit à la différence* led to uniformity. In terms of the left-wing, *gauchist* ideology, all affiliated groups were different in the same way: they were all victims of capitalism. The FHAR adopted the slogan "their struggle is our struggle," effectively erasing any possible distinction between their own struggle and those of other groups.

In the end, *le droit à la différence* proved to be an inadequate slogan in a political arena where differences between groups were considered undesirable. The ideology of difference was therefore effectively exiled to the (politically) invisible subculture and to the higher spheres of culture and science, which were inhabited by numerous French intellectuals who impressed the world with their views on difference (Masques 1981). This popularity of the ideology of difference among intellectuals is paradoxical in a country that is largely intolerant toward political differences (certainly in comparison to other Western European countries). Whereas after the 1980s French intellectuals like Foucault, Derrida, Irigaray, and Cixous fell into partial oblivion among the French feminist and gay movements, they were wholeheartedly embraced by emancipatory movements in the capital of multiculturalist politics: the United States.

Besides a look at the political culture, an analysis of the political opportunities for social movements also requires a look at the *political structure*. The political structure in France is characterized by a centralized state system that is strikingly impermeable. The central government is still very dominant (despite decentralization reforms during left-wing cabinets), while the Parliament, based on a majority system, is much less accessible to new and small parties than are systems based on proportional representation. In France, these structural conditions led to a freeze in the relationship between political parties, with a right-wing bloc facing a left-wing bloc. The most radical parties in these blocs (the Gaullists on the right, the Communists on the left) have long held a dominant position, leading to the previously mentioned old cleavages that still influence French politics and leave less room for new political issues than in many other European countries. The French Greens did not achieve their breakthrough until the second half of the 1990s.

It is important to place this political stagnation in the right context. The fact that certain structural and cultural factors lead to conservatism in French politics and a peculiar dynamics of collective action does not imply that French society as a whole has stagnated. The relationship between society and politics is more complex. While the rapid changes throughout the world during the late 1960s did not exclude France, they led to fewer political innovations there because the left was so strongly dominated by communist (i.e., Marxist) organizations. The predominance of traditional issues in French politics might surprise readers who were led to believe that the winds of change had blown through the corridors of power in May 1968, heralding the breakthrough of new political ideas. The fact of the matter is that the events of May 1968 were not prototypical for the new protest movements that emerged in Europe and the United States; they were in fact atypical. The vehemence of protest in France should be attributed primarily to the volatile alliance between students and millions of striking workers, not to the inherent strength of the new movements.

New social movement sympathizers remained relatively marginal in party politics, too. When they eventually joined the Socialist Party, this "second left" (as the nonstatist left was called) (Hamon and Rotman 1982), gave rise to some openness toward social movements such as the antinuclear movement (which emerged in France as early as it did elsewhere). It was unable, however, to shield these movements and many other new political issues (e.g., homosexuality) from being inundated by orthodox leftist class issues, particularly when the Socialist Party started cooperating closely with the Communists for electoral reasons.

The lack of prospects for the new social movements eventually caused the downfall of the "second left" in French society. While elsewhere, such as in the Netherlands, a "green" subculture developed, the left-libertarian sentiments in France evaporated during the 1980s. Many leftist movements split into countless splinter groups. This process resulted in part from the decreasing support for these movements emanating from French society, which, in turn, was caused by the impossibility of political success. We have analyzed this extensively in the case of the antinuclear movement. It turned out that support for this movement decreased as the political arena—and especially the political parties on the left—distanced itself from it (Koopmans and Duyvendak 1995). The problems faced by new movements, such as the gay and lesbian movement, were attributable to these general characteristics of the French political structure and culture.

In the Netherlands, the traditional political antitheses were pacified a long time ago. As a result, cleavages in state-church and class relations were resolved institutionally (which does not preclude persistent class differences), giving new movements greater access to the political arena (Duyvendak et al. 1992; Kriesi 1993). Furthermore, the legitimacy of identity-based demands in the Netherlands is the product of a completely different tradition: "pillarization," or the organization of society and politics on the basis of sharply defined, separate groups. As a country of minorities—there was no religious denomination to which a majority of the Dutch adhered—the Netherlands generally empathized with specific groups demanding recognition. Such groups could even request state funding to maintain their specificity: these "pillars" had their own schools, broadcasting organizations, and welfare institutions, paid for by the state (Duyvendak 1994; Lijphart 1971, 1974). This pillarization remained intact until the late 1960s. Its gradual erosion ("depillarization") led people to question the tradition. It soon became clear that Dutch pillarized society was hierarchical and undemocratic: consultation was the prerogative of the upper echelons. In addition, individuals found it impossible to break out of their respective pillars. Numerous political customs, implemented during pillarization, nevertheless remained intact after the 1970s. In addition to the custom of funding a wide variety of oppositional groups, the custom to invite all the different organizations to participate in the political process, with the aim of reaching a consensual and peaceful solution of conflicts, also persisted. Thus, the scope of Dutch political culture extends to specific groups that take pride in their "difference." Or, more accurately, tolerance for such difference is greater than it is in France, where assimilation seems to be the best a minority can hope to accomplish.[4]

The Dutch homosexual movement COC (which organizes both gays and lesbians) received invitations to serve on official committees as well as an impressive array of subsidies. As stated, this is a familiar pattern in the open Dutch political *culture*: all kinds of organizations receive government funding, including some with positions that deviate from the "norm" (not only those of radical gay and lesbian activists, but also antinuclear groups and even squatters). New organizations, such as the gay and lesbian one, have benefited from this longstanding tradition.

The relative openness of Dutch politics is reinforced by a few aspects of the political system's *structure*, especially the system of proportional representation. Minority parties, even those obtaining less than 1 percent of the vote, are entitled to congressional representation. Established political parties therefore need to remain especially alert to new trends. They must accommodate new topics and individuals in the party or risk forfeiting votes and seats.

In the Netherlands more opportunities were available to highlight gay pride. Many gay men and especially lesbian women emphasized their distinctive characteristics ("difference"): the homosexual movement was not looking for a spot in the limelight but wanted its own show: its own lifestyle and space for cultural and political expression. The openness of the Dutch public and political arena, however, also subdued the movement's discourse: the relative ease of attaining equal rights in the Netherlands quickly marginalized the emphasis on the "difference" of homosexuals (Duyvendak 1994). This change reveals an interesting paradox with respect to France in that granting minorities latitude and equal rights has reduced the need for identity politics in the Netherlands. Where minorities are not allowed to manifest themselves, however, their identities become more deeply entrenched (France). As for interpreting this paradox, what is the latitude and need for highlighting new identities in both countries?

Old and New Social Movements in France and the Netherlands: The Status of "Identity"

"Traditional" objectives continue to dominate the protest actions of social movements in France, leaving very little room for new objectives. All new movements are confronted with this problem, whether they are predominantly instrumental-oriented (the environmental, peace, and solidarity movements) or identity-oriented (the feminist, squatters, gay and lesbian movements). Identity movements, however, suffer even more from the republican distrust of separate identities. Their sphere of action therefore seems even smaller than that of new, predominantly instrumental movements with less emphasis on identities. But is the prospect for identity movements really that bleak? And, was it always this bleak?

The development of dominant, *old* movements teaches us several lessons. In the first place, we may conclude that the dominant French political discourse is fundamentally opposed to identity-based politics, but that—precisely due to that fact—in political reality identity has been a key issue in traditional conflicts. Corsicans and Bretons, farmers, Catholics, and workers all harbor a deep-seated sense of collective identity. Many even consider acknowledgment of their identity to be the prime objective of their struggle. In light of this, it is easy to refute the contention that identity-based politics are primarily the domain of the new movements. It also seems logical that France—perhaps even more so than elsewhere—should be confronted with political strife based on collective identities. A society that swears by egalitarianism offers disgruntled citizens a powerful discursive weapon for organizing themselves as a group in order to demand equal rights. After all, any French minority group that feels slighted has the right to demand equal treatment.

The older movements pursue a specific type of identity-based strategy: movements based on particular collective identities demand the same rights as the majority. On the one hand, the republican egalitarian tradition grants groups of citizens the freedom to unite temporarily and demand equal rights. On the other hand, this tradition makes it impossible for such groups to maintain their appeal for support and preservation of their specific group culture or identity. Since separate identities are not recognized, it is (and always has been) impracticable to pursue a multiculturalist policy (Gutmann 1992; Seidman 1993; Taylor 1992) in France.

The degree of freedom granted to *new* identity-based movements in France is limited for two reasons. First, the legitimacy of identity-based political action is always temporary and conditional. Such action is tolerated as long as it is directed toward eradicating inequality or erasing the societal discrepancies and disadvantages fueling the group's discontentment. Second, the available space for new movements is limited because the political field is already occupied by the aforementioned traditional identities. According to the prevailing political logic, these traditional political identities should have been temporary. Instead, stagnation of the political system has enabled them to become highly stable entities. The situation has resulted in another intriguing paradox: *Although the French political system makes no provision for the permanent accommodation of specific collective identities, these identities have proved extraordinarily persistent, owing to the obstructive dynamics of the political system.*

These circumstances not only force new movements to formulate their demands in terms of the republican rhetoric of universalism and egalitarianism (a rhetoric emphasizing equality, as in many other liberal countries) but also dictate that they should forge alliances with the dominant discourse of the older movements. This prompted many new movements to seek shelter under the wings of traditional leftist parties and movements, where they learned to speak the language of the left-wing political family, which stresses specific "old" identities (Duyvendak 1995a:203–9).

However, even in France there is scope for new issues, despite the fact that they must be formulated in terms of the traditional antitheses. Yet *new* organizations making an independent bid to place their issues on the political agenda fail, almost without exception.[5]

The situation in the Netherlands is quite different: effective resolution of old issues has cleared a lot of space on the political agenda for new ones. As argued above, the space for new topics is attributable to old political *traditions*: new groups easily achieve political acknowledgment (financial or institutional), and new issues quickly enter the political arena. The strength of these longstanding traditions is the only possible reason for the predominantly positive reception of homosexual emancipation in the Netherlands, even when the Christian democrats were included in the coalition governments. In contrast to France, there are (and were) no "hard" identities in Dutch politics gays and lesbians had to compete with: since many other groups had been recognized and appeased before the gay and lesbian movement emerged, these "old" identities were not as persistent as the old ones in France. Due to the fact that there are provisions for the permanent accommodation of specific collective identities in the Netherlands, these groups are much more "open" and willing to accept others than are comparable groups in France still desperately seeking recognition.

Finally, I will further illustrate the differences between the two countries by presenting two relevant episodes in the history of the French and Dutch gay and lesbian movements.

Two Episodes in the History of the French and Dutch Gay and Lesbian Movements: AIDS Politics and the Recognition of Homosexual Relationships

Political tradition has had a profound effect on the development of the gay and lesbian movement in France.[6] It has even dictated the political language the movement uses to formulate its objectives. The far-reaching influence of the universalist republican tradition on the gay and lesbian movement was proved once more when AIDS reared its ugly head (Favre 1992). Whereas many other Western countries soon realized the need to combat AIDS in a differentiated manner, the French government refused to design prevention campaigns directed at male homosexuals (Altman 1988; Duyvendak and Koopmans 1991; Duyvendak 1996). The development of a target-group policy proved to be almost impossible in a republican country (Arnal 1993; Pollak 1988). Even the organizations founded to assist HIV-infected people and AIDS patients tried to avoid being labeled homosexual, despite the fact that almost all of their members and patients were homosexual, especially at the start of the epidemic (Hirsch 1991; Pollak and Rosman 1989). Ernst analyzed the situation as follows: "The enduring influence of the French republican model of citizenship and politics is evident in the gay community's response to AIDS. The reluctance of AIDS organizations to 'own' the disease, and to interpret it as a civil rights issue, and to instead view it as a health problem is testament of the degree to which identity-based politics remain illegitimate in France. While French AIDS organizations certainly recognize the ways in which the disease poses a threat to civil rights, this threat is viewed as a general one. AIDS poses a threat to the universal human rights of all French citizens, not to the right of French gays" (1995:17). Groups of citizens have neither political nor social opportunities to permanently manifest themselves as being different. They therefore see themselves primarily as individuals, whose only common denominator is that they are French. "Unlike the US which allows, indeed encourages group differences to flourish in civil society, and unlike the Dutch state which recognizes groups as political agents, the French state often approaches groups with an eye to privatizing and suppressing them or subjecting social differences to hierarchical, normalizing control. France may be a nation of individuals, but before such individuals are men or women, bourgeois or proletariat, straight or gay, Catholic or Muslim, they are, or should be, French" (Seidman 1997:252).

The AIDS epidemic made abundantly clear that differentiation among groups (and thinking in terms of groups) is necessary, even in France, not because AIDS strikes only homosexuals, but because certain groups obviously run a greater risk of contracting the disease than others. This awareness sparked a vociferous antirepublican reaction, in particular through ACT-UP Paris, which presented itself as a community organization that wanted to have its "uniqueness" recognized, an unprecedented phenomenon in France. On the one hand, the rhetoric employed by ACT-UP Paris was very similar to that of the left-wing movements of the 1960s and 1970s (in its denunciation of sexual repression) but at the same time radically different by virtue of its call for the foundation of a homosexual *community*, something no other French movement had ever sought to attain.

The two goals adopted by ACT-UP Paris (politicization of AIDS and identity-building) did not suit the associational and political establishment, and after 1991 ACT-UP started to become the object of fairly virulent attacks in both these areas, highlighting the difficulty of establishing a homosexual movement on a communitarian basis in France. Frédéric Martel, for example, as his book *Le Rose et le noir. Les homosexuels en France depuis 1968* (1996) shows, felt compelled to defend the republican model against the communitarian tendencies developing in gay AIDS organizations in France. And he was not alone: most French associations reacted negatively to ACT-UP's attempt to found a homosexual movement on the basis of the American identity/community model. These reactions indicated that the goals of ACT-UP directly contested the attachment of the French left to the classic republican model, in which "minority politics" is not tolerated, on its own terms.[7]

An interesting analogy to this struggle can be found in the development in the early 1980s of movements like SOS-Racisme, which asserted (like the FHAR for gays and lesbians in the 1970s) a *droit à la différence* for French people of immigrant parents (Blatt 1995).

The severe resistance ACT-UP has experienced to this day in France attests to the fact that an action model and discourse that fit a movement in one country—the tremendous impact of ACT-UP in the United States is a good example—may diffuse to other countries but will not necessarily take hold there. Because ACT-UP demanded recognition as a community organization, it was not able to expand its appeal in France. Its antirepublican battle cries made it easier for the French authorities to ignore its demands, even those for equal treatment.

In that sense, one would expect the current struggle to allow partnership registration as an alternative to marriage for couples to have a better chance of succeeding, as it demands the same rights for heterosexual and homosexual couples, irrespective of their differences. This discussion reflects, however, the selective nature of republicanism's universalism. From the reactions to the proposal for this registration option, it is evident that "universal" in France refers to what is commonly accepted as "normal." Thus, only heterosexuals seem to qualify for institutions sanctioned by the state. How ironic to find a heterosexual group "right" in a land so proud of its universalism.

In the Netherlands both AIDS policy and marriage legislation are entirely different. Dutch homosexuals figured prominently in fighting the epidemic (Duyvendak 1996). In fact, they (i.e., the leaders of their organizations) were in a position to select the prevention strategy they expected would yield the best results. This situation reveals the risks of complete "self-administration," since the information message chosen ("stop engaging in anal intercourse") long persisted in that format, even after profound doubts had arisen regarding its resonance and effectiveness. Since this message had been "approved" by homosexuals themselves, however, it did not instigate a reaction among other groups. At any rate, because of the major role of a homosexual "elite" in AIDS policy, the "average" gay man had (or felt) no cause to mobilize, let alone engage in a radical or demonstrative form of action.

In the debate about legislation concerning relationships between homosexuals, the differences between France and the Netherlands took a surprising turn as well. The deep political appreciation of minorities in the Netherlands led to greater willingness to adapt legislation concerning relationships. Registered partnerships were approved in 1998, and same-sex civil marriages are likely in the near future as well. Respect for minorities enables their equality in politics and before the law. In republican France, the persistent prohibition of marriages between homosexuals is a striking contrast to the practice in the Netherlands. In keeping with its tradition, France is the scene of heated debates and demonstrations, this time primarily by those opposing legislation that would allow homosexuals to legalize their relationship. The right wing and the Catholics in France are flooding the streets by the hundreds of thousands: hardened identities are up in arms, and new groups are paying the price.

Comparing the two cases shows that the space for identity politics greatly differs in France and the Netherlands. In France, the dominant republican rhetoric precludes recognition of groups. Even at the height of the AIDS epidemic, the fact that AIDS primarily struck among certain groups was ignored. In response, a "communitarian" ideology evolved among French homosexuals: the negation of their existence led them to emphasize their distinction from other groups in dramatic terms. In contrast, the Dutch strategy for combatting AIDS makes clear that when there is space for a group to exist, that group will not need to stress its particular identity and "differentness" in strong terms. The almost immediate recognition within the political and social arena that HIV primarily struck among homosexuals—and, therefore, that this group should be the prime actor in the fight against AIDS—explains why no radicalization of the gay and lesbian movement and no "queering" of gay and lesbian identities took place in the Netherlands (Duyvendak 1996).

Moreover, the example of homosexual marriage shows that the dominant group actively represses gay and lesbian identities. Ironically, in a republican France proud of its universalist flag, the dominant majority turns out to have a strong identity as well: women, migrants, and homosexuals who want to organize themselves are disqualified as unrepublican by a dominant group consisting primarily of white, heterosexual men. In France, this dominating group has, at least compared to the Netherlands, a surprisingly conservative face, partly due to the logic of solidified identities described earlier: the majority values class, heredity, region, religion, and political affiliation, because those are the identities that have occupied France during the past century. In the Netherlands, on the other hand, politics is much less defined by "a face": the tradition of tolerance for organizing minorities (stemming from the fact that everyone belongs to a minority) prevents rights that exist for one group from being withheld from another. Paradoxically, it seems that equality prospers through the recognition of difference.

Notes

Special thanks are due to Mark Blasius and David Rayside for their insightful and constructive commentary.

1. The research data presented in this paragraph, dealing with protest in France from 1975 through 1989, are discussed more extensively in Duyvendak 1995a. My study of French social movements formed part of a broader, international comparative study (see Giugni 1992; Koopmans 1995; Kriesi et al. 1992, 1995).

2. Although the Socialist Party initially expressed some support for this movement (implying that it was not completely insensitive to new social movements), it ceased supporting the antinuclear movement as soon as it came to power in 1981. As a

result, France is the only country in Europe that has carried out its original nuclear energy program from start to finish (Koopmans and Duyvendak 1995).

3. The FHAR published the *Rapport contre la normalité* (1971).

4. Contrasting the Netherlands with France shows that there are other ways of dealing with difference than the French way. A comparison with the situation in Canada would have probably resulted in a similar contrast (which is not to say that France is exceptional in its denial of group identities).

5. In fact, only one organization has been partly successful: the left-wing, Catholic Trade Union (CFDT) (Hamon and Rotman 1982). Since 1968, this union has criticized the dominant political culture that makes broaching new issues so difficult. Even the Parti Socialiste (PS) was unsuccessful in this regard, largely because of its effort to compete with the Communist Party by emulating it as much as possible. As a result, the PS was the most dogmatic socialist party in Western Europe until the early 1980s, thus obstructing the emergence of a New Left and granting hardly any latitude to the "new social movements." The CFDT took a different approach. It tackled the dominant position of the Communist Trade Union (CGT), by being "different." The CFDT broached various nontraditional trade-union issues, such as *autogestion* (autonomy), environmental policy, women's rights, and the dangers of nuclear energy. The CFDT presented itself as mouthpiece for the antistatist *deuxième gauche,* as "le parti de la société civile" (Esprit 1980).

6. For a more extensive empirical description of the history of the French gay and lesbian movement, see Duyvendak (1995c) and Fillieule and Duyvendak (1999). For the history of AIDS organizations, see Fillieule (forthcoming) and De Busscher and Pinell (1996).

7. See also the editorial of Gérard Dupuy in *Libération*, June 24, 1995 ("Visibles"), an article of Pascal Bruckner in *Le Monde*, June 23, 1995 ("La Démagogie de la détresse"), and the public debate started by the publication of *Le Rose et le noir. Les homosexuels en France depuis 1968* by Frédéric Martel (*Le Monde*, April 15, 1996: "Les homosexuels se divisent sur la question du communautarisme"; *Le Nouvel Observateur,* April 25, 1996, etc.) For an analysis of the reasons why France is fundamentally reticent about the communitarian model, in the tradition of republican principles of the République, see also the sophisticated analysis of Ernst (1995).

Works Cited

Adam, B. D. 1995. *The Rise of a Gay and Lesbian Movement*. New York: Twayne.

Altman, D. 1988. "Legitimation through Disaster: AIDS and the Gay Movement." In *Aids, the Burdens of History*, ed. E. Fee and D. M. Fox, 301–15. Berkeley: University of California Press.

Ambler, J. S. 1971. *The Government and Politics of France*. Boston: Houghton Mifflin.

Arnal, F. 1993. *Résister ou disparaître? Les homosexuels face au sida. La prévention de 1982 à 1992*. Paris: L'Harmattan.

Blatt, D. S. 1995. *Immigration Politics and Immigrant Collective Action in France, 1968–1993*. Ph.D. diss., Ithaca: Cornell University.

Brand, K.-W. 1985a. *Neue soziale Bewegungen in Westeuropa und den USA. Ein internationaler Vergleich*. Frankfurt: Campus.

————. 1985b. "Vergleichendes Resümee." In *Neue soziale Bewegungen in Westeuropa und den USA. Ein internationaler Vergleich*, ed. Brand, Frankfurt: Campus. 306–34.

De Busscher, P. O., and P. Pinell. 1996. "La création des associations de lutte contre le Sida." In *Sida et vie psychique: approche clinique et prise en charge*, ed. S. Hefez. Paris: La Découverte.

Duyvendak, J. W. 1994. *De verzuiling van de homobeweging*. Amsterdam: SUA.

————. 1995a. *The Power of Politics: New Social Movements in France*. Boulder, CO: Westview Press.

————. 1995b. "Gay Subcultures between Movement and Market." In *New Social Movements in Europe*, by Kriesi et al., 165–80.

————. 1995c. "From Revolution to Involution: The Disappearance of the French Gay Movement." *Journal of Homosexuality* 29/4:369–85.

————. 1996. "The Depoliticization of the Dutch Gay Identity, or Why Dutch Gays Aren't Queer." In *Queer Theory/Sociology*, ed. S. Seidman, 421–38. Cambridge: Blackwell.

Duyvendak, J. W., and R. Koopmans. 1991. "Weerstand bieden aan AIDS. De invloed van de homobeweging op de ontwikkeling van AIDS." *Beleid en Maatschappij* 3:237–45.

Duyvendak, J. W., H. A. van der Heijden, R. Koopmans, and L. Wijmans, eds. 1992. *Tussen verbeelding en macht. 25 jaar nieuwe sociale bewegingen in Nederland*. Amsterdam: SUA.

Ernst, C. 1995. "AIDS and the French Gay Community: *Dédramatisation* and Gay Identity." Paper delivered at the Western Political Science Association Annual Meeting.

Esprit. 1980/4. *La CFDT et la crise du syndicalisme*. Paris.

Favre, P., ed. 1992. *SIDA et politique. Les premiers affrontements (1981–1987)*. Paris: L'Harmattan.

FHAR. 1971. *Rapport contre la normalité*. Paris: Champ Libre.

Fillieule, O., ed. Forthcoming. *Activisme et guerre contre le sida. Regards sur les Act-Up d'Europe et des USA*. Paris: L'Harmattan.

Fillieule, O., and J. W. Duyvendak. 1999. "Gay and Lesbian Activism in France: Between Integration and Community-Oriented Movements." In *The Global Emergence of Gay and Lesbian Politics: National Imprints of a Worldwide Movement*, ed. B. D. Adam, J. W. Duyvendak, and A. Krouwel, 189–213. Philadelphia: Temple University Press.

Giugni, M. 1992. *Entre stratégie et opportunité. Les nouveaux mouvements sociaux en Suisse*. Ph.D. diss., University of Geneva.

Gutmann, A. 1992. Introduction to *Multiculturalism and "The Politics of Recognition": An Essay by Charles Taylor*, ed. A. Gutmann. Princeton: Princeton University Press.

Hamon, H., and P. Rotman, 1982. *La Deuxième Gauche. Histoire intellectuelle et politique de la CFDT*. Paris: Ramsay.

Hazaseeringh, S. 1994. *Political Traditions in Modern France*. Oxford: Oxford University Press.

Hirsch, E. 1991. *Solidaires, AIDES*. Paris: Les Éditions du Cerf.

Hoffmann, S., CH.-P. Kindleberger, L. Wylie, J.-R. Pitts, J.-B. Duroselle, and F. Goguel. 1963. À la recherche de la France. Paris: Seuil.

Koopmans, R. 1995. Democracy from Below: New Social Movements and the Political System in West Germany. Boulder, CO: Westview Press.

Koopmans, R., and J. W. Duyvendak. 1995. "The Political Construction of the Nuclear Energy Issue and Its Impact on the Mobilization of Anti-nuclear Movements in Western Europe." Social Problems 42, no. 2:235–51.

Kriesi, H. 1993. Political Mobilization and Social Change. The Dutch Case in Comparative Perspective. European Centre Vienna/Aldershot: Avebury Press.

Kriesi, H., and J. W. Duyvendak. 1995. "National Cleavage Structures." In New Social Movements in Europe, by Kriesi et al., 3–25.

Kriesi, H., R. Koopmans, J. W. Duyvendak, and M. Giugni. 1992. "New Social Movements and Political Opportunities in Western Europe." European Journal of Political Research 22:219–44.

———. 1995. New Social Movements in Europe: A Comparative Analysis. Minneapolis: University of Minnesota Press.

Lijphart, A. 1971. "Comparative Politics and the Comparative Method." American Political Science Review 65, no. 3:682–93.

———. 1974. "Consociational Democracy." In Consociational Democracy: Political Accommodation in Segmented Societies, ed. K. McRae, 70–89. Toronto: McClelland and Stewart.

Martel, F. 1996. Le Rose et le noir. Les homosexuels en France depuis 1968. Paris: Éditions du Seuil.

Masques. 1981/9–10. Homosexualités 1971–1981. Paris.

———. 1985/25–26. Années 80. Mythe ou Libération. Paris.

Pollak, M. 1988. Les Homosexuels et le SIDA: Sociologie d'une épidémie. Paris: A. M. Métaillié.

Pollak, M., and S. Rosman. 1989. Les Associations de lutte contre le SIDA: Éléments d'évaluation et de réflexion. Paris: EHESS/CNRS.

Schuyf, J., and A. Krouwel. 1999. "The Dutch Lesbian and Gay Movement: The Politics of Accommodation." In The Global Emergence of Gay and Lesbian Politics: National Imprints of a Worldwide Movement, ed. B. D. Adam, J. W. Duyvendak, and A. Krouwel, 158–83. Philadelphia: Temple University Press.

Seidman, S. 1993. "Identity and Politics in a 'Postmodern' Gay Culture: Some Historical and Conceptual Notes." In Fear of a Queer Planet: Queer Politics and Social Theory, ed. Michael Warner, 105–42. Minneapolis: University of Minnesota Press.

———. 1997. Difference Troubles: Queering Social Theory and Sexual Politics. Cambridge: Cambridge University Press.

Taylor, C. 1992. "The Politics of Recognition." In Multiculturalism and "The Politics of Recognition," ed. A. Gutmann, 25–73.

Tielman, R. A. P. 1982. Homoseksualiteit in Nederland: studie van een emancipatiebeweging. Meppel: Boom.

Tocqueville, A. de. 1968. De la Démocratie en Amérique. Les grands thèmes. Ed. J. P. Mayer. Paris: Gallimard.

———. 1988. L'Ancien Régime et la révolution. Ed. F. Mélonio. Paris: Flammarion.

THREE

LESBIAN-FEMINIST ACTIVISM AND LATIN AMERICAN FEMINIST *ENCUENTROS*

Juanita Díaz-Cotto

S OCIAL SCIENCE STUDIES of women in Latin America,[1] whether written by lesbians or heterosexual women, have tended to ignore the experiences and contributions of lesbians to their societies. Such exclusion has been the result not only of heterosexism and internalized lesbophobia but also of the repression to which Latin American lesbians have been subjected throughout the centuries by social forces on all sides of the political spectrum.

This article discusses the emergence of a distinctive lesbian-feminist politics in the context of the larger Latin American feminist *encuentros*.[2] The overall issue is the relationship between Latin American feminist political identities and perspectives and lesbian-feminist organizing. Such discussion will take place through an analysis of the role played by lesbians in six of the eight Latin American and Caribbean feminist encuentros held between 1980 and 1999. Brief references will be made to three of the five Latin American and Caribbean lesbian-feminist encuentros held between 1987 and 1999.

In order to situate lesbian-feminist organizing within a historical context, the article will briefly discuss the emergence of contemporary Latin American feminist movements and explore some of the main themes characterizing the encuentros. It will end with a discussion of the emergence of a distinct lesbian-feminist politics within each of the encuentros in order to measure the growth of lesbian activism within Latin American feminist movements.

Contemporary Feminist Movements in Latin America

The second wave of feminist movements in Latin America emerged and thrived during the mid-1970s within national, regional, and international contexts, including growing national debts, austerity measures imposed by international monetary agencies, active anti-imperialist movements, and severe political changes (e.g., military dictatorships, guerrilla movements, leftists revolutions, liberalization, and redemocratization).

Feminism was embraced by lesbians and heterosexual women despite the existence of widespread stereotypes about who feminists were and what their goals were. These stereotypes were often accompanied by ridicule and the ever-present threat, and sometimes use, of physical violence. Such rejection partly resulted from the belief of many men and women that feminists were "man-haters" and, by implication, lesbians. The fact that feminists openly questioned traditional gender roles and women's oppression and that by the 1980s, a small number of feminists across the region began to openly identify themselves as lesbians, bolstered these stereotypes.

Those on the right saw feminists as threatening the foundations of the family and, hence, the religious and sociopolitical structure itself. Many on the left argued that feminists were among the most privileged and "Americanized" of the women's population in their countries; that their concerns had little to do with the realities facing most women in the region. Feminist "male bashing" also threatened to drive an irreconcilable wedge between the sexes and, as a result, served as a tool of "yankee imperialism." The fact that many women who became publicly identified as feminists were white and middle class and that many Latin American feminists had been influenced by the development of feminist movements in the United States and Europe exacerbated those fears. In spite of such backlash, Latin American feminists have continued to make their demands for equality and justice known in multiple ways. Moreover, their ranks have expanded among the working classes and poorest sectors of the urban and rural populations (e.g., factory workers, domestic workers, peasant women, and women from the favelas). These sectors, nonetheless, challenged mainstream feminists to broaden their definition of feminism and become more racially aware and class-conscious.

The resurgence of Latin American feminisms, as the variants of the feminist movements are referred to in the region, took place alongside the grassroots struggles waged by women's groups, frequently affiliated with the left, the Catholic Church, and/or human rights organizations that did not consider themselves feminist. As such, "contemporary Latin American feminists . . . form but one part of a larger multifaceted, socially and politically heterogeneous women's movement."[3] Most important, many feminists formed an integral part of grassroots struggles. "From the moment the first feminist groups appeared in the mid-1970s, many Latin American feminists . . . joined forces with other opposition currents in denouncing social, economic, and political oppression and exploitation."[4]

Close collaboration among diverse groups of women was possible because many feminists had originally formed part of the leftist opposition in their countries. In fact, many became convinced of the need to create organizationally and economically "autonomous" feminist movements only after repeated disillusionment with the sexist politics of leftist male leaders. Feminists argued that unless women struggled for the elimination of women's oppression from the outset they would not be conferred an equal role in the development of their countries once socialism was achieved.

In spite of these differences, feminist movements continued to support the anti-imperialist and anticapitalist objectives of the left; a position that differentiated them from mainstream feminist movements in the United States and Europe. Moreover, a significant number of feminists continued to argue for the need to practice "double militancy"—the simultaneous participation of women in organizations of the left and in feminist-identified groups. Only in this manner would women be assured that whatever transformation took place in their societies would produce a significant redistribution of power, wealth, and resources.

The presence of Latin American feminisms has been evident in the formation of working-class women's groups, the opening of women's research centers, and the sponsoring of legislation in support of women's rights. In addition, "The number of feminist magazines, film and video collectives, centers for battered women and rape victims, feminist health collectives, lesbian rights groups, and other gendered feminist projects steadily expanded throughout the 1980s."[5]

Equally important was the organizing during the 1980s and 1990s of feminist encuentros, one of the most significant arenas for feminist debate. At the gatherings, women living inside and outside the region sought to obtain support for their local struggles and devise and coordinate strategies across geographic boundaries. The encuentros also offered an opportunity to make feminist issues the center of national debates. Furthermore, the encuentros have themselves been one of the many strategies used by Latin American feminists to broaden the scope of their movements.

> [They] . . . have served as springboards for the development of a common Latin American feminist political language and as staging grounds for often contentious political battles over what would constitute the most efficacious strategies for achieving gender equality in dependent, capitalist, and patriarchal states.[6]

With the participation of representatives from the Cuban and Nicaraguan Revolutions, the discussion extended to the means by which women could have their concerns addressed under socialist regimes.

Many Latin American lesbians who had participated in leftist and progressive social movements (but hid their sexual orientation/preference in the face of widespread lesbophobia and repression) found that the heterosexual-dominated encuentros provided a safer haven in which to discuss issues such as heterosexism, lesbophobia, lesbian relationships and sexuality, lesbian parenting, internalized lesbophobia, and violence against lesbians.

However, the attitudes and behavior of heterosexual feminists toward their lesbian peers varied. While lesbian-feminists supported gender-specific issues prioritized by heterosexual feminists (e.g., violence against women, reproductive rights, equal pay for equal work), the latter were reluctant to incorporate lesbian demands for an end to heterosexism and lesbophobia into their organizational and movement agendas. Heterosexual feminists and closeted lesbian-feminists frequently reiterated some of the arguments used by opponents of feminism to oppose the open inclusion of lesbian concerns and organizations in feminist groups and coalitions. Some argued that lesbian concerns were alien to the realities of most Latin American women. Others claimed that Latin American peoples were not "ready" to discuss such issues; that such debates could lead to the further alienation and repression of feminist movements. Still others influenced by Catholicism, the mass media, and the psychiatric establishment considered lesbians to be sick, deviants, or perverts. Although women who transgress social norms have generally been labeled "man-haters" and lesbians, the fact such labeling was used to keep women from uniting with one another was generally ignored.

The practical manifestations of lesbophobia varied. In some cases open lesbians were not allowed to join heterosexual-dominated groups or coalitions or they were expelled when they came out of the closet. Feminist organizations have denied meeting spaces to lesbian groups. They have publicly attacked lesbians in the mass media or denied them the right to publish articles in feminist publications. In some instances heterosexual feminists were willing to accept lesbians in their groups and coalitions, but the latter were welcome only as long as they did not discuss lesbianism and/or demand the inclusion of their concerns in the group's platform. In other cases, heterosexual women appeared supportive of lesbian issues at the encuentros, but were not so supportive upon their return home. And in at least one instance, heterosexual women in Argentina went as far as to physically force the lesbian contingent out of the International Women's Day march that year.

Though it is not within the scope of this article to discuss the relationship of lesbians to the gay male movement in Latin America, it is important to indicate both that mixed lesbian and gay groups existed parallel to autonomous feminist and lesbian-feminist groups, and that lesbians also formed autonomous lesbian groups in reaction to the sexism of the men in these groups. Moreover, although feminist movements allowed Latin American lesbians to achieve a measure of visibility within their societies, such visibility was also the result of joint activities with gay males (e.g., litigation, lobbying for criminal law reform, lesbian and gay pride marches and demonstrations, participation in international lesbian and gay events).

In some countries, lesbians also achieved visibility through their participation in leftist political parties. While the left generally considered lesbians and gays to be "decadent bourgeois," primarily Trotskyists affiliated with the 4th Socialist International supported lesbian and gay struggles in various Latin American countries and in Mexico sponsored open lesbian and gay candidates for political positions during the 1980s and 1990s.[7]

However, though Latin American lesbian activism can be traced through joint activities with gay males and leftist political parties, the feminist encuentros have been chosen as the sites for study because they are the major arenas in which lesbians from diverse countries have been able to meet periodically to discuss issues of concern and plan strategies for combatting heterosexism and lesbophobia. The nature of the encuentros will be discussed briefly below to provide a context from which to understand the participation of lesbian-feminists within them.

Latin American and Caribbean Feminist Encuentros

The six Latin American feminist encuentros held between 1980 and 1993 shared many common themes, one of which concerned the composition of encuentro participants. Between 1980 and 1993 participation in Latin America's feminist encuentros became increasingly diverse. Participants in the 1st Feminist Encuentro (1st-FE) (1980) tended to be women from feminist organizations, feminist members of leftists parties, and unaffiliated women. By the 6th Feminist Encuentro (6th-FE) (1993) participants also included women active in nonleftist political parties, women who worked for the state, union women, Catholic feminists, members of lesbian-feminist groups, and members of what in the region are called "women's movements" (e.g., housewives' associations, mothers' clubs, neighborhood groups).[8]

As more women who did not consider themselves feminists began to participate both as organizers of and delegates to the encuentros, the frustration of longtime feminists increased. They felt that the encuentros were losing their feminist character and becoming meeting places for nonfeminist "popular sector" and political party women whose only concern was to divert the energy of the movement to their respective causes. Underlying these disagreements was also the issue of whether class or gender should be prioritized when analyzing women's condition. As a result of these conflicts, at each encuentro discussions ensued about how feminism should be defined and how women who were not feminists should be incorporated within feminist movements.

The issue of whether the feminist movements should remain autonomous resurfaced in some form or another at each encuentro. The discussion at the encuentros during the beginning of the 1980s centered on the relationship between feminist movements and leftist political parties. As women began to participate in the civilian governmental structures and state-sponsored organizations and programs created during the 1980s, many sought the support of organized feminist sectors. However, a significant number of feminists questioned women's participation in civilian governments with close ties to the same military sectors responsible for the torture and murder of thousands of people during military dictatorships.

The role played by national and international private and governmental funding agencies in helping to finance encuentros and feminist organizing efforts was also hotly debated at each of the encuentros. Moreover, as feminists continued to form Non-Governmental Organizations (NGOs) and receive external funding,[9] they came under criticism by other feminists who argued that access to such funding created an "elite" group that determined the agenda and research interests of their organizations. They believed that with the funding also came attempts by the donor agencies to limit the scope of group activities and that such restrictions compromised the autonomy of the organizations receiving funds. It was additionally argued that because funders required being kept abreast of local organizing efforts, they had the potential to play a surveillance role for national and international security agencies.

Another theme prevalent during the organizing of the encuentros was the relationship between women living inside and outside the region. Many Latin American women living in the United States and Europe sought to forge alliances with their sisters back home in order to combat their common experiences of racial, ethnic, and class discrimination and economic exploitation. However, the reaction of some encuentro organizers and participants was less than welcoming. In some encuentros Latin American women living abroad were charged the same registration fees as Anglo/European women despite the different access to resources among both groups of women. In at least one encuentro quotas were set for foreign participants in which Latin American women living outside the region had to compete with non-Latinas for entrance into the encuentro. Ironically, some encuentro organizers developed closer ties with their white Anglo/European women funders than with Latin American women living abroad. Thus, the alliance between Latin American women living inside and outside the region was continually frustrated.

Other themes that resurfaced at the encuentros were the ways in which each of the gatherings was structured, how to maintain continuity between encuentros, and the manner in which privileges based on race/ethnicity, color, class, and heterosexuality kept women separated.

In spite of the differences among feminists, the resolutions passed at each of the six encuentros supported national liberation struggles, anti-imperialist movements around the world, and an end to human rights violations. Workshop and panel resolutions called for an end to the oppression of poor and working-class peoples, ethnic/racial minorities, and women, and for full inclusion of these sectors in all spheres of economic, political, and social life.

Like their heterosexual peers, Latin American lesbian-feminists helped create and sustain organizations covering a wide range of issues generally identified with feminism. As such, Latin American lesbians, both from inside and outside the closet, formed an integral part of women's movements, human rights groups, and self-identified feminist groups. Some had been militant in left-wing political parties and collectives. Furthermore, in countries such as Argentina, Brazil, and Chile, many lesbians were "disappeared" by military regimes along with their gay brothers. Others died in guerrilla struggles waged in countries like Nicaragua and El Salvador. Still others participated in revolutionary governments in Cuba and Nicaragua. While throughout the period studied some continued to support "double militancy," others supported the existence of both autonomous feminist and autonomous lesbian-feminist movements.

Once feminist movements emerged as viable political forces and provided spaces, such as the encuentros, in which women could discuss a number of controversial issues, lesbians demanded that these spaces be available for them to discuss the nature of their particular oppression, to network among themselves, and to seek the support of heterosexual women to end hetero-sexism and lesbophobia. Partly because the concerns of lesbian-feminists could not be fully addressed within the heterosexual-dominated encuentros, lesbian-feminists decided to organize separate lesbian-feminist encuentros. Ultimately, lesbian activists sought to carry out permanent changes, not only on behalf of lesbians and other women in their societies, but also on behalf of other marginalized and oppressed groups. The means by which lesbian-feminists gradually took advantage of heterosexual-dominated encuentros to network and lobby on behalf of their agendas will be discussed below. A brief discussion of the lesbian-feminist encuentros as well as their impact on the heterosexual-dominated encuentros will also be provided.

Lesbian Activism and the Latin American and Caribbean Feminist Encuentros

1st Latin American and Caribbean Feminist Encuentro: Bogotá, Colombia (1980)

The 1st-FE was attended by three hundred women representing eleven Latin American countries in addition to Curaçao, Canada, the United States, and European countries. Although those attending included lesbians as well as heterosexuals, the specific concerns of lesbians were not officially addressed by organizers in any of the scheduled workshops/panels. In view of such omission, a Canadian lesbian mother argued that time be allotted to discuss the oppression to which lesbians were subjected.[10] The response of encuentro organizers was to cancel all scheduled workshops and to hold a plenary session on lesbianism. The fact that many heterosexual women were curious about lesbian sexuality became evident when 80 percent of the women present attended the plenary. Basic themes discussed included: myths about lesbians; coming out; lesbian mothers; role-playing and feminism; and lesbian sexuality.

The closest the 1st-FE came, however, to publicly supporting lesbian-feminists was the passing of a resolution stating, "We denounce the social pressure exerted on women who reject the traditional roles imposed on them."[11] Nonetheless, the lesbian presence had made itself felt at the encuentro and was to become a visible component of all subsequent encuentros.

2nd Latin American and Caribbean Feminist Encuentro (2nd-FE): Lima, Peru (1983)

The 2nd-FE was attended by over six hundred women living in at least eight Latin American countries, the United States, Curaçao, and Europe. While encuentro organizers scheduled nineteen workshops narrowly organized around the theme of patriarchy, neither heterosexism, lesbophobia, nor lesbian sexuality were included in the official program. Within this context, two lesbian activists from Mexico and two Latina immigrants to the United States (including myself) sought to schedule an impromptu lesbian workshop. Although some lesbians felt that the topic of lesbianism might be better discussed in the "sexuality" workshop, in consultation with others we decided to schedule a separate "mini-workshop" called "Lesbianism and Patriarchy," and I agreed to participate as an open lesbian in the sexuality workshop. Participation in the sexuality workshop would be geared toward establishing that lesbianism was a valid and healthy sexual option for women. The workshop on lesbianism would allow lesbians to counter the assumption that lesbianism was solely about sex.

In the end, the lesbianism workshop was led by a Cuban immigrant to the United States, myself, a Puerto Rican immigrant to the United States, and a Mexican lesbian activist. The workshop was attended by half of the women in the encuentro. The overwhelming attendance of heterosexual-identified women at the workshop illustrated how curious they were about lesbian relationships and sexuality and the alternatives these offered women who wanted to break out of traditional roles.

Basic themes discussed during the workshop included: myths about lesbians; coming out; role-playing; lesbian mothers; heterosexism and lesbophobia; and the relationship between lesbianism and feminism. Other subjects discussed included how lesbians were being forced by heterosexism and lesbophobia to form autonomous lesbian organizations.

Most of the lesbians who openly shared their personal experiences were Latin American immigrants to the United States. A few others lived in Mexico, Peru, and Brazil. At the time, the only lesbian group represented at the

2nd-FE was Grupo de Acao Lésbica-Feminista Sao Paulo (GALF-Sao Paulo, Brazil). The overall individual participation of lesbians at the workshop indicated the early stages lesbian organizing efforts were at inside and outside the region.

The participation of sisters living abroad was crucial because many lesbians living in the region were hesitant to come out of the closet in front of heterosexual women from their own countries. Some feared that if they came out publicly, heterosexual members of their delegations would discriminate against them and maybe even fire some of them from their jobs once they returned home. However, the prominent participation of Latin American immigrants to the United States led one closeted Peruvian lesbian to argue that the discussion was framed in a North American and foreign context (i.e., my being Puerto Rican). She argued that in Latin America the population was basically either heterosexual or bisexual. These remarks evidenced not only the speaker's internalized lesbophobia but also the hostility that some Latin American lesbians felt toward women living in the United States and Puerto Rico, a U.S. colony. Yet, other Latin American lesbians living in the region argued that lesbians were also oppressed in Latin America. The fact that Latin American lesbians from several countries came out of the closet at an international gathering itself challenged assumptions that lesbianism was irrelevant to the realities of the lives of Latin American women.

Another consequence of the workshop was that although some heterosexual women threatened to leave the encuentro because of the presence of open lesbians and others refused to be housed with lesbians, a significant number of heterosexual women took the opportunity to explore their sexuality. Closeted lesbians were also able to come out safely in the presence of other lesbians. Furthermore, a significant number of lesbians became convinced of the need to create autonomous lesbian-feminist organizations that could serve as more effective vehicles for challenging heterosexism inside and outside feminist movements.

The lesbian resolution submitted and adopted at the final plenary and printed up as part of *Las Memorias*, or minutes of the encuentro, found the following: heterosexuality was imposed on all women; lesbianism was a global phenomenon; lesbians, like other minority groups, have been oppressed and marginalized throughout history; and lesbians have been an integral part of feminist movements. As a result, lesbianism and lesbian oppression fell within a feminist framework. The resolution called for the questioning of compulsory heterosexuality and for heterosexual-dominated feminist movements to openly support the right of women to be lesbians. It also demanded that in subsequent encuentros lesbian oppression form an integral part of all discussions on women's oppression.[12] Moreover, lesbians emphasized the need for open lesbians to become more visible within feminist movements. However, although the lesbian resolution was printed in *Las Memorias*, its presentation in the document remained tainted with mixed images of lesbians. The title page of the resolution showed a lesbian facing the wall as if lesbians had something to hide from or be ashamed of.

3rd Latin American and Caribbean Feminist Encuentro (3rd-FE): Bertioga, Brazil (1985)

The 3rd-FE was attended by over 850 women living in fourteen Latin American countries, the Dutch Antilles, the United States, Canada, and Europe. Workshops and resolutions tended to reflect those held at earlier encuentros. [13] Two major innovations were that for the first time a workshop on lesbianism and one on racism were officially scheduled by encuentro organizers. The open inclusion of lesbians and lesbian concerns was made possible because for the first time some encuentro organizers were lesbians active in lesbian-feminist organizations in Brazil, which had a visible lesbian and gay civil rights movement.

The 3rd-FE saw the active participation of three lesbian groups: GALF-Sao Paulo (Brazil), Colectivo de Lesbianas (Spain), and Grupo de Auto Conciencia de Lesbianas Feministas (GALF-Peru), the latter created after the 2nd-FE. Members of these organizations and independent lesbians held a caucus that organized four workshops. Three of these were: "Lesbianism: Notes for a Feminist Discussion," "The Lack of Lesbian Presence in Publications," and "Organizing Ourselves as Lesbians." The workshops discussed compulsory heterosexuality, lesbophobia within feminist movements, lesbian invisibility in the media, and the need for women occupying government positions to propose and support lesbian and gay rights legislation. Participants also discussed internalized lesbophobia, the relationship between lesbianism and feminism, and difficulties confronted in organizing lesbians.

The issues of heterosexism and lesbophobia were also brought up in other workshops, such as one on sexuality and one on the Sandinista Revolution in Nicaragua. In the latter, lesbians challenged the statements of one of the panelists who, while acknowledging the contributions of lesbians and gays to the Sandinista Revolution and Nicaraguan society, denied the continued oppression of lesbians and gays under the Sandinista Revolution.

Conflicts arose with heterosexual women when the lesbian caucus defended the decision to hold some closed sessions in order to discuss the strategies and tactics needed to organize lesbians and to counteract lesbophobia, particularly within feminist movements. Many lesbians resented having to spend the limited time available answering the questions of heterosexual women concerning lesbian identity and sexuality. Lesbian resolutions reiterated those of the previous encuentros and called for the inclusion of lesbian concerns throughout future encuentro activities.

4th Latin American and Caribbean Feminist Encuentro (4th-FE):
Taxco, Mexico (1987)

The 4th-FE was attended by 1,500 women from nineteen Latin American countries, Haiti, Europe, and the United States. The turnout reflected the strength and interest feminism had awakened in women throughout the region, particularly among Central American women from the women's movements. The latter were motivated to organize around gender-specific concerns as a result of the sexism they experienced both in national liberation struggles and in the civilian governments being constructed during the 1980s.

Though resolutions resembled those of previous encuentros, participants at the 4th-FE also called for the organizing of national and/or subregional encuentros and for peasant women, women domestic workers, and prostitutes to be represented at the next encuentro. They also called for the creation of women's lands, for a broader definition of feminism, the development of closer ties between theoretical feminism and women's movements, and for liberation theology to support the liberation of women.[14]

This time a significant number of lesbians came to the encuentro with agendas resulting from their participation at the 9th Conference of the International Lesbian Information Services (ILIS) in Geneva (March 1986),[15] and, most important, at the 1st Lesbian-Feminist Encuentro (1st-LFE) held in Cuernavaca a few days prior to the 4th-FE in Taxco.

The convening of the 1st-LFE attended by over 240 lesbians demonstrated the growth in the number of lesbian-feminist groups created between the 3rd-FE (1985) and 4th-FE (1987). Present were women from thirteen Latin American lesbian groups representing Brazil, Peru, the Dominican Republic, Chile, Costa Rica, Mexico, and the United States, as well as non-Latina representatives from Holland. Also present were unaffiliated lesbians and/or lesbian members of mixed groups from these countries and from Colombia, Argentina, Honduras, Nicaragua, Panama, and Trinidad and Tobago.

Despite the commonalities between lesbians organizing inside and outside the region, the 1st-LFE was plagued by a host of conflicts that hindered unity efforts.[16] The conflicts reflected the personal and political rivalries that characterized the increasingly diversified Latin American lesbian communities. They centered on the role diverse groups of lesbians should play and the rights they should have in future lesbian-feminist encuentros and in La Red de Lesbianas Latinoamericanas y del Caribe (hereafter La Red), the Latin American lesbian network created during the ILIS conference. Issues debated were the role of: members of lesbian groups; unaffiliated lesbians; lesbians living outside the region; and lesbian members of mixed groups. Particularly destructive were the conflicts that arose between lesbians living inside and outside the region and among Mexican lesbians. Although Latin American lesbians living in the United States were expected to provide funding for the

1st-LFE, some living in the region feared that those living abroad would set the agenda for lesbian organizing in the region if their numbers were too large. The conflicts among Mexican lesbians were based on longstanding personal and political rivalries.

To these conflicts were added those concerning the role to be played by European lesbians and international funders (i.e., ILIS, the Dutch government). Some lesbians resented the fact that Latin American lesbians had been partially prompted to organize the 1st-LFE and La Red because they had been told during the 9th ILIS Conference that in order to receive funding they must hold a lesbian-feminist encuentro and form a "network" (what became La Red). Those supporting foreign funding maintained that Latin American lesbian visibility was bolstered by developing ties with international lesbian and gay rights organizations such as ILIS and the International Lesbian and Gay Association (ILGA). Such affiliations could also reduce the isolation of Latin American lesbians and allow them access to funding to support local organizing and regional networking efforts.

Despite the existence of widespread differences among them, when the 1st-LFE ended those lesbians planning to attend the 4th-FE which followed left the gathering firmly committed to making sure that the concerns of lesbians were addressed by heterosexual feminists. The ability of lesbians to work together during the 4th-FE was facilitated by the fact that a significant number of lesbians who attended had not been at the 1st-LFE. Also, the fact that at the 4th-FE the number of Latin American lesbians living abroad was minimal meant that they no longer represented the threat to lesbians living in the region that they had at the 1st-LFE. Lesbians present at the 1st-LFE made sure that the workshops that had not be held there were held during the 4th-FE.

Once at the 4th-FE, the growth of Latin American lesbian activism made itself evident when, during the opening ceremonies, nine delegations indicated that they included lesbians among them. These delegations represented Brazil, Chile, Costa Rica, Dominican Republic, Mexico, Nicaragua, Peru, Puerto Rico, and the United States. Although some of these lesbians belonged to lesbian-feminist groups in their countries, also present were unaffiliated lesbians and lesbians from mixed groups from these countries and from Argentina, Ecuador, Guatemala, Honduras, and Venezuela.

For lesbians, the 4th-FE represented the second time encuentro organizers had officially scheduled lesbian workshops. The first was titled "Lesbianism and Politics: The Political Relations between the Lesbian-Feminist Movements and the Heterosexual Feminist Movements," the second, "Body Politics: Sexuality. The Unconscious—The Body. Seduction. Cultural Roles. Growing Old. Lesbianism." Nonetheless, lesbians continued to feel these topics confined them to discussions that were of primary interest to heterosexual women or discussed lesbians solely as sexual beings. Consequently, lesbians meeting in a caucus decided to both participate in the scheduled workshops and hold closed sessions.

While scheduled plenaries and workshops took place in two locations simultaneously, lesbians met as one group for four consecutive days, seeking to strengthen their ability to network and strategize, which had been severely shaken during the 1st-LFE. Sessions included "Lesbianism and Politics," "Myths, Roles, and Sexuality," "Lesbian Mothers," and "Lesbianism and Repression."

While the discussions during the first three workshops resembled those of earlier encuentros, the workshop titled "Lesbianism and Political Repression" began with the showing of a news clipping of a 1987 raid of a lesbian bar in Peru in which seventy-five women were arrested and mistreated by police officers. The television networks, insensitive as to how the public exposure of lesbians would affect them, had aired the news clipping three times. Although at the time there was a government-imposed curfew, many women were released from the police station shortly after midnight. Women present at the workshop discussed the occurrence of similar incidents in their own countries. They also examined the manner in which lesbians were oppressed by internalized lesbophobia and their own alcoholism.

During the 4th-FE lesbians also exchanged visual and written materials including the newly published *Compañeras: Latina Lesbians (An Anthology)*.[17] The fact that the book documented the lives of forty-seven Latin American lesbians born in ten different countries allowed lesbians living inside and outside the region to compare their experiences.

As in the case of the previous two feminist encuentros, the conclusions of the various lesbian workshops were included in *Las Memorias*.[18] In addition to the themes included in earlier gatherings, lesbian resolutions at the 4th-FE called for the following: denouncing human rights violations against lesbians before international organs; the creation of groups to lobby for the repeal of anti-lesbian and anti-gay legislation; and the formation of coalitions to fight all forms of oppression. Lesbians also resolved to use La Red to both disseminate information about the repression of lesbians and solicit support.

In spite of the attempts to foster unity during the encuentro among lesbian participants, there were two separate lesbian contingents at the march held at the conclusion of the 4th-FE. Members of the Seminario Marxista Leninista Feminista de Lesbianas (Mexico) had been asked by organizers to march at the end because their banner was considered too large. But few lesbians were willing to march behind them both because of political positions members had taken during the 1st-LFE and 4th-FE and because their banner had the picture of a woman with a rifle in her hands and her breasts exposed. In the end, a small number of lesbians chose to march with the Seminario because it was dangerous to let them march alone at the end where they could be easily attacked both because they were lesbians and openly supported armed struggle.

Once the 4th-FE ended, organizers asked Rebeca Sevilla, a Peruvian lesbian activist, and me if we were willing to participate as open lesbians in a press conference along with heterosexual-identified women and several closeted lesbians. It was the first time open lesbians were included at an encuentro press conference in a Spanish-speaking country. By such inclusion organizers publicly acknowledged and supported the presence and participation of lesbians at the encuentro and in feminist movements. These lesbians and others from Peru and Mexico were also interviewed for German radio stations, thus giving Latin American lesbian concerns more exposure.

5th Latin American and Caribbean Feminist Encuentro (5th-FE): San Bernardo, Argentina (1990)

The 5th-FE, organized by feminists from Argentina and Uruguay, was attended by three thousand women from thirty-eight different countries, the most heavily attended of all the encuentros. Notable was the participation of women legislators from Argentina, Venezuela, and Uruguay, many of whom did not consider themselves feminists. As in the case of the 3rd-FE and 4th-FE, a "Lesbianism" workshop was officially scheduled. Also, racial and religious minorities as well as lesbians and other "marginalized groups within the patriarchy" were allotted a time slot and a room to meet each day. Lesbian-feminists took advantage of these open spaces, made sure that lesbian concerns were raised in other workshops, and also met in closed sessions during the four days of the encuentro.

During the 5th-FE, members of Costa Rica's lesbian-feminist group, Grupo Lésbico-Feminista Costarricense Las Entendidas, discussed the lack of support they had received from heterosexual feminists during the organizing of the 2nd Lesbian-Feminist Encuentro (2nd-LFE) held in Costa Rica earlier that year. At the time, conservative forces throughout Central America and as far away as Peru but particularly right-wing newspapers, television stations, legislators, and religious leaders in Costa Rica, had launched an extensive attack against encuentro organizers.[19] The attacks, which began weeks prior to the holding of the 2nd-LFE, accused lesbians of attempting to corrupt and pervert the minds of young girls. Conservatives argued that lesbians were going to have a "satanic orgy." They feared lesbians and gays would consequently hold lesbian and gay pride marches and demand an end to the legal and social discrimination against them.

The impact of the widespread publicity intensified the lesbophobia/homophobia already made acute in Costa Rica by anti–AIDS sentiments. AIDS phobia had led to the closing of gay male bars and made women's bars more vulnerable. It also encouraged acts of violence against lesbians and gays. Although a few organizations did support 2nd-LFE organizers before the holding of the event, the controversy revealed the widespread lack of support for lesbians among Costa Rican heterosexual feminists.

As a result of a press conference held after the 2nd-LFE by lesbians living outside the country (at the request of Costa Rican lesbians) and a letter written by 150 influential Costa Ricans criticizing the treatment lesbians had received from the media, the media's portrayal of lesbians changed somewhat for the better.

In spite of the controversy, during the 2nd-LFE lesbians living in Costa Rica, Ecuador, Peru, Argentina, Puerto Rico, the United States, Spain, and Germany were able to solidify La Red. Participants left knowing that representatives of Aquelarre Lésbico, Puerto Rico's lesbian-feminist group, had taken responsibility for organizing the 3rd-LFE in 1992. In Costa Rica, Latinas living in the U.S. also began filming a documentary on Latin American lesbians.

Events surrounding the organizing of the 2nd-LFE, however, had a profound negative effect on the lesbian community of Costa Rica. The publicity had led some 2nd-LFE organizers not to attend the encuentro for fear that they would lose their jobs. Other lesbians were pushed back into the closet. Although after the encuentro some of those who had withdrawn from Las Entendidas following the eruption of the controversy rejoined the group or attended its events, they were resented by many of those who felt they had been forced by circumstances to come out of the closet. The fact that the overwhelming number of heterosexual feminists had not offered their support disillusioned many lesbians who looked to feminist movements for support. Still, Las Entendidas continued to advocate on behalf of lesbians for a few more years.

Partly as a response to the events described above at the 5th-FE, members of Las Entendidas presented a paper summarizing the concerns of lesbian-feminists expressed in previous encuentros. Titled "From the Lesbian Experience to the Fifth Feminist Encuentro with Love and Knowledge," the document traced the history of lesbophobia within feminist movements in Latin America and provided a theoretical basis for the need to examine women's oppression using a lesbian-feminist perspective as a point of departure.[20] The document reiterated the need to incorporate lesbian-feminism into the central themes of future encuentros. It also called for analyzing the interrelationship among ethnicity, class, gender, and sexuality.

The experiences of Las Entendidas illustrated the struggles lesbian-feminists have continually had to wage both within and outside feminist movements. They showed the isolation lesbians faced in their countries and, hence, the urgency for them to unite across local, national, and international borders.

The solidarity among the lesbians present at the 5th-FE, however, was tested when in a workshop facilitated by a Mexican lesbian and a Spanish lesbian, the latter supported sadomasochism, pedophilia, and pornography as healthy alternatives. It was the first time such issues had been debated within a lesbian-feminist workshop in the encuentros. As a result of the lack of support among Latin American lesbian-feminists for these positions, such arguments have not been raised at subsequent encuentros.

A less serious controversy ensued when several lesbians became upset because a Puerto Rican lesbian held a session titled "Lesbophobia Workshop for Heterosexual Women." While several lesbians present chose to share their diverse personal and political experiences, others resented the organizer for what they perceived as "catering" to heterosexual women.

Despite the differences among them at the 5th-FE, lesbians continued to network and socialize with one another. Moreover, regional networks formed by lesbians and heterosexual women who shared similar interests (e.g., eliminating racism, health concerns, media) were further strengthened. It was also at the 5th-FE that members of La Red met to further discuss the 3rd-LFE planned for 1992. I also took the opportunity to continue filming encuentro proceedings and conducting interviews for a forthcoming video documentary on Latin American lesbians.

At the end of the 5th-FE, lesbians were encouraged by organizers to hold their own press conference. While the press conference allowed lesbians to share their views on lesbian oppression in different parts of the western hemisphere, it also allowed heterosexual women to distance themselves somewhat from "the lesbians" at the gathering. Unlike the case of the 4th-FE where lesbians marched in two separate contingents, in the 5th-FE they marched together. The contingent also included the participation of members of the Comunidad Homosexual Argentina, a local lesbian and gay organization.

6th Latin American and Caribbean Feminist Encuentro (6th-FE): Costa del Sol, El Salvador (1993)

The 6th-FE was the first encuentro to be organized by a subregional organizing commission. Although the politically tense situation in El Salvador and the vocal resistance to the encuentro expressed by conservative forces in Central America reduced the number of participants, over 1,200 women attended the event.

Encuentro workshops included the customary topics as well as discussions of Mapuche (indigenous peoples) politics and the forthcoming United Nations Conference on Women in Beijing, China, in 1995. It was in El Salvador that workshops concerning Latin American women in the diaspora were most heavily attended by women living inside the region. The attendance reflected a recognition of the solidarity work Latin American women in the

United States and Europe have carried out on behalf of national liberation movements in Latin America.

Prior to the 6th-FE, the commitment on the part of a significant number of encuentro organizers to support lesbian-feminists had become evident in a number of ways. In a pre-encuentro gathering held in March 1992, organizers reiterated their commitment to supporting several decisions taken at the 5th-FE, including the incorporation of lesbian-feminist issues as one of the thematic cores of the encuentro. This commitment led to the deliberate inclusion of members of lesbian-feminist groups in the encuentro's organizing commission despite the resistance of some organizers.[21]

For lesbian-feminists, another significant development was the manner in which organizers responded to several attacks made by conservatives opposed to the holding of the 6th-FE. As early as five weeks prior to the encuentro, articles published by the Salvadoran Feminine Front[22] and by Salvadorans living in San Francisco claimed that the 6th-FE was a gathering of lesbians and gays[23] as well as supporters of the Committee in Support of the People of El Salvador (CISPES) and the Farabundo Marti National Liberation Front (FMLN), the former guerrilla army turned political party. A notice published by the Association of Salvadoran Women a week prior to the 6th-FE summarized some of major positions:

> A group of foreign women—with the support of CISPES—is organizing for October 30 through November 3, the 6th FEMINIST CONGRESS under the guise of defending the rights of Central American women. But in reality, it is a CONGRESS OF LESBIANS, HOMOSEXUALS, BISEXUALS AND PERVERTS (queers), like they have in other countries. This would crush our moral, religious and civic values, in addition to endangering the health of Salvadoran women. For this reason, we alert our compatriots not to allow themselves to be surprised concerning the real aims of the 6th FEMINIST CONGRESS.[24]

The attempts to discredit the 6th-FE continued, as indicated by an article published a few days prior to the encuentro, which stated that encuentro organizers promoted abortion and the discussion of lesbianism.[25] The articles were accompanied by personal threats to organizers as well as threats to local business owners in Costa del Sol, where the 6th-FE was to be held. The threats led one hotel to cancel its contract with organizers.[26]

CISPES and encuentro organizers refused to be intimidated by such tactics. While CISPES admitted that it had organized a delegation to attend the 6th-FE, it denied that it had anything to do with the organizing of the event. CISPES accused right-wing sectors, who opposed the peace negotiations then taking place in El Salvador, with trying to discredit the 6th-FE as well as trying to disrupt the process of democratization. It asked ONUSAL to take precautions to ensure the personal safety of encuentro organizers and threatened to take judicial measures to stop the campaign of defamation against it and other organizations.[27]

The efforts of CISPES were complemented in the United States by those of private citizens, legislators, religious entities, publications, legal groups, women's groups, and lesbian and gay organizations who voiced their concerns that the 6th-FE take place without difficulties.[28] The International Gay and Lesbian Human Rights Commission (San Francisco) also called for lesbian and gay activists to send letters of protest to the government of El Salvador.[29]

In the meantime, encuentro organizers sought to meet with the president of El Salvador, representatives of ONUSAL, and the presidents of the legislative and judicial bodies in order to ensure the safety of encuentro participants.[30] Organizers rejected the claims that they had any ties with the FMLN or any other political party or with the lesbian and gay delegation being sponsored by CISPES. They also exposed the fact that several newspapers had denied encuentro organizers the right to respond to the attacks made against them.

Encuentro organizers also stated, "Sexual preference is not asked as part of the enrollment. We do not deny that lesbian women will come."[31] However, they observed that "lesbian issues are only a small part of the encuentro, which will also focus on physical abuse of women, abortion and labor rights, and political organizing skills."[32] According to one organizer, the aim of the event was to advance the construction of the feminist political force. This translated into "achieving respect for women with respect to race, sexual options, and the right to abortion."[33] Fliers announcing the 6th-FE continued to state that feminist discussions at the gathering would include the issue of struggling "for a sexuality free of prejudices."[34]

One of the positive developments that took place during the controversy was the creation of the Salvadoran lesbian-feminist collective, Colectiva Lésbica Feminista Salvadoreña de la Media Luna and the publication of the first issue of its newsletter *Luna de Miel* just prior to the 6th-FE.[35] The growth in the number of lesbian organizations in the region was reflected at the 6th-FE by the participation of representatives from Media Luna (El Salvador), Colectivo de Lesbianas Feministas "Ciguay" (Dominican Republic), Colectivo Lésbico Homosexual (Nicaragua), Convocatoria Lesbiana (Argentina), El Closet de Sor Juana (Mexico), Las Entendidas (Costa Rica), Rede de Información Lésbica Um Outro Olhar (Brazil), and Tal Para Cual (Ecuador). Also present were representatives of the Latina Lesbian History Project (U.S.), the Colectivo de Feministas Lésbicas (Spain), *LSD*—Grupo de Lesbianas Feministas de Madrid (Spain), ILIS (Holland), the Movimiento Homosexual de Lima (Peru), and the International Gay and Lesbian Human Rights Commission (U.S.). Unaffiliated lesbians and/or lesbians from mixed groups also came from these countries as well as Bolivia, Chile, Colombia, Guatemala, Honduras, Argentina, Canada, and England.

Prior to the 6th-FE a few members of lesbian groups in Latin America had participated in several ILGA conferences, most significantly the one held in

1991 in Acapulco, Mexico, amid vocal resistance by conservative sectors. The controversy, combined with ILGA's stipulation that local gay leaders include lesbians in the organizing process, had significantly increased lesbian visibility in Mexico.[36] During the ILGA conference Latin American lesbians, some of whom had participated in lesbian-feminist encuentros, were able to meet once again. Although conflicts arose over personal and political differences, in particular the nature of La Red, the immediate threats and dangers posed by conservative forces in Mexico somewhat united lesbians at the event.

In addition to attending the 1991 ILGA conference, some of the lesbians present at the 6th-FE had participated in the 3rd-LFE held in Puerto Rico during 1992.[37] The 3rd-LFE had witnessed a series of conflicts that once again hindered the ability of Latin American lesbians to fully work together. The fact that a significant number of Latin American lesbians at the encuentro lived in the United States contributed to the resurgence of tensions between lesbians living outside and inside the region. The latter resented the presence of lesbians living abroad and the chauvinism exhibited by two lesbians living in the United States. Some of those living outside the region argued in turn that lesbians in Latin America needed to stop using them as scapegoats and start analyzing their own racial, ethnic, and class privilege in relation to other women in their countries. As had occurred at the 1st-LFE in Mexico, such conflicts were used as a reason by lesbians living in the region to hold a "closed workshop" from which those living outside the region were excluded. A meeting was subsequently held to bridge the gap between the two groups but the wounds have been slow to heal.

Added to these conflicts were those arising from personal and political differences between members of the Brazilian delegation. Conflicts also arose between lesbians who wanted to be able to bring their small children to subsequent lesbian-feminist encuentros and those who opposed it. The 3rd-LFE ended without any specific country taking responsibility for organizing a 4th-LFE. However, representatives of Coordinadora del Tercer Encuentro de Lesbianas Feministas (CELF) (Puerto Rico), Colectivo Ciguay (Dominican Republic) and Las Entendidas (Costa Rica) agreed to hold a regional consultation to discuss the matter in the future.

The regional consultation, which also came to include representatives of Tal Para Cual (Ecuador), El Closet de Sor Juana (Mexico), and Um Otro Olhar (Brazil), took place in the Dominican Republic in June 1993, just months prior to the 6th-FE. It concluded that although Brazil was the most logical site for the next lesbian-feminist encuentro, the final decision concerning the host country was to be made by the lesbians attending the 6th-FE.[38]

At the 6th-FE, tensions based on personal and political differences continued to plague the lesbian caucus, where some argued that international funding from Anglo/European lesbian and gay organizations, such as ILGA and

ILIS, was creating a self-perpetuating Latin American lesbian "elite" concerned with monopolizing such funding for their own self-aggrandizement.

In spite of such differences, lesbians workshops at the 6th-FE were held under the headings of "Lesbianism," "Coming Out as a Lesbian," and "Lesbianism, Compulsory Heterosexuality, and Human Rights." Lesbian-feminists also continued meeting in closed sessions throughout the gathering, now under the label of "Organized Lesbians." Additionally, an Anglo lesbian filmmaker was authorized by encuentro organizers to film a discussion among lesbians for inclusion in her documentary about the encuentro. 6th-FE Resolutions continued to reflect lesbian concerns.

Conclusion

Latin American lesbians, like their heterosexual peers, participated in a number of social movements that sought to bring about a fundamental change in the sociopolitical and economic structure of their societies. As such, they formed an integral part of women's movements, human rights groups, and feminist organizations. When feminists began to organize regional encuentros, lesbian-feminists made their voices heard within them.

The open participation of lesbians within the feminist encuentros developed gradually. At first, lesbians were afraid to come out in their countries and in the feminist encuentros for fear that they would be rejected by their heterosexual peers. However, because a number of Latin American lesbians living inside and outside the region consistently took the initiative to come out at the encuentros, more lesbians were encouraged to do the same. Lesbians participated as organizers of encuentros, as workshop leaders and participants, and as cultural workers. They carried out documentation projects, distributed literature, helped create special-interest regional networks, marched in lesbian contingents, and participated in press conferences.

Once lesbians came out of the closet within feminist organizations and regional gatherings, heterosexual feminists and closeted lesbian-feminists responded in diverse ways. While some heterosexual feminists embraced lesbianism and/or lesbian goals without reservation, others excluded lesbians and lesbian concerns, and some went so far as to verbally and physically attack lesbians. Still others exhibited an ambivalent attitude, being willing to include open lesbians in their organizations and coalitions but demanding that they not come out publicly nor demand the incorporation of lesbian concerns into their agendas.

Lesbians responded to the heterosexism and lesbophobia of heterosexual feminists by joining mixed lesbian and gay groups, participating in leftist parties supportive of lesbian and gay rights, and by forming autonomous lesbian organizations. They also sought the political and financial support of international lesbian and gay organizations.

However, once lesbians began to organize within their own countries and across national boundaries, they were confronted with a number of personal and political conflicts resulting from the increasing diversity of the lesbian community. Ironically, a great deal of the solidarity exhibited by Latin American lesbians was carried out not at the lesbian-feminist encuentros but during the feminist encuentros. In these latter meetings, although lesbians felt most threatened by the lesbophobia of heterosexual women, lesbians living in the region felt the least threatened by the participation of lesbians living abroad.

While during the second half of the 1990s additional feminist and lesbian-feminists encuentros were held in the region, limitations of space combined with the complicated events surrounding the organization of the encuentros prevented such discussions from taking place here. Nonetheless, Latin American lesbians continued to participate in the organization of feminist and lesbian-feminist encuentros and to form lesbian-feminist groups. They repeatedly sought to consolidate a Latin American lesbian identity and agenda as well as solidify a regional lesbian network that could be called upon for support in times of local crisis.

Notes

I would like to thank Rosalind Ruth Calvert for her editing suggestions.

1. Latin America as used here includes Brazil, South and Central America, and the Caribbean.

2. *Encuentros* as used in the region signifies a meeting between individuals or groups designed for the interchange of ideas and experiences.

3. Nancy Saporta Sternbach, Marysa Navarro-Aranguren, Patricia Chuchryk, and Sonia E. Alvarez, "Feminisms in Latin America: From Bogotá to San Bernardo," *Signs* 17, no. 2 (Winter 1992): 393–434.

4. Ibid., 397.

5. Ibid., 404.

6. Ibid., 396.

7. See Norma Mogrovejo, "Un amor que se atrevió a decir su nombre: La lucha de las lesbianas y su relación con los movimientos homosexual y feminista en América Latina" (Ph.D. diss., Universidad Autónoma de México, 1998).

8. Sternbach et al., "Feminisms," 418.

9. Funders included private and governmental agencies from the Netherlands, England, West Germany, the United States, and various Latin American countries. See F.M.U. and M.C.V. "II Encuentro Feminista Latinoamericano y del Caribe," *brujas* (1983); Comissao Organizadora do III Encontro Feminista Latino Americano e Do Caribe, *Memoria, III Encuentro Feminista Latino-Americano e do Caribe* (Sao Paulo, Brazil, 1985), 99–100; and newsletter of Comité Preparatorio del VI Encuentro Feminista Latinoamericano y del Caribe, Centro América, "Descenredándonos: Recordando de San Bernardo a Montelimar," 1993.

10. "Latin America's *Encuentro Feminista*," *Connexions* no. 3 (Winter 1982); and Marysa Navarro, "The First Latin American Women's Conference," *Signs* 8 (1982): 154–57.

11. Author's translation. ISIS Internacional and Colectivo Coordinador del II Encuentro, *II Encuentro Feminista Latinoamericano y del Caribe* (Rome, 1984), 130.

12. Ibid., 56–57.

13. *Memoria del III Encuentro Feminista.*

14. Coordinadora del IV Encuentro Feminista Latinoamericano y del Caribe, *Memoria del IV Encuentro Feminista Latinoamericano y del Caribe* (Taxco, México, 1987).

15. "Conferencia Lésbica em Genebra," *Chana com Chana* 10 (Sao Paulo) (June 1986): 24–27.

16. L.A.L., "Mexicanas Organisan Conferencia Lesbiana," *Womanews* (November 1986), 4; Elena Popp, "First *Encuentro* of Lesbian Feminists," *Off Our Backs* 18, no. 3 (March 1988): 32–33; and Mogrovejo, "Un amor."

17. Juanita Ramos, ed., *Compañeras: Latina Lesbians (An Anthology)* (New York: Routledge, 1994; originally published by Latina Lesbian History Project, 1987).

18. *Memoria del IV Encuentro Feminista.*

19. Grupo Lésbico-Feminista Costarricense Las Entendidas, *Memoria de un Encuentro Inolvidable: II Encuentro Lésbico Feminista de América Latina y el Caribe* (San José, Costa Rica, 1990).

20. Las Entendidas, "Desde la experiencia lésbica, al V Encuentro con amor y sabiduría" (xeroxed document).

21. Comité Preparatorio del VI Encuentro, "Desenredándonos."

22. Frente Femenino Salvadoreño, "Voz de Alarma," *El Diario Hoy* (San Salvador), September 25, 1993.

23. See "Alerta sobre convención de apoyo a homosexuales," *El Mundo* (San Salvador, September 21, 1993.

24. Author's translation. Asociación de Mujeres Salvadoreñas, "¡Alerta, Mujeres Salvadoreñas!", October 23, 1993.

25. "Encuentro Feminista promueve el aborto" (author unknown).

26. Tim Johnson, "Lesbians' Planned Trip to Salvador Sparks Threats," *Miami Herald*, October 20, 1993, p. 10A; and "Hoteles no se prestarían para reunión homosexuales," *El Diario Hoy* (San Salvador), October 24, 1993, p. 29.

27. Comité en Solidaridad con el pueblo salvadoreño, "A La opinión pública salvadoreña," *La Prensa Gráfica*, October 5, 1993; "CISPES reafirma su compromiso con el pueblo salvadoreño y con su lucha para la democracia y la paz con justicia social," September 27, 1993; and Johnson, "Lesbians' Planned Trip."

28. Paul Wellstone et al., "Carta Abierta de ciudadanos norteamericanos para la seguridad e integridad del VI Encuentro Feminista Latinoamericano y del Caribe" (Instituto de Investigación, Capacitación y Desarrollo de la Mujer), 1993.

29. Johnson, "Lesbians' Planned Trip."

30. "Denuncian campaña de difamación contra sexto encuentro," *Diario Latino*, September 29, 1993, p. 3.

31. Johnson, "Lesbians' Planned Trip."

32. Ibid.

33. Author's translation. "Encuentro Feminista promueve el aborto."

34. Author's translation. Comité Regional Preparatorio del VI Encuentro Feminista Latinoamericano y del Caribe (flier).

35. Colectiva Lésbica Feminista Salvadoreña de la Media Luna, *Luna de Miel* (October 1993): 2 (newsletter).

36. Mongrovejo, "Un amor."

37. Irene León, trans. Miriam Martinho, "Lésbicas Em Borinquen: III Encontro de Lésbicas Feministas Latino-Americanas e do Caribe," *Um Outro Olhar* 19/20, no. 7 (Fall/Winter 1993): 24–26.

38. Personal and political differences among lesbians in Brazil that were apparent at the 3rd-LFE prevented the 4th-LFE from being held there.

FOUR

GLOBAL GAZE/GLOBAL GAYS

Dennis Altman

"What was fundamentally invisible is suddenly offered to the brightness of the gaze, in a movement of appearance so simple, so immediate that it seems to be the natural consequence of a more highly developed experience."[1]

IT IS EASY to point to the artifice of "Asia" to say that any concept which includes Uzbekis, Koreans, and Bangladeshis might as well find room for Australians. But this argument ignores the historical and racial ties of settler Australia to the Western world, ties that make our claim for inclusion in "Asia" sound ignorant of history and look like a new form of colonialism. Some readers of the first draft of this paper complained that the term "Asian" was too broad to be of value, yet it is frequently invoked by the groups themselves to stress certain communities in their history and experience.

This paper grew out of research I had begun on the development of identities and communities in archipelago Southeast Asia. This research, in turn, developed out of both my involvement in the development of regional community AIDS networks and the larger debate in Australia during the 1990s about that country's relationship to Asia.[2] I came to this research as a privileged white Australian gay intellectual, with access to considerable resources (intellectual, economic, political). But I am also very dependent on those I am researching, who have far greater cultural and linguistic knowledge than I possess, and whose explanations of phenomena reflect as much as mine a particular set of emotional and intellectual positions. In this situation I see myself as coresearcher, ultimately dependent on both the goodwill and self-interest of my informants.

The anthropologist can usually assume her "otherness" from the subject of her study. In my interactions with Southeast Asian gay men this assumption fails to hold up. My research builds on social interactions with people in a variety of settings, ranging from sitting on the beach in Bali to meetings in air-conditioned halls at AIDS conferences in New Delhi and Yokohama, and is predicated on my sharing a certain common ground—sexual, social, political—with those of whom I speak. I would argue that the best understandings of the gay worlds have come out of this way of work—see, for example,

Edmund White's account of pre–AIDS gay America, *States of Desire*[3]—but both academically and ethically this sort of "participant observation" poses dilemmas.

In researching the development of "Asian" (specifically archipelago Southeast Asian) gay worlds, I am both outsider and insider: indeed, I have had the experience of meeting Asian men, engaged in gay political work, who have been influenced by my own writings. Thus I am engaging with men where there is a complex power dynamic at work: I represent the power, prestige, and wealth of the West, but because we are meeting on a terrain of shared sexuality where mutual desire is an acknowledged possibility and where I depend on their goodwill, the power dynamics are not simply unidimensional. My relations with "Asian" "lesbians" reflects a greater distance, and so far I have not been able to make more than very superficial contacts (not least because of the ways in which international AIDS politics have opened up space for homosexual men but not women). I constantly have to balance what I seem to be seeing against an awareness that my "informants" are both telling stories for which I am the intended audience—and, often, which fit their desires to see themselves as part of a "modern" gay world.

These relationships are further complicated by two contradictory trends. On the one hand Asian gay men, by stressing a universal gay identity, underline a similarity with Westerners. Against this, the desire to assert an "Asian" identity, not unlike the rhetoric of the "Asian way" adopted by authoritarian regimes such as those of China, Indonesia, and Malaysia, may undermine this assumed solidarity. Moreover, the ubiquity of Western rhetoric means that many of the informants use the language of the West to describe a rather different reality. For example, the "Gay Men's Exchange," a "zine" (i.e., four-page photocopied newsletter) produced in Manila includes a two-page "Gay Man's Guide to Coming Out," reproduced from a popular American publication.[4] The sort of language of this and other Western publications helps determine not only the language used in groups but also who feels comfortable in discussions and how they explain their own feelings to themselves. Some years ago in Manila I watched the film *Victor/Victoria* on local television. Although it is ostensibly set in Paris in the 1930s, its characters speak of "coming out" as "gay." Such politically correct historical anachronisms presumably sends messages to the large audience who would have seen the film on prime time television.

Western lesbian/gay theorists and activists gradually are beginning to perceive the problems of claiming a universality for an identity that developed out of certain historical specificities. In his introduction to a book on "queer theory," Michael Warner wrote: "In the middle ground between the localism of 'discourse' and the generality of the subject is the problem of international—or otherwise translocal—sexual politics. As gay activists from nonwestern contexts become more and more involved in setting agendas, and as the rights discourse of internationalism is extended to more and more cultural contexts, Anglo-American queer theorists will have to be more alert to the globalizing—and localising—tendencies of our theoretical languages."[5]

It is interesting that none of the contributors to this particular book take up this challenge—despite its title, *Fear of a Queer Planet*. American "queer theory" remains as relentlessly Atlantic-centric in its view of the world as the mainstream culture it critiques. Equally interesting is the apparent lack of interest in "queer" theory in most of the non-Western world, and the continued usage by emerging movements of the terminology "lesbian" and "gay."

Sex/Gender/Sexuality in "Gay Asia"

In late June 1994 there was a very large demonstration in New York City to commemorate the twenty-fifth anniversary of Stonewall, the riots at a New York bar claimed as the birthplace of the modern gay/lesbian movement. The organizers went to some trouble to invite groups from the rest of the world—including the developing world—to participate, obviously believing that the events being celebrated were of universal relevance. In ways that would shock many anthropologists, a claim to the universality of "gay" and "lesbian" identities is emerging in the rhetoric of groups such as (to speak only of Asia) Bombay Dost, OCCUR in Japan, Ten Percent in Hong Kong, Pink Triangle in Malaysia, the Library Foundation in the Philippines, and the lesbian group Anjaree in Thailand.[6]

It could be objected that these groups represent only a very small part of the homosexual populations of these countries and that their use of language and symbols derived from overseas means they will be unable to mobilize significant numbers within their own societies. But twenty years ago the gay movements of North America, Australasia, and Western Europe similarly spoke for very few, and their growth was unpredictably rapid. Of course this happened where the largely American symbols could be made relevant to local conditions (as with Sydney's Gay and Lesbian Mardi Gras, which has become a uniquely Australian version of what elsewhere are "gay pride parades"). But in a world where more and more cultural styles are imported and assimilated, there seems to be no reason why a Western-style gayness should not prove as attractive as have other Western identities.

The question is how to balance the impact of universalizing rhetoric and styles with the continuing existence of cultural and social traditions. Let me cite an encounter with a young Filipino in a bar in Quezon City, Metro Manila, in the mid-1990s. Ricardo had just come from a meeting of his university gay group and was full of excitement at the prospect of an upcoming campus gay event. He spoke with enthusiasm of a march the university gay group was organizing in the neighborhood and of a play that had recently been presented in the bar where we were sitting.

The bar itself requires description: Cinecafe combines elements of a café, a bar, a porn video showroom, and a backroom for sex. All of this is contained in a very small, three-story building, hidden away in a back street far removed from the tourist hotels of Makati and Ermita, with a clientele that is almost entirely Filipino. At the same time there are certain aspects of Cinecafe that very clearly link it to a larger global gay world: the posters, the magazines, and the films themselves (exclusively French and American) were the same one might find in different but similar establishments in Zurich, Montreal, or Sydney. In many ways it is a third-world version of male sex-on-premises venues in such Western cities, although Cineclub is far smaller and less well appointed.

Ricardo himself (like so many middle-class Filipinos as fluent in English as in Tagalog) sounded remarkably like the young men I had known in the early 1970s in America, Australia, and Western Europe, and spoke indeed of gay liberation in phrases that were very familiar. This encounter raised a whole set of questions about the meaning of terms like "gay" and "gay liberation" in very different cultural contexts. For the streets outside were the streets of an undeniably third-world country, and the men in Cinecafe, while in many ways shaped by Western influence, were themselves part of Filipino society, seeking each other out in ways similar to the ways homosexuals seek each other out in the West and not there (as some versions of the globalization of sexuality would have it) to meet Westerners or foreign tourists.

There are equivalents to Cinecafe in other parts of Asia; the past decade has seen the growth of a commercial gay world beyond its few existing bastions such as Bangkok and Tokyo to cover most of the countries of Asia where there is sufficient economic and political space. Both affluence and political liberalism seem required for a commercial gay world to appear: that it appears to be bigger in Manila than Singapore is due to a number of factors of which comparative political tolerance is perhaps the most essential.

In recent years gay film festivals and magazines have appeared in Hong Kong, Korea, and India; in Malaysia the HIV/AIDS group Pink Triangle is a de facto gay organization, which engages in a constant round of community development activities (and now provides some space for lesbians as well); and in Indonesia the gay organization KKLGN (Working Group for Indonesian Lesbians and Gay Men) has groups in about eleven cities[7] and has held three national meetings. Films and novels with gay themes have begun appearing, especially in East Asia.[8] Thailand has the most developed gay infrastructure in Southeast Asia, including a Thai gay press (clearly not aimed at tourists) and several well-appointed saunas whose clientele is largely Thai.[9] It is sometimes claimed that lesbians remain almost invisible; it might be more accurate to recognize that they are less linked to gay men than they are in many Western countries. While the universalizing rhetoric of human rights is one that blunts gender differences, talking of both "lesbian" and "gay" (and sometimes of "lesbian," "gay," "bisexual," and "transgender") as if they were inherently coupled, the itinerary toward new forms of homosexual identities/ behaviors/communities will not necessarily be the same for women and men. One would expect lesbian movements to develop in conjunction with the development of middle-class feminism, not necessarily to be linked to developments among homosexual men, which seems to be the case for both Thailand and the Philippines. Except in Indonesia, it is my impression that only very tentative steps have been taken to establish a mutual sense of lesbian/ gay cooperation.

Such "modern" forms of gay life coexist with older forms (often linked to ritualized expressions of transgender) or hybrid forms—for example, the annual "Miss Gay Philippines Beauty Pageant."[10] Yet a certain blurring of the sex/gender order may not be that different from developments in the West, as revealed in ideas of the "third sex" that were dominant in the early stages of a homosexual consciousness In Europe and more contemporary popular images such as the successful play/musical/film *La Cage aux Folles*. Western images of sex/gender in Asia often stress transgender images, as in the popularity of the play/film *M Butterfly* with its story of the French diplomat's love for a Chinese man he allegedly believed to be a woman. But to see transvestism as a particular characteristic of Asian cultures is to miss the role of drag in all its perverse and varied manifestations in Western theater, entertainment, and commercial sex.

Western fascination with these images may reflect a greater acceptance of transgendered people (more accurately, transgendered males) in many Asian countries, as suggested in a report that the Indonesian entry in the 1994 Gay Games in New York included an all-transsexual netball team—the national champions.[11] In many countries such transgendered communities are institutionalized and have won an accepted, if marginal, social status, often as providers of personal services (hairdressers, beauticians, etc.), which may include prostitution. In Indonesia during the 1990's, the national association of *waria* had as patron the minister for women's affairs. In the Philippines local dignitaries will attend *bacla* fashion shows.

There are differences as well as similarities between groups such as Indonesian *waria* or *banci*, Filipino *babaylan* or *bac(k)la*, Malay *maknyah* or Thai *kathoey*, which goes beyond the scope of this paper. What they appear to have in common is a conceptualization of the sex/gender order that has no simple equivalent in the dominant language or social arrangements of Western societies. In translating the term *kathoey* Peter Jackson makes clear the range of concepts the word conveys: "1: originally a male or female hermaphrodite; 2: male or female transvestite, or transsexual; 3: male homosexual or (rarer) a female homosexual."[12] And referring to similar groups in

Polynesia, Niko Besnier writes, "Sexual relations with men are seen as an optional consequence of gender liminality, rather than its determiner, prerequisite or primary attribute."[13] In general the new "gay" groups reject a common identity with more traditional identities and define themselves as contesting sexual rather than gender norms. This is not to deny the significance of gender; as Richard Parker wrote of similar developments in Brazil, "It would be more accurate to suggest that, rather than replacing an earlier system of thought, this newer system has been superimposed on it, offering at least some members of Brazilian society another frame of reference for the construction of sexual meanings. In the emphasis on sexuality, as opposed to gender, sexual practices have taken on significance not simply as part of the construction of a hierarchy of men and women, but as a key to the nature of every individual."[14] The existence of several "systems of thought" leads to a certain ambivalence; thus some Filipinos who belong to gay groups might also see themselves in particular contexts as *bacla*.[15] Clearly the divisions are related—though not identical—to those of class, much as American or Australian men who twenty years ago defined themselves as "gay" were largely from relatively privileged backgrounds.

Often the way in which homosexuality is discussed in contemporary Asia will combine quite distinct traditional and modern discourses. Consider this sentence in a report on the first Filipino lesbian congress: "Rep. Reynaldo Calalay's bill seeking the appointment of a congressional representative for the third sex and Rep. Geraldo Espina's that criminalises discrimination against gays have stirred some ripples."[16] In these two attempts to use the power of the state, one sees the ongoing confusion between those who see homosexuality as the result of gender divergence (a "third sex") and those who see sexuality as a distinct category ("gays"). This confusion is not of course unknown in the West; indeed it is only in the past two decades that the Western understanding of homosexuality has become largely divorced from gender—that is, that lesbians are seen as other than women who want to be men, and male homosexuals as other than effeminate men wanting to be women. These changes were expressed in the creation of gay/lesbian communities and political movements since the 1970s in most Western countries, which tended to marginalize "drag queens" and "butch dykes" in favor of more mainstream styles of being homosexual, including exaggerated masculine ("macho") and feminine ("lipstick lesbians") modes.

The ambiguities between the local and the global, the traditional and the postmodern, are constantly there. In a recent trip to Manila I was half-listening to the radio in a taxi when I heard an unmistakably queeny voice proclaim: "I'm a girl dropped in a man's body" followed by several sentences in Filipino, then: "I'm a girl with something extra." That same day, in *The Evening Paper*, a somewhat upmarket newspaper, I read the weekly "Gayzette" page, where readers were asked to identify the authors of a list of twenty books ranging from *To Anaktoria* (Sappho) to *A Place I've Never Been* (David Leavitt)—only one of them (Ameng of Wu's *The Cut Sleeve*) not from the West. The quiz, headed "queer now, queer then" was designed to discover "how much you know about your world. Are you a real queen? Or a mere princess? Is the baby now a fairy?"

In much of urban Southeast Asia it is easy to see parallels with the West of several decades ago: existing ideas of male homosexuals as would-be women are being replaced by the assertion of new self-concepts; more men are attracted to the idea of primary homosexual relationships rather than marrying and engaging in "homosex" on the side; there is a development of more commercial venues (but simultaneously, perhaps, there is less public cruising as "gay" makes homosexuality more specialized); in both organizations and media there is the emergence of a gay political consciousness. The mock-femininity of Thai or Indonesian "queens" and the mock-macho pose of hustlers is eerily reminiscent of John Rechy's novel of the early 1960s, *City of Night*, as is the fluctuation between overt queeniness and a certain prudery, public campiness, and great secrecy vis-à-vis families and workmates.[17]

There is, as well, a certain vulnerability and fragility underlying much of the new gay life—not, of course, without its parallels elsewhere. For many of the young men who become part of the growing gay worlds of Asian cities there is a rupture with family, village, religion, and social expectations that can be very painful. It is not uncommon to meet young men whose growing sense of themselves as gay has led to interruptions of study, to breaks with family, and to a general feeling of being stranded between two worlds (where an older Western man will often be cast in the role of protector). Guilt, self-hatred, and even suicide are not uncommon for those who feel themselves irretrievably homosexual in societies that deny open discussion of sexual difference even while allowing for certain variations much less acceptable in the West.

It is tempting to accept the Confucian and other "Asian" discourses about the significance of the family, and forget that similar experiences are very common for homosexuals in most countries, even those in northwest Europe that have moved furthest toward official acceptance. American research, for example, suggests the rate of suicide among adolescent homosexuals is far higher than the average. It is true that most homosexuals in Asian (and South American, Eastern European, and African) cities are still likely to be more integrated into family roles and expectations than would be true in Sydney, San Francisco, or Stuttgart. But we are speaking here of gradations, not absolute differences, and the growing affluence of many "developing" countries means possibilities for more people to live away from their families and a gradual decline in pressure to get married. One of the key issues is how gay identities will change as "Asians" recuperate Western images and bend them to their own purposes.

To see oneself as "gay" is to adhere to a distinctly modern invention, namely the creation of an identity and a sense of community based on (homo)sexuality. Most homosexual encounters—this is probably true even in the West—take place between men or women who do not define themselves as "gay" or "lesbian," and certainly do not affiliate to a community. The development of such identities and communities began in the nineteenth century, although some historians claim evidence for it at least in London, Paris, and Amsterdam in the eighteenth century. My focus is very clearly on those men who perceive themselves—and increasingly present themselves to others—as having a consciousness and a politics related to their sexuality. They may or may not be behaviorally bisexual; what matters for the purpose of this discussion is their sense of identity. Often such men appear more comfortable within an international homosexual world, which they have often encountered firsthand through travel and study, than they are with the traditional sex/gender order described by anthropologists and still existing in rural areas of their countries.

What characterizes a gay community? Writing of Hungary (where the political restraints until recently were similar to those of authoritarian Asia) Laszlo Toth argued, "There is a specific gay social institution system—from a specific non-verbal communication system to gay publications—which enables homosexuals to communicate with other gays, supporting gay, community consciousness."[18] Despite the emphasis on communication, this is an institutional rather than a discursive view of community, recognizing that genuine community requires the existence of specific institutions within which a common consciousness can be expressed, which may include a community-specific language (true of many homosexual subcultures, and now apparent in the emergence of clearly defined gay slang[s] in Indonesia and the Philippines).

The gay worlds of Bangkok, Jakarta, Hong Kong, Manila, or Seoul are obviously different from those of Budapest, Johannesburg, Hobart, Minneapolis, or Sao Paulo, yet in all these cities—covering all continents and both "developed" and "developing" countries—there are similarities that seem important and I would hypothesize have more to do with common urban and ideological pressures than they do with the cultural backgrounds of, say, Thais, Hungarians, and Brazilians. There is a great temptation to "explain" differences between homosexuality in different countries by reference to cultural tradition. What strikes me is that *within* a given country, whether Indonesia or the United States, Thailand or Italy, the *range* of constructions of homosexuality is growing, and that in the past two decades there have emerged a definable group of self-identified homosexuals—to date many more men than women—who see themselves as part of a global community, whose commonalities override—but do not deny—those of race and nationality.

This is *not* to present a new version of an inexorable march toward "development," with the end point defined in terms of building American-style gay ghettos across the world. Stephen Murray has warned that "there are obstacles to the globalization of an egalitarian (gay) organization of homosexuality even in the relatively industrialised and 'modern' capitals of 'developing' countries."[19] But globalization, in both its cultural and economic manifestations, impinges on the very creation and experience of sexual behavior and identities.

The reasons for these developments lie in both economic and cultural shifts, which are producing sufficiently large and self-confident groups of men (and some women) who wish to live as homosexuals in the Western sense of that term—that is, expressing their sexual identity openly, mixing with other homosexuals, and having long-term primary relations with other homosexuals. Thus the Japanese or Thai tradition that married men are reasonably free to have discrete homosexual liaisons on the side seems as oppressive to the young radicals of OCCUR or FACT (Fraternity for AIDS Cessation in Thailand) as it did to French or Canadian gay liberationists of the 1970s.

It is sometimes assumed that the notion of "a homosexual identity forged through shared lifestyles" has been, as Chilla Bulbeck put it, "almost exclusive to the west."[20] In fact the evidence for homosexual identities, lifestyles, and subcultures in a number of "developing" countries, most particularly in South and Central America, dates back to the early years of the century and arguably before that, at least in Brazil. Similar historical work has yet to be done for cities like Bangkok and Manila; almost certainly there are recognizable subcultures whose history has not been recorded.

A political expression of homosexuality is far more recent. Tony Perez's collection, *Cubao*, first published in 1980, was subtitled (in Tagalog): "The first cry of the gay liberation movement in the Philippines." The first self-conscious gay groups appeared in Indonesia (Lambda 1982) and Japan (JILGA 1984) in the early 1980s, just before the advent of AIDS was to change the terrain for gay organizing in ways that would make it more urgent while opening up certain overseas sources of funding. In the past decade there has been a proliferation of gay (sometimes lesbian and gay) groups, and many other AIDS organizations do a certain amount of gay outreach or even community development.

It is clear that the language of HIV/AIDS control, surveillance, and education has been a major factor in spreading "gay identities" and facilitating the development of gay consciousness (as it has also contributed to the creation of self-conscious identities of "sex workers" and "People with AIDS"[21]). It is impossible to know how far the dispersal of Western-style gay identities would have occurred without AIDS, which has opened up both space and resources for gay organizing and increased the influence of both Western cultures and surveillance. Consider the large numbers of Western, or Western-trained, epidemiologists, anthropologists, and psychologists who have used HIV/AIDS as a reason to investigate sexual behaviors across the world, and by so doing have changed the ways in which the participants themselves understand what they are doing.

The relationship is summed up in a flyer announcing a party at the 1995 AIDS in Asia Conference in Chiang Mai (Thailand):

> Chaai Chuai Chaai is an NGO based in Chiang Mai. Our aim is to increase safer sex among gay and bisexual men, and male sex workers and their partners, through street outreach, bar outreach and one-on-one peer education. We are a non-profit voluntary organization staffed and run by the gay community in Chiang Mai.

Here the language of "gay" identity and gay-defined HIV education ("outreach," "peer education") are conflated to suggest a community which many Thais would claim is irrelevant to continuing cultural assumptions. Matthew Roberts has argued that AIDS has been the essential catalyst for these developments, although I suspect he falls into the trap of assuming a linear development toward the Western model: "At Stonewall 50 we will likely find ourselves an open and proud community globally, efficaciously practising safe sex . . . and with notable advances in our civil rights across the globe."[22]

Neocolonial "Sex Wars"

A large-scale construction of a lesbian/gay identity as a central social one—what Stuart Hall calls a master identity[23]—developed in the Western world beginning at the end of the 1960s, and clearly Asians who adopt lesbian/gay identities are conscious of and in part molded by Western examples. In both North America and Europe, gay liberation grew out of the counterculture and other radical movements, most particularly feminism. To some extent this is also true of the developing gay worlds of the south, but more significant is the global explosion of communications. One example: several years ago I walked into a hotel room in Buenos Aires and turned on the television to see a live broadcast from the Lesbian/Gay Rights March in Washington, D.C. In the same way the opening of the 1994 Gay Games in New York was on the front page of the *Jakarta Post*, and large numbers of young Asians are learning about lesbian/gay/queer worlds from the proliferation of youth-oriented television and rock videos. (Of course print media served to disperse news of the rise of Western gay movements before the days of MTV and CNN, although less effectively.)

Michael Tan links the rise of gay identities/organizations to Western influence and a growing "middle class" and claims there is "a global Sexual Revolution, involving a gradual shift in transcending the view of sex-as-reproduction toward sex and sexuality as consent and commitment, respect and respectability."[24] Yet as Tan recognizes, "modernity" in the countries under discussion is rather different from its Western models, for it coexists with other and sometimes actively competing forces. Tan and others have suggested that the absence of the sort of hostility toward homosexuality found in Anglo-Saxon societies may also retard the development of gay political movements. This argument can go overboard, as in Walter Williams's argument that "Indonesian values—social harmony, peacefulness, and the national motto 'unity in diversity'—seem to protect gays from mistreatment more completely than western notions of individual rights."[25] Such protection would not extend to those whose "gayness" took on political forms deemed harmful to the Indonesian state.

The importation of certain concepts of sexualities is not, of course, new: missionaries, anthropologists, government officials, and travelers all played their role in simultaneously interpreting and obscuring existing realities. In terms of importing homosexual identity, a significant Western influence dates from at least the early years of this century. Western models of homosexuality have come to Asia through both large cultural forces and the influence of individuals, who were often attracted to "the East" because of its apparent liberality. This is particularly true of Bali, which from the 1920s on was constructed by rich European homosexuals as a "paradise" because of the seeming beauty and availability of young Balinese men. This is most clearly expressed in the life of Walter Spies, a German painter, who was responsible in part for the Western discovery and fetishization of Balinese art, and who eventually fell foul of a colonial moral drive just before World War II. Indeed, as Adrian Vickers claims, "It was not the Second World War but Bali's reputation as a homosexual paradise which ended the golden era of European Bali."[26]

Yet after World War II and independence there was something of a rebirth of Bali's reputation, and a number of gay foreigners, among them the painter Donald Friend, settled for a time in Bali. Today there is a considerable expatriate gay population in Bali, as there is in Thailand, the Philippines, and Sri Lanka, drawn by the lure of "available" young men and "tolerant" social mores. It is easy to condemn these men in the tones that are increasingly being used in a blanket fashion to demonize all sex tourists, and it is undeniable that there are some very ugly aspects to gay sex tourism. At one level there is the same exploitation of young Asians common in the much larger heterosexual scene[27]: beach prostitution in Kuta (Bali) or take-out bars in Bangkok are not particularly attractive, and young men face many of the same threats to health and integrity as do young women in the sex industry.

Without denying the ugliness born of larger economic inequities, one has to recognize a somewhat more complex pattern of relationships at work. In many cases young men are able to use their sexual contacts with (usually older) foreigners to win entry into the Western world, either through the acquisition of money, skills, language, or, most dramatically, the possibility of emigration. Some young men have made a conscious decision to use their sexuality as a means for social mobility, settling for a "housewife" role with a richer and older Westerner out of a mixture of glamor and calculation.

Nonetheless, these relationships are inevitably shaped by colonial structures, which are almost impossible to escape. Racism and colonial scripts of superiority/inferiority are replicated within structures of desire, in ways neither side is comfortable in admitting. (One reader of the manuscript assumed that I was speaking here of active/passive or top/bottom role-playing; I have something more complex in mind. As Genet showed, such roles may well be reversed in an unconscious transgression of colonial assumptions.) Ironically the assertion of "gayness" among middle-class Asian young men is beginning to erode their willingness to play the script an older generation has used to enter the Western homosexual world.

There is a danger of both moral indignation and over-romanticization getting in the way of fully understanding the dynamics of Western/Asian homosexual contacts. This is compounded by the immaturity of many of the expatriate Westerners themselves, who import their own fractured sense of self along with their material advantages. Undoubtedly many Westerners desire in Asians (both men and women) the deference and servitude unavailable at home, and for some the colonial/racist framework of their relationships allows them to act out their own sense of self-hatred. Although there is an extensive literature of the gay expatriate—from late nineteenth-century Frenchmen in North Africa to Anglo-American writers such as Angus Wilson and Francis King and, more recently, Christopher Bram, Neil Miller, and Peter Jackson[28]—there is virtually nothing written from the point of view of the "local," and there is a great need to hear those voices.[29]

But this is only part of the story: the gay men one sees in Western-style discos at Legian (Bali) or bars in Bangkok are not the only ones. There are many venues in Bangkok, Tokyo, or Manila that cater almost exclusively to locals; indeed, a number of gay bars in Japan deliberately discourage foreigners, and the one gay sauna in Manila explicitly excludes them. In both cases fear of AIDS is the ostensible reason; the larger underlying motives are clearly more complex and operate on a number of levels. Long-lasting relationships exist between Asian homosexuals, marked by a certain equality, and part of the creation of "modern" gay identity appears to be a desire to open up the possibility of such relationships without their being framed by differences in age, status, or race.

"The personal is the political" for lesbian/gay politics in "developing" countries as much as it remains the case in Western countries. But where there is a legacy of colonialism, which has infused sexual relationships as much as other interactions, that slogan takes on particular meanings. In conversations among gay activists, particularly in the Southeast Asian region, there has been some discussion of "Asian empowerment," by which is meant a reversal of the traditional assumption that Asian men are sexually available for Westerners. Such conversations suggest particular forms of self-assertion and involve a rejection not only of the image of Asian men as "available" but also of the dominant stereotype of them as "feminine" or "passive."

Just as Western gay movements have asserted a certain masculinity in their constructions of male homosexuality, so Asian gays, having to counteract both indigenous and imported perceptions of them as men-who-want-to-be-women, are likely to be attracted to some variant of the western "macho" style. (For example, gay men are beginning to attend gyms in the richer cities of the region.) In gay discussion groups in Manila and Kuala Lumpur, there is talk of "Asian" men learning to eroticize each other as a way of overcoming a deeply internalized sense of inferiority vis-à-vis Europeans.

The sexual-political relations of colonialism means that for many gay men in Asia the phallus is white and must be rejected, sometimes leading to a rejection (more in rhetoric than practice) of European men as sex partners in the belief that they inevitably bear certain racial and colonial prejudices. To quote the Filipino-American poet R. Zamora Linmark:

> They like you because you eat dog, goat and pig's blood . . .
> They like you because you kneel hard, bend over quick and spread wide . . .
> They like you because you're a potato queen . . .
> They like you because you take it in, all the way down
> They like you because you ask for it, adore it
> They like you because you're a copycat, want to be just like them
> They like you because, give it a couple more years, you'll be just like them
> And when that time comes, will they like you more?[30]

Linmark himself (Filipino-born but U.S.–based) illustrates a further factor now at work, which is the development of significant communities of "gay Asians" in the diaspora. A self-conscious Asian gay consciousness has emerged over the past decade in the United States, Canada, Australia, and Britain, expressed through a burgeoning of social and political groups.[31] In this sense the image presented in the film *The Wedding Banquet* is remarkably out of date; the film opposes a (white) gay world to a traditional (Taiwanese) heterosexual one, but nowhere recognizes the existence in a city like New York of a very significant and increasingly visible East Asian gay community. Gay Asian expatriates are playing a role of some importance in the furthering of gay groups and identities "back home," even though, as Richard Fung has warned, they often seek to "conflate the realities of Asians in the diaspora with those living in Asian countries."[32]

Globalizing Influences on Asian Sexual Identities

There are three dominant scripts in which the globalization of gay identities is commonly described. The first sees Southeast Asia as possessing a "natural" tolerance for sexual fluidity and expression before the onset of colonialism and places great emphasis on the continuing traditions of both homosexual and transgender cultures. Thus Frederick Whitham wrote: "The Philippines, as is generally true of Southeast Asian and Polynesian societies, has maintained a longstanding tradition of tolerance for its homosexual populations."[33] This view led to some parts of Asia—Thailand, Sri Lanka, Bali—becoming seen in the twentieth century as homosexual paradises. The second script grows out of this, namely a strong emphasis on the impact of colonialism and tourism in creating homosexual worlds. This in turn feeds a third script, which places its emphasis on the impact of modernity, and argues for the current development of "gay" identities, communities, and organizations across Asia as part of a larger pattern of economic and cultural globalization. As two Indonesian AIDS workers wrote: "Globalisation and economic growth have allowed Indonesian youth unprecedented access to information and media about sex."[34]

It is constantly important to find a balance between the view of globalization as a new stage of imperialism and the triumphalist discourse of globalization as the creation of a new world society, characterized by Simon During as "magic":

> "General magic" is an appropriate term because it catches the astonishing cross-cultural reach of the desire for broadcasting, music, camera and video products. This general desire is not "natural." . . . Desires are produced by transnational advertising campaigns, while the technologies are shaped by data gathered through ethnographic market research.[35]

While I accept the role of economic and cultural globalization as crucial to the development of new sexual identities, such explanations must build on existing sex/gender regimes and values, just as the contemporary gay worlds in the West built on preexisting traditions and cultures. But I suspect that the emergence of gay groups and commercial worlds in modern Asia has relatively little to do with precolonial cultural formations, although these often continue to coexist with newer forms. The comment of Clark Taylor that "[h]omosexual Mexicans often prefer their way of interacting to the U.S. forms because of cherished, cultural values" ignores the other factors at play.[36]

This is not to deny the powerful symbolic and psychological reasons for exploring such connections: one of the benefits of a postcolonial approach is to unravel the ways in which colonial practices have denied cultural tradition. It is ironic that in many developing countries religious and gay interpretations present bitterly opposed views of the "traditional" status of homosexuality. Recently Iran and China—with several thousand years of literary exploration of homosexual love—have seen bitter persecution of "decadence." (The desire of developing elites to deny their own sexual histories because of imported moralities, and the resulting persecution of homosexuals, has been explored by Bret Hinsch for China.[37])

Sexual identity politics grow out of modernity but also show the way to postmodernity, because they both strengthen and interrogate identity as a fixed point and a central reference. The claiming of lesbian/gay identities in Asia or Latin America can be as much about being Western as about sexuality, symbolized by the co-optation of the word "gay" into Thai, Indonesian, etc., and the use of terms such as "moderno" (in Peru) and "internacional" (in Mexico) to describe "gayness." As Alison Murray writes: "Jakarta is now gayer than ever, and despite the dominant discourse, gay is a modern way to be. This has undoubtedly been influenced by western trends and internationalisation of gay culture, and in the process, the distinctive position of the *banci* has tended to be subsumed within the definition of gay."[38]

Of course existing cultural and political patterns will influence the extent to which global market forces and images can shape a new sort of public sexual identity. In both Singapore and Hong Kong one feels a large gay presence about to burst forth; in both cities one meets large numbers of young men who identify as gay, but who are restrained by familial and government pressures from the lifestyle that affluence and global media increasingly hold up before them. Even in the most apparently liberal environments there will be restrictions that seem odd if we expect a wholesale replica of the Western model. Thus I once gave a couple of copies of the Australian gay magazine, *Outrage*, to the manager of the Kuala Lumpur sauna. This sauna is unambiguously a meeting place for gay men in K.L., and a great deal of sex routinely takes place on the premises. Nevertheless I was told firmly there could be no open display of something as overtly homosexual as these magazines—which are routinely sold in most Australian newsagents.

A New Gay/Lesbian Politics?

The first draft of this paper was written at a time when Southeast Asia seemed set upon a pattern of constant and rapid economic growth, which was, depending on how one saw these developments, either opening up increasing space for greater individual choice or rapidly destroying traditional kinship and communal ties. Leaders such as Malaysian prime minister Mahathir have of course sought to have it both ways, regretting the decline of "traditional values" while simultaneously pushing for a rapid economic modernization that places great stress on such values. Equally, the moves to democratic regimes, most pronounced in the Philippines and Thailand, seemed likely to expand to much of Southeast Asia along with economic affluence and liberalization.

After the crash of 1997–98, the pattern of continual growth looks far more problematic, as do any easy assumptions that affluence will offer growing opportunities for adopting "modern" lifestyles. One concrete example: if in Kuala Lumpur I had been told that it was increasingly possible for young people to leave home and live on their own, then the economic downturn would almost certainly have cut off this option for many. Equally, the large commercial world of Bangkok was clearly affected by the economic turndown. Currently, the future of Indonesia in particular is unclear, but a rise in fundamentalism could have considerable impact on slowing the development of lesbigay life in that country. Yet in the euphoria following the overthrow of Suharto and the election of President Wahid it was also possible to foresee a strengthened democracy that would also sweep away restrictions on organizing in Malaysia and Singapore.

This paper was also begun before the Internet had become a major means of communication. As part of the economic growth of Southeast Asia, the possibilities of computer-based communications have been grasped with enormous enthusiasm and created a new set of opportunities for the diffusion of information and the creation of (virtual) communities. Whereas the gay movements of the 1970s in the West depended heavily on the creation of a gay/lesbian press, in countries such as Malaysia, Thailand, or Singapore the Internet offers the same possibilities, with the added attraction of anonymity and instant contact with overseas, thus fostering the links with the diaspora already discussed. Work by Chris Berry and Fran Martin has shown the enormous importance of the net in creating social bonds between young homosexuals in Taiwan and South Korea.[39]

At a more conventional level there are only occasional examples of Asian gay groups engaging in political activity of the sort associated with their counterparts in the West. Although Hong Kong decriminalized homosexuality in 1990[40] and there has been some campaigning against the British-derived laws in India,[41] there has been no political agitation to repeal such laws in Singapore and Malaysia, though the issue has been discussed within both Pink Triangle and People Like Us (Singapore), and allegations of sodomy against former Malaysian deputy prime minister Anwar Ibrahim in 1998 meant the issue was put on the public agenda. Several small gay and lesbian political groups have been established in the Philippines in recent years, and since 1996 there has been an annual gay pride march in Manila. Though these groups have involved a number of groups, ProGay (the Progressive Organization of Gays in the Philippines), as its name suggests, is concerned with drawing links between specifically gay issues and larger questions of social justice. The early gay liberationist debate about the extent to which homosexual freedoms were bound up in larger social transformation, largely abandoned by mainstream Western gay and lesbian groups, thus remains in evidence in the Filipino movement.

The development of political movements among people whose identities are being defined in terms of their sexuality will reflect larger features of the political culture of their society. It is not surprising that there is a more politicized gay world in Manila than in Bangkok, despite the latter's huge commercial gay scene; the political culture of the two countries would lead us to expect this. Gay politics in both Indonesia and the Philippines reflects the class structures of the countries; in both, there are powerful upper-class figures whose homosexuality is widely known but who refuse any public identification with a "movement." In Indonesia in particular there is some evidence of the emergence of gay activism based among lower-middle-class people who have less to lose. My impression is that there are certain tensions between developing groups around class position, often correlated with access to the English language and the outside world, but at this stage this is only a tentative suggestion based on limited observation.

Although the assertion of gay identities and community in the West took a particular political form, associated with the development of gay liberation movements in the early 1970s, this does not mean that groups in other parts of the world, whose sense of "gayness" is fueled by somewhat different sources, will necessarily follow the same itinerary. We must avoid what Michael Connors has termed the "narcissistic transition narrative in 'diffusion,' whereby the trajectory of the Third World has already been traversed by the First."[42]

The best example of Western-style political activism has come from the Japanese group OCCUR, which has engaged in lobbying various ministries, persuaded the Japanese Society of Psychology and Neurology to declassify homosexuality as a mental illness, and succeeded in a court case against the Tokyo metropolitan government in winning the right to use public educational facilities for meetings. Despite these gains OCCUR has warned:

> There are many obstacles to lesbian and gay organizing in Asia and the Pacific islands which do not necessarily exist elsewhere in the world. These include not only the existence of governments repressive of human rights, but also problems that stem from cultural, historical and social differences with the West. For OCCUR this has meant resisting a direct importation of models of lesbian and gay activism developed in the West and developing instead an original form of activism that reflects Japan's specific social and political context.[43]

Nonetheless, OCCUR and several other lesbian/gay groups from Asia and other developing areas participate in international networks such as ILGA (International Lesbian and Gay Association) and IGLHRC (International Gay and Lesbian Human Rights Commission), thus increasing their own links to the West and furthering the idea of a universal identity with claims to civil and political rights that transcend other cultural and national boundaries. That this is highly contested was obvious in claims for lesbian inclusion at the 1995 World Conference on Women in Beijing, and in counterclaims such as that of Singapore's foreign minister at the 1994 Human Rights Conference in Vienna that "[h]omosexual rights are a western issue, and are not relevant to this conference."[44]

I am optimistic enough to believe that these sort of arguments will lose in the long run. In the words of former UN Secretary-General Butros Butros Ghali, "We must remember that forces of repression often cloak their wrong-doing in claims of exceptionalism. But the people themselves time and again make it clear that they seek and need universality. Human dignity within one's culture requires fundamental standards of universality across the lines of culture, faith and state."[45] The discourses of global rights that Ghali invokes provide new weapons for groups in non-Western countries to adopt.[46]

This does not mean, however, the adoption of a Western-style lesbigay political activism. In late 1996 controversy erupted in Thailand after the governing body of the country's teacher-training colleges decreed that "sexual deviants" would be barred from entering the colleges. Though there was considerable opposition to the ban (subsequently dropped) other than Anjaree, most of this came from non-gay sources. As Peter Jackson concluded, "A dynamic gay scene has emerged . . . in the complete absence of a gay rights movement."[47] When I visited Bangkok shortly after this event I visited the "gay center," Utopia, which appeared to be largely the creation of an expatriate American, and the potential for gay activism a couple of years earlier in AIDS work seemed to have disappeared.

Indeed, it may be that a political movement is the least likely part of Western concepts of homosexual identity to be adopted in many parts of the world, even as many enthusiastically embrace the mores and imagery of Western queerdom. The particular form of identity politics that allowed for the mobilization of a lesbigay electoral pressure in countries like the United States, the Netherlands, or even France may not be appropriate elsewhere, even if Western-style liberal democracy triumphs. (In countries such as the Netherlands or Switzerland, identity politics builds on a long tradition of religious and linguistic difference; in the United States, Canada, and Australia, it is related to certain concepts of multiculturalism.[48]) The need of Western lesbigays to engage in identity politics as a means of enhancing self-esteem may not be felt in other societies.

The Western lesbigay movement emerged in conditions of affluence and liberal democracy, where despite other large social issues it was possible to develop a politics around sexuality, which is less likely in countries where the very structures of political life are constantly contested. Writing of contemporary South Africa, Mark Gevisser notes, "Race-identification overpowers everything else—class, gender and sexuality."[49] In the same way basic questions of political economy and democratization will impact the future development of gay/lesbian movements in Southeast Asia. If the realities of different forms of gay life require us to abandon the idea that the model for the rest of the world, whether political, cultural, or intellectual, need be New York or Paris, and to recognize the emerging possibilities for such models in Bangkok and Johannesburg, we may indeed be able to speak of "a queer planet." We may even recognize the need to question whether "Anglo-American queer theorists" are saying much of relevance to the majority of people in the world who are developing a politics out of their shared sexuality in far more difficult conditions than those within which Western lesbian and gay movements arose.

Notes

Thanks to the Australian Research Council for financial support for the research project reported in this paper, plus a number of people who read various drafts, particularly Ben Anderson, Mark Blasius, Peter Jackson, Shivananda Khan, Suvendrini Perera, Anthony Smith, and Geoffrey Woolcock. The first draft of this paper was presented at a conference titled "Identities/Ethnicities/Nationalities: Asian and Pacific Contexts" held at La Trobe University in Melbourne in July 1994. This draft was largely completed in 1997.

1. Michel Foucault, *The Birth of the Clinic*, trans. A. M. Sheridan (London: Routledge, 1986), 195.

2. I discuss these issues in *Defying Gravity: A Political Life* (Sydney: Allen and Unwin, 1997).

3. Edmund White, *States of Desire* (New York: Dutton, 1980).

4. Wes Muchmore and William Hanson, *Coming Out Right: A Handbook for the Gay Male* (Boston: Alyson, 1991).

5. Michael Warner, ed., *Fear of a Queer Planet* (Minneapolis: University of Minnesota Press, 1993), xii.

6. See "Anjaree—Towards Lesbian Visibility," *The Nation* (Bangkok), September 25, 1994; Kanokwan Tarawan, "Thailand," in *Unspoken Rules: Sexual Orientation and Women's Human Rights*, ed. Rachel Rosenbloom. (London: Cassell, 1996), 197–202.

7. KKLGN produces a monthly publication *Gaya Nusantara* (contact: Jln Mulyosari Timur 46, Surabaya 60112).

8. On film, see Chris Berry, *A Bit on the Side* (Sydney: EM Press, 1994). The best known novels are probably those of Mishima; few others have been translated but see Pai Hsien-yung, *Crystal Boys* (San Francisco Gay Sunshine, 1990) (Taiwan); Johann Lee, *Peculiar Chris* (Singapore: Cannon, 1992); Andrew Koh, *Glass Cathedral* (Singapore: EPB, 1995); Shyam Selvaduri, *Funny Boy* (Toronto M & S, 1994); Neil Garcia and Danton Remoto, *Ladlad: An Anthology of Philippine Gay Writing* (Manila: Anvil, 1994); Thomas Boggs, *Tokyo Vanilla* (London: GMP, 1998), all available in English.

9. See Eric Allyn, *Trees in the Same Forest* (Bangkok/San Francisco: Bua Luang, 1991); Peter Jackson, *Dear Uncle Go: Male Homosexuality in Thailand*, 2nd ed. (Bangkok; Bua Luang Books, 1995).

10. See Mark Johnson, *Beauty and Power: Transgendering and Cultural Transformations in the Southern Philippines* (Oxford: Berg, 1997); Danton Remoto, *Seduction and Solitude* (Manila: Anvil, 1995).

11. Susan Wyndham, "Out on the Streets," *Weekend Australian*, June 18–19, 1994.

12. Jackson, *Dear Uncle Go*, 301. See also Jackson, "*Kathoey*><Gay><Man: The Historical Emergence of Gay Male Identity in Thailand," in *Sites of Desire, Economies of Pleasure*, ed. L. Manderson and M. Jolley (Chicago: University of Chicago Press, 1997), 166–90.

13. Niko Besnier, "Polynesian Gender Liminality through Time and Space," in *Third Sex, Third Gender*, ed. G. Herdt (New York, Zone, 1994), 300.

14. Richard Parker, *Bodies, Pleasures and Passions* (Boston: Beacon, 1991), 95.

15. See Neil Garcia, *Philippine Gay Culture: The Last Thirty Years* (Quezon City: University of the Philippines Press, 1996); Martin Manalansan, "Speaking of AIDS: Language and the Filipino 'Gay' Experience in America," in *Discrepant Histories: Translocal Essays on Filipino Cultures*, ed. V. Rafael (Philadelphia: Temple University Press, 1995), 193–220.

16. See Francine Medina, "Women Who Love Women," *Today* (Manila), December 16, 1996.

17. John Rechy, *City of Night* (New York: Grove, 1964). Compare the detailed historical discussion in George Chauncey, *Gay New York* (New York: Basic Books, 1994).

18. Laszlo Toth, "The Development of Hungarian Gay Subculture and Community in the Last Fifty Years," unpublished paper, Budapest, 1994, p. 12.

19. Stephen O Murray, "The 'Underdevelopment' of Modern/Gay Homosexuality in Mesoamerica," in *Modern Homosexualities*, ed. Ken Plummer (London: Routledge, 1992), 29.

20. Chilla Bulbeck, "Exploring Western Sexual Identities through Other Sexual Identities," paper presented to Australian Sociological Association Conference, Adelaide, December 1992, p. 5.

21. I have deliberately limited the discussion of AIDS in this paper as I have discussed it at length elsewhere. See Dennis Altman, *Power and Community* (London: Taylor and Francis, 1994); "Political Sexualities: Meanings and Identities in the Time of AIDS," in *Conceiving Sexuality*, ed. J. Gagnon and R. Parker (New York: Routledge, 1994), 97–106; "Globalization, Political Economy and HIV/AIDS," *Theory and Society* 28, no. 4 (August 1999): 559–84.

22. Matthew Roberts, "Emergence of Gay Identity and Gay Social Movements in Developing Countries: The AIDS Crisis as Catalyst," *Alternatives* 20 (1995): 261.

23. Stuart Hall, "The Question of Cultural Identity," in *Modernity and Its Discontents*, ed. S. Hall, D. Held, and T. McCrew (London: Polity Press, 1993), 280.

24. Michael Tan, introduction to *A Different Love*, by Margarita Singco-Holmes (Manila: Anvil, 1994), xii.

25. Walter Williams, *Javanese Lives* (New Brunswick, NJ: Rutgers University Press, 1991), 181.

26. Adrian Vickers, *Bali: A Paradise Created* (Melbourne: Penguin, 1989), 124.

27. See Sandra Sturdevant and Brenda Stoltzfus, *Let the Good Times Roll* (New York: New Press, 1992).

28. Christopher Bram, *Almost History* (New York: Donald Fine, 1992); Peter Jackson, *The Intrinsic Quality of Skin* (Bangkok: Floating Lotus, 1994); Francis King, "A Corner of a Foreign Field," in his *One Is a Wanderer* (Harmondsworth: Penguin, 1985); Neil Miller, *Out in the World* (New York: Random House, 1992); Angus Wilson, *As If by Magic* (New York: Viking, 1973).

29. A Western attempt to make "the boys" central to the story is Kent Ashford, *The Singalong Tribe* (London: GMP, 1986).

30. R. Zamora Linmark, "They Like You Because You Eat Dog," in *Charlie Chan Is Dead*, ed. Jessica Hagedorn (New York: Penguin, 1993), 266.

31. See Siong-huat Chua, "Asian-Americans, Gay and Lesbian," in *Encyclopedia of Homosexuality*, ed. Wayne Dynes (New York: Garland, 1990), 84–85; Russell Leong, ed., *Asian American Sexualities* (New York: Routledge, 1996).

32. Richard Fung, "Looking for My Penis: The Eroticized Asian in Gay Porn Video," in *Asian American Sexualities*, ed. Leong, 126.

33. Frederick Whitham, "Bayot and Callboy: Homosexual—Heterosexual Relations in the Philippines," in *Oceanic Homosexualities*, ed. Stephen O. Murray (New York: Garland, 1992), 234.

34. See Desti Murdijana and Priyadi Prihaswan, "AIDS Prevention in Indonesia," *National AIDS Bulletin* (Canberra), April 1994, pp. 8–11. This theme was developed in a cover story in *Asia Week*: "Sex: How Asia is Changing," June 23, 1995, and in *The Economist*: "It's Normal To Be Queer," January 6, 1996.

35. Simon During, "Postcolonialism and Globalization," *Meanjin* 51, no. 2 (1992): 341.

36. Clark Taylor, "Mexican Male Homosexual Interaction in Public Contexts" in *The Many Faces of Homosexuality*, ed. Evelyn Blackwood (New York: Harrington Park Press, 1986), 117.

37. Bret Hinsch, *Passions of the Cut Sleeve* (Berkeley: University of California Press, 1990), 165–66.

38. Alison Murray, "Dying for a Fuck: Implications for HIV/AIDS in Indonesia," paper presented at Gender Relations Conference, Canberra, 1993, p. 6.

39. Chris Berry and Fran Martin: "Queer 'n' Asian on the Net: Syncretic Sexualities in Taiwan and Korean Cyberspaces," *Inqueeries* (Melbourne) 2, no. 1 (June 1998): 67–93.

40. "After 10 Years' Debate, HK's Gay Free to Love in Private," *Australian*, July 13, 1990.

41. For details, see Sherry Joseph and Pawan Dhall, "Lesbigay Voices from India," in *Different Rainbows*, ed. Peter Drucker (London: GMP, 2000).

42. Michael Connors, "Disordering Democracy: Democratization in Thailand," unpublished paper, Melbourne University, 1995, p. 12.

43. OCCUR, "HIV/AIDS and Gay Activism" brochure, Tokyo, June 6, 1995.

44. Quoted in Berry and Kelly, "Queer 'n' Asian on the Net," 73.

45. Butros Butros Ghali, "Democracy, Development and Human Rights for All," *International Herald Tribune*, June 10, 1993.

46. See, e.g., Margaret Keck and Kathryn Sikkink, *Activists beyond Borders* (Ithaca: Cornell University Press, 1997); Dennis Altman, "The Emergence of 'Modern' Gay

Identities and the Question of Human Rights," in *Human Rights and Gender Rights*, ed. Maila Stivens et al. (London: Routledge, 2000), 211–28.

47. Peter Jackson, "Beyond Bars and Boys: Life in Gay Bangkok," *Outrage* (Melbourne), July 1997, pp. 61–63.

48. See my "Multiculturalism and the Emergence of Lesbian/Gay Worlds," in *Australian Civilisation*, ed. Richard Nile (New York: Oxford University Press, 1994), 110–24.

49. Mark Gevisser, "Gay Life in South Africa," in *Different Rainbows*, ed. Peter Drucker (London: GMP, 2000).

FIVE

SEXUAL RIGHTS

INVENTING A CONCEPT,

MAPPING AN INTERNATIONAL PRACTICE

Rosalind Pollack Petchesky

"SEXUAL RIGHTS" is the newest kid on the block in international debates about the meanings and practices of human rights, especially women's human rights. That such a concept and lively discussions about it have finally surfaced in large international forums—in spite or because of the pervasive climate of resurgent fundamentalisms in the world—surely in itself marks a historic achievement that feminist and gay and lesbian movements should proudly claim. Yet at this stage the concept is far from clear, not only among its staunch opponents but also among many of its advocates. It may be that "sexual rights" has become *both* a progressive wedge, opening up new space in the human rights lexicon for acknowledgment of diverse sexualities and their legitimate need for expression; *and* a kind of code that, like "reproductive rights," means different things to different speakers, depending on their power position, sexual orientation, gender, nationality, and so on. Moreover, the risks, ambiguities, and potential misunderstandings of trying to negotiate sexuality through the arcane channels of international human rights procedures are troublesome. When it comes to sex, a chasm still separates the local and the global.

In what follows I will lay out some general reflections on the tenuous place where sexual rights discourse and politics currently hang suspended. First, I will briefly review developments in the 1990s international conferences—particularly the world population conference in Cairo and the women's conference in Beijing, in 1994 and 1995 respectively—that have given birth to a still infantile (if not embryonic) sexual rights language. Second, I will consider some of the difficulties in promoting a positive, or affirmative, concept of sexual rights, one that goes beyond the urgent but also more acceptable struggle to combat the discriminations, abuses, and horrors committed against sexual minorities (including women who stray from dominant gender norms). The larger context for such difficulties, as I will show, is shared by all affirmative approaches to rights as goods, entitlements, and, ultimately, transformed social arrangements, not just defenses against discrimination or bodily harm. Third, I will attempt to outline some basic elements of what such an affirmative approach to sexual rights might involve and its implications for social rights generally.[1] Finally, I will speculate about why even feminist, human rights, and other progressive groups have often been complicit in suppressing positive definitions of sexual rights, either actively or by omission; what factors in our ideological and political legacy contribute to this silence; what we have to lose from continuing this evasive or complicit practice; and what we have to gain from coming out in favor of sexual rights in a positive, liberatory sense.

Without going into details, let me review at least the outcomes of the 1990s United Nations conference debates that began to craft an incipient sexual rights concept. Significantly, *no international instrument relevant to human rights prior to 1993 makes any reference whatsoever to the forbidden "S" word* (other than "sex," as in biological sexes); that is, *prior to 1993 sexuality of any sort or manifestation is absent from international human rights discourse.* This may seem unremarkable when we consider the rigid division between public and private spheres that, as feminist critics have repeatedly pointed out, prevails in human rights implementation and enforcement mechanisms (Bunch 1990; Cook 1994; Copelon 1994; Freedman and Isaacs 1993; Romany 1994; Sullivan 1995). Yet, even if we confine human rights only to the responsibilities of states, leaving out those of private persons or other institutions, it must be said that, in fact, there never has been a sharp division between "private" and "public" in accepted human rights principles. Every major human rights document going back to the Universal Declaration of 1948 has much to say about the rights of persons in their private and personal lives: to marry and form a family, to express their beliefs and religion, to educate their children, to be respected in their privacy and homes, etc.— but nothing about expressing and being secure in their sexuality. Moreover, neither do any of the women's conference declarations refer to women's sexuality, much less sexual rights, prior to 1992—not the Women's Convention (Convention on the Elimination of All Forms of Discrimination Against Women, 1981) nor the Nairobi Forward Looking Strategies (1985), which refer to sexual equality and women's right to control their fertility but not to sexual freedom or the rights of lesbians. In other words, in most human rights discourse until very recently, sexual life is acknowledged only implicitly, and then confined within the bounds of heterosexual marriage and reproduction (see Cook 1995; Copelon and Hernandez 1994).[2]

A major turning point came in 1993 with the World Conference on Human Rights in Vienna, where, thanks to the concerted efforts of a well-organized women's human rights lobby, the Declaration and Programme of Action called on states to eliminate "gender based violence and all forms of sexual harassment and exploitation," including trafficking in women, "systematic rape, sexual slavery, and forced pregnancy" (paras. 18 and 38). The Declaration on the Elimination of Violence Against Women, passed by the General Assembly that same year, contains even more explicit condemnation of various forms of "physical, sexual and psychological violence against women" (para. 2) and makes it clear—thanks again to the work of feminist international legal scholars—that this prohibition is not something new but rather stems directly from time-honored principles embedded in international human rights law. These include, among others, the rights to life, liberty, and security of the person (Universal Declaration, Art. 3; European Convention on Human Rights, Art. 2); to the inviolability of the person and physical and mental integrity (African Charter on Human and Peoples' Rights, Arts. 4 and 6; American Convention on Human Rights, Art. 5); and to freedom from torture and cruel and inhuman punishment (Cook 1995). Indeed, feminist scholars have established a clear link between torture and rape or other forms of sexual violence, whether in the context of war or domestic relations (Copelon 1994).

The Vienna Declaration and the Declaration on Violence Against Women were important not only because they gained recognition of sexual violence as a human rights violation but also because they finally initiated "the sexual" into human rights language. Yet not until the International Conference on Population and Development (ICPD) in Cairo in 1994 would sexuality begin to sneak into international documents as something positive rather than always violent, abusive, or sanctified and hidden by heterosexual marriage and childbearing. As Yasmin Tambiah puts it, "the Cairo Document is indisputably one of the most progressive statements acknowledging sexual activity as a positive aspect of human society to emerge recently through global consensus" (1995). Many government delegates at the Cairo conference (particularly those from Islamic or Catholic countries where fundamentalists have a strong political influence) made no secret of their complete aversion to letting the bad "S" word appear anywhere in the ICPD Programme of Action; it remained bracketed until nearly the final hour. Yet, in the document's final version, references to "sex" and "sexuality" appear numerous times, and for the first time in any international legal instrument, the ICPD Programme explicitly includes "sexual health" (if not sexual pleasure) in the array of rights that population and development programs should protect. Chapter 7 adopts the World Health Organization's official definition of "sexual health" as an integral part of reproductive health, requiring "that people are able to have a satisfying and safe sex life" as well as to decide "if, when and how often" to reproduce. It defines the purpose of sexual health as "the enhancement of life and personal relations, and not merely counselling and care related to reproduction and sexually transmitted diseases" (para. 7.1).

There is little doubt that the concerns of many delegations, especially those from sub-Saharan Africa, about the devastating health and social consequences of HIV-AIDS played a crucial role in bringing sexuality into the ICPD document—at least as important as the role of the women's human rights coalition in foregrounding women as victims of sexual violence. Nonetheless, the extent to which "a satisfying and safe sex life" as an affirmative and not only a disease-preventive goal appears in the Programme is surprising. One does not want to overstate this; nowhere did freedom of sexual expression and orientation gain recognition as a human right, either at the Cairo conference or anyplace since. Yet, while there is no explicit reference to sexual rights for gays, lesbians, or unmarried persons (or anyone else for that matter), neither does paragraph 7.2 expressly limit its principle of self-determination, safety, and satisfaction in sexual life to heterosexuals, married couples, or adults (Copelon and Petchesky 1995). Indeed, other provisions in chapter 7 refer to "the limited power many women and girls have over their sexual and reproductive lives" and urge governments to provide adolescents with a full array of sexual and reproductive health services and education "to enable them to deal in a positive and responsible way with their sexuality." While "voluntary abstinence" is offered as one means toward the goal of men "[sharing] responsibility with women in matters of sexuality and reproduction," so too are condoms (that nefarious and finally unbracketed "C" word) (paras. 7.3, 7.41, 7.44, 7.45, and 8.31). Finally, and most controversially as it turned out, signatory governments to the ICPD Programme pledge in chapter 5 that their laws and policies will take into account the "plurality of [family] forms" existing in most societies (paras. 5.1 and 5.2).

The Platform for Action produced by the Fourth World Women's Conference (FWWC) in Beijing in 1995 went a number of steps further toward formulating a concept of sexual rights as part of international human rights principles. There a complicated negotiation process involving delegates, the Vatican-led fundamentalists, some wily chairs, and the women's nongovernmental organization (NGO) coalition hammered out the following historic paragraph:

> The human rights of women include their right to have control over and decide freely and responsibly on matters related to their sexuality, including sexual and reproductive health, free of coercion, discrimination and violence. Equal relationships between women and men in matters of sexual relations and reproduction, including full respect for the integrity of the person, require mutual respect, consent and shared responsibility for sexual behavior and its consequences. (para. 96)

This text is remarkable for both its utterances and its silences, what it makes explicit in the repertoire of international declarations (which are nonbinding but morally incumbent on their signatories), and what it leaves hidden. Notice that for the first time women are acknowledged as sexual as well as reproductive beings, with human rights to decide freely about their sexuality without any express qualification regarding age, marital status, or sexual orientation. But notice too that the original formulation of the paragraph, which had been bracketed in the draft, stated *not* "the human rights of women" but *"the sexual rights of women."* In the final version of the Beijing Platform, the phrase "sexual rights" disappears altogether; the phrase "sexual orientation" (much less lesbian or gay) never even made it into the draft, whereas "reproductive rights"—"the capability to reproduce and the freedom to decide if, when and how often to do so"—is now indelibly codified, through both Cairo and Beijing, in human rights treaty language.[3] Moreover, the phrase "respect for the integrity of the person" was introduced to replace any reference to "bodily integrity" or the body in any form (which some feminists feared would be applied to the fetus); nowhere in the Beijing Platform do sexualized female bodies or nonheterosexual bodies, claiming pleasures rather than fending off abuses, appear.

Of course this absence is the outcome of a complex drama in the halls of the United Nations. In that drama the fine points of language become a critical terrain for the contestation of power—and of the meanings of sexuality—through endless spirals of domination, resistance, and reconstitution of discourse (see Petchesky 1995a, 1997). A formidable coalition of feminist NGOs from both the south and the north working tirelessly at the Cairo and Beijing conferences was able to stake new ground on this terrain, in the face of much stronger forces among fundamentalists and the more conservative population groups and governments. Even in Cairo, the feminist coalition had succeeded in transforming the discourse of "reproductive rights" from a Westernist code for abortion into an international United Nations language denoting women's human right to self-determination over their fertility, motherhood, and, to a limited degree, sexuality. It was inevitable that this victory would call forth a backlash in the immediate aftermath of the ICPD, revealing where the hard lines would be drawn. For there is no doubt that underneath the aversion to sexual rights lurks the taboo against homosexuality, bisexuality, and alternative family forms. Note these typical reservations to the final ICPD Programme of Action registered by dissenting delegations. Holy See: "With reference to the term 'couples and individuals,' the Holy See reserves its position with the understanding that this term is to mean *married couples and the individual man and woman who constitute the couple."* And Egypt: "Our delegation called for the deletion of the word 'individuals' since it has always been our understanding that all the questions dealt with by the Programme of Action . . . relate to harmonious relations between couples united by the bond of marriage in the context of . . . the family as the primary cell of society" (UN 1994:144–46).

This drift continued in the prelude to Beijing. Having basically lost the verbal contest in Cairo, including on the question of "diverse family forms," the Vatican-led fundamentalist alliance conducted a concerted media campaign leading up to the FWWC designed to taint the concepts of "reproductive and sexual rights" with the labels of "individualism," "Western feminism," and lesbianism. This campaign not only opposed the language of "reproductive rights" and "diverse family forms" but, for a period of time, also succeeded in bracketing all references to the word "gender." The reason for this puzzling maneuver, as feminists involved in the Third Preparatory Meeting learned, was that Vatican agents had obtained a women's studies course packet from the United States containing readings that not only explained gender as a social construct (rather than a biological given) but also evoked the possibility of changing genders, multiple genders, and other shocking heresies. Hence the Vatican delegation's insistence that "sex," not "gender," should be the official terminology.

In Beijing itself, the fundamentalist campaign against "gender" and "sexual rights" fronted as a crusade on behalf of "parental rights"; its real targets were clearly the sexuality of all unmarried adolescents and lesbian sexuality. A flier distributed at the conference by a group of North American Vatican-aligned women called Coalition for Women and the Family makes perfectly plain the homophobia that Holy See delegates are far too politic to display in official United Nations sessions. Titled "Sexual Rights and Sexual Orientation— What Do These Words Really Mean?" the flier associates "these words" with not only homosexuality, lesbianism, and sexual relationships outside marriage and among adolescents, but also "pedophilia," "prostitution," "incest," and "adultery." And it engages in gay-baiting and fear-mongering (e.g., the statement, "Homosexuals have claimed protection for behaviors which everyone knows spread HIV/AIDS"). Yet the fundamentalist position goes even deeper than the issues of sexual and bodily self-determination for women and gays, challenging the ethical and epistemological basis of these claims to rights. In his *Evangelium Vitae* encyclical—released to the media precisely to coincide with the March Preparatory Committee Meeting (Prep Com) before Beijing—the pope condemns ideas and practices asserting reproductive and sexual autonomy by associating them with "a hedonistic mentality unwilling to accept responsibility in matters of sexuality" and "a self-centered concept of freedom" (Catholics for a Free Choice 1995; *Evangelium Vitae* 1995).

But we cannot blame the Vatican alone for the ambiguity that remains in the Beijing Platform's sexual rights formula. In a world historical moment of religious patriarchal revivalism, accusations of "selfishness" and admonitions to self-sacrifice directed toward women have a powerful appeal. In such a climate, liberal groups also become susceptible to the backlash and begin to retreat or curb their demands. The U.S. delegation in Beijing, for example— made up mostly of women Democrats allied with the Clinton administration and very nervous about the power of right-wing conservatives back home— tempered its usual support for reproductive rights and women's rights by submitting an interpretive statement during the deliberations on paragraph

96 of the platform, cited earlier. In its statement, the United States emphasizes three different times the phrase "relationships *between women and men*"
as well as "freedom from coercion, discrimination and violence," thus seeming to deflect from any possible interpretation that would highlight lesbian
identity or women's right to sexual pleasure.[4]

In the face of not just evasion but outright antagonism and "a sexphobic
right wing that drew its strength from a multi-religious base" (Tambiah
1996), women's groups from around the world involved in the official Beijing
conference also found it necessary to compromise on any affirmative and
more controversial formulation of sexual rights. In March 1995, a petition
signed by thousands of women and groups from sixty countries in all the
world's regions had been presented to Gertrude Mongella, the conference's
secretary-general, calling on member states "*to recognize the right to determine
one's sexual identity; the right to control one's own body, particularly in establishing intimate relationships; and the right to choose if, when, and with whom to bear
or raise children as fundamental components of the human rights of all women
regardless of sexual orientation.*" Given the rancorous climate of the late-night
deliberations on the final wording of paragraph 96, however, women's
groups and their government allies found it difficult if not impossible to
argue for such explicitly feminist and affirmative values.[5]

But why? Why is it so much easier to assert sexual freedom in a negative
rather than an affirmative, emancipatory sense; to gain consensus for the
right not to be abused, exploited, raped, trafficked, or mutilated in one's
body but not the right to fully enjoy one's body? Aside from tactical positions
and defenses against overt homophobia, is there a larger social, political, and
economic context, as well as a particular ideological baggage, that makes
such an approach still quite elusive in this historical moment? Before attempting to answer these questions, let me say emphatically how important
is the ground that feminist organizations, especially in the south, have
opened up toward winning recognition of reproductive and sexual rights as
human rights. Women's and gay rights movements in countries where the
Catholic Church is powerful—the Philippines, Nigeria, Brazil, Mexico, Peru,
and elsewhere in Latin America—have struggled (still unsuccessfully in most
cases) to legalize abortion, reduce maternal mortality, and educate about
safer sex and condom use. In Bangladesh, according to Sajeda Amin and Sara
Hossain (1995), women's organizations have publically countered brutal attacks on women accused by Islamic religious tribunals of transgressing sexual norms. In Egypt, Sudan, Somalia, Kenya, and Nigeria, the campaigns by
women's groups against female genital mutilation have focused simultaneously on the procedure's erosion of women's sexual pleasure as well as its
severe risks to their health (Toubia 1995; Tambiah 1995).

All these efforts nourished the forcefulness of the women's coalitions in
Vienna, Cairo, and Beijing and their success in merging the language of sex-

ual and reproductive health with the language of women's human rights. The synthesis they created has in turn rearticulated a feminist ethics of bodily integrity and personhood that permeates the Cairo and Beijing documents and directly challenges the moral arsenal of Catholic, Jewish, and Islamic fundamentalists. This ethics postulates not only that women must be free from abuse and violation in their bodies, including their fertility and sexuality, but also that they must be treated as principal actors and decision makers, as the ends and not the means of population, health, and development programs. Moreover, it applies this principle not only to states and their agents but to every level where power operates—in the home, the clinic, the workplace, the church, synagogue or mosque, and the community (Corrêa and Petchesky 1994; Corrêa 1994; Sen and Snow 1994).

Yet I find something disturbing in the way this shift to a feminist ethic of self-determination over our bodies, which has indisputably become a shared discourse across south and north, has opened up through negations, denials, and litanies of violence and abuse behind which the claims to pleasure remain ever silent. Of course human rights language, especially with the second- and third-generation rights, is supposed to embody affirmative entitlements and not just protections from abuse or discrimination; they are two sides of a coin (I cannot enjoy my sexual body if I am subjected to the constant fear of battering or unwanted pregnancy) (Heise 1995a, 1995b; Copelon 1994). Still, the campaigns around women's human rights have generally gained the widest attention when they parade the worst horrors (genital mutilation; mass rape as a weapon of war; forced abortion or sterilization; sexual trafficking; murder of women for sexual or gender "deviance"). They therefore capitalize on the image of women as victims.[6] Given this tendency in feminist human rights discourse, it is no accident that in both the health and human rights sections of the Beijing Platform, the specter of sexualized bodies claiming pleasures lurked *behind* the debates, present only in the absence of "bodies" and "sexual rights" in the final text. And this victimizing tendency is troubling to the extent that it evades, or even mirrors, fundamentalist patriarchal images of women as weak and vulnerable.

To be sure, the problem with such negative constructions of sexual rights is one that pervades human rights discourse in general. Historically, it has always been the case that the human rights violations that receive the most attention and have the greatest possibility of being vigorously combatted have been those involving blatant discrimination or physical abuse, the paradigm situations being those of torture victims and mistreated political prisoners. It is much more difficult to achieve anything but lip service from governments to their treaty commitments under the International Covenant on Economic, Social and Cultural Rights (ICESCR), which includes many important provisions subsequently incorporated in the Cairo and Beijing documents. For example, article 12 of the ICESCR recognizes "the right of everyone to the enjoyment of the highest attainable standard of physical and mental health," now a major underpinning of the principles of reproductive and sexual health rights. But framing health in affirmative human rights terms means "conceptualizing [it] as a social good" basic to human dignity and well-being "and not solely a medical, technical, or economic problem" (Leary 1994). And this implies major obligations and redirection of resources on the part of governments. They must take positive action to make sure that decent health care becomes both a legitimate entitlement and an accessible reality for all people under their jurisdiction; that is, they must create the necessary social conditions for health to become a social right. If very few societies in a world now dominated by capitalist markets take this view (as opposed to the view of health care as a private commodity), should we be surprised that only one country on earth, South Africa, has a constitution that recognizes the right to freedom of sexual orientation?

I do not wish to be misunderstood here. The rape, forced marriage, forced slavery, mutilation, and other forms of sexual violence imposed on thousands of women as part of the Rwandan genocide is only the most shocking recent example of a pattern of "hatreds" (to use Zillah Eisenstein's word) that inter- sects almost everywhere with racial and national antagonisms (Eisenstein 1996; Human Rights Watch 1996; Center for Women's Global Leadership 1996; Rosenbloom 1995). Less dramatic but just as insidious in the long run are the criminalization of lesbianism in many countries and mounting pres- sure from conservatives for the enforcement of criminal bans in some of these.[7] My intention is certainly not to deny or diminish the magnitude of such atrocities against women and sexual minorities, committed and con- doned by states and communities throughout the world. Rather, I am simply making the argument that focusing on such cases—however horrifying and important in bringing media attention to the legitimacy of sexual rights as human rights—at best gets us to the level of liberal tolerance. The negative, exclusionary approach to rights—sometimes expressed as the right to "pri- vacy" or to be "let alone" in one's choices and desires—can never in itself help us to construct an *alternative vision* or lead to fundamental structural, social, and cultural transformations. Even the feminist slogan "my body is my own," while rhetorically powerful, may also be perfectly compatible with the hegemonic global market insofar as it demands freedom from abuse but not from the economic conditions that compel me to sell my body or its sexual or reproductive capacities (Pateman 1988; Petchesky 1995b).

What, then, would such an alternative, positive vision of sexual rights look like? I would suggest it contains two integral and interlocked compo- nents: a set of *ethical principles* (the substance, or ultimate ends, of sexual rights) and a wide range of *enabling conditions* without which those ends could not in practice be achieved (Corrêa and Petchesky 1994). The ethical principles I have in mind include sexual diversity, habitational diversity (or "diverse family forms"), health, decision-making autonomy (personhood), and gender equality. *Sexual diversity*, or "multisexualism," implies commitment to the principle that diverse types of sexual expression (not only heterosexual or conjugal) are not only tolerable but a positive benefit to a just, humane, and culturally pluralistic society. This principle places optimum value on the ethical goods of caring, affection, support, and mutually consensual erotic stimulation, assuming that the particular forms or relationships through which these activities get expressed—whether heterosexual, homosexual, or bisexual—are secondary to the importance of a cultural climate that encourages their expression. (I am assuming here a broad definition of "consent" that would preclude adult-child incest and various other sexual relations between persons in grossly different power positions, such as prison guards and inmates or doctors and their patients.) A wealth of ethnographic and historical examples of such diversity existing in numerous societies and cultures is certainly available to us from the rich scholarship of gay and lesbian (or queer) studies of the past decade.[8] One might surmise that, from a broad cross-cultural and historical perspective, conjugal heterosexuality is far from a universal practice and argue that rights, while not governed by social and cultural practices, ought at least to take their diversity into account.

A second and closely related principle I am calling *habitational diversity* in order to separate it from procreation, which it may but does not necessarily involve. This principle already has a precedent in the ICPD Programme of Action's repeated recognition of "diverse family forms," which created such havoc among the Vatican and its fundamentalist allies. While specifically mentioning only female-headed households, the Cairo document acknowledges that people cohabit, raise children, and sustain affective relations in many types of arrangements across the world's societies and cultures; implies that the patriarchal, conjugal, heterosexual kind of family is neither exclusive nor inherently superior; and suggests that all sorts of families or cohabiting groups, regardless of their structure, are "entitled to receive comprehensive protection and support" from the state (ICPD, para. 5.1). Probably the fears of the fundamentalists that this language would sanction gay and lesbian families and marriages say more about the hysteria of fundamentalists than the intentions of member states. Nonetheless, the recognition of "diverse family forms" in the ICPD Programme does put the "right to marry and found a family," hallowed in major human rights instruments, in a rather new light.

The third ethical principle contained in my affirmative vision of sexual rights is that of *health*, and it too has already received international human rights codification. When we combine "the right of everyone to the enjoyment of the highest attainable standard of physical and mental health" with the Cairo document's recognition that "sexual health" is a part of reproductive rights and involves a "satisfying" as well as a "safe" sexual life, then we are approaching something that starts to look like pleasure as a positive good. Of course the link to reproduction limits the scope of this principle, but not if it is taken in conjunction with sexual and habitational diversity. The point is that there is already some basis in existing international agreements for asserting the right to sexual pleasure as a part of basic health and well-being necessary to human life—a concept recognized in several major world religions (including Islam and Judaism) as well as many traditional cultures.[9]

Fourth is the principle of *autonomy*, or *personhood*, implying the right of individual persons—children and youth as well as adults—to make their own decisions in matters affecting their bodies and health. It is expressed eloquently in the pre-Beijing petition I cited earlier ("Put Sexuality on the Agenda at the World Conference on Women"): "*the right to determine one's sexual identity; the right to control one's own body, particularly in establishing intimate relationships.*" Clearly this principle is rooted in basic concepts of liberty and democracy and is fundamental to citizenship (or pre-citizenship[10]) rights. In other words, as feminist and other human rights advocates have stressed so often, so-called civil and political rights and economic, social and cultural rights are interdependent and indivisible (Sen 1990; Human Rights Watch 1996; Copelon and Petchesky 1995). How can I act responsibly as a citizen and a member of my kin group and community if my body and sexuality are defined and controlled by others—by my husband, parents, religious authorities, or the state?

But, especially in the domain of sexual rights, we have to see the autonomy or personhood principle as inseparable from that of *gender equality*, when we recall the thousands of ways in all societies that the law of sexual norms is infused with a gender code as well as a family code. Yasmin Tambiah, in her splendid analysis "Sexuality and Human Rights," encapsulates the inequities in the situation of the girl child in so many societies, the "contradictory messages" that cripple the development of her sexuality:

> She is instructed to devalue her own body lest she be responsible for inciting unwarranted male attention. Simultaneously she is expected to cultivate the ability to hold male attention as a desireable wife. She is kept ignorant about her body because it is alleged that the less she knows about it, the less likely she is to explore her sexuality and therefore compromise her virginity. At the same time, however, she is expected to develop a healthy and knowledgeable attitude toward motherhood. (1995:374)

Tambiah's observation that the girl child is thus "compelled into heterosexuality, being denied the opportunity to develop an understanding of her sexuality and eventually to exercise an informed, autonomous choice" (375) confirms some of the findings of the International Reproductive Rights Research Action Group (IRRRAG) in a recent study we conducted in seven countries in Africa, Asia, the Americas, and the Middle East.[11] We were discouraged to find that older generations of women—denied other channels of authority or outlets for self-assertion—are even more likely than men in many communities to be the ones who police the boundaries of other women's (and their own daughters') sexual behavior. As is well known, women may acquire a certain privileged status or respectability from upholding traditional practices and codes of honor.[12] Likewise, Tambiah's description of women's *normative* condition, heterosexual marriage, as one fraught with dangers, both physical and social, and the need to constantly walk a fine line with regard to sexuality, echoes the findings of our researchers. In one country study after another, we found women making "trade-offs," negotiating their sexual pleasure and autonomy in exchange for other gains. For example, in the Philippines, Mexico, and Egypt, women accept unwanted marital sex in exchange for husbands' cooperation in housework or to stave off quarrels or domestic violence. In Egypt, they adapt to female genital mutilation or a wedding-night defloration ritual they find painful and humiliating in order to secure public respectability and the freedom to come and go.[13] In Brazil, fear of domestic violence limits the physical and sexual mobility of rural women, while fear of pregnancy and losing their jobs keeps domestic workers effectively celibate. And the majority of women we interviewed everywhere still believe that expressing their need for sexual satisfaction, much less their entitlement to it, will bring them shame.

But at the same time we encountered these sad and more familiar examples of sexual self-denial, IRRRAG's research also disclosed some voices of poor women, across diverse cultures and situations, who articulated an affirmative sense of entitlement to sexual pleasure as women. Sometimes this is vicarious: mothers who begin to identify with their daughters and seek sexual autonomy and pleasure for and through them, giving the trade-off strategy an intergenerational form. This was particularly true of working-class Brazilian housewives who rejected for their daughters the rigid virginity codes that had been ingrained in them as young girls. My favorite respondent in our whole study is the São Paulo mother who tells her daughter, "You have to obey your mother and be a good girl. Even if you have sex, do it carefully, use a condom. Know what you are doing. . . . because, if afterwards you have a child, who will take care of your children? There are so many ways to avoid it." While obviously reflecting fear of the widespread risk of HIV-AIDS and other sexually transmitted diseases (STDs) in urban Brazil, such mothers are also taking the traditional definition of a "good girl" and turning it upside down (Portella et al. 1998).

In other examples, affirmative expressions of sexual entitlement among grassroots women may be indirect—for example, the maquilladora worker from Sonora in Mexico who complained that women "don't have the chance to like [sex]" because men are always so aggressive and overbearing and "only care for their own satisfaction" (Ortiz-Ortega et al. 1998). Elsewhere they are more direct, such as the nineteen-year-old woman in northern Nigeria who defiantly announced, "Whenever I feel like sleeping with my boyfriend, I go to him" (Osakue and Hilber 1998); or the forty-year-old farmworker from the Sertão region of Brazil who certified that concepts of sexual freedom are not the sole property of urban, middle-class activists:

> [I]t's a matter of choice. If someone feels better with a man, she should keep to him. . . . If I like a woman, it's my business. I've got to think of myself, not of what others may say. . . . Everyone has the right to choose what is right for herself.[14] (Portella et al. 1998)

Yet these affirmative sexual claims by grassroots women have to be seen at the present time more as wishes or aspirations than concrete realities. For most women, their realization in practice depends on the other crucial component of sexual rights I mentioned earlier, that of *enabling conditions*. Particularly given the huge cutbacks and privatization of social services that women in all seven IRRRAG countries—and throughout the world—are facing, the five ethical principles I sketched will remain useless abstractions without global economic, social, and structural changes. How is decision-making autonomy over one's sexuality possible without full information about safer sex, sexuality, one's body, contraceptive methods, and ways to avoid STDs? How is sexual health possible without access to preventive, caring, and good quality services and methods? How is habitational diversity possible if one lacks commodious housing, a place and space to be intimate? More profoundly, how are sexual diversity and gender equality possible without a cultural revolution in how societies, the media, and institutions envision "women" and "men"? In other words, if we ask (in human rights lingo) what would be the minimal criteria for developing indicators whereby United Nations agencies and governments could establish standards for measuring compliance with sexual rights principles, we begin to see that an affirmative approach to sexual rights opens up enormous transformational visions that would affect men as well as women, all of society and not only its sexual minorities.

But if this is the case, why indeed have many progressive organizations, including women's and human rights groups, been so tentative about mobilizing behind an affirmative and comprehensive sexual rights program? In particular, why are so many of us complicit in maintaining the invisibility of sex as pleasure? There are many reasons, some hidden and some obvious, and no space here to explore them at length. Short of outright homophobia (which, unfortunately, still contaminates many organizations), they partly involve a certain ideological baggage: the legacy of the left, its economistic biases and suspicions of "bourgeois individualism"; the legacy of nationalism and its suspicions of Western cultural imperialism; and the legacy of Foucauldian postmodernism, which both "discovered" and inscribed the agentic sexual self to be an illusion of the European Enlightenment. There is also the political contradiction built into the feminist and gay rights movements, to the extent that both these movements seek at the same time to transform societies and to find "a place at the table." Aspiring to power and influence in the public realm, including power over the terms of human rights rhetoric, always contains risks of compromise and co-optation; risks that necessarily contributed to the ambiguities as well as the strengths in the final Beijing document over the meanings of "sexual rights." What we can say is this: the body evokes the fetal body for some and women's sexualized body, including the lesbian body, for others; either way, it remains dangerous and commands silence. Sexual self-determination and sexual rights imply both the negative freedom against unwanted intrusions, violations, and abuses, and also the positive capacity to seek and experience pleasures in a variety of ways and situations, including (for women) without a man. But the latter is still too dangerous to permit affirmative reiteration among many women's movements.

While I am convinced that affirmative constructions of rights need more of our attention, as both intellectuals and activists, the "liberatory" approach to sexual rights poses its own dilemmas. First, am I overly dichotomizing the "pleasure" and "danger" sides of sexuality and thus ignoring the dialectical way in which the affirmative and negative dimensions of rights are intertwined? Amartya Sen, addressing the concept of freedom more generally, makes a powerful argument that "the social commitment to individual freedom has to be concerned with both positive and negative freedoms, and with their extensive interconnections" (1990:50). Not only does a person's right to fully develop and enjoy her body and her erotic and emotional capacities depend on being free from abuse and violence, as well as having the necessary enabling conditions and material resources discussed earlier, it may also be the case that awareness of affirmative sexual rights comes as a result of experiencing their violation.[15] An interesting life trajectory discovered by IRRRAG researchers in several countries was one in which a woman had been beaten or systematically subjected to unwanted sex by her husband over many years and had finally resisted effectively (sometimes wielding a knife), after which she gained a sense of empowerment that led to new forms of independent earning, a new relationship, or both.

Second, as an umbrella category attempting to be inclusive and universal, sexual rights can become a totalizing language that actually excludes and obscures. The now mainstreamed elision of the phrase "sexual and reproductive rights" among feminist reproductive health advocates too often tends to bury the sexual, folding it discretely into marital/heterosexual and childbearing relations (see IPPF 1996; Cook 1995). Nowhere do any of the existing

human rights instruments, including the Cairo and Beijing documents, articulate freedom of sexual orientation or diverse sexualities; thus, to the extent
that "sexual rights" continues to rely on interpretations of these instruments
or to collapse the "sexual" into the "reproductive," the specific rights and
situations of lesbians, bisexual women, and a whole range of culturally specific sexual minorities may remain invisible. How do we create a general
rights framework that also addresses these specificities?[16] Moreover, reticence
about making sexual practices and their diversity explicit may affect not only
human rights interpretation but also the accuracy of field research. Surely it
says more about the sensitivities of IRRRAG's researchers than the practices
of our respondents that in almost none of our seven studies is lesbian sexuality anywhere to be found.

At the same time, it is crucial to recognize that these silences I find disturbing—including in IRRRAG's own research—are as much based on strategic calculation as they are on deep inner conflict. In many countries and
communities still, to speak openly of women's right to varied sexual pleasures is to invite the closing down of your organization, ostracization of its
members, verbal and physical attacks, or even death. The spiral of resistance
is still, as always, constrained by power; and these power dynamics are reproduced in the souls of all of us, however radical our vision. In this political
context, to begin to speak of sexual rights, even tentatively, is a big step. In
the research context, to begin to map out women's often compromising strategies for negotiating their sexual entitlements can show us which conditions
must change before we can help to empower the women we interview, and
ourselves, to reach for strategies that are more daring.

By 1999, it was possible to append a more positive note to this article, based
on developments that occurred during the "Cairo + 5" process in the United
Nations to review implementation of the Programme of Action (POA).[17] Toward the end of that process, it was clear that *sexual rights* had now become
an official and indelible part of the international human rights lexicon, regardless of the absence of the actual words from any document. Even the
Holy See, in its final interpretive statement to the General Assembly in July
1999, unwittingly reinforced this discourse when it announced its reservations to any provision making access to abortion part of "sexual health, sexual rights, reproductive health or reproductive rights."

This achievement at the level of language was the result of persistent efforts by women's health and human rights NGOs. Despite an antifeminist
backlash during the 1999 meetings, led by the Vatican and a few of its
fundamentalist allies, Women's Coalition NGOs participating in Cairo + 5
worked in many resourceful ways to make their presence and ideas felt.
These included numerous press conferences and interviews, an effective alliance with the Youth Coalition, forceful speeches before the conference plen-

aries, an "Open Letter to the Vatican" signed by dozens of Latin American NGOs and others from the Women's Coalition, and a vigorous international petition campaign ("See Change") over the Internet, launched by Catholics for a Free Choice (CFFC), to challenge the Vatican's status at the UN.[18] Most dramatic of all perhaps was a "silent" demonstration during the Prep Com in March in which Women's and Youth Coalition members lined up outside the delegates' meeting room to protest against the stalling tactics being carried out by certain delegations and to insist that the review process move forward. That security guards were immediately deployed to remove the hundred or so demonstrators signifies that silence in UN corridors may sometimes speak louder than words.[19]

In fact, I would argue that by 1999 women's transnational NGOs had become far more sophisticated than they were in 1994 about the need for effective strategies to address the *structures of power* underlying existing patterns of global governance. (CFFC's organized challenge to the Vatican's status as a "nonmember state permanent observer" at the UN is just one vibrant example.) This sophistication has made the quiet legitimation of sexual rights language more than a symbolic victory. A recent compilation of the work of the five UN human rights treaty bodies relevant to reproductive and sexual health indicates numerous instances since the Cairo and Beijing conferences in which the human rights committees have cited countries for their failure to prevent sexual and other forms of violence against women, or to provide sex education, sexual and HIV/AIDS counseling for men, women, and adolescents, or more funds for sexual health services.[20] Slowly but steadily, sexual rights are making their way into the institutionalized mechanisms of international human rights law.

Notes

This article has also been published in *Framing the Sexual Subject: The Politics of Gender, Sexuality, and Power*, ed. R. G. Parker, R. M. Barbosa, and P. Aggleton (Berkeley: University of California Press, 1999), 81–103. For much of the thinking in it (though not for its flaws), I gratefully acknowledge stimulating discussions with Roxanna Carrillo, Sonia Corrêa, Susanna Fried, Claudia Hinojosa, Rachel Kyte, Ilana Landsberg-Lewis, Adriana Ortiz-Ortega, Rachel Rosenbloom, Yasmin Tambiah, the New Visions Faculty Seminar on Human Rights at Hunter College, and most especially the ideas and support of Rhonda Copelon. I also gratefully acknowledge the participants in the seminar "Reconceiving Sexuality: International Perspectives on Gender, Sexuality and Sexual Health," Rio de Janeiro, April 1996, where I presented an earlier version of the paper, and the support of Regina Barbosa and Richard Parker, convenors of the seminar.

1. Some of this analysis is drawn from a previous article I wrote with Sonia Corrêa; see Corrêa and Petchesky 1994.

2. On one level, this should not be surprising. Despite Foucault's (eurocentric) insistence on characterizing modernity by its incessant preoccupation with sex talk, in fact we know how consistently such talk, even in the West, has been veiled, ambivalent, guilt-laden or scandal-ridden. Only at the end of the twentieth century and the beginning of the new millennium, largely due to the global HIV-AIDS pandemic, have international relations become a domain where sexuality can be somewhat openly discussed. See Parker and Gagnon 1995, especially the editors' introduction and article by Altman in that volume; and Foucault 1978.

3. Both the ICPD Programme (para. 7.2) and the Beijing Platform (para. 95) define "reproductive rights" as "[resting] on the recognition of the basic right of all couples and individuals to decide freely and responsibly the number, spacing and timing of their children and to have the information and means to do so, and the right to attain the highest standard of sexual and reproductive health. It also includes their right to make decisions concerning reproduction free of discrimination, coercion and violence, as expressed in human rights documents."

4. Thanks to Rhonda Copelon for providing me with a copy of this statement (dated September 14, 1995, submitted to the Main Committee of the FWWC in Beijing).

5. See Rosenbloom 1995, appendix A, for the full text of the petition. While I attended some earlier sessions of the official conference, I was not present at the meeting described. Many thanks to Roxanna Carrillo, Rhonda Copelon, Rachel Kyte, and Ilana Landsberg-Lewis for sharing their impressions of this historic moment.

6. This emphasis is very much present in two otherwise excellent and invaluable publications that offer chilling testimonies of the kinds of sexual abuse and violence that brutalize women (and gay men) throughout the world (Center for Women's Global Leadership 1996; Rosenbloom 1995).

7. For the case of recent anti-gay and lesbian legislation and campaigns by fundamentalists in Sri Lanka, see Tambiah 1996. According to the International Gay and Lesbian Human Rights Commission, eighty-six countries outlaw gay male homosexuality, compared to forty-four that criminalize lesbianism; clearly, lesbianism is seen as less of a threat, but only because of its "social invisibility" and the denial by lawmakers that it even exists (Rosenbloom 1995:xiii).

8. For just a few examples, see Parker and Gagnon 1995, especially articles by Lutzen, Herdt and Boxer, Tan, Lancaster, Zalduondo and Bernard, and Weeks.

9. Aihwa Ong (1994) notes that the *kampung* women she interviewed in Malaysia—apparently more influenced by *adat*, or village tradition, than by contemporary fundamentalist versions of Sharia'a law—considered sex "essential to good health and only viewed negatively when indulged in excessively or with an unsuitable partner."

10. In the case of children or immigrants.

11. See IRRRAG, *Negotiating Reproductive Rights: Women's Perspectives Across Countries and Cultures*, ed. R. Petchesky and K. Judd, (London: Zed Books, 1998). IRRRAG's interdisciplinary research teams—made up of social science researchers, women's health movement and human rights activists, and health providers—carried out intensive qualitative research among low-income urban and rural women in Brazil, Egypt, Malaysia, Mexico, Nigeria, the Philippines, and the United States in 1993 and 1994. The purpose of the research was to find out the circumstances and areas in

which such women—varying in age, marital status, ethnicity, religion, and occupation—begin to develop a sense of entitlement and self-determination around sexual and reproductive decision making.

12. In Nigeria, for example, we repeatedly observed how older rural and urban market women maintained and elevated their status in the community by enforcing traditional practices such as widowhood rites and female genital mutilation. In Egypt we found that mothers were more likely than fathers to want to enforce the *baladi dokhla*, or wedding-night ritual proving virginity, and to control their daughters' choice of marriage partner; apparently these are arenas where they feel they can maintain some kind of authority in the household. In several countries, mothers were unwilling to impart sexual knowledge to their daughters prior to their marriage, for fear of "opening their eyes" and risking the family's honor.

13. Ironically, men interviewed in Egypt see this ritual as an "invasion of privacy"; only women feel compelled to trade their bodily integrity for economic and civil rights that legally belong to them. See Aida Seif El Dawla, Amal Abdel Hadi, and Nadia Abdel Wahab, "Women's Wit over Men's: Trade-Offs and Strategic Accommodations in Egyptian Women's Reproductive Lives," in Petchesky and Judd 1998.

14. Of course this woman's ideas are in no sense "pure" or unmediated; they probably have some connection to the work of feminist health organizers in Pernambuco (particularly the work of the organization SOS-Corpo with grassroots women in the agricultural workers' union). Still, her sincerity in embracing the ideas is not in doubt.

15. Thanks to Susanna Fried for calling my attention to this point.

16. The *IPPF Charter on Sexual and Reproductive Rights* is the best example of a thorough, thoughtful compendium of basic principles and the existing instruments from which they derive that uses very broad language to imply—but not specify. The closest it comes to articulating an affirmative approach to sexual pleasure is under principle 2, "The Right to Liberty and Security of the Person," where it states: "All persons have the right to be free to enjoy and control their sexual and reproductive life, having due regard to the rights of others." Also, "All persons have the right to be free from externally imposed fear, shame, guilt, beliefs based on myths, and other psychological factors inhibiting their sexual response or impairing their sexual relationships." Compare the HERA action sheet on sexual rights, which states: "Sexual rights are a fundamental element of human rights. They encompass the right to experience a pleasurable sexuality, which is essential in and of itself and, at the same time, is a fundamental vehicle of communication and love between people. Sexual rights include the right to liberty and autonomy in the responsible exercise of sexuality." Within this definition, HERA lists ten points, among them "the right to happiness, dreams and fantasies"; "the right to explore one's sexuality free from fear, shame, guilt, false beliefs and other impediments to the free expression of one's desires"; "the right to choose one's sexual partners without discrimination"; "the right to full respect for the physical integrity of the body"; and "the right to be free and autonomous in expressing one's sexual orientation" (HERA 1998). HERA is a transnational network of women's health activists from all the world's regions who work to advocate, design, and implement strategies for guaranteeing sexual and reproductive rights and health within the broader context of human rights and sustainable development. For more information, contact the HERA secretariat, c/o International Women's Health Coalition, 24 East 21st St., New York, NY 10010.

17. The ICPD + 5 review process consisted of three stages over a five-month period in 1999. The Hague Forum (preceded by a simultaneous Youth and NGO Forum) in early February was sponsored by the United Nations Population Fund (UNFPA) and was mainly convened to finalize background documents reviewing progress and obstacles in implementing the POA within countries. This was followed in March by a two-day meeting of the UN Committee on Population and Development (CPD) in New York, which transformed itself into a Prep Com for the later UN General Assembly Special Session (UNGASS), held in late June–early July to review the Secretary-General's Final Report on Key Actions for Further Implementation of the ICPD POA. See http://www.unfpa.org for documents, speeches, and further information.

18. The Open Letter (July 1, 1999) asked: "Given that the Vatican is not a nation-state, is not involved in the implementation of the Cairo Programme of Action and, by its very nature, does not have women or children or sexual and reproductive problems, why is the Vatican delegation interested in blocking advances in contraception, sexual education, and HIV prevention that are beneficial to millions of women, especially . . . poor women?" For more information about CFFC's "See Change" campaign, see http://www.cath4choice.org.

19. A dynamic, skilled, and very vocal Youth Coalition, representing 132 NGOs in 111 countries, participated in all the ICPD + 5 meetings. It argued that adolescents have the same sexual and reproductive rights, and the same right to participate in decisions that affect their lives, as adults. This was an important and exciting change from previous UN meetings.

20. The major human rights treaty bodies at the UN are the Committee on Social, Economic and Cultural Rights; the Committee on the Elimination of all Forms of Racial Discrimination; the Committee on the Elimination of Discrimination Against Women; the Committee on the Rights of the Child; and the Human Rights Committee. See the compilation of their work on sexual and reproductive health rights in *The Application of Human Rights to Reproductive and Sexual Health: A Compilation of the Work of UN Treaty Bodies*, ed. Julie Stanchiere, Isfahan Merali, and Rebecca J. Cook (Program on Reproductive and Sexual Health Law, Faculty of Law, University of Toronto, Canada, June 1999).

Works Cited

Altman, Dennis. 1995. "Political Sexualities: Meanings and Identities in the Time of AIDS." In *Conceiving Sexuality*, ed. Parker and Gagnon, 97–106.

Amin, Sajeda, and Sara Hossain. 1995. "Women's Reproductive Rights and the Politics of Fundamentalism: A View from Bangladesh." *American University Law Review* 44:1319–43.

Bunch, Charlotte. 1990. "Women's Rights as Human Rights: Toward a Re-Vision of Human Rights." *Human Rights Quarterly* 12:486–98.

Catholics for a Free Choice. 1995. *The Vatican and the Fourth World Conference on Women*. Available from Catholics for a Free Choice, 1436 U Street NW, Suite 301, Washington, DC 20009.

Center for Women's Global Leadership. 1996. *From Vienna to Beijing: The Global Tribu-*

nal on Accountability for Women's Human Rights, ed. Niamh Reilly. New Brunswick, NJ: Rutgers University Press.

Cook, Rebecca, ed. 1994. *Human Rights of Women: National and International Perspectives*. Philadelphia: University of Pennsylvania Press.

——. 1995. "Human Rights and Reproductive Self-Determination." *American University Law Review* 44:975–1475.

Copelon, Rhonda. 1994. "Recognizing the Egregious in the Everyday: Domestic Violence as Torture." *Columbia Human Rights Law Review* 25:291–367.

Copelon, Rhonda, and Berta Esperanza Hernandez. 1994. "Sexual and Reproductive Rights and Health as Human Rights: Concepts and Strategies." International Women's Human Rights Law Clinic. New York: City University of New York.

Copelon, Rhonda, and Rosalind Petchesky. 1995. "Toward an Interdependent Approach to Reproductive and Sexual Rights as Human Rights: Reflections on the ICPD and Beyond." In *From Basic Needs to Basic Rights: Women's Claim to Human Rights*, ed. Margaret A. Schuler, 343–67. Washington, DC: Women, Law and Development International.

Corrêa, Sonia. 1994. *Population and Reproductive Rights: Feminist Perspectives from the South*. London: Zed Press.

Corrêa, Sonia, and Rosalind Petchesky. 1994. "Reproductive and Sexual Rights: A Feminist Perspective." In *Population Policies Reconsidered*, ed. Gita Sen, Adrienne Germain, and Lincoln Chen, 107–23. Cambridge, MA: Harvard University Press.

Eisenstein, Zillah. 1996. *Hatreds: Racialized and Sexualized Conflicts in the 21st Century*. New York: Routledge.

Evangelium Vitae. 1995. "Pope's Letter: A 'Sinister' World Has Led to 'Crimes against Life.'" *New York Times*, March 31:A12–13.

Foucault, Michel. 1978. *The History of Sexuality*. Vol. I, *An Introduction*. Trans. Robert Hurley. New York: Pantheon.

Freedman, Lynn P., and Steven L. Isaacs. 1993. "Human Rights and Reproductive Choice." *Studies in Family Planning* 24:18–30.

Heise, Lori L. 1995a. "Violence, Sexuality, and Women's Lives." In *Conceiving Sexuality*, ed. Parker and Gagnon, 109–34.

——. 1995b. "Freedom Close to Home: The Impact of Violence against Women on Reproductive Rights." In *Women's Rights, Human Rights: International Feminist Perspectives*, ed. Julie Peters and Andrea Wolper, 238–55. New York: Routledge.

HERA (Health, Empowerment, Rights and Accountability). 1998. *Women's Sexual and Reproductive Rights and Health Action Sheets*. New York: International Women's Health Coalition.

Human Rights Watch. 1996. *Shattered Lives: Sexual Violence during the Rwandan Genocide and Its Aftermath*. New York: Human Rights Watch.

IPPF (International Planned Parenthood Federation). 1996. *IPPF Charter on Sexual and Reproductive Rights*. London: IPPF.

Leary, V. 1994. "The Right to Health in International Human Rights Law." *Health and Human Rights* 1:24–56.

Ong, Aihwa. 1994. "State versus Islam: Malay Families, Women's Bodies, and the Body Politic in Malaysia." In *Women's Reproductive Rights in Muslim Communities and Countries: Issues and Resources*, 26–36. Cairo: Women Living Under Muslim Laws.

Ortiz-Ortega, Adriana, Ana Amuchastegui, and Marta Rivas. 1998. "'Because They

Were Born from Me': Negotiating Women's Rights in Mexico." In *Negotiating Reproductive Rights*, ed. Petchesky and Judd, 145–79.

Osakue, Grace, and Adriane Martin Hilber. 1998. "Women's Sexuality and Fertility in Nigeria: Breaking the Culture of Silence." In *Negotiating Reproductive Rights*, ed. Petchesky and Judd, 180–216.

Parker, Richard G., and John H. Gagnon, eds. 1995. *Conceiving Sexuality: Approaches to Sex Research in a Postmodern World*. New York: Routledge.

Pateman, Carole. 1988. *The Sexual Contract*. Stanford: Stanford University Press.

Petchesky, Rosalind. 1995a. "From Population Control to Reproductive Rights: Feminist Fault Lines." *Reproductive Health Matters* 6 (November): 152–61.

———. 1995b. "The Body as Property: A Feminist Re-Vision." In *Conceiving the New World Order*, ed. F. D. Ginsburg and R. Rapp, 387–406. Berkeley: University of California Press.

———. 1997. "Spiralling Discourses of Reproductive and Sexual Rights: A Post-Beijing Assessment of International Feminist Politics." In *Women Question Politics*, ed. K. Cohen, K. Jones, and J. Tronto, 569–87. New York: Routledge.

Petchesky, R., and Karen Judd, eds. (for the International Reproductive Rights Research Action Group). 1998. *Negotiating Reproductive Rights: Women's Perspectives across Countries and Cultures*. New York: St. Martin's Press, London: Zed Books.

Portella, Ana Paula, Cecília de Mello e Souza, and Simone Diniz. 1998. "Not Like Our Mothers: Reproductive Choice and the Emergence of Citizenship among Brazilian Rural Workers, Domestic Workers and Housewives." In *Negotiating Reproductive Rights*, ed. Petchesky and Judd, 31–68.

Romany, Celina. 1994. "State Responsibility Goes Private: A Feminist Critique of the Public/Private Distinction in International Human Rights Law." In *Human Rights of Women*, ed. R. Cook, 85–115.

Rosenbloom, Rachel, ed. 1995. *Unspoken Rules: Sexual Orientation and Women's Human Rights*. San Francisco: International Gay and Lesbian Human Rights Commission.

Seif El Dawla, Aida, Amal Abdel Hadi, and Nadia Abdel Wahab. 1998. "Women's Wit over Men's: Trade-Offs and Strategic Accommodations in Egyptian Women's Reproductive Lives." In *Negotiating Reproductive Rights*, ed. Petchesky and Judd, 69–107.

Sen, Amartya. 1990. "Individual Freedom as a Social Commitment." *New York Review of Books*, June 14:49–52/79–80.

Sen, Gita, and Rachel C. Snow, eds. 1994. *Power and Decision: The Social Control of Reproduction*. Cambridge, MA: Harvard University Press.

Sullivan, Donna. 1995. "The Public/Private Distinction in International Human Rights Law." In *Women's Rights, Human Rights: International Feminist Perspectives*, ed. Julie Peters and Andrea Wolper, 126–34. New York: Routledge.

Tambiah, Yasmin. 1995. "Sexuality and Human Rights." In *From Basic Needs to Basic Rights: Women's Claim to Human Rights*, ed. Margaret A. Schuler, 369–90. Washington, DC: Women, Law and Development International.

———. 1996. "Sexual Rights, the State and Democratic Process: Issues for South Asian Women." Paper presented at the Association for Women in Development Conference, Washington, DC, September 5–8.

Toubia, Nahid. 1995. *Female Genital Mutilation: A Call for Global Action*. New York: RAINBO. Available from Women, Ink, 777 United Nations Plaza, New York, NY 10017.

United Nations. 1994. *Report of the International Conference on Population and Development*. Cairo, Egypt. September 5–13.

———. 1995. *Platform for Action of the Fourth World Conference on Women*. Beijing, China. September 4–15.

PART TWO

POLITICALLY THEORIZING HOMOSEXUALITY

SIX

AN ETHOS OF LESBIAN AND GAY EXISTENCE

Mark Blasius

POLITICS INVOLVES A "PROBLEMATIZATION" or a calling into question of power relations in society *by* a social movement, *through* transformation of techniques that are used to govern people—exercising and submitting to power relations, and a production of knowledge (writing, reflection, scientific or other statements that make claims to truth) about the meaning of this phenomenon *as* political.[1] In this essay, I primarily analyze one aspect of this "political problematization," the production of knowledge, by the contemporary lesbian and gay movement. However, the analysis will deal by implication with the other components of politicization, for the political knowledge that the movement is producing is both constitutive of and an expression of what I call an *ethos* of lesbian and gay existence. Thus the knowledge produced through this ethos at once gives meaning to lesbian and gay existence as political and is a form and site of resistance within hegemonic relationships of power of contemporary society; as such, it influences them.

I begin by arguing that lesbian and gay existence should be conceived as an ethos rather than as a sexual preference or orientation, as a lifestyle, or *primarily* in collectivist terms, as a subculture, or even as a community. While lesbian and gay existence may include some elements of these conceptualizations, "ethos" is a more encompassing formulation, better suited for understanding lesbian and gay existence *politically*. I argue that the key to understanding ethos is through the lesbian and gay conceptualization of "coming out," understood as a process of *becoming* in which the individual enters into a field of relationships that constitute lesbian and gay community. Through this process, the individual participates in a collective problematization of self, of types of normativity, and of what counts as truth. It is in the relationship that the individual creates with her- or himself and with others in this practice of the self that is called coming out that an ethos emerges. Finally, I discuss the "politicalness" of this ethos, in particular, its present-day imbrication with the production of knowledge both about what politics is (ontology) and what the limits of politics are (epistemology).

One further remark: I use as my point of departure Eve Kosofsky Sedgwick's statement: "The *special* centrality of homophobic oppression in the twentieth century . . . has resulted from its inextricability from the question of knowledge and the processes of knowing in modern Western culture at large."[2] I will leave to others the deconstruction of "modern Western culture at large." However, since the present essay is, like a section of the Names Project AIDS quilt, a patchwork of ideas from a larger work,[3] I must give a summary of the lesbian and gay political problematic of hegemonic power relations. These constitute what Sedgwick calls "homophobic oppression." By *homophobia* I mean an individual's revulsion toward homosexuality and homosexuals, and often the desire to inflict punishment on the latter as retribution, or to cure them. This is the other side of the coin from *heterosexism*, a structure of power in society (as racism and sexism are) that privileges as superior (natural, more healthy, normative) heterosexuality over homosexuality and, through a variety of procedures of subjectification, creates homophobic subjects (who can even engage in homosexuality themselves—hence the concept of the "self-hating homosexual"). Thus heterosexism is a form of domination and within it and as a support for it as a structure of domination, subjection is the construction of homophobic subjects. Together they constitute what Adrienne Rich termed "compulsory heterosexuality."[4]

To be sure, the knowledge produced through lesbian and gay political problematization is a way of protecting oneself from homophobia taken to its genocidal extreme, as in the complete elimination of homosexuality or of homosexuals. I use the adjective genocidal advisedly and not hyperbolically (even former U.S. Surgeon General Koop spoke of the possibility of homosexual genocide). One conceptualization of genocide, drawn from the experience of the AIDS epidemic and one with which the former surgeon general might agree, is that of U.S. social historian Robert Dawidoff: "Genocide does not ever happen in the same way to the same people, but it always means the wiping out of a despised people through active malevolence or the manipulation of the accidental, plus the denial of its targeted community, and the indifference of the world and its acquiescence in the horror."[5] However, even this conceptualization is misleading because it requires subjective intentionality from those who "target" a particular community. The systematic obliteration of masses of people is an ever-present possibility of modern government where power is exercised as biopower, that is, across two axes of human existence—anatomically through individual bodies and biologically through the populations that they comprise. Thus the processes of life become the object of modern techniques of government that, unlike "the ancient right to *take* life or *let* live [are characterized by] . . . a power to *foster* life or *disallow* it to the point of death," according to a formulation of Michel Foucault.[6] In the context of this historical hypothesis, knowledge is produced by lesbians and gay men both to juxtapose against culturally endemic homophobic distortion and to reveal and stop the systemic disallowance of their lives (as well as to demonstrate how they should be fostered).

It is this historical imperative to produce the truth of and for one's own existence that motivates me; however, this is not to say that it is truth in and of itself that can protect us or anyone. The limitations of the knowledge produced by the lesbian and gay movement are obvious to any lesbian and gay person: When the psychiatric definition of homosexuality-as-illness was overturned through political problematization of the power of psychiatrists by the lesbian and gay movement, the AIDS epidemic then allowed for the remedicalization of homosexual sex as disease producing, generating yet another political problematization through AIDS activism. If truth is created through communal life as an objectification of the values that the members of the community share, then the creation of truth—not only about lesbian and gay existence but, from that vantage point, about what politics is today—refocuses contemporary human reality in a new way. What will protect and enable lesbians and gay men to flourish is an ethos that serves as a condition of possibility for politics, understood both in the creation of community among and between lesbians and gay men as well as the transformation of institutionalized power relations to the extent that lesbians and gay men visibly occupy positions of sociocultural power and authority. Thus what is significant in the production of knowledge by the lesbian and gay movement is not only an antihomophobic discourse, which is Sedgwick's project, but the way in which a lesbian and gay ethos produces knowledge that transforms the world in which all human beings live, as well as the way people understand themselves as living in that world.

Sexual Orientation, Lifestyle, and Community

Sexual Preference or Alternative Lifestyle?

My claim is that living as a lesbian or a gay man today consists in more than a sexual orientation, a lifestyle, or even being a member of a community. It consists in an ethos, by which I mean a shared way of life through which lesbians and gay men invent themselves, recognize each other, and establish a relationship to the culture in which they live. The emergence of a distinctive lesbian and gay ethos is analyzed later in this essay; first, I discuss the limitations of the conventional ways of understanding lesbian and gay existence today.

"Sexual preference," for example, suggests that same-sex eroticism is merely analogous to one's preference for a particular flavor of ice cream and that lesbians and gay men are the same as nongays except for what they do in bed. If this were true, there would be no need for the institutions of the lesbian and gay community that have been built specifically to counter oppression and create safe spaces wherein women can come out as lesbians and meet each other and men can come out as gay and meet each other too, by means of activities that extend far beyond sexual encounters. If the term "sexual preference" is trivializing, "sexual orientation," rooted as it is in the psychiatric discourse that formerly posited homosexuality as a mental illness, suggests that sexual object choice is fixed at a very early age, perhaps pre-natally, and therefore is not amenable to change except through extraordin-ary means. The orientation hypothesis may be etiologically true or not. Be-cause many people who are same-sex "oriented" may not act out this orientation or may do so only furtively, what is important (as in nature/nurture discourse generally) is what one *does* with this orientation, how one "works on" one's sexuality, as I will demonstrate. This is why I have chosen Adrienne Rich's formulation of lesbian and gay *existence*: it indicates both the historical fact of the presence of people who understand themselves as les-bian and gay and their continuing creation of the meaning of that existence.[7]

Further, it is not just the homosexual sexual act itself that precipitates the fear and hatred of those who engage in this kind of sexual behavior on the part of those who do not; rather, it is what these latter people call the "gay lifestyle." Such a fear and hatred may be manifest on the level of individual "homosexual panic" (the fear that one will lose one's gender identity[8]) or in the anxiety that the gay lifestyle, ultimately a stereotype, is causing the downfall of Western civilization. An example of the latter are Norman Pod-horetz's comments on the "central role homosexuality played" in the interwar period in England where upper-class youths, in schools where only "state-subsidized undergraduates [were] generally heterosexual" and where "dan-dies" and

> aesthetes . . . through their writings, their political activities, and the way of life they followed . . . Added to the antidemocratic pacifism of the interwar ethos: a generalized contempt for middle-class or indeed any kind of heterosexual adult life. . . .
>
> . . . For whatever else homosexuality may be or may be caused by, to these young men of the English upper class it represented . . . the refusal of father-hood and all that fatherhood entailed: responsibility for a family and therefore an inescapable implication in the destiny of society as a whole. And that so many of the privileged young of England "no longer wanted to grow up to become fathers themselves" also meant that they were repudiating their birthright as successors to their own fathers in assuming a direct responsibility for the fate of the country. . . .
>
> Anyone familiar with homosexual apologetics in America today will recognize these attitudes.[9]

A resentful Midge Decter, writing in the same publication, *Commentary*, re-veals—indeed, endorses—the stereotyping of a gay lifestyle. Decrying the "mocking effect on heterosexuals . . . of homosexual style, invented by homosexuals and serving the purpose of domination by ridicule," she implores her readers to "*[k]now them as a group*. . . . [O]ne cannot even begin to get at *the truth about homosexuals* without this kind of generalization."[10]

No other aspect of existence for lesbians and gay men comes under such intense scrutiny by others as that of their lifestyle, if not as homophobically as the above, often as though they are some exotic non-Western tribe newly discovered by anthropologists and sensationalized by the media. Their "lifestyle" is simultaneously the point on which gay and lesbian people are attacked most frequently by nongays and a central focus of the movement's problematization of what it means to be lesbian or gay. It is through this problematization of their putative "lifestyle" that the possibility of an ethos emerges with as great an importance as freedom of erotic choices and the struggle for lesbian and gay legal rights. What is at stake in this problematization is not simply a sexual orientation or an alternative lifestyle (one among others in the context of a pluralistic culture) but the question of "how shall I live?"

There are other significant reasons for the intense problematization by lesbians and gay men themselves of their own manner of existing. The condition of compulsory heterosexuality, what Christopher Isherwood called "the heterosexual dictatorship," makes simply living every day a serious problem for lesbians and gay men. All laws, forms of culture (rituals, symbols, etc.), and the most mundane social expectations make one an alien in the world. It is for this reason that the "gay ghetto" exists. Gay and lesbian commercial establishments, social institutions, neighborhoods, resorts, and cruising areas as well as cultural "spaces" or events of art, music festivals, lesbian and gay literature, athletic leagues, conferences, and informational and friendship networks such as those spawned through AIDS activism all constitute a "liberated zone" where lesbians and gay men can feel at home in and at peace with the world. To be sure, the ghetto exists because lesbians and gay men, to the extent that they come out, have been forced by societal rejection to find other means of livelihood, other sources of emotional sustenance, and other institutional frameworks within which to pursue their life objectives; the gay ghetto is significantly a manifestation of forced ghettoization.

Nevertheless, the birth, since the Stonewall riots of 1969, of a lesbian and gay "counterculture" within the stifling larger culture is somewhat of an illusion. Most lesbians and gay men do not live in a gay ghetto,[11] and the possibility of establishing a gay nation-state is unlikely and probably unwise.[12] Some recent analysis even sees nationalism as part and parcel of the logic of social reproduction and a growth economy dependent on heterosexuality, biological reproduction, and generational transmission of culture and capital, in which the self would be fulfilled *through* identification with these processes.[13] Gay men and lesbians are therefore in the situation of constituting themselves as a political community that is dispersed throughout society, fighting homophobia wherever it occurs.

The contemporary lesbian and gay movement since Stonewall has made living one's life as an openly gay or lesbian person a criterion of "liberation." The debate between lesbian and gay separatism and integration (indeed, including lesbian separatism within the lesbian/gay separatist position) has also been continuous since then. But should such a life be lived in as much isolation from nongay society as possible (which would allow, it is said, for a greater richness of personal and communal development), or should lesbians and gays integrate themselves *as gays* and *as lesbians* (forceably or using legal means if feasible) into the warp and woof of the fabric of the society in which they live? An exemplary statement of the first of these positions is in Howard Brookner's film *Burroughs*, where William Burroughs argues the case for a gay state where gays in the diaspora will always be able to count on having a homeland; a statement of the second is in AIDS activist Larry Kramer's Arendtian parallels between Jewish and gay male political experience, Kramer states:

> For a while, San Francisco was the gays' Israel. For decades, gays migrated there, and in time they attained great power in the political structure of that city. No mayor there would consider *not* consulting with gay leaders. And this gay power was sufficient to keep most local heterosexual opposition in check. Tragically, with the devastation of AIDS, gay power in San Francisco has waned considerably; many of the leaders have died.
>
> . . . We don't have Zionism as a hopeful haven from the world's hatred of us. And, as Arendt pointed out, Zionism's solution was not one of fighting anti-Semitism on its own ground, that is, wherever it existed, but to escape it. . . .
>
> . . . As Arendt wrote to support her thesis: "The simple truth is that Jews will have to fight anti-Semitism everywhere or else be exterminated everywhere."[14]

A most eloquent statement of the lesbian separatist position has been made by Marilyn Frye, but even she discovers conditions of possibility for a community of both lesbians and gay men, to the extent that sexism among gay men subsides: "If there is hope for a coordination of the efforts and insights of lesbian feminists and gay men, it is . . . when we are working from chosen foundations in our different differences."[15]

From Lifestyle to Community

The concept of lifestyle is a characteristic way through which, in modernity, individuals come to understand themselves, their relations with others, and their life course and choices; it is as well a principal site at which we have all come to be governed. The problematization of their own lifestyle, indeed more broadly, their way of life, has been based on a conscious imperative among lesbians and gay men to invent the self and ways of relating to others. In spite of the historical and cross-cultural prevalence of homosexuality, both lesbians and gay men must create a self out of (or rather despite) the hetero-sexual self that is culturally given to them (and, due to the suppression and falsification of the historical record, imposed on them as "natural").[16] They must invent ways of relating to each other because there are not ready-made cultural or historical models or formulas for erotic same-sex relationships as there are for different-sex erotic relationships. They must do so, further, in a cultural environment of extreme prejudice, which denies their existence out-right or, at best, allows them to exist by passing, that is, by adopting a heterosexual persona or, if openly gay or lesbian, by adopting a mode of relating to each other that mimics heterosexual "couples." Thus contempo-rary gay men and lesbians live in a situation where, due to their sexual and affectional attractions, they must create relationships and networks of rela-tions with each other against the void in which they have historically and culturally found themselves.

Lesbians and gay men virtually invent a way of life through which they create and re-create the self continually within sexual affectional relation-ships. These relationships differ in kind and vary in intensity. However, these relationships and the way of life that they contribute to creating have, of course, nothing to do with any intrinsic qualities of homosexuals but, rather, with the lack of cultural models of historical traditions for contemporary lesbians and gay men to fall back on and inform their relationships. Contem-porary lesbian and gay existence involves, therefore, the creation of a way of life—understood as a primary means of creating one's own self in and through one's relations with others. Indeed, the extreme creativity that must be exercised by lesbians and gay men just to live day to day, not to mention flourish, cannot be overemphasized. It is the possibility of a lesbian and gay way of life that maps out the contemporary battlegrounds for lesbian and gay existence: the right to make one's own erotic choices, the freeing of a space for a lesbian and gay relational culture that arises out of such erotic choices, and the objectification of these as value in the order of truth and their insti-tutionalization as knowledge. All of these presuppose, for their realization, the emergence of a lesbian and gay way of life more encompassing than a lifestyle, what I call an ethos.

However, in modernity, power has come to be exercised as biopower; as the object of government, the processes of life are now mastered through the control of how the individual lives and of how the individual manages his or her own life in relations with others. Techniques of government, broadly understood, are both the more or less deliberate and institutionally organized exercise of power over individuals and collectivities *and* the capacity to set the framework within which individuals themselves shape their own conduct and produce their own individuality. These techniques ultimately tend to focus on fostering or disallowing various elements of one's lifestyle.[17]

Now, as the concept of a lifestyle has become in modernity an object for government, it has concomitantly become a primary way through which people generally understand and identify themselves to others, that is, that part of one's life that is the principal object of self-reflection and self-creation (what I call ethical self-constitution—working on oneself to create oneself as a subject of one's actions). The concept of one's lifestyle in contemporary Western societies comes to overshadow, even as it incorporates, more traditional sources of identity such as race, religion, ethnicity, class, and occupation in people's self-understanding; indeed, in recent years it has become a general category of sociological and even epidemiological analysis.[18] Further, the modern self is obliged, not by law but within the sphere of consumption and through a market of expertise, to construct a life by choosing among alternative conducts, values, and aspirations, to understand one's own life in terms of the outcomes of such choices, and to account for one's life in terms of the reasons for one's choices.[19] Thus to the extent that lesbians and gay men understand themselves as living a specific lifestyle, they are participating in a way of thinking about themselves that is at once characteristic of modernity and a principal modality through which power has come to be exercised over all of us.

However, the concept of lifestyle is not quite adequate as descriptive of, or as a hermeneutic approach to, the self-understanding involved in lesbian and gay existence or as a basis for (collective) self-reflection. Lifestyle implies consumerism, where the individual "speaks not only with his clothes, but with his home, furnishings, decoration, car and other activities which are to be read and classified in terms of the presence or absence of taste," which is itself an embodiment of social status, reflecting class, gender, ethnicity, region, and even political ideology.[20] Instead, the way of life of lesbian and gay people is much more a function of an ascetic *becoming gay* or *becoming lesbian* through a learning approach to life in the context of lesbian and gay community. Here, working on the self—that is one's *life itself* according to criteria specific to the way one lives it through the relationships that constitute that community—is the object of ethico-aesthetic work rather than its material accoutrements determined through individualistic criteria. (To be sure, the concept of an *ascetic* becoming needs to be differentiated from the "asceticism" our culture inherited from Christianity that involves the devaluing of erotic desire and the mortification of the flesh. Rather, lesbians and gay men participate in the "self-help" or self-shaping techniques, discourses, and institutions of the lesbian and gay communities through which one forms oneself as an ethical subject of one's own actions. As we shall see, such a lesbian and gay erotic ascetic is the basis for their ethos.)

Therefore, a lifestyle can have a largely evanescent quality, as a product of individual whim or fashion—"Today there is no fashion: there are only *fashions*[.] 'No rules, only choices[.]' 'Everyone can be anyone—'."[21] The fact that homoerotic practices are transmitted from generation to generation in spite of familial and cultural suppression does indeed suggest something like a sexual orientation or predisposition. However, the fact that contemporary lesbian and gay people can adapt to radically changing circumstances and treatment of them within a given society (sexual codes, secret societies) suggests that survival is made possible through something collective that is distinct from a mere lifestyle. (Anthropologist Gilbert Herdt, for example, has identified both the era of AIDS and the development of the lesbian and gay community as ushering in "for the first time an institutionalized process of initiating and socializing [lesbian and gay] youths."[22])

However, a lifestyle can also be a category for the analysis of, and indeed can designate the suppression of, individuality within the context of a collectivity with collectively held values to which the individual is held accountable. I am reminded of some New Left writers' suggestions to fashion one's life into a vehicle for political transformation, a kind of politically correct lifestyle, and of a recent proposal by gay male writers for a new gay lifestyle organized around a "Self-Policing Social Code," because the present gay lifestyle is "unworkable . . . diminish[es] the quality of gay life, and make[s] us look bad to straights . . . [because it is] devoid of the values that straight society, with such good reason, respects."[23] Their social code, reproduced here (see figure 6.1), would be enforced through gay social censure—by the gay victim of and gay bystander to "gay misbehavior." I include it here to demonstrate how moral discourse about lifestyle has arisen within lesbian and gay communities but how its content, shaped as it is by the desire to conform to existing heterosexist norms rather than to create lesbian and gay criteria for existence, results in the untenable paradox of either its own abstract moralism or what it suggests as the alternative: gay nihilism.

I have been arguing, therefore, that sexual orientation, derived as it is as a response to a psychiatric diagnosis of homosexuality-as-illness, is inadequate to describe the contemporary lesbian and gay condition. The concept of lifestyle, also, is inadequate both to describe how lesbians and gay men think of themselves in relation to each other (as sharing a lifestyle) because (1) there is nothing about lesbian and gay existence that makes lifestyle uniquely informative about it or empowering and (2) there exist many different lesbian and gay lifestyles, ways of living as gay or lesbian (e.g., lipstick/fashion dyke, lesbian feminist, leatherfolk, queer, butch/femme, gay republican, and the Hannah Arendt Lesbian Peace Patrol of Western Massachusetts, to name but a few almost at random).

Rules for Relations with Straights

I Won't Have Sex in Public Places.

I Won't Make Passes at Straight Acquaintances,
or at Strangers Who Might Not Be Gay.

Wherever Possible and Sensible, I Will Come Out—Gracefully.

I Will Make an Effort, When Among Straights, Not to Live Down
to Gay Stereotypes.

I Won't Talk Gay Sex and Gay Raunch in Public.

If I'm a Pederast or a Sadomasochist, I'll Keep It Under Wraps,
and Out of Gay Pride Marches.

I'll Graciously Decline Invitations to Model Lingerie for "Oprah" or "Donahue."

Rules for Relations with Other Gays

I Won't Lie.

I Won't Cheat on My Lover—or with Someone Else's.

I'll Encourage Other Gays to Come Out, But Never Expose Them
Against Their Will.

Tested or Otherwise, I'll Practice Safe Sex.

I'll Contribute Money in Meaningful Amounts to the Gay Cause.

I Will Not Speak Scornfully or Cruelly of Another's Age, Looks, Clothing,
or Social Class, in Bars or Elsewhere, Lest I Reveal My Own Insecurities.

When Forced to Reject a Suitor, I Will Do So Firmly but Kindly.

I'll Drop My Search for Mr. Right and Settle for What's Realistic.

I Won't Re-Enact Straight Oppression by Name-Calling
and Shouting Down Gays Whose Opinions Don't Square with Mine.

Rules for Relations with Yourself

I'll Stop Trying to Be Eighteen Forever and Act My Age;
I Won't Punish Myself for Being What I Am.

I Won't Have More Than Two Alcoholic Drinks a Day; I Won't Use
Street Drugs at All.

I'll Get a Stable, Productive Job and Become a Member
of the Wider Community Beyond the Gay Ghetto.

I'll Live for Something Meaningful Beyond Myself.

When Confronted by Real Problems, I'll Listen to Common Sense, Not Emotion.

I Will Not Condone Sexual Practices I Think Harmful to Individuals
or to the Community Just Because They're Homosexual.

I'll Start Making Some Value Judgments.

Figure 6.1 A Self-Policing Social Code

Source: From Marshall Kirk and Hunter Madsen, *After the Ball: How America Will Overcome Its Fear and Hatred of Gays in the 1990s*, 360. Copyright © 1989 Doubleday, New York. Used by permission.

Subculture and Community

Is lesbian and gay subculture and community a basis for hermeneutic description of, or self-reflection on, lesbian and gay existence? Lesbian philosopher Sarah Lucia Hoagland, acknowledging the influence of Julia Penelope, makes a distinction between subculture and community: "A lesbian subculture is a group we become part of automatically by declaring ourselves lesbian—but a group 'wholly defined negative terms by an external, hostile culture that sees us as deviates from their "norm".'"[24] Further, the bonds formed among people in a subculture that struggles against oppression are better conceived as alliances; these bonds will not necessarily prevail beyond the immediate struggle. On the other hand, membership in lesbian and gay *community* (Hoagland, as a separatist, is writing of *lesbian* community) is voluntary. She continues:

> If we are to form an enduring community it will not be on the basis of outside threats. Further, it will not be on the basis of a rich tradition nor of what we find here (though we do have crone-ology). If we are to form an empowering community, it will be on the basis of the values we believe we can enact here: what we bring, what we work to leave behind, and what we develop as we engage each other. If we are to transform subculture into community, it will be on the basis of what we create, not what we find. And attempts to control each other won't hold us together; instead, they actually undermine our ability, particularly our moral agency.[25]

Thus, from this perspective, subculture is a negative community, in existence as a reaction to a common threat or, like what has been called the gay ghetto, to provide cultural nourishment to people who are aliens in the larger culture. The kind of community that Hoagland conceptualizes for lesbians, however, does not exist for lesbians yet. They represent themselves in writing more commonly as making up communi*ties* with shared affinities and working alliances among them.[26] Further, to the extent that such a concept of community implies sharing primary group membership (e.g., intimate friendships, living arrangements), there is, arguably, more like an alliance between gay men and lesbians through the organizations and publications they have formed for political expediency (one such organization, the Human Rights Campaign, is the ninth largest PAC in the United States). In the relational dimension of everyday life, there is still a delicate balance between separatism and friendship between lesbians and gay men (this is even more the case in urban areas where the lesbian and gay community has become more elaborated).

However, despite this caveat, there is an ongoing creation of a common lesbian and gay male culture that includes the construction of a history, an anthropology, and, more generally, a scholarly and public discourse about lesbian and gay existence (besides crone-ology).[27] There are other indicators of the development of community between lesbians and gay men: concentration in space (based on residence but also through participation in community institutions); learned and shared norms; institutional completeness within the community serving both lesbians and gay men (including basic social services—health services, bookstores, religious organizations, travel agencies, charities, and political clubs); collective action (street demonstrations, lesbian and gay pride marches, lobbying efforts, etc.); a sense of a shared history; and commitments that go beyond private life and into public endeavors (two examples: the election of African-American mayors in New York, Chicago, and Philadelphia has been attributed, by voting behavior specialists, to lesbian and gay political mobilization and voting, and a number of U.S. cities and states have openly lesbian or gay elected officials).[28] Finally, and also following Hoagland, membership in this community is a consequence of voluntary participation (joining organizations, financially supporting political initiatives, etc.). Inversely, the community is not held together through laws or even informally through a self-policing social code; attempts of lesbians and gays to "try to control each other," especially by excluding people from membership whose erotic object choice is the same sex but are different in other ways (e.g., into sadomasochism, are involved in cross-generational relationships, do drag) have been notoriously divisive and unsuccessful. Both lesbians and gay men remain ambivalent about the desirability of *communitas*, the experience on a subjective level of undifferentiated harmony; this is partially due, no doubt, to their own prior experience of heterosexist community, with its homophobia and sexism from which many of them fled.

Nevertheless, by standard sociological indicators, lesbian and gay community exists, especially in the urban areas to which lesbians and gay men have most often fled. What is most important about it, though, is not communitas, unanimity of fellow feeling (which is not necessary to serve the purpose the community does in fact serve, to which we shall return), but the fact that this sociologic community *does* facilitate the creation of what Hoagland variously calls moral agency and lesbian be-ing, that is, the creation of a specific kind of subjectivity. This distinctive lesbian and gay subjectivity requires an appropriate descriptive category. This is because lesbian and gay people are "everywhere," as they have blood ties with nongay people, and because of the particular kind of community they form with each other. It is territorial but also nonterritorial, the latter forming a public sphere (writing, media, community centers, public/town meetings, organizations and their leadership, and the formation of a lesbian and gay *public*). This is why the descriptive category that most closely approximates what lesbian and gay existence is today is *ethos*: the creation of ethical agency within and through a lesbian and gay community. This ethos is lived and acted beyond the community into the larger world, even though it is dependent on the community and its public sphere for its conditions of possibility.

Coming Out and the Emergence of an Ethos

The condition of existence for community is coming out. This term designates more than the narrow meaning usually attributed to it as a single act whereby an individual declares his or her identity as homosexual, gay, or lesbian to family, friends, or coworkers who previously assumed the person to be nongay. As I conceptualize it, coming out is a lifelong process of *becoming* lesbian or gay. As such, it is a practical creation of the self that involves working on a specific aspect of oneself, using external sources of authority as guidance for such a work on oneself, deploying specific techniques—objective practices through which one forms oneself and makes oneself appear to others, and fashioning oneself toward a goal to which one aspires.[29] If coming out is a condition for the existence of community, then that community becomes a condition of possibility for a lesbian and/or gay ethos, being able to live one's life *as* a lesbian or *as* a gay man, which is the goal of the coming out process.

Coming out refers to an ontological recognition of the self by the self. It involves recognition of one's sexuality (whether subjectively understood as a Freudian bisexual potential, an innate homoeroticism, or a chosen imperative), *and starting from this recognition*, working on one's sexuality so that the self appears and becomes. Coming out is also the fundamental political act. It involves, first, the rejection of one's own subjection (being "in the closet," "passing," treating others homophobically, etc.) as the product of historical processes of domination (by heterosexism) and, second, through recognition of and by other lesbian and gay people, the cognizing or thinking over and thinking differently of oneself and one's relations with others—the creation of oneself under *different* historical conditions in relation to, as a member of, a community.

However, one does not come out once and for all, and coming out is not just a disclosure of one's gay or lesbian identity to others. Rather than being an end-state in which one exists as an "out" person, coming out is a process of becoming, a lifelong learning of how to become and of inventing the meaning of being a lesbian or a gay man in this historical moment. A lesbian and gay community can only exist to the extent that people come out into it—understand themselves and identify themselves to others as lesbian and gay; these acts of self-disclosure and, as we shall see, public self-creation, and the mutual recognition attendant on them, create a community as distinct from a subculture or a "lifestyle enclave" based on "the narcissism of similarity" in patterns of leisure and consumption.[30]

The process-character of coming out can be gleaned from some of the "meanings-in-use" that define it: *coming out* to those who did not know one is gay or lesbian; *coming out* to a lesbian/gay pride march or in joining a lesbian or gay organization; *coming out* professionally, by writing a lesbian/ gay-themed novel, through one's choice of research topics, or by teaching a lesbian/gay-oriented lesson or course; *coming out* as PWA (person with AIDS) or as being HIV-positive or as someone affected by AIDS and doing something about it; *coming out*—whether experienced as the crossing of a sexual frontier, a new experience of the body and what counts as sexual pleasure— or experienced through a ritual marking acceptance into, for example, the leather culture (leather people speak of it as "a second coming out . . . rest[ing] on an experience of intense personal discovery and acceptance . . . a form of birth, a replacement of one world and a good deal of its values with those more attuned to the demands of a Gay person"[31]); *coming out* by holding hands with one's lover in a public place (an action that frequently elicits lesbian/gay bashing). Obviously, not all of these uses of coming out are exclusive to lesbian and gay existence—Magic Johnson "came out" as HIV-positive and there has been enough linguistic slippage that people now speak of coming out as incest survivors or coming out as recovering substance abusers. However, what is specific to lesbian and gay existence about coming out is that the aspect of the self that one is concerned about recognizing in oneself and sharing with others is one's *sexuality.*

Let us analyze more closely the process of coming out as a public creation of the self through one's relationships with others that constitute lesbian and gay community. First, the part of oneself that the self is concerned about, that one is working on, is one's sexuality, understood as one's erotic choices (that would include object choice, what counts as erotic pleasure, what motivates one—feelings, desires, what one thinks is "sexy," etc.)[32] Second, why we care about our sexuality involves sources of incitation and authority external to ourselves; in the most fundamental way, we are "hailed" by various cultural authorities to recognize our sexuality as either homo, hetero, or bi, and to the extent we discover it is possible to be "gay" or "lesbian" (as distinct from being an isolated and deemed unnatural, sinful, or diseased "homosexual"), the lesbian and gay community serves as a source of sexual information as well as providing criteria for recognizing and working on that aspect of ourselves that is our sexuality. Third, how do we use our sexuality in living our lives? This aspect of self-constitution would involve how we use sexuality in creating our self (e.g., specific erotic practices), the kinds of relationships we form based on our sexuality (e.g., a lesbian "care" ethic and gay male "tribes"—networks of friends, "fuckbuddies," current and exlovers and their friends, etc.), and the ways we use such relationships to elaborate our sexuality (e.g., how lesbian and gay couples integrate sexual freedom into their relationships). The narrow meaning of coming out also lies here—self-disclosure is a specific public practice with regard to one's self-creation through sexuality. Fourth, in fashioning oneself, one aspires to constitute oneself as an agent through one's erotic relationships with others. Constitution of oneself as subject of one's actions is what ethics is, and doing so with scrupulous deliberateness (what was referred to earlier as ascetics) in and through a community results in an ethos. This is the goal of coming out; crafting a way of life through one's homoeroticism.

Through all of these four components of coming out, one enters into a specific discourse and practices about what it means to be lesbian or gay that the existence of community has made possible and through which one voluntarily forms oneself as an ethical subject in relation to the values of that community. To be sure, coming out is a recognition of one's homoeroticism as a basic element of one's being; how one acts on that recognition (to camouflage it, to participate in community institutions in order to shape one's sexuality, to enter into conversion therapy) is a matter of choice.

Now, historically, the concept of ethos has not always been applied in this erotic sense. It is erotic among lesbian and gay people because, in the context of cultural domination and subjection, the part of themselves they have had to pay most attention to ethically, and that hence centers the way they live their lives, is their sexuality and their erotic relationships. Etymologically,[33] ethos connotes something deeply embedded in one's existence—indeed, for the Stoics it was the *source* of behavior—that, while learned, is not based on adherence to a belief system (even though it may be a conscious practice) but is habitual. For example, in Plato's *Phaedo* (82b), "happiest are those who have cultivated the goodness of an ordinary citizen [the political excellences] which is acquired by habit and practice, without the help of philosophy and reason." Similar usages are found in Thucydides, Sophocles, Aeschylus, and in Aristotle, where ethos is the outcome of moral rather than intellective understandings. Nietzsche associated ethos with the stylizing of one's behavior, which Michel Foucault later took up as an "aesthetics of existence."[34] Max Weber, in his introduction to *The Protestant Ethic and the Spirit of Capitalism*, conceptualizes ethos as the "spirit" of an economic system; Protestantism's worldly asceticism gave rise to, in his view, the ethos of capitalism.[35] Heidegger, who associated ethos with "poetical dwelling," wrote, "The tragedies of Sophocles preserve the *ethos* in their sagas more primordially than Aristotle's lectures on 'ethics.'" He credits Hölderlin with reclaiming the tragedians' conception of ethos as a poetical dwelling place, the touchstone for his notion of authentic existence, which requires poetical thinking and dwelling.[36] Heidegger relies on the poetical somewhat as a reaction, it appears, to what he perceived as modern philosophy's "degradation" of ethos into ethics having its origin in an atomistic moral subject possessing values as "personality traits": ethos "denotes not mere norms but mores, based on freely accepted obligations and traditions; it is that which concerns free behavior and attitudes, the shaping of man's historical being, the *ethos* which under the influence of morality was later degraded to the ethical."[37]

Therefore, just as ethos needs to be understood apart from social scientific reductionism to the individual as a carrier of moral interests and values, so it also needs to be understood apart from mere aestheticism—that which finds expression in the notion of a homosexual sensibility that Susan Sontag and others emblematized as *camp*: "a private code, a badge of identity even . . . the consistently aesthetic experience of the world . . . a victory of 'style' over 'content,' 'aesthetics' over 'morality,' of irony over tragedy."[38] Even though ethos incorporates such stylized comportment, it is at once an ethico-political category that, as a living ethical practice that both gives rise to responsibilities yet is voluntary and contingent, avoids the dualism of abstract normativism with moral yardsticks, such as the self-policing gay social code, and moral relativism or nihilism. Rather, ethos is a type of existence that is the consequence of coming out—understood as the process of entering into and creating oneself through the field of relationships that constitutes the lesbian and gay community. From this process of self-creation arise *freely chosen* responsibilities, conceptions of what is proper and fitting, that get constituted as selfhood, as what it means to be lesbian and gay.

Yet this ethos is *historical* both in a biographical and a communal sense. As a type of subjectivity, formed through coming out into the relationships that constitute community, its formation does not have an end point for the individual but continues throughout the life course. At the same time, individuals, through their self-constitution and crafting of an ethos, preserve, amend, reassess, and displace elements of this ethos: a lesbian and gay ethos is historically constructed and historically changing. For example, people such as Jean Genet, Quentin Crisp, and Gertrude Stein lived a homosexual ethos (if it can even be called that, since their ways of living were invented without participation in a lesbian or gay community that historically had not yet come to exist) of, respectively, defiant self-assertion (Genet), flaunting (Crisp), and cosmopolitan bohemianism (Stein). Nevertheless, elements of their ethos are preserved in the contemporary lesbian and gay one—in the reclaiming of them as lesbian and gay historical predecessors, through the recognition of "outsider" status in the context of continuing heterosexism, in the will to develop a way of life that does not mimic its norms—to be militantly "queer"—and through participation, translocally and transnationally in what has been called lesbian and gay *Gesellschaft* or the "queer nation."[39]

Finally, ethos more than just informs politics; it *is* political in a fundamental way. Ethos, as the development of one's ethical agency through entering into the discourse of what it means to be lesbian or gay in the practice of coming out, is at the same time the development of what Plato called "the political excellences." Because ethos is a sexual and relational one shared with others by virtue of one's participation in—indeed, creation of oneself through—the lesbian and gay community, the morale and destiny of that community is at stake in being able to live one's own ethos. Thus, in the formation of an ethos, the earlier posed "How shall I live?" becomes inextricably connected to "How shall we live?" The stake that one has in the morale and destiny of local lesbian and gay communities (as these are inflected by the crossing oppressions of race, gender, and ethnicity, in, for example, African-American lesbian feminist community), that make one's "self" possible, becomes stake in civic involvement in wider sociohistorical existence in all aspects of such existence that may affect one's ability to come out and live a lesbian and gay ethos—particularly in the wider lesbian and gay culture that exists by virtue of national and international lesbian and gay communities, the totality of which is *Gesellschaft*. (That is one reason why we should be concerned about, for example, racism, sexism, class, ableism, and ageism within any lesbian and gay community: these affect the morale of that community and hence one's ability to live within it, as well as the possibility of those so disempowered to come out into lesbian and gay communities.

An ethos, then, while formed in community, is enacted throughout the fabric of "everyday life." It is not enacted only in relations with other lesbian and gay people, not just in gay neighborhoods, but, as the formation of an attitude uniting character and behavior, it both relates lesbian and gay people to each other beyond their local gay *Gemeinschaft* into a *Gesellschaft*, and indeed, is an attitude—the so-called openly gay man or avowed lesbian—that they carry into whatever social environment they happen to be in and, importantly, whatever position of sociocultural power or authority they occupy. This attitude involves giving one's life distinctive form through a relation to oneself where one is inventing oneself—coming out, through a relation to others where one is recognized and appreciated through the style one gives to one's existence (as one lesbian describes herself, "A Fully Revolting Hag in the Department of Philosophy").[40] But this attitude is also a relation to the present, where in one's own way and through one's own life, one confronts and displaces compulsory heterosexuality. Unlike the self-policing social code that prescribes moral rules of good and bad behavior, a lesbian and gay ethos emerges not so much from moral as from existential criteria—the discourse of lived experience of lesbians and gay men about the diverse meanings of what it means to be lesbian and gay in the present moment. And more than the criteria of whether lesbians and gays should assimilate or be separatist, or whether individual adherence to a liberal or a conservative political ideology will advance "the cause," what is a *distinctive* criterion of existence is a lesbian and gay ethos, understood as both coming out and integrating one's homoerotic relationships within all one's social relationships. Therefore, an emergent lesbian and gay ethos would consist in an ethico-political choice, not to discipline others and oneself on behalf of a code of behavior, but rather (1) to stylize one's own existence toward the elaboration of selfhood as lesbian or gay, (2) the recognition by others as such, and (3) also as such, *publicly* introducing a change in the order of compulsory heterosexuality.

Ethos and Politics

An ethos of lesbian and gay existence serves as a condition of possibility for politics (understood as both creating and as placing limits on what is conceived as being political). First, the concept of coming out can be crystallized into three axes of experience, corresponding also to the three "moments" of political problematization mentioned at the beginning of this essay. There is the axis of *subjectivity*—one's relation to oneself—in coming out to oneself through experiencing sexual pleasure with others of the same sex, corresponding to practices that link individual to collective identity from which a social movement comes into existence. There is coming out to others *socially* (in family, occupation, and other social interactions), corresponding to the axis of experience that consists in exercising and submitting to power in relations that engage the legal system and other institutions, corresponding to the second moment of political problematization—the assertion of lesbian and gay rights. Finally, there is coming out in one's imagination or understanding of the world *the way it is lived as a lesbian or gay person* (as distinct from having a subjected or "colonized" understanding due to the culture that privileges heterosexuality). The creation, by lesbians and gays themselves, of the "truth about homosexuality" corresponds to the moment of political problematization where compulsory heterosexuality is displaced in the order of knowledge. This truth then becomes infused into the knowledge of human actuality—it corresponds to the axis of experience that is one's relation to what is established as true—and how it is established—in the world in which one lives.[41] As such, coming out is a preeminently *political* experience. As a lifelong process it is more than an initial realization, a public assertion that one is lesbian or gay, as well as a later adaptation to the historically changing norms of the lesbian and gay community. Rather, it is the continuous process of individual and collective empowerment in the historical context of heterosexist domination and homophobic subjection, even though its ultimate goal may be a world in which same-sex eroticism is integrated into psyche and society and coming out is no longer necessary.

A second generalization: in all of the meanings-in-use of coming out, coming out marks at once a redefinition of the self, a rite of passage in one's relationships with other lesbians and gay men (and with nongays), and an act of *volition*. It is truly a cultivation of the self through which the self appears and becomes, through working on an ethical substance (one's sexuality), through sources of authority (*now* the lesbian and gay community), through specific erotico-social practices that one engages in (practices through which sexuality is integrated into, rather than being a "parenthesis" within, everyday life), with the goal of living a lesbian or gay way of life, or ethos.

As such a process of becoming, one does not come out passively or accidentally. Thus one can never really be "outed" by another (except in the very narrow sense of exposing sexual behavior that had been kept secret). To be sure, the cultivation of oneself by working on one's sexuality in coming out is also a choice to participate in and be treated by others in relation to collective values, since the meanings-in-use of coming out that I have mentioned are criteria that lesbians and gay men use to define their collective existence. As I have argued, lesbians and gay men can share an ethos— a very strong structure of existence—without relying on moral injunctions or even coercive means of imposing it on each other. A lesbian and gay community therefore cannot be *produced* through outing. One cannot be forced to enter into a process of becoming that is coincident with the life course itself, and an ethos consists in freely chosen responsibilities as well as traditions; as the old adage goes, you can lead a horse to water, but you cannot make it drink. Outing is best conceived as a political strategy rather than, categorically, a "gay/lesbian issue" (all closeted lesbians and gays should be outed). If one is engaged in homoerotic sex secretly, considering our historical context of heterosexism and homophobia, one has an ethical responsibility to come out. It is arguable whether someone like Malcolm Forbes should be threatened with outing unless he (or she) contributes as much to the community as she or he benefits from it (in the sense of using community institutions in order to be able to engage in sexual relationships). However, if one is currently engaging in or has in the past engaged in homoerotic sex, and wages war against the lesbian and gay community or is actively indifferent to the waging of war by others when one could make a palpable difference, that community has the political right to defend itself by exposing the hypocrisy at the very least. (Examples of this latter case include such people s the late leader of homophobic conservatism, closeted Terry Dolan, and the alleged lesbian clerk to the Supreme Court justice who claimed, while voting with the majority in *Bowers v. Hardwick*, that he did so in part because he had never knowingly met a lesbian or gay man.) Thus outing is best conceived as a strategy of ensuring accountability among policymakers (broadly conceived) or public figures. Such a person's sexual orientation could *become* a "lesbian and gay issue" if that person's policies or public pronouncements negatively impacted on lesbians and gay men; in which case, outing might be a significant way by which the affected constituency could attempt to shape policy or public opinion.

Political Ontology

An ethos of lesbian and gay existence, then, is a basis for a political ontology and epistemology. As an ontological source of politics, this ethos is a self-disclosure, a public creation of the self in coming out, and is also the identi-fication of one's freedom to do so—indeed, one's personal destiny—with that of other gay men and lesbians, the lesbian and gay community. This conceptualization of coming out also places limits on the possibility of poli-tics. Politics is limited by the fact that one cannot force another to be free, to come out. Remaining in the closet and allowing oneself to be dominated by society's heterosexism and, ultimately, subjected by homophobia, is a per-sonal ethical choice too, just as is that of coming out. Because coming out is such a personal ethical choice, made freely and deliberately, the existence of lesbian and gay people as *a people*, a *community*, and the possibility of les-bians and gay men individually to come out and become gay or lesbian is limited by the freedom of each individual to decide for her- or himself whether to come out and become lesbian or gay. The ontological possibility of lesbian and gay community is limited by the extent that lesbians and gay men come out into it.

Again, its ontological possibility is conditioned by the extent to which lesbians choose to form themselves as subjects through participation in insti-tutions that include gay men or, in separatist fashion, through the institu-tions of the (lesbian and nonlesbian) women's community. It is also condi-tioned by the extent to which people of color choose to come out through participation in the lesbian and gay community as distinct from, through their racial and ethnic communities of birth, being "out" publicly within and identifying themselves primarily as members of those communities.[42] It is indispensable to underscore that what we have been analyzing here are the *conditions* for lesbian and gay community, which can allow for the *emergence* of an ethos.

Political Epistemology

Just as coming out is a condition of possibility for politics in an ontological sense, what counts as a "gay issue," epistemologically, are all the power rela-tions that keep them from coming out in this expanded sense, from *becoming* lesbian or gay through living their ethos. The categories of political cognition that have been discussed in this essay are all attempts to make intelligible the experience of lesbians and gay men as political: domination (by heterosex-ism) and subjection (homophobia, including gay/lesbian "self-hatred"), the concept of "gay and lesbian community" in both its local *Gemeinschaft* and wider *Gesellschaft* dimensions, giving rise to a lesbian and gay public sphere; and my formulation of coming out and ethos. This politicalness is condi-tioned by the historico-temporal character of compulsory heterosexuality, the institutionalized power relations that constitute heterosexism and promote homophobia, as well as by the spatial dimensions of its public sphere. As such, conceptualizing lesbian and gay existence as an ethos understands a *historical* ontology of politics. The possibility of politics is conditioned by the historical character of the political action lesbians and gays engage in (and, indeed, the categories of "lesbian" and "gay" are themselves historical). Its possibility is also conditioned by the historical emergence of a public sphere within which lesbian and gay people can appear to each other, debate, and act, making possible a "we," of acting together.

An ethos of lesbian and gay existence is also a source for the production of truth, where by truth I mean procedures for producing, regulating, distributing, and circulating statements about homoeroticism historically and about the experience of it as lesbian or gay today. Indeed, ethos, as coming out in recognition of and in the context of a lesbian and gay community, motivates the production of truth in order to counter the representation of lesbian and gay existence by its enemies and because, as Nietzsche said, "[i]t is our needs that interpret the world,"[43] and a way of life produces the knowledge it needs in order to exist in the world at a particular historical moment. This ethos necessitates the production of knowledge, understood not just as theory but including practical guides to and reflections on living, self-help—medical, legal, relationship, and so forth—manuals, fiction, auto- and biography as well as scientific research. This knowledge is both a truth-in-visibility (that destroys stereotypes) and a *techné*, broader than skill or technology, that is the objectification of the values of the community, the putting to work of its being and stabilizing it in something present (to draw a gloss on Heidegger).[44] Such knowledge allows the community collectively (and the members of it, individually) to exercise power through which heterosexism can be undermined and homophobia prevented or discredited.[45] This knowledge consists of a history of the present constructed from contents of the past that have been deliberately suppressed or disguised within a methodological privileging of heterosexuality, combined with the discourse of lived experience about contemporary lesbian and gay existence by lesbians and gay men themselves. This is a kind of knowledge production that, even when institutionalized through the university, media, writing, and the state (thereby giving it broader legitimation and empowering lesbians and gay men), is not centralized within these established institutions for the production and distribution of knowledge, even though a political struggle is now under way concerning its status within them (as was previously the case with women's studies, for example).[46]

Political Logic

Finally, a word is in order about how lesbian and gay people through their ethos create a politics of sexuality. In modernity, sexuality is a *political* issue because it is constituted at the point of intersection of the two axes across which biopower is exercised: through the performances of individual bodies but with attention to the processes of life of populations (of all women, of gay men, of "men who have sex with men" but do not consider themselves gay, of sex partners of IV drug users, to give examples of some populations).[47]

An ethos arises, fundamentally, from the erotic experiences of lesbian and gay people. Within lesbian existence and gay male existence, sexual relationships are immediately translated into social relationships, and social relationships are experienced as potentially or actually sexual ones. Lesbian and gay erotic practice involves integrating the sexual pleasure of the other into one's own pleasure; it is a sexual ethic of "I get off getting you off." Sexual relationships are therefore social relationships that become reciprocal because there are, historically, few other supports for the relationship (lineage or marriage, for example) than the willingness of the partners themselves to remain in the relationship.[48] The result of this reciprocity is to create equality and intense affectional ties among lesbians and among gay men. I call this characteristic form of bonding among lesbians and among gay men *erotic friendship*.[49]

"Friendship consists in community,"[50] wrote Aristotle, but, by definition, it is not erotic friendship alone that can create community *between* lesbians and gay men and thus it would appear that the ethos of lesbians and the ethos of gay men are constructed differently by virtue of their erotic object choices. Lesbians and gay men are similarly situated (through sexism and homophobia that affects them) with respect to power structured as heterosexist domination and homophobic subjection, and as such, they may work in *alliance* to transform those power relations. However, can their respective sexualities also make possible an ethos that lesbians and gay men can share with each other?

Lesbian and gay male erotic practices displace gender roles and therefore create the possibility for a community of equals between women and men. Lesbian and gay erotics tends to accomplish the inverse of Catherine MacKinnon's dictum: "Sexuality appears as the interactive dynamic of gender as an inequality. . . . Gender emerges as the congealed form of the sexualization of inequality between men and women."[51] Lesbian eroticism breaks with the gender subordination involved in heterosexual eroticism and its reproduction through heterosexual desire. At the same time, and within the space of equality that is lesbian eroticism, essential psychic femininity can be "deprogrammed" through, as Judith Butler suggests, a radical proliferation of gender positions and their enactment as performance—as imitations without an original.[52] By comparison and parallel, gay men are in the paradoxical situation of erotically desiring the signs and symbols of masculinity while at the same time undermining it.[53] Masculinity derives its meaning from its relationship of superiority to femininity incarnated and subjectively edified in heterosexual sexuality. Male homoeroticism eroticizes masculinity without involving the subordination of women. This gay male eroticization of gender equality ("man to man") at the same time undermines manhood that is defined through the eroticization of gender inequality in the subordination of women. It is at once being a man and desiring other men and refusing to be a man as defined through heterosexuality and the subordination of women. In this context, and as a result, we can return to Marilyn Frye's words: "To the extent that gay male culture cultivates and explores and expands its tendencies to the pursuit of simple bodily pleasure . . . it could nurture very radical, hitherto unthinkable new conceptions of what it can be to live as a male body."[54] The habitual practice of homoeroticism ("living as a gay man," "living as a lesbian")—what Butler might call subversive repetition—is an ethos where gender as an inequality can be displaced since a principal experience that produces it within individual subjectivity, sexuality, ceases to do so any longer.

To sum up this politics of sexuality, lesbians and gay men, for reasons of survival, work together in alliance. *Among* lesbians and *among* gay men, homoerotic relationships generate reciprocity and equality and tend to undermine gender as a fixed essence of being a man or a woman. *Between* lesbians and gay men, in the absence of compulsory heterosexuality through which the values and norms of gender as an inequality are enforced and perpetuated, an ethos can emerge from their respective homoeroticisms to the extent that they have allowed for the creation of *social* relations of equality within the lesbian and gay community. (This does not mean that gay men will automatically give up their cultural baggage of the expectation of gender privilege either on the subjective level or on that of its institutionalization.) At the same time, homoerotics works *through* gender not necessarily to abolish it on behalf of androgyny but to render it transparent, to de-essentialize it. The perfection of equality between lesbians and gay men, to the extent that it becomes a part of their shared ethos, can contribute to a problematization of gendered social relationships that engage nongay people as well.[55]

Conclusion

Ethos is the moral dwelling place made possible through the coming out of lesbian and gay people, within which they constitute themselves as ethical beings—as subjects of their actions through erotics—and thereby serve as conditions for the becoming of each other. Ethos is at once a goal of lesbian and gay existence and a condition of possibility for its politics. To be sure, we have not directly addressed specific "issues" of lesbian and gay politics here, such as new definitions of family, the right to reproduce without sexuality, the increase in anti-gay and anti-lesbian violence and the persistence of discrimination, the reconfiguring of health care generally consequent on the

AIDS epidemic, and the legal recognition these imply. However, lesbian and gay people, through an emerging ethos, have created a transnational public sphere within which political action around these, among other issues, has become possible.

Political action, made possible by the creation of a lesbian and gay public sphere, effects state policies but is not itself only statist in orientation; such political action is directed at power *relations*—power as it is exercised in everyday life through procedures of subjection and the forms of domination that support them. (For example, lesbians and gays have, through AIDS activism and patient self-help and empowerment, problematized domination over people's bodies by medical power and its corresponding subjection through the doctor-patient relationship, as well as the direction of the medical research agenda itself.) Biopower, as the *novum* of the contemporary world, has resulted in politics being concerned with not merely constitutional issues—how power relations are codified by the state—but with more broadly constitutive issues: the shape or fabric of human life on the planet—*how* shall we live?—is the substance of politics. It is in this sense that lesbian and gay politics, made possible by but also furthering the conditions for the creation of an ethos, is paradigmatic of politics in our time. . . .

In conclusion, I will briefly discuss the status and meaning (as goal or intent) of gay and lesbian political philosophy from four perspectives.[56] First, I address the question of whether gay and lesbian theory is "merely" the attempt to analyze a situation of social inequality by members of an interest group expressing a subjective preference for change. Second, I deal with a standard sociobiological counterargument to such a sociology of knowledge and show its inadequacy from empirical analysis and contemporary political realities. Third, I demonstrate how current lesbian and gay "identity theory," resurgent in a conceptualization of a "third sex/gender," is an inadequate alternative from a *theoretical* point of view to the kinds of claims critics have suggested. I conclude by formulating what I think are the status and goal of lesbian- and gay-inflected political philosophy that reflect the politics of knowledge today.

Some critics have suggested that this essay conceptualizes knowledge as a direct product of social activity: what is significant in terms of knowledge production, quoting me, is the "transformation of the world in which all human beings live, as well as the way people understand themselves as living in that world."[57] But is not knowledge always directly related to social activities? For example, this relation can involve, first, the application of existing knowledge to social life, as in the Manhattan Project. It can involve, second, the production of new knowledge, motivated by social conditions and which has an effect on them: the development of solar and fusion energy sources as response to dwindling fossil fuels which could result in consequences for the social conditions that produced the knowledge that led to their development. On a more narrowly social level, the production of knowledge about AIDS through HIV transmissability allowed for the invention of safer sex techniques that then transformed what sexual excitement was perceived to be.[58] Third, knowledge could be produced through a reconstruction of knowledge that had existed previously, for example, of homoerotic relationships, but was lost because of historical censorship or methodological disguising in a privileging of heterosexuality.

For such critics, however, knowledge produced from a lesbian and gay perspective is solely to achieve a given political objective in practice. As such, it is no different than "interest" and is therefore not "theoretical" (cannot explain or understand social reality). The status of perspectival *theory* is commonly accepted in political science and political philosophy: dependency theory and feminist theory are certainly theories, for example, in that they seek to explain or understand a situation of social inequality. Feminist theory is not only descriptive of the interests of women but also explanatory of relations between women and men. Dependency theory may be descriptive of the interests of "have nots" but is clearly also explanatory of relationships between "haves" and "have nots." (Critique of these theories tends to focus on their methodological rigor and the extent of their explanatory efficacy, not on whether their truth claims are valid because women or people from economically less-advantaged societies may [but not necessarily] be doing the theorizing.) My argument is that lesbian and gay theory is not only descriptive of political interests of lesbians and gays but explanatory of how sexuality is related to political life. The intent of such theorizing is to understand the politicalness of the contemporary lesbian and gay ethos, that is, how the values that are constitutive of collective existence arise from erotic— broadly conceived—expression and relationships. Therefore, analyzing such an ethos of lesbian and gay existence as a "problematization," "a form and site of resistance within hegemonic relationships of power in contemporary society" yields understanding of what politics is.

Some insist that if theory is conceived as analysis of how people problematize social relations and conventional ways of thinking about them (including thinking they are not power relations), it is already interested political "know-how," not truly theory, since it is not a "questioning" of all interest. Rather, by analyzing in an open-ended way how people (gays, lesbians, and others) have made sexuality a political problem, my theoretical intention is precisely to question their interest in doing so; if by so analyzing I formulate explanatory statements that enable an understanding of politics generally, I have achieved in my analysis *theoretical* status. Some say sexuality is not political, that it is a preferred (private) lifestyle and sexual preference or orientation and cannot provide either an understanding of politics or knowledge for engaging in politics. In the foregoing analysis I explained how it *is* political: sexuality involves at once a social technology of government through which power has historically come to be exercised and a site at which people constitute themselves ethically—as agents of action—and thus position themselves to change the power relations that condition the ways in which they may act. (But this "positioning" takes place in and through socio-cultural and legal power relations, not "outside" them in an essentialized realm of "intimate relations" or privacy.) Further, in analyzing how and why people problematize their own sexual ethics, the power relations (e.g., norms and institutions) that encourage or inhibit sexual behavior, and ways of thinking about both of these—ethics and power—one is not necessarily taking sides and making prescriptive statements. Both advocates for change as well as for retrenchment of sexual norms and institutions can share the recognition of their objective existence in society and their problematization by various social movements on behalf of certain truth claims; they differ in what conclusions to draw about such problematization.[59] But maligning all theoretical products of participants in the lesbian and gay movement because they are merely activist polemic (as many critics of the politics of sexuality do) reflects a conception of theory that is at best naive, and at worst disingenuous about relationships between political philosophy and political action.

Sociobiological theory also makes claims about the politics of sexuality, at levels of both explanatory status and intention. Theoretically, and based on speculative and contested studies, it explains homosexuality as largely deter-mined anatomically, hormonally, and/or genetically. Its intention is to address the question of to what extent and why lesbians and gays deserve political consideration. Richard Posner answers this question in his *Sex and Reason*[60] by presupposing (at least partial) biological determination: "There is no rea-son to think that repression, psychotherapy, behavior modification, or any other technique of law or medicine can . . . [change homosexual preference] in a large enough number of cases to warrant the costs . . . that legal and social discrimination imposes" (308). Sociobiological defenses of the "natu-ralness" of homosexuality as a basis for social tolerance have been proferred by gays and lesbians themselves (as well as their political allies) at least since the middle of the nineteenth century when the term *homosexual* was coined by Austro-Hungarian writer Karl Maria Kertbeny and used by later pa-thologizers and advocates of this form of love. Thus, the political effects of these truth claims have been both repressive as well as protective. As such, these claims cannot be the basis for homosexuality becoming irrelevant to governmental regulatory tolerance or for gays and lesbians to achieve a polit-ical status equal to people whose lives are defined through their heterosexual relations. Posner even admits this. For him, the life prospects for homosex-uals are *intrinsically* (and by "nature") grimmer than for heterosexuals. He approvingly suggests that "there is a bare chance that the formation of homo-sexual preference can be prevented," but since homosexuals' social disadvan-tage is biologically determined, from a cost-benefit perspective homosex-uality can be socially tolerated but never treated by society as *acceptable* (308–9, 311–12).

The logic of sociobiological arguments can always be reversed, as they were in a play by Jonathan Tolins that revolves around a gay man's liberal Jewish sister deciding whether or not to abort a fetus that has been determined through amniocentesis to have a 90 percent genetic probability of later becoming gay. One can imagine, as this playwright stated, that a future society may not need the public power a Nazi state did to exterminate homosexuals; rather, the same effect will be achieved preventatively through a "private" decision made by prospective parents in consultation with their physician. Even if it is an immutable characteristic, homosexuality still requires social acceptance if gay fetuses are to be brought to term.

An alternative theory has recently been articulated by a group of historians and anthropologists led by Gilbert Herdt in a conceptualization of lesbians and gays as a "third sex/gender."[61] Modern Western culture has polarized all individuals by fitting them into complementary dimorphic male/female categories grounded in what these theorists term a "cultural ontology" of reproductive sexuality. For them, biological maleness and femaleness is conceptualized on a continuum, with most individuals clustering toward the extremes but many others in between (one estimate by sex researchers is that 4 percent of live births in the United States are to some extent intersexed or hermaphroditic by a combination of biological criteria). Other cultures have, in fact, created social roles for these "in-betweens," such as the berdache in Native America and the Hijra in traditional and contemporary India. The problem with this "third sex" theoretical endeavor is that contemporary individuals who identify as gay or lesbian are not necessarily transsexual, transvestite, biologically intersexed, transgender-identified, nor even androgynous. Third-sex/gender theorists recognize that female to male transvestism is often an attempt to change status in a gender-based status system, and that people who change biological sex often do so because there are no social roles available for them alternative to the polar male-female ones. This theory, therefore, recognizes the institutionally enforced power of a sex-gender-reproductive cultural ontology but fails in explanation. It has as its goal the explanation of the lived experience of gays and lesbians in our (contemporary Western) society; the superimposition on such experience of models that explain either homosexual role in other societies or that which existed in our society in a previous historical period does not achieve this goal.

If a goal of gay and lesbian political philosophy is explaining on what basis gays and lesbians claim political rights, third-sex theory is on a very precarious footing. That there was acceptance of certain types of social-sexual behaviors in other cultures and other times does not per se make a case for their acceptance here and now. The nineteenth-century formulation of the third-sex category by German attorney-turned-activist Karl Ulrichs to gain tolerance for gays and lesbians (later pathologized by German neurologist Richard von Krafft-Ebing and recuperated by German gay sexologist Magnus

Hirschfeld) was apologetic. Such "urnings" were congenital but not equal to "real" males and females; it was by virtue of their being "less" masculine and feminine that they constituted a third category.[62] Herdt says that the historical emergence in Western modernity of "individual and private desire" (72ff.) allows for the creation of a third-sex category parallel to those existing historically and cross-culturally. However, he admits that from a structural analysis of culture, third terms in such bipolar systems are inherently unstable and cultural roles based on them are difficult to maintain.

A more secure empirical footing on which to theorize political action coalescing around gay, lesbian, bisexual, trans-, and cross-gender sexual identities (using here nomenclature of the 1993 March on Washington) would be the emergence of a new ethical subjectivity—of what it means to *be* an individual. This would move beyond and, in so doing, challenge a socially imposed definition of the self through biological sex, gender, and reproductive sexuality. (I refer to "sexual identities" because, even though trans- and cross-gender are seemingly gender identities, such individuals have demanded recognition within a movement that has arisen within the rubric of the "right" to freedom of sexual expression. Even as this social movement asserts a right to nondiscrimination/equal protection of the laws, the discrimination it seeks to protect against is that based on erotic subjectivity that may be related to gender in complex ways, *sexual* behavior, and cultural creation (ethos) arising from these—this is where the orientation versus behavior distinction breaks down.) This fourth approach analyzes the collective problematization of one's experience of selfhood, relationships with others, and their imbrication with "truth." This imbrication is the definition of selfhood in terms congruent with the organization of society through what Herdt terms the "reproductive paradigm" based on the "principle of sexual dimorphism" (25–26). In this essay, I have called it a technology of government that, through a structure of power and, within it, a construction of subjectivity, makes heterosexuality relatively compulsory. The social movement fosters individuals creating meaningful lives for themselves through sexuality as an experimentation on, and elaboration of, selfhood within relationships with others different from relationships derived from the "truth" of sex-gender-reproductive complimentarity. In doing so, the "reproductive paradigm" (Herdt) or my "technology of government of compulsory heterosexuality" are displaced. This is the stuff of lesbian and gay politics—its contesting received ideas about sexed-gendered-sexualized subjectivity, conceiving how power is exercised through "intimate" relationships that then makes visible the fluidity between what is deemed public and private in relation to sexuality, and engaging in a politics of sexuality that challenges our understanding of what political knowledge is about.

What can theorizing lesbian and gay politics explain that is true and not just the expression of a passionate interest? Such theory need not necessarily be produced by lesbians and gays themselves, but it must reflect how they have questioned the forms of knowledge and practices of expertise that have dominated their life chances relative to others. Thus, analytical work by lesbians and gays may generally carry more weight than that of others. Its truth, therefore, will depend on how their questioning, or political problematization, is reflected in theorizing and how well the theorizing explains to what extend our *common* life has historically come to be constituted through the social technology that lesbians and gays call compulsory heterosexuality or "heteronormativity." The demonstration of how our common life is constituted rests on a criterion of truth status—"is the theory true?"—for which both gays and non-gays can be critics.

Lesbian and gay political theory therefore would not be merely an interest-group theory; it would involve something other than accounting for a sociobiological externality in the management of society; it would be more comprehensive than simple addition of a third-sex category to our knowledge about human diversity. Theorizing about lesbian/gay/bisexual/transgender or (what some have termed) "queer" reflects a transformation in our conception of human agency and the implications of that transformation for how we organize our collective life. This transformation of agency, queer agency, challenges the scope and validity of all conceptions of the relationship between liberty and authority to the extent they are defined by the "reproductive paradigm." Such agency becomes intelligible according to practical-aesthetic criteria of an art of living rather than according to criteria that destine one through a human nature. In this essay I theorized the constitution of agency through analysis of a contemporary lesbian and gay ethos and its expression in lesbian and gay politics. This constitution involves giving one's life form— here derived from lesbian and gay community–inflected value or ethos—as a source of practical knowledge for others in how to live a fulfilling life. As an emergent ethos this includes, for example, (1) the self's subjective experience of agency created agonistically in relation to how the "truth" of sex/ gender/reproductive complementarity is interpersonally and culturally constituted, that evokes a reconceptualization of the sources of autonomy and the meaning of equality; (2) caring and affectional relationships that arise from sexuality but decenter "family values" and relationships derived from reproduction as what gives rise to the political (as in many civil society-state conceptions); and (3) criteria of personal worth or accomplishment and concomitant cultural value that cannot be reduced to economic or scientific rationality (as in the valorization of "coming out" within the lesbian and gay ethos).[63] Lesbian, gay, bisexual, transgender, and queer political philosophers such as myself are trying to explain the inadequacies of our political order to the extent it is grounded in ideas about human nature as heterosexual, as well as to explain how such an ethos regarding sexuality can be of benefit to nongays and to how we conceive politics, too.

Notes

An earlier version of pages 143–66 of this essay was published in *Political Theory* 20, no. 4 (November 1992): 642-71. Copyright © Mark Blasius. Reprinted by permission. An earlier version of pages 166–71 of this essay was published in *Political Theory* 23, no. 3 (August 1995) 520–26. Copyright © Sage Publications, Inc. Reprinted by permission. Thus, the combined texts were written during 1991–94. Very few changes, for content of the argument or even updating, have been made for publication here (2000). I have refrained from major rewriting, showing how far activism and theory have come since then (emblematized by the present queer "postidentitarian" politics of sexuality) and thereby showing my own reflections upon a particular historical moment. The reader may judge what of the original withstands the test of time.

1. This formulation of what politics is, "political problematization," was suggested to me by Michel Foucault. We spent many hours, with many friends, in many different places discussing gay politics and culture. At the time of his death in 1984, I was working on my dissertation in consultation with him and the reader will no doubt recognize his influence on my thinking. However, I must clarify at the outset that, first, in my opinion, he came to his ideas about gay politics and culture primarily through his encounters over many visits with North American lesbian and gay thinkers, and second, that while his work and our conversations influenced the way I think about lesbian and gay existence, I am not presenting an exposition and interpretation of his ideas about it here.

2. Eve Kosofsky Sedgwick, *Epistemology of the Closet* (Berkeley: University of California Press, 1990), 33–34 (emphasis in original).

3. Mark Blasius, *Gay and Lesbian Politics: Sexuality and the Emergence of a New Ethic* (Philadelphia: Temple University Press, 1994). The book contains more elaborate explanation of my usage of the terms "lesbian" and "gay" (as distinct from "queer," including bisexuals, etc.). Here, suffice it to say that when I refer to "gay people" as well as lesbians, I want to include women who understand themselves as "gay women," in addition to gay men. My aim throughout has been to create a framework for dialogue between lesbians and gay men by drawing upon theoretical concepts arising in the writings of both.

4. The term homophobia was "coined" in Dr. George Weinberg, *Society and the Healthy Homosexual* (Garden City, NY: Doubleday/Anchor, 1973); my formulation of the term is based on that earlier one. The term "compulsory heterosexuality" is from Adrienne Rich, "Compulsory Heterosexuality and Lesbian Existence," in *Powers of Desire: The Politics of Sexuality*, ed. Ann Snitow, Christine Stansell, and Sharon Thompson (New York: Monthly Review Press, 1983), 177–205. The analysis of these phenomena as forms of domination and procedures of subjection is undertaken in chapter 1 of my *Gay and Lesbian Politics*.

5. Robert Dawidoff, "Memorial Day, 1988," in *Personal Dispatches: Writers Confront AIDS*, ed. John Preston (New York: St. Martin's, 1989), 177. The former surgeon general's use of the concept is in Maureen Dowd, "Dr. Koop Defends His Crusade on AIDS," *New York Times*, April 6, 1987, p. B8. For a historical analysis of the Nazi extermination of gays, see Richard Plant, *The Pink Triangle: The Nazi War against Homosexuals* (New York: Holt, 1986).

6. Michel Foucault, *The History of Sexuality*, Vol. 1, *An Introduction*, trans. Robert Hurley (New York: Pantheon, 1978), 138 (emphasis in original). Biopower is defined on 139ff.

7. Rich, "Compulsory Heterosexuality," 142.

8. The relationship between gender and sexuality as it motivates homosexual panic is too complex to discuss here. Also, the literature on male homosexual panic is more developed than that on its female counterpart. An interesting structural approach to the former is Eve Kosofsky Sedgwick, *Between Men: English Literature and Male Homosocial Desire* (New York: Columbia University Press, 1986), 83–96, and Sedgwick, *Epistemology*, 182–212.

9. Norman Podhoretz, "The Culture of Appeasement," *Commentary* 64, no. 4 (October 1977): 30, 31.

10. Midge Decter, "The Boys on the Beach," *Commentary* 70, no. 3 (September 1980): 39, 40–41, (emphasis mine).

11. For accounts of the diversity of ways of living as a lesbian or a gay man throughout the United States, see Neil Miller, *In Search of Gay America* (New York: Atlantic Monthly Press, 1989); Martha Barron Barrett, *Invisible Lives: The Truth about Millions of Women Loving Women* (New York: Morrow, 1989); and, for an earlier account, Edmund White, *States of Desire: Travels in Gay America* (New York: Dutton, 1980).

12. William Burroughs proposed the establishment of a gay state analogous to Israel in an interview in Howard Brookner's film about him, *Burroughs*. He later abandoned the idea and proposed instead organizations within existing states modeled after the Chinese Tongs, which he called Gay Protection patrols (GPs; after San Francisco's groups to protect gays against street violence). However, they would also provide services to GP members: assistance in employment and housing, legal advice and assistance, medical aid, protection from extortion, and meeting and recreational facilities. Most of these services have come to be offered in a decentralized manner by the gay communities of large U.S. cities, including orientation sessions to lesbians and gay men who have just migrated from the hinterlands. Burroughs sees the necessity for these kinds of organizations in even the smallest towns nationwide. Dennis Altman argued (in 1985) that

> the past decade and a half has seen the creation of a gay and lesbian "nation," much as nineteenth-century Europe saw the creation of Czech and Roumanian "nations." To be gay has taken on meanings that go far beyond sexual and affectional preference, binding us through a whole set of communal, religious, political and social activities with other gays.

See William S. Burroughs, "Thoughts on a Gay State," in *Gay Spirit: Myth and Meaning*, ed. Mark Thompson (New York: St. Martin's, 1987), 20–24, and Dennis Altman, "What Price Gay Nationalism?" in ibid., 16–19, at 18–19.

13. This is the hypothesis of Michael Warner, "Introduction: Fear of a Queer Planet," *Social Text* 29 (1991): 3–17. See also George L. Mosse, *Nationalism and Sexuality: Middle-Class Morality and Sexual Norms in Modern Europe* (Madison: University of Wisconsin Press, 1985) and Introduction to *Nationalisms and Sexualities*, ed. Andrew Parker, Mary Russo, Doris Sommer, and Patricia Yaeger (New York: Routledge, 1991).

14. Larry Kramer, *Reports from the Holocaust: The Making of an AIDS Activist* (New York: St. Martin's, 1989), 254, 257.

15. Marilyn Frye, *The Politics of Reality* (Freedom, CA: The Crossing Press, 1983), 128–151, at 150.

16. The best analysis of the suppression of and even falsification of historical data on homosexuality remains John Boswell, *Christianity, Social Tolerance, and Homosexuality: Gay People in Western Europe from the Beginning of the Christian Era to the Fourteenth Century* (Chicago: University of Chicago Press, 1980), passim, but particularly the overview of the problem on 17–22. For example, on 20–21 he writes,

> Sometimes their anxiety to reinterpret or disguise accounts of homosexuality has induced translators to inject wholly new concepts into texts, as when the translators of a Hittite law apparently regulating homosexual marriage insert words which completely alter its meaning or when Graves "translates" a nonexistent clause in Suetonius to suggest that a law prohibits homosexual acts.

17. The government of lifestyle has historically been an important strategy in both the United States and the former Soviet Union. For example, in the United States, one motive was the "Americanization" of immigrants through programs to train them in the "American way of life"; similarly, the Bolsheviks gave themselves the task of creating the new Communist Man. The consequences in both societies were that

> the individual's "private" life and "personal" activities were now matters of the well-being of the population: they entered into a calculus of social costs and needed to be governed.

See Keith Gandal and Stephen Kotkin, "Governing Work and Social Life in the U.S.A. and U.S.S.R.," *History of the Present* (February 1985): 4–14.

18. See, for example, Michael E. Sobel, *Lifestyle and Social Structure: Concepts, Definitions, Analyses* (New York: Academic Press, 1981); Mike Featherstone, "Lifestyle and Consumer Culture," *Theory, Culture & Society* 4 (1987): 55–70; and Bryan S. Turner, *Status* (Minneapolis: University of Minnesota Press, 1988), chapter 4, "Mass Culture, Distinction, and Lifestyle." For lifestyle as a category of epidemiological analysis, and its failure (due to its stereotypical character) to account for AIDS etiology, see Gerald M. Oppenheimer, "In the Eye of the Storm: The Epidemiological Construction of AIDS," in *AIDS: The Burdens of History*, ed. Elizabeth Fee and Daniel M. Fox (Berkeley: University of California Press, 1988), 267–300.

19. Nikolas Rose, *Governing the Soul: The Shaping of the Private Self* (London: Routledge, 1990), 227.

20. Featherstone, "Lifestyle," 59, 64.

21. Ibid., 55 (emphasis in original).

22. Gilbert Herdt, "Coming Out as a Rite of Passage: A Chicago Study," in *Gay Culture in America: Essays from the Field*, ed. Gilbert Herdt (Boston: Beacon, 1991), 34.

23. Marshall Kirk and Hunter Madsen, *After the Ball: How America Will Conquer Its Fear and Hatred of Gays in the 1990s* (New York: Doubleday, 1989), 305.

24. Sarah Lucia Hoagland, *Lesbian Ethics: Toward New Value* (Palo Alto: Institute for Lesbian Studies, 1989), 146.

25. Ibid., 155.

26. The theory of "identity politics" that individuals have cross-cutting identities (woman, Native American, lesbian, etc.) that structure both their subjective social experience as well as their loyalties to others, also places limits on the possibility of "community" between lesbians and gay men. My formulation of ethos is an attempt to theorize lesbian and gay existence beyond identity politics, without denying the latter

as one factor in political problematization—how something becomes a political issue. For theoretical discussions of identity politics, see Shane Phelan, *Identity Politics: Lesbian Feminism and the Limits of Community* (Philadelphia: Temple University Press, 1989), and Diana Fuss, *Essentially Speaking: Feminism, Nature and Difference* (New York: Routledge, 1989), chapter 4.

27. At the time of this writing, there is a lesbian and gay book series at Columbia University Press, at NAL, and at St. Martin's, and several exclusively lesbian and gay presses exist. There is a lesbian and gay studies center at the City University of New York (as well as academic programs elsewhere). There have been several annual national academic conferences—three at Yale, one each at Harvard and Rutgers, and one at the University of Iowa, as well as numerous regional and topical ones—annual national lesbian and gay writers' conferences, and numerous common lesbian/gay publications, and 1991 saw the founding of a North American lesbian and gay studies association.

28. These "technical social science" indices of community are from Stephen O. Murray, "Components of Gay Community in San Francisco," in *Gay Culture*, ed. Herdt, 113–16. This research on gay and lesbian voting behavior is being led by Robert W. Bailey of Rutgers University and other members of the Gay and Lesbian Caucus for Political Science.

29. My analysis of coming out follows Michel Foucault's formulation of ethical self-formation in his *History of Sexuality*, vol. 2, *The Use of Pleasure*, trans. Robert Hurley (New York: Pantheon, 1985), 25–32.

30. This conception of lifestyle is that of Robert N. Bellah et al., *Habits of the Heart* (Berkeley: University of California Press, 1985), as cited in Murray, "Gay Community," 114.

31. Geoff Mains, *Urban Aboriginals: A Celebration of Leathersexuality* (San Francisco: Gay Sunshine Press, 1984), 24, 25.

32. There is not enough space here to elaborate "sexuality" as a historical specific component of our experience of "self." I do so, however, in chapter 2 of my *Gay and Lesbian Politics*, where I analyze sexuality as a technology of government—the point of intersection between power relations and ethical self-creation.

33. I want to acknowledge and thank Dante Germino for his assistance in documenting for me the Greek etymology of ethos.

34. "[T]he idea of a morality as obedience to a code of rules is now disappearing, has already disappeared. To this absence of a morality, one responds, or must respond, with a research which is that of an aesthetics of existence." Michel Foucault, "An Aesthetics of Existence," in *Foucault Live*, trans. John Johnston and ed. Sylvere Lotringer (New York: Semiotexte, 1989), 311.

35. Max Weber, *The Protestant Ethic and the Spirit of Capitalism*, trans. Talcott Parsons (New York: Scribner, 1958), 27.

36. Cited in Calvin O. Schrag, *Communicative Praxis and the Space of Subjectivity* (Indianapolis: Indiana University Press, 1986), 210. My discussion of ethos is informed by Schrag's excellent chapter, "Ethos, Ethics, and a New Humanism."

37. Martin Heidegger, *An Introduction to Metaphysics* (Garden City, NY: Doubleday, 1961), 13 (emphasis in original).

38. Susan Sontag, "Notes on 'Camp,'" in *Against Interpretation and Other Essays* (New York: Dell, 1966), 275, 287.

39. For a discussion of gay *Gemeinschaft* and *Gesellschaft*, see Herdt, *Gay Culture*, 11–12.

40. This lesbian is Claudia Card, as self-described in her contributor's biography to *Lesbian Philosophies and Cultures*, ed. Jeffner Allen (Albany: State University of New York Press, 1990), 407.

41. Each of these axes of political experience receives an entire chapter of analysis in Blasius, *Gay and Lesbian Politics*.

42. For a discussion of the tensions between understanding oneself as a black gay man or as a gay black man, see Essex Hemphill, ed., *Brother to Brother* (Boston: Alyson, 1991). For an analogous discussion from the perspective of women of color, see the relevant essays in Barbara Smith, ed., *Home Girls: A Black Feminist Anthology* (New York: Kitchen Table, Women of Color Press, 1983) and Carla Trujillo, ed., *Chicana Lesbians* (Berkeley: Third Woman Press, 1991).

43. Friedrich Nietzsche, *The Will to Power*, trans. Walter Kaufmann and R. J. Hollingdale (New York: Vintage, 1968), no. 481.

44. Heidegger, *Metaphysics*, 133–34. Heidegger states that *techne* "denotes neither art nor technology but a knowledge, the ability to plan and organize freely, to master institutions (cf. Plato's *Phaedrus*). *Techne* is creating, building in the sense of a deliberate pro-ducing" (13–14). See also Michel Foucault's discussion of the ancient *techne tou biou*—knowledge, practices, and institutions for the cultivation of the self—which was the theme of the third volume of his history of sexuality. He also stated in interviews his belief that the development of such a techne, an art of living, was integral to contemporary lesbian and gay existence and, I would add, to the creation of an ethos that links ethical agency with political action. See Michel Foucault, *The History of Sexuality*, vol. 3, *The Care of the Self*, trans. Robert Hurley (New York: Pantheon, 1986), 43–45, 88–92; and Bob Gallagher and Alexander Wilson, "Michel Foucault, An Interview: Sex, Power and the Politics of Identity," *The Advocate* 400 (August 7, 1984): 26–30, 58.

45. Examples of this would include the now nearly universally promulgated safer-sex guidelines, which were an invention of gay men to maintain the kinds of relationships they were engaging in in the face of AIDS, as well as lesbian insemination as reproduction without [hetero] sexuality, and the lesbian and gay redefinition of family.

46. Thus there is a permanent tension between the "unqualified" character of this knowledge (it is "interested"—not objective or sufficiently distanced from subjective experience—or it is not always the product of scientific inquiry or not adequately theorized) and the drive toward codification by, for example, lesbian and gay studies programs, and by the professionalization of lesbian and gay activists when they strive to cooperate with established institutions in order to change their policies.

47. For a discussion of sexuality as a distinctively *political* issue, see Blasius, *Gay and Lesbian Politics*, chapter 2.

48. For an elaboration of this point and an excellent general discussion of lesbian and gay kinship, see Kath Weston, *Families We Choose: Lesbians, Gays, Kinship* (New York: Columbia University Press, 1991), 21–41.

49. For a similar perspective, see Hoagland, *Lesbian Ethics*, 172–74.

50. Aristotle, *Nichomachean Ethics*, trans. Martin Ostwald (Indianapolis: Bobbs-Merrill, 1962), 1159b31–32. 47. This argument is made in greater detail in Blasius, *Gay and Lesbian Politics*, chapter 2.

51. Catherine A. MacKinnon, *Feminism Unmodified: Discourses on Life and Law* (Cambridge, MA: Harvard University Press, 1987), 6.

52. Judith Butler, "Imitation and Gender Insubordination," in *Inside/Out: Lesbian Theories, Gay Theories*, ed. Diana Fuss (New York: Routledge, 1991), 21ff.

53. Brian Pronger, *The Arena of Masculinity: Sports, Homosexuality, and the Meaning of Sex* (New York: St. Martin's, 1990), 75.

54. Frye, *Politics of Reality*, 148.

55. Parallel to my argument here, Allan Berube has analyzed the complement to coming out, "fitting in," that is, how lesbians and gay men integrate their homoerotic relationships into their relationships with non-gays, such as those with families of origin, with coworkers, in neighborhood organizations. His research was presented as "'Fitting In': Expanding Queer Studies Beyond Gay Identity and Coming Out," Fourth Annual Lesbian, Bisexual, and Gay Studies Conference, Harvard University, October 26–28, 1990.

56. This section was originally published in a slightly different form as a separate essay, "The Meaning and Status of Gay and Lesbian Political Philosophy: A Rejoinder to E. Robert Statham, Jr.," *Political Theory* 23, no. 3 (August 1995): 520–26, in a critical exchange with Statham's "Political Philosophy as Political Action: A Response to Mark Blasius," *Political Theory* 23, no. 3 (August 1995): 517–19. For a critique of my work and that of Judith Butler along these lines see Jerry Z. Muller, "Coming Out Ahead: The Homosexual Moment in the Academy," *First Things: A Monthly Journal of Religion and Public Life* 35 (August/September 1993): 17–24.

57. See Statham, "Political Philosophy."

58. See Edward King, *Safety in Numbers: Safer Sex and Gay Men* (New York: Routledge, 1994).

59. For example, both Roger Scruton and I recognize that homosexual erotic expression involves something different than male-female complementarity; but while he views it as "an obscenity," I do not. Scruton, *Sexual Desire: A Moral Philosophy of the Erotic* (New York: Free Press, 1986), 305–11.

60. Richard Posner, *Sex and Reason* (Cambridge, MA: Harvard University Press, 1992), throughout, esp. 291–323.

61. Gilbert Herdt, ed., *Third Sex, Third Gender: Beyond Sexual Dimorphism in Culture and History* (New York: Zone Books, 1994).

62. See the writings by Karl Ulrichs, Karoly (Karl) Maria Kertbeny, and Magnus Hirschfeld in *We Are Everywhere: A Historical Sourcebook of Gay and Lesbian Politics*, ed. Mark Blasius and Shane Phelan (New York: Routledge, 1997).

63. For an extended discussion of these themes, see my *Gay and Lesbian Politics: Sexuality and the Emergence of a New Ethic* (Philadelphia: Temple University Press, 1994).

SEVEN

QUEER THEORY, LESBIAN AND GAY RIGHTS, AND TRANSSEXUAL MARRIAGES

Paisley Currah

A T THE CLOSE of the twentieth century, there has perhaps never been as great a dichotomy between the legal strategies of U.S. mainstream gay and lesbian politics and the queer knowledges produced in the academy: while the largest, most well funded of the gay and lesbian political groups celebrated its constituents' dedication to "faith and family" at a "millennial" rally in Washington, the still-institutionalizing field of lesbian and gay studies churns out largely negative assessments of identity politics.[1] While mainstream gay rights activists seek to improve the legal and social status of gays and lesbians by demanding that equal rights be extended to (partially) disenfranchised gay and lesbian (and sometimes bisexual) people, queer theorists reject such devotion to the regulatory mechanisms of the liberal state, including its production of citizens, individuals, and, in the discourse of today's regime of official multiculturalism, the corollary identity group categories of "gay," "lesbian," "homosexual," "straight."[2] Instead, queer theorists have argued that identity-based political claims ultimately fail to undermine the very categories—homosexuality and heterosexuality, in this case—upon which such subjection is based. However, the opposition between the strict identity fundamentalism of mainstream lesbian and gay rights advocates and the full-throttled identity iconoclasm of queer theorists obscures the potential that could result from a "marriage" between these two very different discursive regimes—however fraught such an alliance may be.[3] This provisional coalition could also undermine the tendency of some of the work produced within the field of queer theory to belittle state-directed political intervention, a tendency that wrongly imagines the law to be set apart from the culture that produces it. I suggest in this article that there are good reasons for the civil rights strategies of sexual minorities to be informed by some of the insights about identity generated in the field of queer theory, even if those insights require some translation before they can be effectively deployed in the legal/political arena.

In the United States, the new field of queer theory emerged out of twentieth-century Continental social theory and has become rooted largely in the disciplines of the humanities.[4] Its proponents have been especially influenced by that tradition's critiques of the "sovereign subject" of liberalism. The axioms of queer theory have implicitly and often explicitly challenged the political usefulness of the kind of essentialist identity claims posited by gay and lesbian rights advocates and refuted by gay and lesbian rights opponents.[5] Indeed, anti-gay ideologues of the Christian right and queer theorists, though using very different languages, have produced congruent nonessentialist accounts of homosexuality: Judith Butler, for example, reads homosexuality and heterosexuality in relation to gender norms, which are themselves not anchored to any secure, incontestable foundations, since gender is actually "a set of repeated acts within a highly rigid regulatory frame that congeal over time to produce the appearance of substance, of a natural sort of being."[6] Located historically, according to Butler, such repetitions produce for each time and place a set of coded actions that define the parameters of normative gender. Similarly, an analyst for the Family Research Council, a large anti-gay organization in the United States, notes that "the central distinguishing characteristic of homosexuality is not identity, but a set of behaviors."[7] (Unfortunately, the religious right's analysis of the institution of heterosexuality is not nearly so sophisticated, relying as it does on God and nature.[8]) As mainstream gay and lesbian rights advocates devise counterarguments to the homophobic rhetoric of their opponents, they often follow the path of least resistance and rebut these nonfoundationalist accounts of homosexuality with essentialist narratives.[9] My argument here, however, demonstrates the costs of this strategy to sexual minorities; this article is part of a larger project that attempts to illustrate liberalism's potential elasticity in accommodating nonnormative notions of identity.

Much of the work done in the emerging field of queer theory has pointed out the ways in which notions of personal identity rely on essential ideas of selfhood that reify the very hierarchies of race, class, gender, and sexuality produced during the ascendancy of the modern liberal state. As Eve Sedgwick points out, "queer" undermines and exceeds the identity categories of gender and sexuality: "[R]ace, ethnicity, postcolonial nationality criss-cross with these *and other* identity-constituting, identity-fracturing discourses."[10] In this view, basing the rights claims of sexual minorities on essentialist notions of "homosexual," "gay," or "lesbian" identity reproduces the transgressions of identity politics. For example, Michael Warner argues:

> What we may be less prepared to recognize is that the form of identity politics itself belongs to Anglo-American traditions and has some distorting influences. It seems impossible in this context to raise the possibility of sexual conflict or diversity except by appealing for the homosexual minority and by making comparisons to other minority movements. In the United States, the default model for all minority movements is racial or ethnic. . . . Despite its language of post-

modernism, multiculturalism tends to rely on very modern notions of authenticity, of culture as shared meaning and the source of identity.[11]

Queer legal theorist Lisa Bower has referred to identity-based rights claims as a "politics of official recognition," an attempt to "fit the 'queer other' within some space already acknowledged by the liberal nation-state."[12] In opposition to such reformist "We're just like you" goals, queer theorists have focused their attention on identity's contingency, fluidity, and constructedness, and suggested that it is in the destabilization of identity categories that effective political practice is to be found. Accompanying this dismissal of the identity-based politics of official recognition has been the abandonment of the state as "the site of privileged political action."[13] Instead, "cultural contestations" have become, in queer theory, the locus of effective political intervention.

But the rights advocates of sexual minorities must make their arguments intelligible to the jurists who are arbitrators of equal protection within the American political system, which does emanate from the Anglo-American liberal tradition, and which does construe identity and the division of the public and private realms in the supposedly naive—but incontrovertibly powerful —formulations of Anglo-American liberalism. Thus the rhetoric surrounding the rights claims of gays and lesbians almost inevitably devolves into claims of "a people" unjustly denied its rightful place in the American dream, like the other groups (African Americans, women) whose struggles have gone before. The leader of the largest gay and lesbian rights group in the United States explicitly locates the quest for gay and lesbian rights as another stepping-stone in the long, venerable tradition of the civil rights struggles: "And in 1995, 150 years after the fact, the Southern Baptist Convention—the same institution that has now condemned gays—repented for defending slavery and condoning racism. I believe and we believe at the Human Rights Campaign, it is how we work, that someday they will repent their homophobia. Not soon, but we are a patient people."[14] On its face, then, if the insights of queer theory were to be seriously integrated into the reasoning of the rights advocates of sexual minorities, those advocates would find themselves facing something of a quandary: how to articulate a rights claim on behalf of an identity that is, in fact, radically contingent—an illusion, a fiction, or at best, an only occasionally coherent narrative.

Some of the implications of a marriage between queer theory and the civil rights strategies of sexual minorities are tellingly revealed in an examination of the very different treatment of transgenderism in those discourses. The practices of transsexuality and transgenderism have played a central role in queer theorists' readings of the destabilizing effects of cultural contestations of gender categories, as Ki Namaste points out:

In recent years, the field known as queer theory has witnessed a veritable explosion of essays, presentations, and books on the subjects of drag, gender, performance, and transsexuality. Yet these works have shown very little concern for those who identify and live as drag queens, transsexuals, and/or transgenders. . . . Why is it that transgendered people are the chosen objects of the field of queer theory, and why does the presentation of these issues ignore the daily realities of transgendered people?[15]

Even queer theorists who do examine the legal construction of proper liberal subjects use the problems that transgender people face when they deal with administrative agencies issuing birth certificates and marriage licenses, family courts denying custody, and police brutalizing trans people to demonstrate the margins, boundaries, and limits of a politics of identity, and fail to attend to the immediate, material violence engendered by the situation. For example, Bower's reading of Karen Ulane's sex-based discrimination lawsuit against Eastern Airlines (she was fired after undergoing sex-change surgery) describes the deconstructive possibilities of "articulating a non-identity": "*Granted* both Ulane and Hardwick 'lost' their cases, but the legal decisions can be interpreted to suggest the instability of sex and sexual identities and the capacity of ambiguous identities to create contestation in the legal field."[16] Yet Ms. Ulane might not—indeed, did not in her Title VII complaint—describe herself as a "non-identity": she described herself as a woman; moreover, she would probably not have put quotation marks around the word "lost" when describing the outcome of her case. Similarly, the first thought to come to the mind of Dee Farmer (a preoperative male-to-female transsexual prisoner who was beaten and raped when placed in a federal penitentiary's male general population) when she found out she lost her Eighth Amendment–based case was probably not that at least her challenge constituted a blow to the hegemonic system of gender classification.[17] Finally, in Missouri, Sharon Boyd, a transsexual woman, lost joint custody of her sons and had her visiting rights severely restricted because, in part, the court did not have "substantial evidence" that the "father's" sex reassignment surgery would have no effect on the children's "moral development."[18] While noting the incoherence embedded in legal regulation of the relationship among genitalia, gender identity, and gender expression, it is also vital that we not lose track of the material consequences of such regulation. As Robert Cover has written, "A judge articulates her understanding of a text, and as a result, somebody loses her freedom, his property, his children, even his life."[19] Transsexual, transgender, and gender-variant people are thus besieged on both sides—by queer theorists' readings of transgender subjectivity, which poses transgender people and their rights claims as interesting only insofar as their very subjectivity works to deconstruct categories, rather than as identity-bearing subjects who might wish to enjoy freedom from state-sponsored violence and discrimination, and, simultaneously, by advocates for lesbian and gay rights who perceive such gender-crossing practices and identities as too radically other, too inauthentic, or too marginal to hegemonic U.S. gender norms to be included in the politics of official recognition that seeks legislative and judicial remedies for identity-based discrimination.[20]

One of the reasons why transsexual and transgender people do not yet have a permanent seat on the freedom train that is the U.S. mainstream lesbian and gay rights movement is that movement's reliance on the identity category of sexual orientation, a term that remains intelligible only if sex and gender remain relatively stable categories.[21] (Gender nonconforming identities and practices, of course, constitute an assault on the naturalized coherence of these categories, *regardless of the intention* of those who engage in gender-variant practices or whose gender identity does not "match" the sex assigned to them at birth.) In fact, some lesbian and gay rights advocates have taken the assumption that sex secures sexual orientation to its logical extreme, arguing that sexual orientation discrimination is best understood as a type of sex discrimination. This strategy is particularly apposite since neither the courts at the federal circuit level nor the Supreme Court has found that sexual orientation constitutes a suspect or quasi-suspect class, and thus has not required that laws discriminating on the basis of sexual orientation be subject to a higher level of judicial scrutiny.[22] Basing the rights claims of lesbians and gay men on a definition of homosexuality as constituted by same-sex object choice at first glance appears to be a solid tactical move, since rights claims need to be articulated in terms that are intelligible to the judiciary. What could be more intelligible than sexual object choice, since that choice is supposedly premised on the biological sex of one's partner, rather than on the sexual practices that the opponents of gay and lesbian rights relish probing? Certainly sex is a category that seems reassuringly solid and knowable—unlike homosexuality itself, which opponents of lesbian and gay rights tend to depict in behavioral terms.

The sexual orientation discrimination as sex discrimination strategy has been articulated very clearly in the Hawaii same-sex marriage case: the challengers of the ban on same-sex marriage there based their most successful judicial claim on an article of Hawaii's constitution prohibiting state-sanctioned discrimination in the exercise of a person's civil rights on the basis of sex. Although the state of Hawaii attempted to argue that the plaintiffs had no rights to "enter into state-licensed homosexual marriages" because as homosexuals they "are neither a suspect nor a quasi-suspect class and do not require heightened judicial solicitude," the majority opinion of Hawaii's Supreme Court noted that "'Homosexual' and 'same-sex' marriages are not synonymous," finding that "it is immaterial whether the plaintiffs . . .

are homosexuals."[23] According to the majority's reasoning, then, it is the sex of the marriage license applicants that is at issue, not their sexual orientation, and absent a compelling state interest, refusing marriages licenses to applicants of the same sex is unconstitutional under the Hawaiian constitution. Such a sex-based approach ends the reliance of gay and lesbian rights advocates on the difficult suspect class argument—which involves trying to prove that homosexuality constitutes an immutable characteristic, rather than merely a behavior or set of practices. Instead, the more discrete, already quasi-suspect category of sex becomes the operative identity in this civil rights claim. Thus it is not the homosexuality of the plaintiffs that is at issue, but rather the sex of their partner. Figured this way, many, though not all,[24] homosexual rights claims boil down to sex. Mark Fajer observes:

> Unlike the suspect class argument, a gender-based equal protection argument avoids the immutability controversy. While immutability is not a litmus test for heightened scrutiny, courts and commentators discussing classifications based on sexual orientation generally seem to rely heavily on it. Many who support heightened scrutiny argue that sexual orientation is immutable; some who reject heightened scrutiny argue it is not. Because mutability is a difficult issue, gay advocates are better off avoiding it if possible. To the extent that the gender-based argument rests on immutability, it is the immutability of gender, not of orientation.[25]

Certainly, the "common sense" knowledge of sex produces a narrative in which biological sex is immutable, is limited to two categories, and is determined by the body—and in which gender, although socially constructed, is produced in a predictable relation to sex. This model posits that the sex assigned to the infant at birth by a doctor's visual check of the genitalia will accurately predict the child's gender identity, or sense of being male or female. As Suzanne Kessler and Wendy McKenna have noted, "Gender attribution is, for the most part, genital attribution."[26] In turn, this model assumes, the child's gender identity will cause the child to begin to organize "his" or "her" behavior to conform to either masculine or feminine patterns of presentation. This developmental milestone is variously described as social sex role, gender behavior, or gender expression.[27] Although a few psychologists are beginning to challenge this model,[28] most do not,[29] and, in the larger social field in which civil rights arguments are made, this model dominates, operating not merely as a description of childhood development but as normative standard of correctness, as how things ought to be arranged. Before homosexuality was removed from the American Psychiatric Association's list of mental disorders in 1973, in the United States this model of sexuality posited a fourth developmental achievement—heterosexuality—which is the culmination of the entire developmental process: infants designated as male will become aware of themselves as boys, learn to act masculine, and develop a heterosexual sexual orientation; infants designated female at birth will learn to label themselves as girls during early childhood, will later present feminine behavior, and will eventually develop a sexual attraction toward the opposite sex.

Opponents of the rights of sexual minorities still adhere to the model that construes heterosexuality as the normative end point of mature human sexuality; conversely, advocates of gay and lesbian rights affirm that heterosexuality, bisexuality, and homosexuality are equally healthy avenues of development. But, as Eve Sedgwick points out in an article titled "How to Bring Your Kids Up Gay," there is a substantive connection, in the minds of homophobes at least, between gender nonconformity and homosexuality. She notes that the elimination of the diagnosis of homosexuality from the American Psychiatric Association's Diagnostic and Statistical Manual in 1973 was followed a few years later with the introduction of a new pathology, "Gender Identity Disorder of Childhood," which pathologizes effeminate boys and overly masculine girls. Thus, homosexuality, defined in terms of same-sex object choice, is uncoupled from the new pathology, which posits that healthy boys and girls exhibit a "Core Gender Identity" consonant with their biological sex. Of course, as Sedgwick observes, "One serious problem with this way of distinguishing between gender and sexuality is that, while denaturalizing sexual-object choice, it radically renaturalizes gender."[30] And the problem with "renaturalizing gender" is that the category of biological sex is fraught with indeterminacy.[31] Apart from visible genitals, other physiological components include hormones, chromosomes, and internal reproductive organs. As Anne Bolin notes, "[T]he more scientific and complex the determinants of biological sex become, the less they can be relied on to indicate gender."[32] A strategy that is based on sex and gender, then, is ultimately unmoored—not only for transgender people, but for nontransgender people as well, since "sex" carries much more cultural freight than it can coherently bear. For example, Sedgwick lists sixteen possible meanings of the term "sexual identity," ranging from "biological sex" to masculinity/femininity to sexual fantasies to cultural or political identification.[33] And, as Steven Seidman has noted, the equation of sexual identity with sexual orientation means that a "vast range of desires, acts, and social relations [such as same-sex S/M, interracial, intergenerational, or commercial sex] are never made into an object of theory and politics."[34]

If sexual orientation is defined by sexual object choice, are equal rights claims based on sexual orientation implicitly premised on the continuation of the binary sex classification system? If so, what are the consequences, not just for lesbians and gay men but also for bisexual, transgendered, and transsexual people, of linking the rights claims of sexual minorities to particular constructions of the relation among sex, gender identity, gender expression, and sexual object choice? I want to suggest that arguments for gay, lesbian, and bisexual civil rights must challenge not only discrimination based on sex and sexual orientation, but also the legal construction of the relationship among sex, gender identity, and gender expression that inheres in the definition of sexual orientation. The end of state-sponsored discrimination on the basis of sexual orientation is unquestionably an important goal. But so is ending the juridical power of the state to enforce any particular definition of sex, gender identity, or sexual orientation. In an article published in 1979, Mary Dunlap made these connections explicitly, arguing that there is a "commonality" among women, homosexuals, mothers of illegitimate children, and sexually reassigned persons "who have suffered from the power of the law to prescribe sex identity, and, correlatively, to enforce sex roles in all areas of life." She concluded, "If the individual's authority to define sex identity were to replace the authority of law to impose sex identity, many of the most difficult problems currently associated with the power of government to probe, penalize, and restrict basic freedoms of sexual minorities would be resolved."[35] While gay and lesbian rights advocates pursue the worthy goal of putting an end to particular kinds of state-sponsored discrimination against sexual minorities, the more radical project of dismantling the state's monopoly of authority to define the relation between sex and gender has sometimes been obscured.[36] Moreover, if the rights claims of lesbian and gay people rely on the deployment of arguments, either implicit or explicit, that reinforce hegemonic U.S. gender norms, including the notion that there is a predictable, normative relationship among visible genitals, gender identity, and gender expression, any ensuing victory might turn out to be something of a pyrrhic one, not only for members of transgender and gender-variant communities but even for those lesbian, bisexual, and gay people who are not transgendered or gender variant. (It is important to note that use of the term "gender" rather than "sex" by gay and lesbian rights advocates does not necessarily indicate an expansive understanding of the term, one that incorporates the more complex and theoretically precise concepts of gender identity and gender expression. Arguing that laws prohibiting same-sex marriages are a form of gender discrimination is a far cry from arguing that discrimination against gender-variant people and practices, such as effeminate men, masculine women, cross-dressers, transvestites, and transsexuals, is also a type of gender discrimination.)

While the recent freedom-to-marry challenge engineered by mainstream lesbian and gay rights advocates is apparently articulated in terms of essentialist notions of sex and gender, it is important to recognize that legal advocates of transsexuals had already been defending "same-sex" marriages for some time.[37] In fact, in some jurisdictions, "same-sex" marriage is already legal, or, more precisely, many states have been unable to regulate very successfully marriages between those whose sexual identity, gender identity, and even sexual orientation confounds the predictable relationship assumed to exist among sex, gender identity, and sexual orientation schema presupposed by many individual state statutes and case law. For example, when Lori Buckwalter, a male-to-female transsexual who had been taking hormones for about a year, announced that she was going to marry her female lover before officially requesting a certificate indicating her sex had been changed, she was also announcing the first public marriage of a "homosexual" couple in Oregon. This officially sanctioned homosexual marriage resulted from the disjunction between her gender identity and the law's assignment of her gender. In Ms. Buckwalter's eyes, as a woman who marries the object of her desire, another woman, the marriage is a homosexual one. At the moment of the marriage, however, the legal categories defined Ms. Buckwalter as a male; therefore the marriage—while a same-gender one—is nevertheless sanctioned by the state as an opposite-sex marriage. When Ms. Buckwalter formally had her gender identity changed, however, an Oregon regulatory agency officially recognized her as a woman, and she was already married to another woman—thus resulting in a legal same-sex marriage. Ms. Buckwalter was able to take advantage of the incoherence of the state's marriage laws—that designate marriage as a union between a man and a woman, and attribute gender based on visible genital sexual characteristics—and marry her lover, a woman, before her sex-reassignment surgery. Of course, since her gender identity, and that of her partner, is female, she already had a same-gender marriage before undergoing sex-reassignment surgery.

These marriage plans reveal the contradictions inherent in legislating what is supposedly natural, organic, and immutable—both the perfect correspondence between the anatomical sex given at birth and gender identity, *and* the universality and normativity of opposite-sex desire. Her plan to marry *before* undergoing surgery confounds any attempt to define and contain the relations among gender identity, anatomical sex, sexual orientation, and sexuality within the particular marriage law of the state she lives in. In Oregon, marriage is entered into by "a male" and "a female."[38] Oregon's laws on the official designation of gender mark surgery as the moment that sex reassignment is completed, as the moment of transition from male to female, in this particular case.[39] Oregon's case law on defining sex, however, is not the final word on that subject since, for the purpose of marriage, the power to define sex is left to the individual states—a power the Defense of Marriage Act does not undermine.[40] As the late transgender legal rights advocate Dee McKellar pointed out, some contradictions arise in comparing statutes and case law across states:

> In Ohio, which will not correct a birth certificate, a post-op TS can marry someone with similar genitals. In Oregon, a pre-op TS can marry someone with com-

plementary genitals. In Texas, a non-op with court-ordered gender correction can marry a person with similar genitals by showing a driver's license, or can show a passport and marry someone with complementary genitals.[41]

Generally the most important instrument for the purposes of marriage is one's birth certificate. Currently, only fifteen states allow postoperative transsexuals to change their birth certificates. Individual states have different statutes and case law on amending birth certificates, resulting in the patchwork of predicaments described above. Some states, such as Arizona, have statutes that allow for the issuance of new birth certificates, while others, such as Colorado, have statutes that allow for the amendment of the original birth certificates.[42] Conversely other states, such as Tennessee, have statutes explicitly prohibiting the retroactive changing of birth certificates[43] or, as in the case of Ohio and Oregon, have case law prohibiting the legal recognition of sex changes.[44] Since the state of Ohio will not allow the legal designation of sex to come into congruence with an individual's sex-reassignment surgery, it is perfectly possible for either a preoperative or a postoperative transsexual woman from Ohio to marry another woman there; but conversely, it is not possible for a postoperative transsexual woman to marry a man in that state.[45] And in Oregon, because that state refused to recognize Lori Buckwalter's female gender identity, Ms. Buckwalter was able to marry her woman lover before she underwent sex-reassignment surgery.[46]

The ontological chaos of the laws on marriage, sex, and gender identity is made even clearer by the response of those opposing this marriage. Upon hearing about Ms. Buckwalter's marriage plans, Lon Mabon, the leader of Oregon Citizens Alliance, announced he would immediately begin organizing a voter referendum that would define marriage as a strictly heterosexual institution and gender as something determined at conception. "It stops this playing around with Mother Nature," Mabon said.[47] Not only does Mabon want to enshrine forever the relation between gender identity and anatomy, he also wishes to define the moment when that relationship is secured, at conception, no less, which would make it impossible for transsexuals to change their gender identity legally to match sex-reassignment therapy or surgery. Recently, an appellate court in Texas affirmed this view when it upheld a lower court's decision to throw out a wrongful death lawsuit made by a postoperative transsexual woman against the doctor whom she believed was responsible for the death of her husband. The reasoning of the court: the marriage between the plaintiff Christine Littleton and her husband was a same-sex marriage and therefore invalid under Texas law because the "male chromosomes do not change with either hormonal treatment or sex reassignment surgery. . . . Biologically, a post-operative female is still a male." The panel in this case found that there were "no significant facts to be decided," only "a pure question of law" to be decided by the court.[48] Similarly, the U.S. Christian right's attempt to defend traditional Western notions about the relation between genitals and gender identity by putting the relation between gender identity and anatomy up to a vote concedes the fundamentally political basis of the identity classificatory scheme. So while the Christian right attempts to legislate (literally) notions about the correct relation between anatomy and gender, Ms. Buckwalter and her supporters enunciate her rights claims in the language of classical Millian liberalism: "[I]t's her life and she can do what she likes," her son reasons; "[I]t allows me to be who I am" and "others' judgment of you shouldn't stop you," Ms. Buckwalter argues.[49] In defense of both her transition and her and her partner's wish to be the first homosexual couple in Oregon to be officially married, Ms. Buckwalter invokes a coherent, immanently rational constellation of conventions, one that resonates strongly with U.S. political vernacular—the language of liberal, individualist rights. She and her family deny her community any right to legislate her gender identity.

Of course, gender transitivity is not the only problem that the Oregon Citizens Alliance sees in this pre-op transsexual marriage. Mabon and other opponents of same-sex marriage claim that the people of Oregon must never officially sanction same-sex marriage for the simple reason that these unions would strike a death blow to the core values of Western culture. The problem, quite simply, is that culture, or at least what is best about "our" culture, would not be reproduced if same-sex marriages were to become legal. For example, a congressman supporting the Defense of Marriage Act (DOMA) argued:

> We live in a free country . . . precisely because we have standards, because our society has successfully socialized most Americans in the values of love, charity, and tolerance; and the institution on which we depend to socialize these values is the institution of marriage. Those who oppose [DOMA] are either seeking no standards or a standard vastly different from that sanctioned by millennia of tradition, the teachings of all the monotheistic religions, and in particular, the teachings of Judeo-Christian religion on which our culture is based.[50]

Indeed, reproduction figures as a recurring motif in these discussions against "gay marriage." Many opponents of same-sex marriage do understand that gender, or, more precisely, gender identity, is not literally reproduced through the body, but through cultural mechanisms. It is because the link between assigned biological sex and gender identity and expression is not secured by "nature" that they are so vociferously in favor of securing that link by law—despite the discursive and physical violence that such state intervention entails.

How exactly is it that same-sex marriage would fail to transmit the cultural heritages of American culture? According to the arguments put forward by the opponents of same-sex marriage, it is by failing to raise children with a firm sense of the "correct" gender identity—one that conforms to the gender assigned to them on the basis of their genitalia—that same-sex marriages would fail to reproduce what is good about (hegemonic) American culture. Thus, one of the arguments put forward by opponents of same-sex marriage in Hawaii addresses the gender identity of the children raised in same-sex households. For example, the minority members of the Hawaii's Commission on Sexual Orientation and the Law (arguing against same-sex marriage) cite testimony asserting,

> One of the most fundamental functions of parenting is to evoke, develop, and reinforce gender identity and then proceed to shepherd the developing child in such a way as to bring his psychological side into harmony with his biological side, and thereby develop a solid sense of maleness or femaleness. . . . [A] child should be brought up with a mother and a father, in order to develop appropriate gender-defined self identity. . . . We must fight back against the social movements which are destructive to our ways of life. . . . This means, above all, preventing the passage of laws which ignore the differences between a male and a female, and which undermine the security and stability of the family and the nation.[51]

In these debates, it is assumed that the institution of heterosexual marriage functions to reproduce traditional gender roles, arrangements, and identities. To prove this claim, opponents of same-sex marriage cite evidence that purports to show that children raised in same-sex households have difficulty developing a gender identity consonant with their assigned gender. It is important to note that in these discussions of children—in same-sex marriages as well as in adoption and custody case law—it is not merely the potential of the children raised in such households to become homosexual that is explicitly under discussion; in addition, the development of the children's gender identity is also questioned, often even more explicitly. But, as Shannon Minter has pointed out, gender-identity problems in youth are invariably yoked to the specter of homosexuality, or "pre-homosexual conditions."[52]

Certainly, the ideologues of the Christian right work hard to associate the gender identity disorder with homosexuality. For example, Robert Knight, of the Family Research Council, argues that "children really do need a mother and a father. A little boy needs to have a mother for that mother love, and to have his growing masculinity affirmed, and to watch both parents interact and see how men should treat women, women should treat men, how they both treat each other as husbands and wives, mothers and fathers, and their relationship with their children."[53] For Knight, inculcating heterosexuality goes part and parcel with establishing a gender identity that conforms to gender norms—learning masculinity, for example, is also learning heterosexuality. So gender normativity—the belief that gender ought to be organized according to traditional and firmly established gender identities, practices, and arrangements—assumes heteronormativity.

Since the crux of the argument against same-sex marriage lies in the linkage of heteronormativity with gender normativity, of gender identity with sexual orientation, gay and lesbian advocates for same-sex marriage have sometimes responded by reasserting the distinction, citing evidence to prove, first, that children raised by same-sex couples or by single lesbians or gay men are no more likely to become gay or lesbian than children raised in opposite-sex households, and second, that the gender identity of children raised in such households is no "less normal" than that of children raised in opposite-sex households. However, basing arguments for same-sex marriage, custody, and adoption on data that suggest that children raised in lesbian and gay households are no "less normal" than children raised in heterosexual households—in terms of their gender identity and sexual orientation—means that the heteronormative aspects of the institution of marriage are challenged by resorting to an argument that suggests that the production of gay, lesbian, bisexual, or transgender children in a same-sex household would be a bad thing. Such an argument ultimately does little to undermine seriously either the heteronormativity or the gender norms upon which arguments about the reproduction of American greatness rest.

The separation of sexual orientation from gender variance, transgenderism, and transsexualism reinforces the idea that gender identity has a stable and predictable relation to the gender assigned at birth on inspection of the visible genitals, which ought not to be changed. We can see now that this disjunction between sexual orientation and gender nonconformity is premised on the idea that gays and lesbians are defined by same-sex desire, which in turn is premised on the notion that sex and gender identity are static, fixed, intransitive. In the case of gays and lesbians, then, one is the same as one's object of desire. But what exactly is it that is the same? Visible genitals? Internal reproductive organs? Chromosomes? Hormones? Or gender identity? And what if one is not the same as one's lover? No doubt basing rights claims on a definition of sexual orientation as constituted by same-sex object choice has the advantage of analytical clarity. But that analytical clarity loses its usefulness when it is forced to apply to particular histories, practices, cultures, and social formations—to the lived experiences of sexual minorities, in short. As the work produced in queer history has pointed out, particular historical configurations around sex, gender-identity expression, and sexuality cannot be contained by an invocation of ahistorical categories that do not take the variability of forms of gender expression into account. For example, in his study of gay life in New York in the first half of this century, George Chauncey points out:

[I]n important respects the hetero-homosexual binarism, the sexual regime now hegemonic in American culture, is a stunningly recent creation. Particularly in working-class culture, homosexual behavior per se became the primary basis for the labeling and self-identification of men as "queer" only around the middle of the twentieth century; before then, most men were so labeled only if they displayed a much broader inversion of their ascribed gender status by assuming the sexual and cultural roles ascribed to women.[54]

There are—and have been—many queer communities and cultures that do engage in practices that undermine traditional gender norms, that do constitute a kind of queerness that is not at all described by the notion of same-sex desire. When the mainstream gay and lesbian rights community's strategies for equality leave intact the legal gender taxonomy created through the regulation of the "correct" relation between genitals and gender identity (via state courts and administrative agencies), the result is a narrow victory: the analytical category of sexual orientation is kept pure at the expense of those whose chromosomes, anatomy, gender identity, and gender expression are not linked according to the mandates of the normative taxonomy, a taxonomy backed by force of law.

While "homosexuality" in particular and sexual orientation in general, defined abstractly as constituted by sexual object choice, has been an important conceptual tool in furthering the rights claims of gay men and lesbians in the heyday of the new social movements and the ascendancy of identity politics, perhaps it is time to reconsider how extensively it is invoked to further the civil rights strategies of increasingly divergent sets of identities, practices, orientations, and to recognize how deeply implicated the concept of homosexuality is in reinscribing the hegemonic sex/gender system. It may be that it is too blunt an instrument for it to further the interests of all gender-transitive, or transgender, constituencies, or any minority group constituted by virtue of its members' sexuality.

This clash of constituencies between mainstream lesbian and gay rights advocates and the gender community—the debate over including transsexuals and transgender people in the proposed federal Equality Non-Discrimination Act is one example—is not as clear-cut as many assume. One constituency, queer and transgender youth, blurs this distinction.[55] While gay and lesbian rights advocates fight for equal rights, children and adolescents exhibiting gender-variant behavior can be pathologized, treated, and in some cases institutionalized for gender-identity disorder to cure them of their pre-homosexual *or* pre-transsexual conditions. One of the leading proponents of the treatment of gender identity disorder in childhood, George Rekers, made this connection quite clearly at a recent conservative conference on homosexuality, according to a reporter covering the event:

> Rekers said lesbians tend to be tomboys in childhood, identify too closely with their fathers, prefer to play with "masculine" toys and demonstrate a "distinct dislike for doll play and various other female activities." Male homosexuals, Rekers said, "report the opposite pattern," preferring the company of girls and

wanting to wear lipstick and dresses. Rekers characterized both behaviors as "gender disturbances" that can be corrected through 18 to 22 months of weekly therapy during childhood and adolescence.[56]

To return to the reproduction of sex, sexual orientation, and gender transitivity, the disavowal of any connection between sexual orientation and gender nonconformity by many lesbian, bisexual, and gay rights advocates has its consequences. While it is certainly true that gender-variant behavior is not primarily reproduced in the family, as the Christian right and other opponents of same-sex marriage assert, it does have to get reproduced somewhere. Launching arguments that reinforce gender norms into that discursive space of the media, broadly construed —which is the actual battleground for the rights claims of gender minorities—plays into the ongoing conservative assaults on minority gender-transitive traditions. Instead, we need to give sustenance to gender-variant traditions, to preserve them, to make sure they get reproduced, not play into the larger ideological erasure of them. We need to contest rather than support ideologies that assert that queer, gay, lesbian, bisexual, questioning, and transgender kids are pathological and that ultimately reinforce heteronormative notions.[57] Putting too much time and energy into making arguments that are implicitly premised on the dominant gender norms (and their relationship to anatomy) merely because they are intelligible in terms of the disciplining powers of the school, the psychiatrist's office, and the family court means that we ignore the larger project of transforming just what is intelligible.

Suggesting that sexual orientation and gender nonconformity are entirely separate issues skirts the problem: the right wing, much of the "general public," and many members of the judiciary do see a link between sexual orientation and gender nonconformity. Moreover, lesbians and gay men, even gender-conforming lesbians and gay men, do suffer material consequences from that link, most notably in cases involving child custody. For example, in Illinois, a court restricted a lesbian mother's visitation with her son, finding that the child has a "gender identity problem" and that "there is no strong evidence . . . that the [lesbian mother] will be more discreet in terms of her exposition of her gay lifestyle in the child's presence, and notwithstanding the child's gender identification problem, which she learned in 1987, [she] took the child to a gay-lesbian parade," where he observed, among other things, male cross-dressers.[58] In Louisiana, a lesbian mother lost joint custody because of concerns about gender identity. The court concluded that "where the sexual preference is known and openly admitted, where there have been open, indiscreet displays of affection beyond mere friendship and where the child is of an age where gender identity is being formed, the joint custody arrangement should award greater custodial time to the father."[59] In New Jersey, an appellate court permitted a second-parent adoption by the same-sex partner of the natural mother, noting with approval that "[e]ach child has a bedroom beautifully decorated in appropriate childhood motifs with M. having a feminine design and Z. a masculine design" and that "[b]oth parents want the children to have good self-esteem and a good sense of gender identity."[60]

Finally, there is the case of Mary Ward, in which a lesbian lost custody of her child to an ex-husband who had been convicted of murdering a previous wife. The trial judge did not rule that Mary Ward's sexual orientation per se meant she would lose custody, but rather considered the effects on the child's living in such a household. However, one of the "facts" that figured largely in the trial court's decision against Ward was that her eleven-year-old daughter, living in a lesbian household, was forgoing age-appropriate behavior such as wearing women's perfume and "preferred instead to wear men's cologne."[61] There may not have been any causal relationship between Ward's same-sex desire and her daughter's supposed gender nonconformity. But the appropriate response of gay and lesbian rights advocates to such a determination is not to reassert a distinction between sexual orientation and gender nonconformity, but to challenge the very notion that there is something wrong with "girls" who act like "boys," with children assigned at birth as female who identify as boys, or with children who want to change their sex. In challenging the sex-based classifications embedded in so much discrimination against gays, lesbians, bisexual, and transgender people, it is vital that we get to the root of the problem and challenge the very premises of the classification system itself, rather than suppose for strategic purposes that these classifications—sex, gender, masculinity, femininity—are anterior to politics.

Moreover, any analysis of identity-based discrimination that is part of an anti-homophobic political project must necessarily be twofold: first, such an analysis must examine the unjust political, social, and economic effects that the identitarian categories themselves engender; and second, the analysis must interrogate the actual production of identitarian categories, including in that interrogation the contingent events, histories, and geographies surrounding those productions, as well as the contradictions and incongruities that inhere in bounding the self from others. Kimberle Crenshaw notes that the same dual approach to identity categorizations can be applied to any antidiscrimination claim: Is the discrimination unconstitutional because the classification is, ultimately, groundless, or because the classification unfairly harms or subordinates a particular group? Analyses of identity-based rights claims often attend more to one aspect of this dual approach than to the other. Extending her analysis of the erasure of black women's narratives from antiracist and antisexist discourses, Crenshaw, for example, argues that an approach that focuses on the effects a system of subordination has on oppressed identity groups may ultimately be more politically empowering: "At this point in history, a strong case can be made that the most critical resistance strategy for disempowered groups is to occupy and defend a politics of social location rather than to vacate and destroy it."[62] The appropriation of queer theory's useful theoretical insights by advocates of gay rights and the rights of sexual minorities requires maintaining a delicate balance between the politics of location and the politics of deconstruction. Thus, it is essential that the relation between identity politics and identity practices be reimagined in order to include practices that do not neatly line up with an identity category recognized in the U.S. rights tradition; to push the bounds of the interpellatory practices of the liberal state and the language of liberal jurisprudence, rather than reject the attempt to enunciate equal protection claims altogether; and, finally, to remain intelligible within a system of gender- and sexuality-based oppression in which populations recognize themselves as individuals yet are controlled through the production of classifications that iterate it rather than enable human freedom.

Notes

This work would not have been possible without the intellectual and political community provided by Monica Barrett, Jennifer Levi, Shannon Minter, and Elizabeth Seaton. I am also indebted to Ellen Andersen, Mark Blasius, Shane Phelan, Jacqueline Stevens, and Martha Umphrey for their comments on earlier versions of this article. This article grew out of my participation in an annual symposium of the *Hastings Law Journal* and was written with the support of the PSC-CUNY Research Award from the Research Foundation of the City University of New York.

1. On February 4, 1997, "the nation's largest gay and lesbian political organization [Human Rights Campaign] and the nation's largest gay faith-based movement [the Universal Fellowship of Metropolitan Community Churches] announced plans today to sponsor a march on Washington in the spring of the year 2000." See HRC press release, "Millennium March on Washington for Equal Rights Announced by National Gay Organizations," February 4, 1997.

2. The terminology used in this article shifts depending on the constituencies, practices, or social movements under discussion. For example, since the largest and most powerful lesbian and gay rights organizations do not include bisexual people in their mission statements (Lambda Legal Defense in the legal arena and HRC in the legislative arena), it would be inaccurate to use "bisexual" to describe the constituencies imagined by these advocates. The term "sexual minorities" is the author's default term for inclusive movements, ones that seek to further the rights of gay, lesbian, bisexual, transgender, transsexual, queer, two-spirited, and intersexed people and practices.

3. Other queer legal theorists have effectively proposed that the civil rights strategies of sexual minorities be informed by queer theory. For a representative sample, see Lisa Bower, "Queer Problems/Straight Solutions," in *Playing with Fire: Queer Politics, Queer Theory*, ed. Shane Phelan (New York: Routledge, 1997) 267–91; Janet Halley,

"The Construction of Heterosexuality," in *Fear of a Queer Planet*, ed. Michael Warner (Minneapolis: University of Minnesota Press, 1993) 82–102; and Carl Stychin, *Law's Desire* (New York: Routledge, 1995).

4. Lauren Berlant and Michael Warner point out that "Queer theory has flourished in the disciplines where expert service to the state has been least familiar and where theory has consequently meant unsettlement rather than systemization." Berlant and Warner, "What Does Queer Theory Teach Us about X?" *PMLA* 110 (1995): 348.

5. Some of the "foundational" texts of queer theory include all volumes of Michel Foucault's *History of Sexuality* (New York: Random House, 1978), Judith Butler's *Gender Trouble* (New York: Routledge, 1990) and *Bodies That Matter* (New York: Routledge, 1993), and Eve Sedgwick's, *Epistemology of the Closet* (Berkeley: University of California Press, 1990). For a sophisticated introduction to queer theory, and some of its implications, see Anna Marie Jagose, *Queer Theory: An Introduction* (New York: New York University Press, 1990).

6. Butler, *Gender Trouble*, 33.

7. Steven A. Schwalm, "Kinsey, Kids, and 'Gay' Sex: Why Schools Are Teaching Your Kids about Homosexuality" (http://www.frc.org:80/podium/pd98i1hs.html), December 1998. For an extended discussion of the similarity between these accounts, see Paisley Currah, "Politics, Practices, Publics," in *Playing with Fire: Queer Politics, Queer Theories*, ed. Shane Phelan (New York: Routledge, 1997), 231–66.

8. See Didi Herman, *The Antigay Agenda* (Chicago: University of Chicago Press, 1997).

9. See Paisley Currah, "Searching for Immutability: Homosexuality, Race, and Rights Discourse," in *A Simple Matter Of Justice*, ed. Angelia R. Wilson (London: Cassell, 1995), 51–90.

10. Eve Kosofsky Sedgwick, *Tendencies* (Durham: Duke University Press, 1993), 9.

11. Michael Warner, introduction, to *Fear of a Queer Planet*, ed. Michael Warner (Minneapolis: University of Minnesota Press, 1993), xvii.

12. Lisa Bower, "Queer Problems/Straight Solutions," in *Playing with Fire: Queer Politics, Queer Theories*, ed. Shane Phelan (New York: Routledge, 1997), 268–69.

13. Ibid., 268.

14. Elizabeth Birch, speech at the Human Rights Campaign's Second Annual Dinner on September 19, 1998, and excerpted in *HRC Quarterly* (Fall 1998), 14.

15. Ki Namaste, "'Tragic Misreadings': Queer Theory's Erasure of Transgender Subjectivity," in *Queer Studies*, ed. Brett Beemyn and Mickey Eliason (New York: New York University Press, 1996), 183–84. See also, e.g., Marjorie Garber, *Vested Interests: Cross-Dressing and Cultural Anxiety* (New York: Routledge, 1992); and Carole-Anne Tyler, "Boys Will Be Girls: The Politics of Gay Drag," in *Inside/Out: Lesbian Theories, Gay Theories*, ed. Diana Fuss (New York: Routledge, 1991), 32–70.

16. Bower, "Queer Problems/Straight Solutions," 285 (emphasis mine).

17. *Farmer v. Brennan*, 114 S.Ct. 1970 (1994).

18. *J.L.S. v. D.K.S., n/k/a/ S.D.S.*, 943 S.W. 2d 766 (Court of Appeals of Missouri, Eastern District, Division Four) (March 11, 1997).

19. Robert Cover, "Violence and the Word," *Yale Law Journal* 95 (1986): 1601.

20. The Employment Non-Discrimination Act of 1997, S. 869, 105th Cong., 1st sess., section 3: "The term 'sexual orientation' means homosexuality, bisexuality, or heterosexuality, whether such orientation is real or perceived."

With the exception of the state of Minnesota, it is only on the local level that legislation that would protect transgender and transsexual people and practices has been proposed, and in twenty-nine municipalities, such legislation has passed. For example, an Iowa City ordinance, passed in October 1995, defines gender identity as: "A person's various individual attributes, actual or perceived, in behavior, practice or appearance, as they are understood to be masculine and/or feminine" (Ordinance No. 95–3697, Ordinance Amending Title 2: "Human Rights," City Code). See Paisley Currah and Shannon Minter, *Transgender Equality: A Handbook of Activists and Policy-makers* (New York: National Center for Lesbian Rights and Policy Institute of the National Lesbian and Gay Task Force, 2000). See also Paisley Currah and Shannon Minter, "Unprincipled Exclusions: The Struggle for Legislative and Judicial Protections for Transgendered People," *William and Mary Journal of Women and the Law* 6 (2000).

21. In celebrating transgressive sexualities and social formations, queer theorizing also runs the risk of becoming too heavily invested in the continued existence of gender normativity itself. In an article titled "Sexualities without Genders and Other Queer Utopias," Biddy Martin has shown how some queer theory actually premises the instability and the deconstructive potential of the homo/heterosexual binarism on the presumed stability of gender distinctions. See Martin, *Femininity Played Straight* (New York: Routledge, 1996), 71–96.

22. See, e.g., Marc A. Fajer, "Can Two Real Men Eat Quiche Together? Storytelling, Gender-Role Stereotypes, and Legal Protection for Lesbians and Gay Men," *University of Miami Law Review* 46 (1992): 511; Andrew Koppelman, "Why Discrimination against Lesbians and Gay Men Is Sex Discrimination," *New York University Law Review* 69 (1994): 197; Sylvia Law, "Homosexuality and the Social Meaning of Gender," *Wisconsin Law Review* 187 (1988): 187; Cass Sunstein, "Homosexuality and the Constitution," *Indiana Law Journal* 70 (1994): 1–28. For a critique of Sunstein's argument for same-sex marriage, see Morris B. Kaplan, *Sexual Justice* (New York: Routledge, 1997), 225–26.

23. *Baehr v. Lewin*, 852 P.2d 44, 51, 52, n. 11, n. 17 (Hawaii Supreme Court, May 5, 1993).

24. There are some exceptions, including discrimination in employment related to gender presentation, expression, or role. See *Price Waterhouse v. Hopkins*, 490 US 228 (1989) and Mary Ann Case, "Disaggregating Sex from Gender," *Yale Law Journal* 105 (1995): 1.

25. Fajer, "Can Two Real Men Eat Quiche Together," 647.

26. Suzanne Kessler and Wendy McKenna, *Gender: An Ethnomethodological Approach* (Chicago: University of Chicago Press, 1978), 11.

27. For a review of the psychological literature on gender identity, see Deborah E. S. Frable, "Gender, Racial, Ethnic, Sexual, and Class Identities," *Annual Review of Psychology* 48 (January 1, 1997): 139. As Anne Bolin suggests, transsexuals skew the entire determinist schematic: "As a social identity, transsexualism posits the analytic independence of the four gender markers—sex, gender identity, gender role or social identity (including behaviors and appearance) and sexual orientation—that are embedded in the Western gender schema as taken-for-granted premises and regarded in a number of scientific discourses as 'naturally' linked." Bolin, "Transcending and Transgendering," in *Third Sex, Third Gender*, ed. Gilbert Herdt (New York: Zone Books, 1994), 459.

28. Most notably Sandra Bem, *The Lenses of Gender* (New Haven: Yale University Press, 1993).

29. As Shannon Minter has pointed out, the psychiatric diagnosis of Gender Identity Disorder (GID) has provided needed cover to psychologists and psychiatrists to treat pre-homosexual, or pre-transsexual children; indeed, he notes, "the great majority of children treated for GID grow up to be lesbian, gay, or bisexual." Minter, "Diagnosis and Treatment of Gender Identity Disorder in Children," in *Sissies & Tomboys: Gender Nonconformity in Homosexual Childhood*, ed. Matthew Rottnek (New York: New York University Press, 1999), 9–34. See also Katherine K. Wilson, "Myth, Stereotype, and Cross-Gender Identity in the DSM-IV," available on the Internet at http://www.transgender.org/tg/gic/awptext.html. See also the National Gay and Lesbian Task Force, "Statement on Gender Identity Disorder and Transgender People," December 11, 1996, http://www.ngltf.org/press/GID.html.

30. Eve Kosofsky Sedgwick, "How to Bring Your Kids Up Gay," in *Fear of a Queer Planet*, ed. Michael Warner (Minneapolis: University of Minnesota Press, 1993), 73.

31. Anna Fausto-Sterling, *Myths of Gender* (New York: Basic Books, 1992).

32. Bolin, "Transcending and Transgendering," 453.

33. Eve Kosofsky Sedgwick, *Tendencies* (Durham: Duke University Press, 1993), 7. The most comprehensive overview thus far of legal attempts to define sex is Julie A. Greenberg's "Defining Male and Female: Intersexuality and the Collision between Law and Biology," *Arizona Law Review* 41 (1999): 265. For a discussion of much of the contradictory case law on sex and gender identity, including cases involving transsexuals, see Katherine M. Franke, "The Central Mistake of Sex Discrimination Law: The Disaggregation of Sex from Gender," *University of Pennsylvania Law Review* 144 (1995): 1. For a detailed examination of the "conflation" between sex, gender, and sexual orientation, see Francisco Valdes, "Queers, Sissies, Dykes, and Tomboys," *California Law Review* 83 (1995): 1. See also Mary Ann Case's discussion of Title VII and effeminate men in "Disaggregating Sex from Gender."

34. Steven Seidman, "Deconstructing Queer Theory," in *Social Postmodernism*, ed. Linda Nicholson and Steven Seidman (Cambridge: Cambridge University Press, 1995), 127.

35. Mary Dunlap, "The Constitutional Rights of Sexual Minorities," *Hastings Law Journal* 30 (1979): 1147–48.

36. John D'Emilio identifies the emergence of identity politics in the 1970s, which became "the organizing framework for oppression and . . . the basis for collective mobilization," as partly responsible for the foundering of the more radical aspects of the gay liberation movement in the United States, which originally sought to challenge the very categories upon which gay oppression was based. D'Emilio, *Making Trouble* (New York: Routledge, 1992), 245.

37. Most notably, Phyllis Frye, a founder of the International Conference on Transgender Law and Employment Policy.

38. 1995 Oregon Revised Statutes, Title II, chapter 106.

39. Oregon state law provides that: "A court that has jurisdiction to determine an application for a change of name of person under ORS 33.410 and 33.420 may order a legal change of sex and grant a certificate indicating the change of sex to a person whose sex has been changed by surgical procedure." Oregon Revised Statutes, Title 3, chapter 33, 33.460. The Oregon Supreme Court, however, has held that birth certifi-

cates cannot be changed for persons who have completed their sex reassignment. *K. v. Health Division* 277 Ore. 371 (1977).

40. The Defense of Marriage Act declares that no state "shall be required to give effect to any public act, record, or judicial proceeding of any other State, territory, possession, or tribe respecting a relationship between persons of the same sex that is treated as a marriage under the laws of such other States." U.S. Code, Title 28, chapter 115, section 1738c. The Defense of Marriage Act did not, however, attempt to define sex.

41. Dee McKellar, "Legal Status." Moreover, the medical establishment's emphasis on the completion of sex-reassignment surgery as the moment of transition from one sex to another poses particular problems for female-to-male transsexuals, who are much less likely to undergo "bottom" surgery than male-to-female transsexuals.

42. Shannon Minter, "Transgendered Parents' Legal Guide to Child Custody" (San Francisco: National Center for Lesbian Rights, 1997).

43. Tennessee Code Annotated, Title 68, chapter 3, section 303: "The sex of an individual will not be changed on the original certificate of birth as a result of sex change surgery."

44. *K. v. Health Division*. An Ohio court, ruling on "whether a post-operative male-to-female transsexual is permitted under Ohio law to marry a male," found that, "There was no evidence that [Elaine Ladrach] at birth had any physical characteristics other than those of a male and he was thus correctly designated 'Boy' on his birth certificate. There was also no laboratory documentation that the applicant had other than male chromosomes." *In re* Declaratory Relief for Ladrach, 513 N.E.2d 828 (1987). See also the English case, *Corbett v. Corbett* (P.D.A. 1970), 2 W.L.R. 1306, in which a judge ruled that the assignment of gender at birth becomes the person's "true sex" that sex-reassignment surgery cannot change.

45. See Patrick O'Donnell, "He Plans to Become a Woman Shortly after Marriage," *The Houston Chronicle*, October 6, 1986, p. 7, describing Denise Smith's plan to marry her fiancée Debi Easterday and then begin a male-to-female sex-change procedure.

46. For another discussion of transsexual marriages, see Mary Coomb, "Trans-genderism and Sexual Orientation: More Than a Marriage of Covenience," *National Journal of Sexual Orientation Law* 3 (1997) (http://metalab.unc.edu/gaylaw/issue5/coombs.html).

47. "Oregon Couple Adds Twist to Love Story," *The Associated Press*, Portland, December 14, 1996.

48. *Littleton v. Prange*, 1999 Westlaw 972986 (October 27, 1999).

49. "Oregon Couple Adds Twist to Love Story."

50. House of Representatives, Hon. James M. Talent of Missouri, 141 *Congressional Record* (Tuesday, July 23, 1996) 1346.

51. Minority Opinion, State of Hawaii Report of the Commission on Sexual Orientation and the Law, December 1995, chapter 5, part 1, p. 16, citing Dr. Harold M. Voth, pp. 14, 16–17.

52. Minter, "Diagnosis and Treatment of Gender Identity Disorder in Children," 15.

53. Robert Knight, "Same-Sex Marriage? Straight Talk from the Family Research Council," August 1996. (http://www.townhall.com/townhall/FRC/net/st96d2.html).

54. George Chauncey, *Gay New York* (New York: Basic Books, 1994), 13.

55. See Teemu Ruskola, "Minor Disregard: The Legal Construction of the Fantasy That Gay and Lesbian Youth Do Not Exist," *Yale Journal of Law & Feminism* 8 (1996): 269; and Elvira R. Arriola, "The Penalties for Puppy Love: Institutionalized Violence against Lesbian, Gay, Bisexual and Transgendered Youth," *Journal of Gender Race and Justice* 1, no. 2 (Spring 1998): 429–70.

56. Rekers advocates the use of aversion therapy in this treatment. Carolyn Lochhead, "Conservatives Brand Homosexuality a 'Tragic Affliction,'" *San Francisco Chronicle*, June 20, 1997, p. A4.

57. In arguing against legal discrimination against homosexuals, Stephen Macedo concedes, "It is not completely unreasonable to regard heterosexuality as preferable to homosexuality. There may even be a 'wavering child' to whom this information is important." Macedo, "Homosexuality and the Conservative Mind," *Georgetown Law Journal* 84 (1995): 292.

58. Post-decree court ruling, quoted in *In re Marriage of Jimmie Pleasant, Jr. v. Sandra Pleasant*, 256 Ill App. 3d 742, 750 (1990). This order was reversed by an appellate court, which found that "there is no evidence that Jimmie has a gender identity problem." However the higher court ruling did not dispute the logic behind the earlier ruling—that the existence of a "gender identity problem" would indicate that the mother's lesbian lifestyle had a detrimental effect on the child; instead, the higher court disputed the finding that the child in question had such a "problem." *In Re Marriage of Jimmie Pleasant, Jr. v. Sandra Pleasant*, 256 Ill. App. 3d 742, 754 (1990).

59. *Francis Walter Lundin v. Gabrielle Howell Lundin*, 563 So. 2d 1273, 1275, 1277 (La. App. 1st Cir. 1990).

In another case in Louisiana, an appellate court affirmed a trial court's decision to take away primary custody from a lesbian mother because, in part, of the assumption that the formation of the boy's gender identity would be affected by the witnessing of open displays of "sexually charged" affection between two women. "Robin . . . argues that . . . the displays of affection between herself and Karri do not exceed the bounds of friendship, and that formation of the boy's gender identity will not be affected . . . Robin asserts that she should not be denied custody because of her admitted homosexuality. We cannot agree." *Robin Scott Nee Rowan v. James Matthew Scott*, 665 S. 2d 760, 766 (La. App. 1st Cir. 1995).

60. *In the Matter of the Adoption of Two Children by H.N.R.*, 666 A.2d 535, 537 (NJ S.Ct. App. Div. 1995).

61. *Ward v. Ward*, 1996 Fla. App. LEXIS 9130 (Court of Appeal of Florida, First District, 1996).

62. Kimberle Crenshaw, "Mapping the Margins: Intersectionality, Identity Politics, and Violence against Women of Color," *Stanford Law Review* 43 (1991): 1298–99, 1297.

EIGHT

PUNKS, BULLDAGGERS, AND WELFARE QUEENS

THE RADICAL POTENTIAL OF QUEER POLITICS?

Cathy J. Cohen

ON THE EVE of finishing this essay my attention is focused not on how to rework the conclusion (as it should be) but instead on news stories of alleged racism at Gay Men's Health Crisis (GMHC). It seems that three black board members of this largest and oldest AIDS organization in the world have resigned over their perceived subservient position on the GMHC board. Billy E. Jones, former head of the New York City Health and Hospitals Corporation and one of the board members to quit, was quoted in the *New York Times* as saying, "Much work needs to be done at GMHC to make it truly inclusive and welcoming of diversity. . . . It is also clear that such work will be a great struggle. I am resigning because I do not choose to engage in such struggle at GMHC, but rather prefer to fight for the needs of those ravaged by H.I.V." (Dunlap).

This incident raises mixed emotions for me, for it points to the continuing practice of racism many of us experience on a daily basis in lesbian and gay communities. But just as disturbingly it also highlights the limits of a lesbian and gay political agenda based on a civil rights strategy, where assimilation into, and replication of, dominant institutions are the goals. Many of us continue to search for a new political direction and agenda, one that does not focus on integration into dominant structures but instead seeks to transform the basic fabric and hierarchies that allow systems of oppression to persist and operate efficiently. For some of us, such a challenge to traditional gay and lesbian politics was offered by the idea of queer politics. Here we had a potential movement of young antiassimilationist activists committed to challenging the very way people understand and respond to sexuality. These activists promised to engage in struggles that would disrupt dominant norms of sexuality, radically transforming politics in lesbian, gay, bisexual, and transgendered communities.

Despite the possibility invested in the idea of queerness and the practice of queer politics, I argue that a truly radical or transformative politics has not resulted from queer activism. In many instances, instead of destabilizing the assumed categories and binaries of sexual identity, queer politics has served to reinforce simple dichotomies between heterosexual and everything "queer." An understanding of the ways in which power informs and constitutes privileged and marginalized subjects on both sides of this dichotomy has been left unexamined.

I query in this essay whether there are lessons to be learned from queer activism that can help us construct a new politics. I envision a politics where one's relation to power, and not some homogenized identity, is privileged in determining one's political comrades. I'm talking about a politics where the *nonnormative* and *marginal* position of punks, bulldaggers, and welfare queens, for example, is the basis for progressive transformative coalition work. Thus, if there is any truly radical potential to be found in the idea of queerness and the practice of queer politics, it would seem to be located in its ability to create a space in opposition to dominant norms, a space where transformational political work can begin.

Emergence of Queer Politics and a New Politics of Transformation

Theorists and activists alike generally agree that it was in the early 1990s that we began to see, with any regularity, the use of the term "queer."[1] This term would come to denote not only an emerging politics, but also a new cohort of academics working in programs primarily in the humanities centered on social and cultural criticism (Morton 121). Individuals such as Judith Butler, Eve Sedgwick, Teresa de Lauretis, Diana Fuss, and Michael Warner produced what are now thought of as the first canonical works of "queer theory." Working from a variety of postmodernist and poststructuralist theoretical perspectives, these scholars focused on identifying and contesting the discursive and cultural markers found within both dominant and marginal identities and institutions that prescribe and reify "heterogendered" understandings and behavior.[2] These theorists presented a different conceptualization of sexuality, one that sought to replace socially named and presumably stable categories of sexual expression with a new fluid movement among and between forms of sexual behavior (Stein and Plummer 182).

Through its conception of a wide continuum of sexual possibilities, queer theory stands in direct contrast to the normalizing tendencies of hegemonic sexuality rooted in ideas of static, stable sexual identities and behaviors. In queer theorizing the sexual subject is understood to be constructed and contained by multiple practices of categorization and regulation that systematically marginalize and oppress those subjects thereby defined as deviant and "other." And, at its best, queer theory focuses on and makes central not only the social constructed nature of sexuality and sexual categories, but also the varying degrees and multiple sites of power distributed within all categories of sexuality, including the normative category of heterosexuality.

It was in the early 1990s, however, that the postmodern theory being produced in the academy (later to be recategorized as queer theory) found its most direct interaction with the real-life politics of lesbian, gay, bisexual, and transgendered activists. Frustrated with what was perceived to be the scientific "de-gaying" and assimilationist tendencies of AIDS activism, with their invisibility in the more traditional civil rights politics of lesbian and gay organizations, and with increasing legal and physical attacks against lesbian and gay community members, a new generation of activists began the process of building a more confrontational political formation—labeling it queer politics (Bérubé and Escoffier 12). Queer politics, represented most notoriously in the actions of Queer Nation, is understood as an "in your face" politics of a younger generation. Through action and analysis these individuals seek to make "queer" function as more than just an abbreviation for lesbian, gay, bisexual, and transgendered. Similar to queer theory, the queer politics articulated and pursued by these activists first and foremost recognizes and encourages the fluidity and movement of people's sexual lives. In queer politics sexual expression is something that always entails the possibility of change, movement, redefinition, and subversive performance—from year to year, from partner to partner, from day to day, even from act to act. In addition to highlighting the instability of sexual categories and sexual subjects, queer activists also directly challenge the multiple practices and vehicles of power that render them invisible and at risk. However, what seems to make queer activists unique, at this particular moment, is their willingness to confront normalizing power by emphasizing and exaggerating their own anti-normative characteristics and non-stable behavior. Joshua Gamson, in "Must Identity Movements Self-Destruct? A Queer Dilemma," writes that

> queer activism and theory pose the challenge of a form of organizing in which, far from inhibiting accomplishments, the *destabilization* of collective identity is itself a goal and accomplishment of collective action.
>
> The assumption that stable collective identities are necessary for collective action is turned on its head by queerness, and the question becomes: *When and how are stable collective identities necessary for social action and social change?* Secure boundaries and stabilized identities are necessary not in general, but in the specific, a point social movement theory seems currently to miss. (403, original emphasis)

Thus queer politics, much like queer theory, is often perceived as standing in opposition, or in contrast, to the category-based identity politics of traditional lesbian and gay activism. And for those of us who find ourselves on the margins, operating through multiple identities and thus not fully served or recognized through traditional single-identity-based politics, *theoretical conceputalizations* of queerness hold great political promise. For many of us, the label "queer" symbolizes an acknowledgment that through our existence and everyday survival we embody sustained and multisited resistance to systems (based on dominant constructions of race and gender) that seek to normalize our sexuality, exploit our labor, and constrain our visibility. At the intersection of oppression and resistance lies the radical potential of queerness to challenge and bring together all those deemed marginal and all those committed to liberatory politics.

The problem, however, with such a conceptualization and expectation of queer identity and politics is that in its present form queer politics has not emerged as an encompassing challenge to systems of domination and oppression, especially those normalizing processes embedded in heteronormativity. By "heteronormativity" I mean both those localized practices and centralized institutions that legitimize and privilege heterosexuality and heterosexual relationships as fundamental and "natural" within society. I raise the subject of heteronormativity because it is this normalizing practice/power that has most often been the focus of queer politics (Blasius 19–20; Warner xxi–xxv).

The inability of queer politics to effectively challenge heteronormativity rests, in part, on the fact that despite a surrounding discourse that highlights the destabilization and even deconstruction of sexual categories, queer politics has often been built around a simple dichotomy between those deemed queer and those deemed heterosexual. Whether in the infamous "I Hate Straights" publication or queer kiss-ins at malls and straight dance clubs, very near the surface in queer political action is an uncomplicated understanding of power as it is encoded in sexual categories: all heterosexuals are represented as dominant and controlling and all queers are understood as marginalized and invisible. Thus, even in the name of destabilization, some queer activists have begun to prioritize sexuality as the primary frame through which they pursue their politics.[3] Undoubtedly, within different contexts various characteristics of our total being—for example, race, gender, class, sexuality—are highlighted or called upon to make sense of a particular situation. However, my concern is centered on those individuals who consistently activate only one characteristic of their identity, or a single perspective of consciousness, to organize their politics, rejecting any recognition of the multiple and intersecting systems of power that largely dictate our life chances.

It is the disjuncture, evident in queer politics, between an articulated commitment to promoting an understanding of sexuality that rejects the idea of static, monolithic, bounded categories, on the one hand, and political practices structured around binary conceptions of sexuality and power, on the other hand, that is the focus of this article. Specifically, I am concerned with those manifestations of queer politics in which the capital and advantage invested in a range of sexual categories are disregarded and, as a result, narrow and homogenized political identities are reproduced that inhibit the radical potential of queer politics. It is my contention that queer activists who evoke a single-oppression framework misrepresent the distribution of power within and outside of gay, lesbian, bisexual, and transgendered communities, and therefore limit the comprehensive and transformational character of queer politics.

Recognizing the limits of current conceptions of queer identities and queer politics, I am interested in examining the concept of "queer" in order to think about how we might construct a new political identity that is truly liberating, transformative, and inclusive of all those who stand on the outside of the dominant constructed norm of state-sanctioned white middle- and upper-class heterosexuality.[4] Such a broadened understanding of queerness must be based on an intersectional analysis that recognizes how numerous systems of oppression interact to regulate and police the lives of most people. Black lesbian, bisexual, and heterosexual feminist authors such as Kimberle Crenshaw, Barbara Ransby, Angela Davis, Cheryl Clarke, and Audre Lorde have repeatedly emphasized in their writing the intersectional workings of oppression. And it is just such an understanding of the interlocking systems of domination that is noted in the opening paragraph of the now famous black feminist statement by the Combahee River Collective:

> The most general statement of our politics at the present time would be that we are actively committed to struggling against racial, sexual, heterosexual, and class oppression and see as our particular task the development of *integrated* analysis and practice based upon the fact that the major systems of oppression are interlocking. The synthesis of these oppressions creates the conditions of our lives. As Black women we see Black feminism as the logical political movement to combat the manifold and simultaneous oppressions that all women of color face. (272)

This analysis of one's place in the world, which focuses on the intersection of systems of oppression, is informed by a consciousness that undoubtedly grows from the lived experience of existing within and resisting multiple and connected practices of domination and normalization. Just such a lived experience and analysis have determined much of the progressive and expansive nature of the politics emanating from people of color, people who are both inside and outside lesbian and gay communities.

However, beyond a mere recognition of the intersection of oppressions, there must also be an understanding of the ways our multiple identities work to limit the entitlement and status some receive from obeying a heterosexual imperative. For instance, how would queer activists understand politically the lives of women—in particular women of color—on welfare, who may fit into the category of heterosexual, but whose sexual choices are not perceived as normal, moral, or worthy of state support? Further, how do queer activists understand and relate politically to those whose same-sex sexual identities position them within the category of queer, but who hold other identities based on class, race, and/or gender categories that provide them with membership in and the resources of dominant institutions and groups?

Thus, inherent in our new politics must be a commitment to left analysis and left politics. Black feminists as well as other marginalized and progressive scholars and activists have long argued that any political response to the multilayered oppression that most of us experience must be rooted in a left understanding of our political, economic, social, and cultural institutions. Fundamentally, a left framework makes central the interdependency among multiple systems of domination. Such a perspective also ensures that while activists should rightly be concerned with forms of discursive and cultural coercion, we also recognize and confront the more direct and concrete forms of exploitation and violence rooted in state-regulated institutions and economic systems. The Statement of Purpose from the first Dialogue on the Lesbian and Gay Left comments specifically on the role of interlocking systems of oppression in the lives of gays and lesbians. "By leftist we mean people who understand the struggle for lesbian and gay liberation to be integrally tied to struggles against class oppression, racism and sexism. While we might use different political labels, we share a commitment to a fundamental transformation of the economic, political and social structure of society."

A left framework of politics, unlike civil rights or liberal frameworks, brings into focus the systematic relationship among forms of domination, where the creation and maintenance of exploited, subservient, marginalized classes is a necessary part of, at the very least, the economic configuration. Urvashi Vaid, in *Virtual Equality*, for example, writes of the limits of civil rights strategies in confronting systemic homophobia:

> [C]ivil rights do not change the social order in dramatic ways; they change only the privileges of the group asserting those rights. Civil rights strategies do not challenge the moral and antisexual underpinnings of homophobia, because homophobia does not originate in our lack of full civil equality. Rather, homophobia arises from the nature and construction of the political, legal, economic, sexual, racial and family systems within which we live. (183)

Proceeding from the starting point of a system-based left analysis, strategies built upon the possibility of incorporation and assimilation are exposed as simply expanding and making accessible the status quo for more privileged members of marginal groups, while the most vulnerable in our communities continue to be stigmatized and oppressed.

It is important to note, however, that while left theorists tend to provide a more structural analysis of oppression and exploitation, many of these theorists and activists have also been homophobic and heterosexist in their approach to or avoidance of the topics of sexuality and heteronormativity. For example, Robin Podolsky, in "Sacrificing Queers and Other 'Proletarian' Artifacts," writes that quite often on the left lesbian and gay sexuality and desire have been characterized as "more to do with personal happiness and sexual pleasure than with the 'material basis' of procreation—we were considered self-indulgent distractions from struggle . . . [an example of] 'bourgeois decadence.'" (54).

This contradiction between a stated left analysis and an adherence to heteronormativity has probably been most dramatically identified in the writing of some feminist authors. I need only refer to Adrienne Rich's well-known article, "Compulsory Heterosexuality and Lesbian Existence," as a poignant critique of the white, middle-class heterosexual standard running through significant parts of feminist analysis and actions. The same adherence to a heterosexual norm can be found in the writing of self-identified black left intellectuals such as Cornel West and Michael Eric Dyson. Thus, while these writers have learned to make reference to lesbian, gay, bisexual, and transgendered segments of black communities—sparingly—they continue to foreground black heterosexuality and masculinity as the central unit of analysis in their writing—and most recently in their politics: witness their participation in the Million Man March.

This history of left organizing and the left's visible absence from any serious and sustained response to the AIDS epidemic have provoked many lesbian, gay, bisexual, and transgendered people to question the relevance of this political configuration to the needs of our communities. Recognizing that reservations of this type are real and should be noted, I still hold that a left-rooted analysis that emphasizes economic exploitation and class structure, culture, and the systemic nature of power provides a framework of politics that is especially effective in representing and challenging the numerous sites and systems of oppression. Further, the left-centered approach I embrace is one that designates sexuality and struggles against sexual normalization as central to the politics of all marginal communities.

The Root of Queer Politics: Challenging Heteronormativity?

In the introduction to the edited volume *Fear of a Queer Planet: Queer Politics and Social Theory*, Michael Warner asks the question: "What do queers want?" (vii). He suggests that the goals of queers and their politics extend beyond the sexual arena. Warner contends that what queers want is acknowledgment of their lives, struggles, and complete existence; queers want to be represented and included fully in left political analysis and American culture. Thus what queers want is to be a part of the social, economic, and political restructuring of this society; as Warner writes, queers want to have queer experience and politics "taken as starting points rather than as footnotes" in the social theories and political agendas of the left (vii). He contends that it has been the absence or invisibility of lived queer experience that has marked or constrained much of left social and political theories and has "posited and naturalized a heterosexual society" in such theories (vii).

The concerns and emerging politics of queer activists, as formulated by Warner and others interested in understanding the implications of the idea of queerness, are focused on highlighting queer presence and destroying heteronormativity not only in the larger dominant society but also in extant spaces, theories, and sites of resistance, presumably on the left. He suggests that those embracing the label of "queer" understand the need to challenge the assumption of heteronormativity in every aspect of their existence:

> Every person who comes to a queer self-understanding knows in one way or another that her stigmatization is connected with gender, the family, notions of individual freedom, the state, public speech, consumption and desire, nature and culture, maturation, reproductive politics, racial and national fantasy, class identity, truth and trust, censorship, intimate life and social display, terror and violence, health care, and deep cultural norms about the bearing of the body. Being queer means fighting about these issues all the time, locally and piecemeal but always with consequences. (xiii)

Now, independent of the fact that few of us could find ourselves in such a grandiose description of queer consciousness, I believe that Warner's description points to the fact that in the roots of a lived "queer" existence are experiences with domination and in particular heteronormativity that form the basis for genuine transformational politics. By transformational, again, I mean a politics that does not search for opportunities to integrate into dominant institutions and normative social relationships, but instead pursues a political agenda that seeks to change values, definitions, and laws that make these institutions and relationships oppressive.

Queer activists experiencing displacement both within and outside lesbian and gay communities rebuff what they deem the assimilationist practices and policies of more established lesbian and gay organizations. These organizers and activists reject cultural norms of acceptable sexual behavior and identification and instead embrace political strategies that promote self-definition and full expression. Members of the Chicago-based group Queers United Against Straight-acting Homosexuals (QUASH) state just such a position in the article "Assimilation Is Killing Us: Fight for a Queer United Front" published in their newsletter. WHY I HATED THE MARCH ON WASHINGTON:

> Assimilation is killing us. We are falling into a trap. Some of us adopt an apologetic stance, stating "that's just the way I am" (read: "I'd be straight if I could.").

Others pattern their behavior in such a way as to mimic heterosexual society so as to minimize the glaring differences between us and them. No matter how much [money] you make, fucking your lover is still illegal in nearly half of the states. Getting a corporate job, a fierce car and a condo does not protect you from dying of AIDS or getting your head bashed in by neo-Nazis. The myth of assimilation must be shattered.

. . . Fuck the heterosexual, nuclear family. Let's make families which promote sexual choices and liberation rather than sexual oppression. We must learn from the legacy of resistance that is ours: a legacy which shows that empowerment comes through grassroots activism, not mainstream politics, a legacy which shows that real change occurs when we are inclusive, not exclusive. (4)

At the very heart of queer politics, at least as it is formulated by QUASH, is a fundamental challenge to the heteronormativity—the privilege, power, and normative status invested in heterosexuality—of the dominant society.

It is in their fundamental challenge to a systemic process of domination and exclusion, with a specific focus on heteronormativity, that queer activists and queer theorists are tied to and rooted in a tradition of political struggle most often identified with people of color and other marginal groups. For example, activists of color have, through many historical periods, questioned their formal and informal inclusion and power in prevailing social categories. Through just such a process of challenging their centrality to lesbian and gay politics in particular, and lesbian and gay communities more generally, lesbian, gay, bisexual, and transgendered people of color advanced debates over who and what would be represented as "truly gay." As Steven Seidman reminds us in "Identity and Politics in a 'Postmodern' Gay Culture," beyond the general framing provided by postmodern queer theory, gay and lesbian—and now queer—politics owes much of its impetus to the politics of people of color and other marginalized members of lesbian and gay communities:

Specifically, I make the case that postmodern strains in gay thinking and politics have their immediate social origin in recent developments in the gay culture. In the reaction by people of color, third-world-identified gays, poor and working class gays, and sex rebels to the ethnic/essentialist model of identity and community that achieved dominance in the lesbian and gay cultures of the 1970s, I locate the social basis for a rethinking of identity and politics. (106)

Through the demands of lesbian, gay, bisexual, and transgendered people of color as well as others who did not see themselves or their numerous communities in the more narrowly constructed politics of white gays and lesbians, the contestation took shape over who and what type of issues would be represented in lesbian and gay politics and in larger community discourse.

While similarities and connections between the politics of lesbians, gay men, bisexuals, and transgendered people of color during the 1970s and

1980s and queer activists of today clearly exist, the present-day rendition of this politics has deviated significantly from its legacy. Specifically, while both political efforts include as a focus of their work the radicalization and/or expansion of traditional lesbian and gay politics, the politics of lesbian, gay, bisexual, and transgendered people of color has been and continues to be much broader in its understanding of transformational politics.

The politics of lesbian, gay, bisexual, and transgendered people of color has often been guided by the type of radical intersectional left analysis I detailed earlier. Thus, while the politics of lesbian, gay, bisexual, and trans- gendered activists of color might recognize heteronormativity as a primary system of power structuring our lives, it understands that heteronormativity interacts with institutional racism, patriarchy, and class exploitation to define us in numerous ways as marginal and oppressed subjects.[5] And it is this constructed subservient position that allows our sisters and brothers to be used either as surplus labor in an advanced capitalist structure and/or seen as expendable, denied resources, and thus locked into correctional institutions across the country. While heterosexual privilege negatively impacts and con- strains the lived experience of "queers" of color, so too do racism, classism, and sexism.

In contrast to the left intersectional analysis that has structured much of the politics of "queers" of color, the basis of the politics of some white queer activists and organizations has come dangerously close to a single oppression model. Experiencing "deviant" sexuality as the prominent characteristic of their marginalization, these activists begin to envision the world in terms of a "hetero/queer" divide. Using the framework of queer theory in which hetero- normativity is identified as a system of regulation and normalization, some queer activists map the power and entitlement of normative heterosexuality onto the bodies of all heterosexuals. Further, these activists naively character- ize all those who stand on the outside of heteronormativity, a monolithic understanding of heterosexuality and queerness has come to dominate the political imagination and actions of many queer activists.

This reconstruction of a binary divide between heterosexuals and queers, while discernible in many of the actions of Queer Nation, is probably most evident in the manifesto "I Hate Straights." Distributed at gay pride parades in New York and Chicago in 1990, the declaration written by an anonymous group of queers begins,

I have friends. Some of them are straight.

Year after year, I see my straight friends. I want to see how they are doing, to add newness to our long and complicated histories, to experience some continuity.

Year after year I continue to realize that the facts of my life are irrelevant to them and that I am only half listened to, that I am an appendage to the doings of a greater world, a world of power and privilege, of the laws of installation, a world of exclusion. "That's not true," argue my straight friends. There is the one certainty in the politics of power: those left out of it beg for inclusion, while the insiders claim that they already are. Men do it to women, whites do it to blacks, *and everyone does it to queers.*

. . . The main dividing line, both conscious and unconscious, is procreation . . . and that magic word—Family. (emphasis added)

Screaming out from this manifesto is an analysis that places not heteronormativity, but heterosexuality, as the central "dividing line" between those who would be dominant and those who are oppressed. Nowhere in this essay is there recognition that "nonnormative" procreation patterns and family structures of people who are labeled heterosexual have also been used to regulate and exclude *them.* Instead, the authors declare, "Go tell them [straights] to go away until they have spent a month walking hand in hand in public with someone of the same sex. After they survive that, then you'll hear what they have to say about queer anger. Otherwise, tell them to shut up and listen." For these activists, the power of heterosexuality is the focus, and queer anger the means of queer politics. Missing from this equation is any attention to, or acknowledgment of, the ways in which identities of race, class, and/or gender either enhance or mute the marginalization of queers, on the one hand, and the power of heterosexuals, on the other.

The fact that this essay is written about and out of queer anger is undoubtedly part of the rationale for its defense (Berlant and Freeman 200). But I question the degree to which we should read this piece as just an aberrational diatribe against straights motivated by intense queer anger. While anger is clearly a motivating factor for such writing, we should also understand this action to represent an analysis and politics structured around the simple dichotomy of straight and queer. We know, for instance, that similar positions have been put forth in other anonymously published, publicly distributed manifestos. For example, in the document *Queers Read This,* the authors write, "Don't be fooled, straight people own the world and the only reason you have been spared is you're smart, lucky or a fighter. Straight people have a privilege that allows them to do whatever they please and fuck without fear." They continue by stating that "Straight people are your enemy."

Even within this document, which seems to exemplify the narrowness of queer conceptions, there is a surprising glimpse at a more enlightened left intersectional understanding of what queerness might mean. For instance, the authors continue, "Being queer is not about a right to privacy; it is about the freedom to be public, to just be who we are. It means everyday fighting oppression: homophobia, racism, misogyny, the bigotry of religious hypocrites and our own self-hatred." Evident in this one document are the inherent tensions and dilemmas many queer activists currently encounter: how does one implement in real political struggle a decentered political identity that is not constituted by a process of seemingly reductive "othering"?

The process of ignoring or at least downplaying queers' varying relationships to power is evident not only in the writing of queer activists, but also in the political actions pursued by queer organizations. I question the ability of political actions such as mall invasions (pursued by groups such as the Queer Shopping Network in New York and the Suburban Homosexual Outreach Program [SHOP] in San Francisco) to address the fact that queers exist in different social locations. Lauren Berlant and Elizabeth Freeman describe mall invasion projects as

> [an attempt to take] the relatively bounded spectacle of the urban pride parade to the ambient pleasures of the shopping mall. "Mall visibility actions" thus conjoin the spectacular lure of the parade with Hare Krishna-style conversion and proselytizing techniques. Stepping into malls in hair-gelled splendor, holding hands and handing out fliers, the queer auxiliaries produce an "invasion" that conveys a different message. "We're here, we're queer, *you're* going shopping."
> (210)

The activity of entering or "invading" the shopping mall on the part of queer nationals is clearly one of attempted subversion. Intended by their visible presence in this clearly coded heterosexual family economic mecca is a disruption of the agreed-upon segregation between the allowable spaces for queer "deviant" culture and the rest of the "naturalized" world. Left unchallenged in such an action, however, are the myriad ways, besides the enforcement of normative sexuality, in which some queers feel alienated and excluded from the space of the mall. Where does the mall as an institution of consumer culture and relative economic privilege play into this analysis? How does this action account for the varying economic relationships queers have to consumer culture? If you are a poor or working-class queer the exclusion and alienation you experience when entering the mall may not be limited to the normative sexual codes associated with the mall, but may also be centered on the assumed economic status of those shopping in suburban malls. If you are a queer of color your exclusion from the mall may, in part, be rooted in racial norms and stereotypes that construct you as a threatening subject every time you enter this economic institution. Queer activists must confront a question that haunts most political organizing: How do we put into politics a broad and inclusive left analysis that can actually engage and mobilize individuals with intersecting identities?

Clearly, there will be those critics who will claim that I am asking too much from any political organization. Demands that every aspect of oppression and regulation be addressed in each political act seem, and are indeed, unreasonable. However, I make the critique of queer mall invasions neither to stop such events nor to suggest that every oppression be dealt with by this one political action. Instead, I raise these concerns to emphasize the ways in which varying relations to power exist not only among heterosexuals, but also among those who label themselves queer.

In its current rendition, queer politics is coded with class, gender, and race privilege, and may have lost its potential to be a politically expedient organizing tool for addressing the needs—and mobilizing the bodies—of people of color. As some queer theorists and activists call for the destruction of stable sexual categories, for example, moving instead toward a more fluid understanding of sexual behavior, left unspoken is the class privilege that allows for such fluidity. Class or material privilege is a cornerstone of much of queer politics and theory as they exist today. Queer theorizing that calls for the elimination of fixed categories of sexual identity seems to ignore the ways in which some traditional social identities and communal ties can, in fact, be important to one's survival. Further, a queer politics that demonizes all heterosexuals discounts the relationships—especially those based on shared experiences of marginalization—that exist between gays and straights, particularly in communities of color.

Queers who operate out of a political culture of individualism assume a material independence that allows them to disregard historically or culturally recognized categories and communities or at the very least to move fluidly among them without ever establishing permanent relationships or identities within them. However, I and many other lesbian and gay people of color, as well as poor and working-class lesbians and gay men, do not have such material independence. Because of my multiple identities, which locate me and other "queer" people of color at the margins in this country, my material advancement, my physical protection, and my emotional well-being are constantly threatened. In those stable categories and named communities whose histories have been structured by shared resistance to oppression, I find relative degrees of safety and security.

Let me emphasize again that the safety I feel is relative to other threats and is clearly not static or constant. For in those named communities I also find versions of domination and normalization being replicated and employed as more privileged/assimilated marginal group members use their associations with dominant institutions and resources to regulate and police the activities of other marginal group members. Any lesbian, gay, bisexual, or transgendered person of color who has experienced exclusion from indigenous institutions, such as the exclusion many out black gay men have encountered from some black churches responding to AIDS, recognizes that even within marginal groups there are normative rules determining community membership and power (Cohen). However, in spite of the unequal power relationships located in marginal communities, I am still not interested in disassociating politically from those communities, for queerness, as it is currently constructed, offers no viable political alternative, since it invites us to put forth a political agenda that makes invisible the prominence of race, class, and to varying degrees gender in determining the life chances of those on both sides of the hetero/queer divide.

So despite the roots of queer politics in the struggles of "queer" people of color, despite the calls for highlighting categories that have sought to regulate and control black bodies like my own, and despite the attempts at decentralized grassroots activism in some queer political organizations, there still exist—for some, like myself—great misgivings about current constructions of the term "queer." Personally speaking, I do not consider myself a "queer" activist or, for that matter, a "queer" anything. This is not because I do not consider myself an activist; in fact I hold my political work to be one of my most important contributions to all of my communities. But like other lesbian, gay, bisexual, and transgendered activists of color, I find the label "queer" fraught with unspoken assumptions that inhibit the radical political potential of this category.

The alienation, or at least discomfort, many activists and theorists of color have with current conceptions of queerness is evidenced, in part, by the minimal numbers of theorists of color who engage in the process of theorizing about the concept. Further, the sparse numbers of people of color who participate in "queer" political organizations might also be read as a sign of discomfort with the term. Most important, my confidence in making such a claim of distance and uneasiness with the term "queer" on the part of many people of color comes from my interactions with other lesbian, gay, bisexual, and transgendered people of color who repeatedly express their interpretation of "queer" as a term rooted in class, race, and gender privilege. For us, "queer" is a politics based on narrow sexual dichotomies that make no room either for the analysis of oppression of those we might categorize as heterosexual or for the privilege of those who operate as "queer." As black lesbian activist and writer Barbara Smith argues in "Queer Politics: Where's the Revolution?":

> Unlike the early lesbian and gay movement, which had both ideological and practical links to the left, black activism and feminism, today's "queer" politicos seem to operate in a historical and ideological vacuum. "Queer" activists focus on "queer" issues, and racism, sexual oppression and economic exploitation do not qualify, despite the fact that the majority of "queers" are people of color, female or working class. . . . Building unified, ongoing coalitions that challenge the system and ultimately prepare a way for revolutionary change simply isn't what "queer" activists have in mind. (13–14)

It is this narrow understanding of the idea of queer that negates its use in fundamentally reorienting the politics and privilege of lesbian and gay politics as well as more generally moving or transforming the politics of the left. Despite its liberatory claim to stand in opposition to static categories of oppression, queer politics and much of queer theory seem in fact to be static in the understanding of race, class, and gender and their roles in how hetero-normativity regulates sexual behavior and identities. Distinctions between the status and the acceptance of different individuals categorized under the label of "heterosexual" go unexplored.

I emphasize the marginalized position of some who embrace heterosexual identities not because I want to lead any great crusade to understand more fully the plight of "the heterosexual." Rather, I recognize the potential for shared resistance with such individuals. This potential not only for coali-tional work but for a shared analysis is especially relevant, from my vantage point, to "queer" people of color. Again, in my call for coalition work across sexual categories, I do not want to suggest that same-sex political struggles have not, independently, played an essential and distinct role in the libera-tory politics and social movements of marginal people. My concern, instead, is with any political analysis or theory that collapses our understanding of power into a single continuum of evaluation.

Through a brief review of some of the ways in which nonnormative het-erosexuality has been controlled and regulated through the state and systems of marginalization we may be reminded that differentials in power exist within all socially named categories. And through such recognition we may begin to envision a new political formation in which one's relation to domi-nant power serves as the basis of unity for radical coalition work in the twenty-first century.

Heterosexuals on the (Out)side of Heteronormativity

In this section I want to return to the question of a monolithic understand-ing of heterosexuality. I believe that through this issue we can begin to think critically about the components of a radical politics built not exclu-sively on identities, but on identities as they are invested with varying degrees of normative power. Thus, fundamental to my concern about the current structure and future agenda of queer politics is the unchallenged assumption of a uniform heteronormativity from which all heterosexuals benefit. I want again to be clear that there are, in fact, some who identify themselves as queer activists who do acknowledge relative degrees of power, and heterosexual access to that power, even evoking the term "straight queers." "Queer means to fuck with gender. There are straight queers, bi queers, tranny queers, lez queers, fag queers, SM queers, fisting queers in every single street in this apathetic country of ours" (anonymous, qtd. McIntosh 31).

Despite such sporadic insight, much of the politics of queer activists has been structured around the dichotomy of straight versus everything else,

assuming a monolithic experience of heterosexual privilege for all those identified publicly with heterosexuality. A similar reductive dichotomy between
men and women has consistently reemerged in the writing and actions of
some feminists. And only through the demands, actions, and writing of
many "feminists" and/or lesbians of color have those women who stand outside the norm of white, middle-class, legalized heterosexuality begun to see
this lives, needs, and bodies represented in feminist theory (Carby; Collins;
hooks). In a similar manner lesbian, gay, bisexual, and transgendered people
of color have increasingly taken on the responsibility for at the very least
complicating and most often challenging reductive notions of heteronormativity articulated by queer activists and scholars (Alexander; Farajaje-
Jones; Lorde; Moraga and Anzaldúa; B. Smith).

If we follow such examples, complicating our understanding of both heteronormativity and queerness, we move one step closer to building the progressive coalition politics many of us desire. Specifically, if we pay attention
to both historical and current examples of heterosexual relationships that
have been prohibited, stigmatized, and generally repressed, we may begin to
identify those spaces of shared or similar oppression and resistance that provide a basis for radical coalition work. Further, we may begin to answer
certain questions: In narrowly positing a dichotomy of heterosexual privilege
and queer oppression under which we all exist, are we negating a basis of
political unity that could serve to strengthen many communities and movements seeking justice and societal transformation? How do we use the relative degrees of ostracization all sexual/cultural "deviants" experience to build
a basis of unity for broader coalition and movement work?

A little history (as a political scientist a little history is all I can offer) might
be helpful in trying to sort out the various ways heterosexuality, especially as
it has intersected with race, has been defined and experienced by different
groups of people. It should also help to underscore the fact that many of the
roots of heteronormativity are in white supremacist ideologies that sought
(and continue) to use the state and its regulation of sexuality, in particular
through the institution of heterosexual marriage, to designate which individuals were truly "fit" for full rights and privileges of citizenship. For example,
the prohibition of marriages between black women and men imprisoned in
the slave system was a component of many slave codes enacted during the
seventeenth and eighteenth centuries. M. G. Smith, in his article on the
structure of slave economic systems, succinctly states, "As property slaves
were prohibited from forming legal relationships or marriages which would
interfere with and restrict their owner's property rights" (71–72). Herbert G.
Gutman, in *The Black Family in Slavery and Freedom, 1750–1925*, elaborates
on the ideology of slave societies, which denied the legal sanctioning of marriages between slaves and further reasoned that blacks had no conception of
family.

The *Nation* identified sexual restraint, civil marriage, and family "stability" with "civilization" itself.

Such mid-nineteenth-century class and sexual beliefs reinforced racial beliefs about Afro-Americans. As slaves, after all, their marriages had not been sanctioned by the civil laws and therefore "the sexual passion" went unrestrained. . . . Many white abolitionists denied the slaves a family life or even, often, a family consciousness because for them [whites] the family had its origins in and had to be upheld by the civil law. (295)

Thus it was not the promotion of marriage or heterosexuality per se that served as the standard or motivation of most slave societies. Instead, marriage and heterosexuality, as viewed through the lenses of profit and domination, and the ideology of white supremacy, were reconfigured to justify the exploitation and regulation of black bodies, even those presumably engaged in heterosexual behavior. It was this system of state-sanctioned, white male, upper-class, heterosexual domination that forced these presumably black *heterosexual* men and women to endure a history of rape, lynching, and other forms of physical and mental terrorism. In this way, marginal group members, lacking power and privilege although engaged in heterosexual behavior, have often found themselves defined as outside the norms and values of dominant society. This position has most often resulted in the suppression or negation of their legal, social, and physical relationships and rights.

In addition to the prohibition of marriage between slaves, A. Leon Higginbotham, Jr., in *The Matter of Color-Race and the American Legal Process: The Colonial Period*, writes of the legal restrictions barring interracial marriages. He reminds us that the essential core of the American legal tradition was the preservation of the white race. The "mixing" of the races was to be strictly prohibited in early colonial laws. The regulation of interracial heterosexual relationships, however, should not be understood as exclusively relegated to the seventeenth, eighteenth, and nineteenth centuries. In fact, Higginbotham informs us that the final law prohibiting miscegenation (the "interbreeding" or marrying of individuals from different "races"—actually meant to inhibit the "tainting" of the white race) was not repealed until 1967:

Colonial anxiety about interracial sexual activity cannot be attributed solely to seventeenth-century values, for it was not until 1967 that the United States Supreme Court finally declared unconstitutional those statutes prohibiting interracial marriages. The Supreme Court waited thirteen years after its *Brown* decision dealing with desegregation of schools before, in *Loving v. Virginia*, it agreed to consider the issue of interracial marriages. (41)

It is this pattern of regulating the behavior and denigrating the identities of those heterosexuals on the outside of heteronormativity privilege, in particular those perceived as threatening systems of white supremacy, male domination, and capitalist advancement, that I want to highlight. An understanding of the ways in which heteronormativity works to support and reinforce institutional racism, patriarchy, and class exploitation must therefore be a part of how we problematize current constructions of heterosexuality. As I stated previously, I am not suggesting that those involved in publicly identifiable heterosexual behavior do not receive political, economic, and social advantage, especially in comparison to the experiences of some lesbian, transgendered, gay, and bisexual individuals. But the equation linking identity and behavior to power is not as linear and clear as some queer theorists and activists would have us believe.

A more recent example of regulated nonnormative heterosexuality is located in current debates and rhetoric regarding the "underclass" and the destruction of the welfare system. The stigmatization and demonization of single mothers, teen mothers, and, primarily, poor women of color dependent on state assistance has had a long and suspicious presence in American "intellectual" and political history. It was in 1965 that Daniel Patrick Moynihan released his "study" titled *The Negro Family: The Case for National Action*. In this report, which would eventually come to be known as the Moynihan Report, the author points to the "pathologies" increasingly evident in so-called Negro families. In this document were allegations of the destructive nature of Negro family formations. The document's introduction argues that

> the fundamental problem, in which this is most clearly the case, is that of family structure. The evidence—not final, but powerfully persuasive—is that the Negro family in urban ghettos is crumbling. A middle-class group has managed to save itself, but for vast numbers of the unskilled, poorly educated city working-class the fabric of conventional social relationships has all but disintegrated.

Moynihan, later in the document, goes on to describe the crisis and pathologies facing Negro family structure as being generated by the increasing number of single-female-headed households, the increasing number of "illegitimate" births, and, of course, increasing welfare dependency:

> In essence, the Negro community has been forced into a matriarchal structure which, because it is so out of line with the rest of the American society, seriously retards the progress of the group as a whole, and imposes a crushing burden on the Negro male and, in consequence, on a great many Negro women as well. . . .
> In a word, most Negro youth are in danger of being caught up in the tangle of pathology that affects their world, and probably a majority are so entrapped. . . .
> Obviously, not every instance of social pathology afflicting the Negro community can be traced to the weakness of family structure. . . . Nonetheless, at the center of the tangle of pathology is the weakness of the family structure. (29–30)

It is not the nonheterosexist behavior of these black men and women that is under fire, but rather the perceived nonnormative sexual behavior and family structures of these individuals, whom many queer activists—without regard to the impact of race, class, or gender—would designate as part of the heterosexist establishment or those mighty "straights they hate."

Over the last thirty years the demonization of poor women, engaged in nonnormative heterosexual relationships, has continued under the auspices of scholarship on the "underclass." Adolph L. Reed, in "The 'Underclass' as Myth and Symbol: The Poverty of Discourse about Poverty," discusses the gendered and racist nature of much of this literature, in which poor, often black and Latina women are portrayed as unable to control their sexual impulses and eventual reproductive decisions, unable to raise their children with the right moral fiber, unable to find "gainful" employment to support themselves and their "illegitimate children," and of course unable to manage "effectively" the minimal assistance provided by the state. Reed writes:

> The underclass notion may receive the greatest ideological boost from its gendered imagery and relation to gender politics. As I noted in a critique of Wilson's *The Truly Disadvantaged*, "family" is an intrinsically ideological category. The rhetoric of "disorganization," "disintegration," "deterioration" reifies one type of living arrangement—the ideal type of the bourgeois nuclear family—as outside history, nearly as though it were decreed by natural law. But—as I asked earlier—why exactly is out-of-wedlock birth pathological? Why is the female-headed household an indicator of disorganization and pathology? Does that stigma attach to *all* such households—even, say, a divorced executive who is a custodial mother? If not, what are the criteria for assigning it? The short answer is race and class bias inflected through a distinctively gendered view of the world. (33–34)

In this same discourse of the "underclass," young black men engaged in "reckless" heterosexual behavior are represented as irresponsible baby factories, unable to control or restrain their "sexual passion" (to borrow a term from the seventeenth century). And, unfortunately, often it has been the work of professed liberals like William Julius Wilson, in his book *The Truly Disadvantaged*, that, while not using the word "pathologies," has substantiated in its own tentative way the conservative dichotomy between the deserving working poor and the lazy, Cadillac-driving, steak-eating welfare queens of Ronald Reagan's imagination. Again, I raise this point to remind us of the numerous ways that sexuality and sexual deviance from a prescribed norm have been used to demonize and oppress various segments of the population, even some classified under the label "heterosexual."

The policies of politicians and the actions of law enforcement officials have reinforced, in much more devastating ways, the distinctions between acceptable forms of heterosexual expression and those to be regulated—increasingly through incarceration. This move toward the disallowance of some forms of heterosexual expression and reproductive choice can be seen in the practice of prosecuting pregnant women suspected of using drugs—nearly 80 percent of all women prosecuted are women of color; through the forced sterilization of Puerto Rican and Native American women; and through the state-dictated use of Norplant by women answering to the criminal justice system and by women receiving state assistance.[6] Further, it is the "nonnormative" children of many of these nonnormative women that Newt Gingrich would place in orphanages. This is the same Newt Gingrich who, despite his clear disdain for gay and lesbian "lifestyles," has invited lesbians and gay men into the Republican Party. I need not remind you that he made no such offer to the women on welfare discussed above. Who, we might ask, is truly on the outside of heteronormative power—maybe *most* of us?

Conclusion: Destabilization and Radical Coalition Work

While all this may, in fact, seem interesting or troubling or both, you may be wondering: What does it have to do with the question of the future of queer politics? It is my argument, as I stated earlier, that one of the great failings of queer theory and especially queer politics has been the inability to incorporate into analysis of the world and strategies for political mobilization the roles that race, class, and gender play in defining people's differing relations to dominant and normalizing power. I present this essay as the beginning of a much longer and protracted struggle to acknowledge and delineate the distribution of power within and outside of queer communities. This is a discussion of how to build a politics organized not merely by reductive categories of straight and queer, but organized instead around a more intersectional analysis of who and what the enemy is and where our potential allies can be found. This analysis seeks to make clear the privilege and power embedded in the categorizations of, on the one hand, an upstanding, "morally correct," white, state-authorized, middle-class, male *heterosexual*, and on the other, a culturally deficient, materially bankrupt, state-dependent, *heterosexual* woman of color, the latter found most often in our urban centers (those that have not been gentrified), on magazine covers, and on the evening news.

I contend, therefore, that the radical potential of queer politics, or any liberatory movement, rests on its ability to advance strategically oriented political identities arising from a more nuanced understanding of power. One of the most difficult tasks in such an endeavor (and there are many) is not to forsake the complexities of both how power is structured and how we might think about the coalitions we create. Far too often movements revert to a position in which membership and joint political work are based on a necessarily similar history of oppression—but this is too much like identity politics (Phelan). Instead, I am suggesting that the process of movement-building be rooted not in our shared history or identity, but in our shared marginal relationship to dominant power that normalizes, legitimizes, and privileges.

We must, therefore, start our political work from the recognition that multiple systems of oppression are in operation and that these systems use institutionalized categories and identities to regulate and socialize. We must also understand that power and access to dominant resources are distributed across the boundaries of "het" and "queer" that we construct. A model of queer politics that simply pits the grand "heterosexuals" against all those oppressed "queers" is ineffectual as the basis for action in a political environment dominated by Newt Gingrich, the Christian right, and the recurring ideology of white supremacy. As we stand on the verge of watching those in power dismantle the welfare system through a process of demonizing poor and young, primarily poor and young women of color—many of whom have existed for their entire lives outside the white, middle-class, heterosexual norm—we have to ask if these women do not fit into society's categories of marginal, deviant, and "queer." As we watch the explosion of prison construction and the disproportionate incarceration rates of young men and women of color, often as part of the economic development of poor, white, rural communities, we have to ask if these individuals do not fit society's definition of "queer" and expendable.

I am not proposing a political strategy that homogenizes and glorifies the experience of poor heterosexual people of color. In fact, in calling for a more expansive left political identity and formation I do not seek to erase the specific historical relation between the stigma of "queer" and the sexual activity of gay men, lesbians, bisexual, and transgendered individuals. And in no way do I mean to, or want to, equate the experiences of marginal heterosexual women and men to the lived experiences of queers. There is no doubt that heterosexuality, even for those heterosexuals who stand outside the norms of heteronormativity, results in some form of privilege and feelings of supremacy. I need only recount the times when other women of color, more economically vulnerable than myself, expressed superiority and some feelings of disgust when they realized that the nice young professor (me) was "that way."

However, in recognizing the distinct history of oppression lesbian, gay, bisexual, and transgendered people have confronted and challenged, I am not willing to embrace every queer as my marginalized political ally. In the same way, I do not assume that shared racial, gender, and/or class position or identity guarantees or produces similar political commitments. Thus, identities and communities, while important to this strategy, must be complicated and destabilized through a recognition of the multiple social positions and relations to dominant power found *within* any one category or identity. Kimberle Crenshaw, in "Mapping the Margins: Intersectionality, Identity Politics, and Violence against Women of Color," suggests that such a project use the idea of intersectionality to reconceptualize or problematize the identities and communities that are "home" to us. She demands that we challenge those identities that seem like home by acknowledging the other parts of our identities that are excluded:

> With identity thus reconceptualized [through a recognition of intersectionality], it may be easier to understand the need to summon up the courage to challenge groups that are after all, in one sense, "home" to us, in the name of the parts of us that are not made at home. . . . The most one could expect is that we will dare to speak against internal exclusions and marginalizations, that we might call attention to how the identity of "the group" has been centered on the intersectional identities of a few. . . . Through an awareness of intersectionality, we can better acknowledge and ground the differences among us and negotiate the means by which these differences will find expression in constructing group politics. (1299)

In the same ways that we account for the varying privilege to be gained by a heterosexual identity, we must also pay attention to the privilege some queers receive from being white, male, and upper class. Only through recognizing the many manifestations of power, across and within categories, can we truly begin to build a movement based on one's politics and not exclusively on one's identity.

I want to be clear that what I and others are calling for is the destabilization, not the destruction or abandonment, of identity categories.[7] We must reject a queer politics that seems to ignore, in its analysis of the usefulness of traditionally named categories, the roles of identity and community as paths to survival, using shared experiences of oppression and resistance to build indigenous resources, shape consciousness, and act collectively. Instead, I would suggest that it is the multiplicity and interconnectedness of our identities that provide the most promising avenue for the *destabilization and radical politicalization* of these same categories.

This is not an easy path to pursue because most often this will mean building a political analysis and political strategies around the most marginal in our society, some of whom look like us, many of whom do not. Most often, this will mean rooting our struggle in, and addressing the needs of, communities of color. Most often this will mean highlighting the intersectionality of one's race, class, gender, and sexuality and the relative power and privilege that one receives from being a man and/or being white and/or being middle class and/or being heterosexual. This, in particular, is a daunting challenge because so much of our political consciousness has been built around simple dichotomies such as powerful/powerless; oppressor/victim; enemy/comrade. It is difficult to feel safe and secure in those spaces where both your relative privilege and your experiences with marginalization are understood to shape your commitment to radical politics. However, as Bernice Johnson Reagon so aptly put it in her essay, "Coalition Politics: Turning the Century," "if you feel the strain, you may be doing some good work" (362).

And while this is a daunting challenge and uncomfortable position, those who have taken it up have not only survived, but succeeded in their efforts. For example, both the needle-exchange and prison projects pursued through the auspices of ACT-UP New York point to the possibilities and difficulties involved in principled transformative coalition work. In each project individuals from numerous identities—heterosexual, gay, poor, wealthy, white, black, Latino—came together to challenge dominant constructions of who should be allowed and who deserved care. No particular identity exclusively determined the shared political commitments of these activists; instead their similar positions, as marginalized subjects relative to the state—made clear through the government's lack of response to AIDS—formed the basis of this political unity.

In the prison project, it was the contention of activists that the government which denied even wealthy gay men access to drugs to combat this disease must be regarded as the same source of power that denied incarcerated men and women access to basic health care, including those drugs and conditions needed to combat HIV and AIDS. The coalition work this group engaged in involved a range of people, from formerly incarcerated individuals, to heterosexual men and women of color, to those we might deem privileged white lesbians and gay men. And this same group of people who came together to protest the conditions of incarcerated people with AIDS also showed up to public events challenging the homophobia that guided the government's and biomedical industries' response to this epidemic. The political work of this group of individuals was undoubtedly informed by the public identities they embraced, but these were identities that they further acknowledged as complicated by intersectionality and placed within a political framework where their shared experience as marginal, nonnormative subjects could be foregrounded. Douglas Crimp, in his article "Right On, Girlfriend!" suggests that through political work our identities become remade and must therefore be understood as *relational*. Describing such a transformation in the identities of queer activists engaged in, and prosecuted for, needle-exchange work, Crimp writes:

> But once engaged in the struggle to end the crisis, these queers' identities were no longer the same. It's not that "queer" doesn't any longer encompass their sexual practices; it does, but it also entails a *relation* between those practices and other circumstances that make very different people vulnerable both to HIV infection and to the stigma, discrimination, and neglect that have characterized the societal and governmental response to the constituencies most affected by the AIDS epidemic. (317–18)

The radical potential of those of us on the outside of heteronormativity rests in our understanding that we need not base our politics in the dissolution of all categories and communities, but we need instead to work toward the destabilization and remaking of our identities. Difference, in and of itself—even that difference designated through named categories—is not the problem. Instead it is the power invested in certain identity categories and the idea that bounded categories are not to be transgressed that serve as the basis of domination and control. The reconceptualization not only of the content of identity categories, but the intersectional nature of identities themselves, must become part of our political practice.

We must thus begin to link our intersectional analysis of power with concrete coalitional work. In real terms this means identifying political struggles such as the needle-exchange and prison projects of ACT-UP that transgress the boundaries of identity to highlight, in this case, both the repressive power of the state and the normalizing power evident within both dominant and marginal communities. This type of principled coalition work is also being pursued in a more modest fashion by the Policy Institute of the National Gay and Lesbian Task Force. Recently, the staff at the task force distributed position papers not only on the topics of gay marriages and gays in the military, but also on right-wing attacks against welfare and affirmative action. Here we have political work based in the knowledge that the rhetoric and accusations of nonnormativity that Newt Gingrich and other right-wingers launch against women on welfare closely resemble the attacks of nonnormativity mounted against gays, lesbians, bisexuals, and transgendered individuals. Again it is the marginalized relation to power, experienced by both of these groups—and I do not mean to suggest that the groups are mutually exclusive—that frames the possibility for transformative coalition work. This prospect diminishes when we do not recognize and deal with the reality that the intersecting identities that gay people embody—in terms of race, class, and gender privilege—put some of us on Gingrich's side of the welfare struggle (e.g., Log Cabin Republicans). And in a similar manner a woman's dependence on state financial assistance in no way secures her position as one supportive of gay rights and/or liberation. While a marginal identity undoubtedly increases the prospects of shared consciousness, only an articulation and commitment to mutual support can truly be the test of unity when pursuing transformational politics.

Finally, I realize that I have been short on specifics when trying to describe how we move concretely toward a transformational coalition politics among marginalized subjects. The best I can do is offer this discussion as a starting point for reassessing the shape of queer/lesbian/gay/bisexual/transgendered politics as we begin the twenty-first century. A reconceptualization of the politics of marginal groups allows us not only to privilege the specific lived experience of distinct communities, but also to search for those interconnected sites of resistance from which we can wage broader political struggles. Only be recognizing the link among th ideological, social, political, and economic marginalization of punks, bulldaggers, and welfare queens can we begin to develop political analyses and political strategies effective in confronting the linked yet varied sites of power in this country. Such a project is important because it provides a framework from which the difficult work of coalition politics can begin. And it is in these complicated and contradictory spaces that the liberatory and left politics that so many of us work for is located.

Notes

The author would like to thank Mark Blasius, Nan Boyd, Ed Cohen, Carolyn Dinshaw, Jeff Edwards, Licia Fiol-Matta, Joshua Gamson, Lynne Huffer, Tamara Jones, Carla Kaplan, Ntanya Lee, Ira Livingston, and Barbara Ransby for their comments on various versions of this paper. All shortcomings are of course the fault of the author.

A version of this essay also appeared in *GLQ: A Journal of Lesbian and Gay Studies* 3 (1997): 437–65. Copyright © 1997 OPA. Reprinted by permission.

1. The very general chronology of queer theory and queer politics referred to throughout this article is not meant to write the definitive historical development of each phenomenon. Instead, the dates are used to provide the reader with a general frame of reference. See Epstein for a similar genealogy of queer theory and queer politics.

2. See Ingraham for a discussion of the heterogendered imaginary.

3. I want to be clear that in this essay I am including the destruction of sexual categories as part of the agenda of queer politics. While a substantial segment of queer activists and theorists call for the *destabilization* of sexual categories, there are also those self-avowed queers who embrace a politics built around the *deconstruction* and/or elimination of sexual categories. For example, a number of my self-identified queer students engage in sexual behavior that most people would interpret as *transgressive* of sexual identities and categories. However, these students have repeatedly articulated a different interpretation of their sexual behavior. They put forth an understanding that does not highlight their transgression of categories, but one that instead represents them as individuals who operate outside of categories and sexual identities altogether. They are sexual beings, given purely to desire, truly living sexual fluidity, and not constrained by any form of sexual categorization or identification. This interpretation seems at least one step removed from that held by people who embrace the fluidity of sexuality while still recognizing the political usefulness of categories or labels for certain sexual behavior and communities. One example of such people might be those women who identify as lesbians and who also acknowledge that sometimes they choose to sleep with men. These individuals exemplify the process of destabilization that I try to articulate within this essay. Even further removed from the queers who would do away with all sexual categories are those who also transgress what many consider to be categories of sexual behaviors while they publicly embrace one stable

sexual identity (for example, those self-identified heterosexual men who sleep with other men sporadically and secretly).

4. I want to thank Mark Blasius for raising the argument that standing on the outside of heteronormativity is a bit of a misnomer, since as a dominant normalizing process it is a practice of regulation in which we are all implicated. However, despite this insight I will on occasion continue to use this phrasing understanding the limits of its meaning.

5. See Hennessy for a discussion of left analysis and the limits of queer theory.

6. For an insightful discussion of the numerous methods used to regulate and control the sexual and reproductive choices of women, see Shende.

7. See Jones for an articulation of differences between the destabilization and the destruction of identity categories.

Works Cited

Alexander, Jacqui. "Redrafting Morality: The Postcolonial State and the Sexual Offences Bill of Trinidad and Tobago." In *Third World Women and the Politics of Feminism*, ed. C. T. Mohanty, A. Russo, and L. Torres, 133–52. Bloomington: Indiana University Press, 1991.

Berlant, Lauren, and Elizabeth Freeman. "Queer Nationality." In *Fear of a Queer Planet*, ed. Warner, 193–229.

Bérubé, Allan, and Jeffrey Escoffier. "Queer/Nation." *Out/Look: National Lesbian and Gay Quarterly* 11 (Winter 1991): 12–14.

Blasius, Mark. *Gay and Lesbian Politics: Sexuality and the Emergence of a New Ethic.* Philadelphia: Temple University Press, 1994.

Butler, Judith. *Gender Trouble.* New York: Routledge, 1990.

Carby, Hazel. *Reconstructing Womanhood: The Emergence of the Afro-American Woman Novelist.* New York: Oxford University Press, 1987.

Clarke, Cheryl. "The Failure to Transform: Homophobia in the Black Community." In *Home Girls*, ed. Smith, 197–208.

Cohen, Cathy J. "Contested Membership: Black Gay Identities and the Politics of AIDS." In *Queer Theory/Sociology*, ed. S. Seidman, 362–94. Oxford: Blackwell, 1996.

Collins, Patricia Hill. *Black Feminist Thought: Knowledge, Consciousness, and the Politics of Sociology Empowerment.* New York: Harper, 1990.

Combahee River Collective. "The Combahee River Collective Statement." In *Home Girls*, ed. Smith, 272–82.

Crenshaw, Kimberle. "Mapping the Margins: Intersectionality, Identity Politics, and Violence against Women of Color." *Stanford Law Review* 43 (July 1991): 1241–99.

Crimp, Douglas. "Right On, Girlfriend!" In *Fear of a Queer Planet*, ed. Warner, 300–320.

Davis, Angela Y. *Women, Race and Class.* New York: Vintage, 1983.

de Lauretis, Teresa. "Queer Theory: Lesbian and Gay Sexualities." *Differences* 3, no. 2 (Summer 1991): iii–xviii.

Dunlap, David W. "Three Black Members Quit AIDS Organization Board." *New York Times* Jan. 11, 1996, p. B2.

Dynson, Michael Eric. *Between God and Gangsta Rap.* New York: Oxford University Press, 1996.

Epstein, Steven. "A Queer Encounter: Sociology and the Study of Sexuality." *Sociological Theory* 12 (1994): 188–202.

Farajaje-Jones, Elias. "Ain't I a Queer." Creating Change Conference, National Gay and Lesbian Task Force. Detroit, Michigan. Nov. 8–12, 1995.

Fuss, Diana, ed. *Inside/Outside*. New York: Routledge, 1991.

Gamson, Joshua. "Must Identity Movements Self-Destruct? A Queer Dilemma." *Social Problems* 42 (August 1995): 390–407.

Gutman, Herbert G. *The Black Family in Slavery and Freedom, 1750–1925*. New York: Vintage, 1976.

Hennessy-Rosemary. "Queer Theory, Left Politics." *Rethinking MARXISM* 7, no. 3 (1994): 85–111.

Higginbotham, A. Leon, Jr. *In the Matter of Color-Race and the American Legal Process: The Colonial Period*. New York: Oxford University Press, 1978.

hooks, bell. *Feminist Theory: From Margin to Center*. Boston: South End, 1984.

Ingraham, Chrys. "The Heterosexual Imaginary: Feminist Sociology and Theories of Gender." *Sociological Theory* 12 (1994): 203–19.

Jones, Tamara. "Inside the Kaleidoscope: How the Construction of Black Gay and Lesbian Identities Inform Political Strategies." Unpublished paper, Yale University, 1995.

Lorde, Audre. *Sister Outsider: Essays and Speeches by Audre Lorde*. New York: The Crossing Press, 1984.

McIntosh, Mary. "Queer Theory and the War of the Sexes." In *Activating Theory: Lesbian, Gay, Bisexual Politics*, ed. J. Bristow and A. R. Wilson, 33–52. London: Lawrence and Wishart, 1993.

Moraga, Cherríe, and Gloria Anzaldúa, eds. *This Bridge Called My Back: Writings by Radical Women of Color*. New York: Kitchen Table/Women of Color, 1981.

Morton, Donald. "The Politics of Queer Theory in the (Post) Modern Moment." *Genders* 17 (Fall 1993): 121–45.

Moynihan, Daniel Patrick. *The Negro Family: The Case for National Action*. Washington DC: Office of Policy Planning and Research. U.S. Department of Labor, 1965.

Phelan, Shane. *Identity Politics: Lesbian Feminism and the Limits of Community*. Philadelphia: Temple University Press, 1989.

Podolsky, Robin. "Sacrificing Queer and Other 'Proletarian' Artifacts." *Radical America* 25, no. 1 (January 1991): 53–60.

Queer Nation. "I Hate Straights" manifesto. New York, 1990.

Queers United Against Straight-acting Homosexuals. "Assimilation Is Killing Us: Fight for a Queer United Front." WHY I HATED THE MARCH ON WASHINGTON (1993): 4.

Ransby, Barbara, and Tracye Matthews. "Black Popular Culture and the Transcendence of Patriarchical Illusions." *Race & Class* 35, no. 1 (July–September 1993): 57–70.

Reagon, Bernice Johnson. "Coalition Politics: Turning the Century." In *Home Girls*, ed. Smith, 356–68.

Reed, Adolph L., Jr. "The 'Underclass' as Myth and Symbol: The Poverty of Discourse about Poverty." *Radical America* 24, no. 1 (January 1990): 21–40.

Rich, Adrienne. "Compulsory Heterosexuality and Lesbian Existence." In *Powers of Desire: The Politics of Sexuality*, ed. A. Snitow, C. Stansell, and S. Thompson, 177–206. New York: Monthly Review, 1983.

Sedgwick, Eve. *The Epistemology of the Closet*. Berkeley: University of California Press, 1990.

Seidman, Steven. "Identity and Politics in a 'Postmodern' Gay Culture." In *Fear of a Queer Planet*, ed. Warner, 105–42.

Shende, Suzanne. "Fighting the Violence against Our Sisters: Prosecution of Pregnant Women and the Coercive Use of Norplant." In *Women Transforming Politics: An Alternative Reader*, ed. C. Cohen, K. Jones, and J. Tronto. New York: New York University Press, 1997.

Smith, Barbara. "Queer Politics: Where's the Revolution?" *The Nation* 257, no. 1 (July 5, 1993): 12–16.

———, ed. *Home Girls: A Black Feminist Anthology*. New York: Kitchen Table/Women of Color, 1983.

Smith, M. G. "Social Structure in the British Caribbean about 1820." *Social and Economic Studies* 1, no. 4 (August 1953): 55–79.

"Statement of Purpose." Dialogue on the Lesbian and Gay Left. Duncan Conference Center in Del Ray Beach, Florida, April 1–4, 1993.

Stein, Arlene, and Ken Plummer. "'I Can't Even Think Straight': 'Queer' Theory and the Missing Sexual Revolution in Sociology." *Sociological Theory* 12 (1994): 178–87.

Vaid, Urvashi. *Virtual Equality: The Mainstreaming of Gay & Lesbian Liberation*. New York: Anchor, 1995.

Warner, Michael, ed. *Fear of a Queer Plant: Queer Politics and Social Theory*. Minneapolis: University of Minnesota Press, 1993.

West, Cornel. *Race Matters*. Boston: Beacon, 1993.

Wilson, William Julius. *The Truly Disadvantaged: The Inner City, the Underclass, and Public Policy*. Chicago: University of Chicago Press, 1987.

PART THREE

SEXUAL-IDENTITY POLITICS

IN THE UNITED STATES

NINE

SEXUAL IDENTITY AND URBAN SPACE

ECONOMIC STRUCTURE AND POLITICAL ACTION

Robert W. Bailey

THE URBAN CHARACTERISTIC of sexual identity is not new. Whether viewed as "gay ghettos," "sexual havens," or even domains of sexual consumerism, the inference drawn from the study of the "gay ghetto" was that each of these communities was the same: almost as if San Francisco were an archetype for all lesbian and gay residential clusters in the United States.

In part this is the result of past explorations of lesbian or gay urban terrains. The initial examinations of these sexual domains were drawn by participant observers who used ethnographic techniques.[1] The results were rich in theory but rested their conclusions on observation and in-depth interviews. Although they identified the meanings of these spaces in terms of the actions of participants (both politically and personally), they did not attempt to characterize sexual domains in larger terms—either for the political or economic status of these communities or for the cities in which they were located.

The first sophisticated quantitative study of spatial patterning by sexual identity was conducted in San Francisco. Manual Castells, working with Don Lee and Karen A. Murphy, examined what he came to call the "gay territory" and its role as a base for a social and political movement built about sexuality.[2] His analysis was part of a larger study of the localizaton of class and other conflicts within large metropolitan areas. Castells was looking to identify such sites as organizational bases for progressive politics. His analysis of the geography of San Francisco is gay community was aimed toward assessing its potential for future radical political action. Yet in pursuing his research agenda, Castells also introduced some misinterpretations of domains of sexual identity that had become part of the literature of urban politics.

To conduct the analysis, Castells and Murphy used five dimensions to identify these sexually identified domains by census tracts.[3] No one of the measures was used to the exclusion of others, and in the end Castells relied on a judgmental assessment of the overlapped maps of spaces identified by these five indicators. Having defined some areas of the city as "gay territory" (and by exclusion others as "non-gay territory"), Castells further analyzed these census tracts in light of several standard census dimensions, specifically referencing the territories against twelve variables. He concluded that indeed "gay territory" had social roots that could be identified. Most important, he found that the percentage of the population under 18 years of age was a strong descriptor of gay vs. non-gay territories. This he termed a "family space" variable.

A second variable describing differences between gay and non-gay territory was what Castells called "property," the census bureau dimension that described the percentage of housing units that were owner-occupied. He found no other relationship in the measures tested and concluded that "gay [male] territory" was culturally based, not economically based. He went on to describe property and family values as "major walls protecting the 'straight universe' against gay influence." Using other techniques, Castells added a "higher rent" scale and an "education" scale to further explain differences in the two "territories."[4] Though gay territory was rental, it was not of the highest rental spaces in the city. Higher rents added a third barrier to expansion of gay territory in San Francisco, concluded Castells.

Although Castells was the first to quantitatively assess the boundaries and character of gay territories, there were problems in his analysis in both method and theory. Gay territory is still focused in the Castro/Eureka Valley district in San Francisco, where there are more men than women and a higher rate of educational accomplishment. But by the 1990s other trends were evident. At least in San Francisco, expansion of "gay territory" was not limited by higher rents as Castells had expected, but by "family territory." There has been gay and lesbian in-migration to the higher-rent, higher-value Pacific Heights area but no in-migration into the higher-income St. Francis Woods area, a domain of upper-middle-class family housing. There has been some expansion out onto the avenues west of Twin Peaks, but conflict between gay entrepreneurs and Latino activists at the perimeter between the Castro and the Mission districts did limit expansion in that direction.

In addition to these relatively minor problems with the analysis, the most controversial aspect of Castells's study was how he defined lesbians as a result of his work. San Francisco's gay male community may have been more visible in the late 1970s than were lesbians, but this was only a matter of degree, not kind. Even in the 1970s and certainly by the early 1980s, there were clear and identifiable lesbian domains, residential clusters of women within the Bay Area. But the real problem with the Castells effort in regard to women was the inference he drew from what he saw as the apparent lack of women's neighborhood spaces: that lesbian spaces could not be found *because women were not territorial.* Castells's generalization about women may be the result of a negative approach to "gay space"—that is, space is seen as defensive, in a sense *space against* other social forms and constructions.

Scholars have already dealt with the male exclusiveness of Castells's work and the implications associated with its conclusion. Women's spaces in other cities have been identified and examined.[5] That women did indeed construct their own identity spaces, even in San Francisco in the 1970s and before, is well documented by now.

The fundamental problem with Castells's work has been addressed by other scholars, but there remains another problem—not from how these domains are seen within gay/lesbian or queer studies, but how they are interpreted within urban studies. If Castells jumped to conclusions about women from his single case, many scholars in urban sociology and politics have similarly jumped to conclusions about the role of gay men and lesbians in urban settings from the single case of San Francisco. The gentrifying role of gay men and the rehabilitation of older Victorian houses in the city is now a legend in urban development policy. The ability of lesbians and gay men to mobilize sexual identity at the polls and through local legislatures has been generalized to other cities. But San Francisco is only one case, and hardly the typical case, neither for the political and economic processes that surround urban transformation nor for the politics of lesbians and gay men. Of course, it was the possibility that San Francisco's gay community might be at the cutting edge of a transformative urban social movement that engaged Castells's interest in the first place. But his observations on the character of gay territory were falsely generalized by others.

The purpose of this chapter is to reexamine and critique Castells's empirical findings based on his study of gay territories in San Francisco through a much broader analysis both in terms of variables analyzed and case studies. Rather than base the analysis on only two primary variables and ten secondary ones, the present study is based on several clusters of variables that in all amount to more than one hundred indicators. Rather than study just one city, the present analysis looks at more than forty metropolitan areas. After establishing a firmer empirical base than available in the past, the chapter goes on to examine the political implications of its central finding—social factors best describe these urban domains of sexual identity, not economic factors.

Finding Sexual Domains in the Urban Setting

To better understand the meaning of these urban domains of sexuality, we must at least attempt to describe "lesbian and gay territories" in a comparative framework. The first step is to establish a surrogate indicator for concentration of lesbian and gay residents, as Castells had done. The second is to study these identified urban spaces in the context of a data set that will allow for comparison.

The decennial census offers little help. At best it provides a surrogate indicator for dedicated same-sex households. But the exclusion of single, noncoresident, partnered gay men and lesbians and those living in other arrangements from the data set introduces a bias that cannot be overcome through weighting. An additional problem is that in its most useful format, the Public Use Microdata Sets' (PUMS)[6] 1 percent and 5 percent samples, the data are linked to geographic areas that are far larger than block groups, census tracts, or even zip codes, the other potential geostatistical boundaries that can be used with census data. The PUMS area for Rochester, New York, for example, covers the entire city.

An alternative method, with its own problems, is used in the present work. The primary data set used in this chapter to identify gay/lesbian residential concentration is not the decennial census but a direct-mail list created from nearly one hundred smaller regional lists and a number of national lists. With more than 525,000 households identified by merging regional lists, the roll is the largest such list in the country directed at lesbians and gay men. Equally important is that the list is not aimed at direct marketing, but at political networking. It includes small as well as large donors to gay candidates for local office, subscribers to lesbian and gay newspapers and magazines, contributors to national gay organizations, and others.[7]

From this source two indicators of residential concentration were constructed. The first was an index of residential concentration that refers to a mean within each individual Metropolitan Statistical Area (MSA). That is, the zip codes within census bureau–defined MSAs were seen as the base of an analysis of regional concentration. After a mean across the region was established, each individual zip code was then compared to this regional average. Those areas where an unusually large number of lesbian or gay male households were present would then be scored high on an index of regional concentration. In some cities the highest level of concentration was as high as 27 or even 35 times the regional mean. The West Village in New York, for example, scored a 27 when compared to the 625 zip codes in all the New York state counties in and about New York City. The second dimension was a simple per capita ratio of households on the list when compared to the total population within each zip code as reported by the census bureau for 1990, what direct mail professions call the area's penetration.

Despite the advantages of using a community-generated mailing list, the list itself is obviously not a randomly generated data set. While its very size ensures that every conceivable subsidiary demographic category would be covered, it is not likely that they are in general proportion to their fraction in society. Even though it is not a direct merchandising list in the standard sense (that is, geared heavily toward higher-income groups), it clearly would cut off the lowest economic groups in the gay community. It can also be assumed to be biased toward men rather than women (though all self-identification indicators show that men out-identify as gay than women as lesbian—about 60 percent to 40 percent) and toward whites than minorities. It is clear, for example, that in New York and Chicago blacks are underrepresented, and in the lower San Francisco Bay Area that Latinos are underrepresented. Thus, the biases of these data must be kept in mind in all circumstances.

Having said this, though, I should repeat that the measures are used to identify spaces or domains, not persons or households. I am seeking the common and differing characteristics of lesbian and gay neighborhoods defined as concentrations of lesbian and gay-male-identified households in whatever proportion, not commonalities of households or individuals. The indicators are nothing more then identifiers of "domains of sexual identity."[8]

Domains of Sexual Identity I:
Social and Demographic Correlates

The defining characteristics of urban domains of sexual identity are primarily social and demographic, not economic. Economic variables play a differing role in the several cities examined, but display no universal influences. These findings are the result of correlation analysis of a merged file of the surrogate indicators of residential concentration of gay men and lesbians described above with over two hundred frequently asked variables from the standard extraction files of the 1990 decennial census. More than forty MSAs were analyzed—essentially all MSAs that had sufficient data to show patterns. The analysis was conducted metropolitan area by metropolitan area at the zip code level of aggregation.

Age and Household Structure

By far the most consistent themes evident among the neighborhoods identified by concentrations of gay residents were age and household structure.

GAY/LESBIAN URBAN ENCLAVES TEND TO BE YOUNG

In nearly all urban spaces that can be identified as centers of strong gay and lesbian presence, the typical resident is young and the household is small in size. In most of the forty MSAs studied, concentrations of gay and lesbian residents correlated positively and significantly with the census bureau–defined 24–35-year-old grouping.[9] Three of the thirteen MSAs where the 25–35-year-old category did not correlate with concentration of gay residents have a large student population—Austin, Albany, and St. Louis. In these cities, the 18–24-year-old category correlated with lesbian and gay presence.

In addition, several of the cities showed strong relationships among both of the younger adult age categories (Birmingham, Milwaukee, Philadelphia, Boston, Cincinnati, and Buffalo). Again, lesbian and gay residential clusters near university communities were important. An analysis of the middle-aged categories reinforces the younger profile of urban "gay territories." In most cities studied there is a negative correlation in the middle-aged brackets. The results vary from city to city, but it is clear that lesbian and gay residents tend to live with, or are themselves, younger urbanites.

PRESENCE OF SENIORS

A surprising finding is the degree to which lesbians and gay men reside side by side with senior citizens. While this was true in cities typically known for having a high proportion of retirees—Honolulu, San Diego, Miami/Ft. Lauderdale, and Tampa/St. Petersburg—it was also true in some of the older cities of the Midwest and South: Chicago (especially in zip code areas with 50 percent or more African-American residents), Minneapolis/St. Paul, Milwaukee, New Orleans, Atlanta, Omaha, Rochester, St. Louis, Cincinnati, and Cleveland all showed positive and significant correlations between the presence of gay men and lesbians and senior citizens. The co-presence of gay men, lesbians, and seniors in the same neighborhood in these older cities is probably a manifestation of changing neighborhoods—older neighborhoods where seniors have remained in changing ethnic communities while younger residents—gay men and lesbians among them—move in.

HOUSEHOLD SIZE AND STRUCTURE

In addition to age, the two other most potent correlates associated with urban spaces of high concentrations of lesbian and gay residents are household size and household structure. Gay "territory" is dominated by single households or couple households without children. In all metropolitan areas studied, the presence of gay and lesbians residents correlated negatively with average household size (the range of correlation coefficients was a low of $r = -0.2212$ in the San Francisco Bay region to a high in Cincinnati of $r = -0.7036$; all at statistically significant levels). It was universally true also that neighborhoods with a strong gay and lesbian presence correlated positively with the percentage of single households and of people living alone (coefficients ranged from $r = 0.41$ to $r = 0.72$). Households in these urban spaces were less likely to be headed by married couples, or be made up of married couples and children. To state it differently, it was universally true in the forty MSAs studied that neighborhoods with a strong presence of lesbian and gay residents are neighborhoods dominated by non-family households (the range was $r = 0.46$ to 0.76).

THE CO-PRESENCE OF FEMALE-HEADED HOUSEHOLDS AND GAY/LESBIAN RESIDENTS

The presence of female-headed households in these spaces adds a further dimension to the profile. A substantial body of urban literature has shown that urban space is being "genderized" and that this has important social and economic implications.[10] In many of the cities studied there was a substantial presence of female-headed households side by side with gay or lesbian households. The relationship ranges from statistically insignificant, to a substantial positive relationship (Baltimore was the highest at $r = 0.6628$). In no city or MSA studied did the presence of lesbian and gay residents correlate negatively with the presence of female-headed households. When the presence of gay and lesbian residents was correlated with the percentage of female-headed households with children, a positive and significant correlation could be found in most of the older Northeast and Midwest metropolitan regions: Chicago, Baltimore, Milwaukee, Philadelphia, Washington, Cleveland, Albany, the Quad Cities, the Twin Cities, Buffalo, Boston, Indianapolis, and New Orleans among them. In fact, in the Northeast, only New York City showed no such relationship. Though the pattern was common in the Northeast, it was also present in some other cities around the country including some of the "sun belt" cities, including Phoenix, Denver, Sacramento, and Tampa/St. Petersburg. The overlap of gender space and spaces associated with sexual identity seems certain.

Sexual Identity and Racial Patterning of Urban Space

The relationship of race to lesbian and gay urban space is more complicated than that of age and household structure to lesbian and gay urban space. On one level there is a methodological issue. Associating some urban spaces with the sexual identity of one grouping and others with a racial identity necessarily imputes an ontology to space as if lesbians or gay men of African descent could not reside in sexual-identity spaces, and non-African lesbians or gay men could not live in urban spaces characterized by the racial identity of the majority of its residents. Obviously the points to be made in the analysis of racial identity, sexual identity, and urban space could be pressed far beyond their practical utility.

The second issue is more one of real conflict over urban space. The initial image of the "gay ghetto" was that it was male, white, and middle class. The "whiteness" of gay communities became a subject of debate first by African-American gay men and lesbians, then Latinos, and most recently by Asians. In much of urban America, the profile of the educated gay white male as the dominant one of the gay movement came into conflict with the economic aspirations of urban African Americans. The combination of real economic issues, traditional affiliation of African Americans with the American Baptists and Methodist denominations, and—later—a refocus on Afrocentrism which viewed homosexuality as a set of behaviors outside African traditions placed the two communities in some cities at loggerheads. In some cases—San Francisco is an example—there also was conflict with the Latino communities' seeing the expansion of neighborhoods with high concentrations of lesbians and gay men as a potential threat to the stability of their own neighborhoods.

LESBIAN AND GAY NEIGHBORHOODS MORE INTEGRATED THAN SURROUNDING METROPOLITAN AREAS

But the racial patterning is more complicated than these images present. In almost all the metropolitan areas studied, "gay and lesbian territory" tends to be more integrated than the urban and suburban areas of the surrounding metropolitan regions. This would be true under most circumstances, since in a great majority of MSAs, gay men and lesbians tend to live in the central city; thus almost by definition those neighborhoods would be more integrated, especially in older center cities. In Philadelphia, Pittsburgh, Baltimore, New Orleans, Washington, Hartford, Sacramento, Albany, the Quad and Twin Cities, Buffalo, Cincinnati, Boston, and Indianapolis, the presence of gay men or lesbians correlates negatively and significantly with percentage of whites regionally. In no broad MSA urban area examined did the presence of lesbian and gay residents by zip code correlate positively with the percentage of white residents.

THE SEPARATION OF "GAY" AND AFRICAN AMERICAN SPACES

Nevertheless, despite the general pattern of sexual domains being better integrated than their surrounding MSAs, is also striking that across the country, gay neighborhoods are more likely to be integrated by Latinos and Asians than by African Americans.[11] Whether the reason is higher mobility among newer immigrants, historic legal discrimination against blacks in cities of the South, Washington, and Chicago, or ascribable to economics, the pattern remains.

In the Chicago MSA, for example, gay domains on the city's north side have large enough numbers of Asians, Latinos, and even Native Americans to result in significant and positive correlations with the presence of lesbians and gay men. But the areas of the Chicago MSA that have a strong lesbian and gay presence do not show a similar and significant presence of African Americans. The Chicago region as a whole has consistently demonstrated a marked cleavage by race in housing, economics, and voting patterns.[12] When taking the city of Chicago out of its two state MSAs and examining it on its own, racial patterning is more extreme and quite evident in even the comparatively integrated gay domains of the Boyztown.

The same pattern can be seen in Washington, D.C. Though zip code areas with a strong lesbian and gay presence show a degree of racial integration when compared with the rest of the metro Washington area, racial patterning within the District itself is obvious—especially in regard to African Americans. While the lesbian and gay presence within the District does correlate negatively with the white population percentage, it is Latinos and Asians who offer the margin of racial integration in the gay domains of northwest Washington, not African Americans. A clustering of lesbian and gay residents in the largely African-American southwest portion of the District is identifiable. Nevertheless, it is clear that the racial divisions in housing patterns that are so evident in the District are also evident among Washington's lesbian and gay residents.

When the five counties of New York City are examined, racial patterning does emerge—though it is not as strong as it is in Chicago or Washington. In the 165 zip code areas of the city there is a mild negative correlation with the presence of African Americans citywide ($r = -0.2302$) and a mild positive one for the presence of whites ($r = 0.2674$). But this citywide analysis can be misleading. When Manhattan is taken out of the calculations, and Queens, the Bronx, Brooklyn, and Staten Island are analyzed separately, no statistically significant correlations against race are found. When Manhattan is studied alone, the zip codes with a high concentration of lesbian and gay residents correlate significantly with the percentage of white residents ($r = 0.5768$) and negatively with the percentage of black residents ($r = -0.4507$).

GEOGRAPHIC DIFFERENCES

The differing patterns between southern cities where separation was strong and older industrial cities of the Northeast and Midwest where it is weak is also striking. For example, despite large black populations in all southern and some sun belt cities, there is no marked sign of overlap among lesbian and gay residential spaces and African-American identified spaces within the cities themselves. In Dallas, Birmingham, Houston, and Atlanta there is no suggestion that zip code areas with higher than average percentages of gay and lesbian residents are more integrated than other neighborhoods in their respective MSA regions. This is a pattern starkly different from the cities of the Northeast. While regionally, almost all metropolitan areas of the Northeast corridor and the Midwest showed that gay space was more likely to be integrated space (in that they significantly and negatively correlated to the presence of whites), there is no such finding at either the regional or city level in the larger southern urban areas analyzed. In fact, when Houston,

Dallas, and Atlanta are looked at as cities, not as urban statistical regions, the opposite is true. Houston demonstrates a negative correlation between the presence of gay men and lesbians and African Americans. The same is true in Atlanta ($r = -0.4087$) but the presence of gay men and lesbians correlates positively with the presence of whites and Latinos. And when the city of Dallas is viewed independently of the greater Dallas/Fort Worth area, the presence of gay and lesbian residents again correlates negatively with presence of African Americans ($r = -0.3038$). These patterns are especially important as both Houston and Atlanta are seen as the new centers of lesbian and gay life in the South, having passed New Orleans two decades ago as the principal center of gay/lesbian presence in the states of the old Confederacy.

Los Angeles, the second largest gay center in the country, also shows racial patterning in relation to sexual identity. The greater Los Angeles/Long Beach/ Riverside MSA demonstrates no statistically significant relationship region-wide between racial categories and measures of lesbian and gay presence at the zip code level. But when Los Angeles County is examined independently of the overall Los Angeles/Long Beach/Riverside MSA (so as to include Santa Monica, Pasadena, and West Hollywood but exclude Riverside County), racially defined housing patterns measured against sexual identity do emerge. There is actually a mildly positive but statistically significant correlation between the presence of gay men and lesbians and the presence of Anglos/whites ($r = 0.2093$). In fact, when Los Angeles city is examined alone it demonstrates a pattern similar to those of Houston, Atlanta, and Dallas.

Whether these patterns of Los Angeles, Dallas, Houston, and Atlanta reflect more their spatial growth and economic change since the close of World War II than factors of race is a question that cannot be answered here, but the results may be related to household income in some cases. As we shall see, gay domains in Atlanta, Los Angeles, Manhattan, and Houston have among the highest per capita incomes of the areas studied. They also show the most separate housing patterns measured against race. Baltimore and Indianapolis, cities that have among the lowest per capita income rates among those studied, are also the two most integrated. And yet economics cannot explain the separation in Queens, where income and race have finally come to a point of noncorrelation, and where large numbers of African Americans and gay men and lesbians live in differing social enclaves.[13] Nevertheless, what is seen here is a wide variation in the degree to which lesbian- and gay-identified space is "race-neutral" space.

Gender, Sexual Identity, and Urban Space

As a counterpoint to the essentialism of Castells that men are more "territorial" than women, several researchers have tried to show that indeed there is a spatial aspect to women's communities. The principle focus of such studies are areas known within the women's community as having a vibrant and large lesbian presence—East San Francisco Bay, greater Park Slope in Brooklyn, Northampton (Massachusetts), Santa Fe, and some medium and smaller cities not usually identified with sexual spaces. The studies of these lesbian identity spaces are in addition to the larger body of research on the genderization of urban space, largely conducted by scholars interested in the interaction of social welfare policy and women's studies. It is apparent that portions of urban space are taking on gender identification due primarily to changes in urban household structures, especially the dramatic increase in female-headed households.

To add to this body of research, an attempt was made to identify differences in urban residential patterns between lesbians and gay men. Again, given the method used here, the sample pool is among those individuals who are sufficiently engaged in some political or social activity in the lesbian/gay community to be on the half-million network mailing list, and thus the warnings given above should be remembered here.[14] Several MSAs were broken out by sex. The six communities analyzed were: Atlanta, Birmingham, Brooklyn, Albuquerque/Santa Fe, Baltimore, and the San Francisco Bay Area (including San Francisco and San Jose cities and the South Bay and East Bay Counties). In each of the six sample areas there was patterning to female-coded households in unsurprising ways, but in some other cases the results are important.[15] Three general themes emerge in this study of men and women.

MORE OVERLAP THAN EXPECTED

There was more overlap in residential patterns than would probably be expected—especially within the lesbian and gay community. In the San Francisco Bay Area, for example, where the East Bay communities of Berkeley and Oakland are typically identified as women's communities, the greatest concentration of resident lesbians in the Bay Area is actually in San Francisco. The zip code with the highest per capita rate of women on the mailing list is thirty times the regional mean, while for men, the same measure is fifty-three times the regional mean. And yet, the peak of concentration is in the same neighborhood—the Castro/Eureka Valley area. In Atlanta also, there is not as much difference between the geographic patterning among gay men and lesbians as might have been expected. In fact, the points of highest concentration among men and women in Atlanta are the same: those zip codes areas of center-northeast Atlanta, between downtown and Piedmont Park and north, focused around Ansley Park, east to Little Five Points, and southeast of midtown into the Grant Park area. Similarly in Albuquerque, the overlap of men's and women's residential patterns is quite strong

($r = 0.9399$; P $= <.001$). There are very few correlations with other so-cial-demographic indicators of any significance that differ for either gay men or women (though the fact that there are more seniors in areas where lesbians concentrate in Albuquerque is statistically significant).

This theme must be understood in terms of degree, however. In Baltimore, gay men and lesbians did not live together as closely as they did in some other cities. The correlation coefficient between the presence of gay men and the presence of lesbians at the zip code level regionally was only moderately strong ($r = 0.6861$), one of the lowest of the six regions examined here. Thus at least some differences between the residential patterns of gay men and lesbians could be expected.

Brooklyn may demonstrate the pattern best. Greater Park Slope Brooklyn has been known for many years as the center of a strong women's community, but the reality is that women and men overlap. When analyzing the more substantial number of gender-coded households from the list (which covers 45,000 homes in New York City), the main theme is similarity between the sexes; but there are some differences. In Brooklyn, the core of the gay community is in western Brooklyn, between Prospect Park and the East River—frequently referred to as the Brownstone Belt of Brooklyn—for both men and women. This broad community is itself often thought of as having two polls historically: one an older, largely gay male residential cluster in Brooklyn Heights (in fact, Chauncey[16] identified it as a gay area earlier in the century); the second focused on Park Slope but stretching west from Boreum Hill and north into Prospect Heights and Fort Green, whose neighborhoods are well integrated or predominantly black. This second section, has also often been associated with the Brooklyn's women's community.[17] But despite these gender identifications (largely by word of mouth), there are overlaps among all of these neighborhoods. When residential patterns in Brooklyn are examined more closely, there are not very many differences in spaces associated with gay men and lesbians. In fact, at least at the zip code level, the overlap between the sexual-identity indexes of the two sexes correlated substantially ($r = 0.8134$).

WOMEN ARE LESS GHETTO-IZED THAN MEN

The second theme is that there does not appear to be as concentrated a residential pattern among women as among men. That is, though the peaks of concentration of gay men and lesbians overlap, at the margins women are more dispersed. In pure statistical terms, gay men were at higher per capita rates (when assessed against a mean established among men) than were lesbians. The lesbian communities stretching across Oakland and Berkeley, for example, are clearly observable as is the one in Noe Valley area, at the border between the Castro and Mission districts and even in the avenues west of

Twin Peaks in San Francisco proper. As in the other cities examined, women identifying with lesbian and gay organizations were more dispersed than gay men in the Bay Area (gay men are more concentrated than women). Within Santa Fe city, there is an strong concentration of both lesbians and gay men on the north side of the city. But when the entire Santa Fe/Albuquerque region is looked at, there is a stronger residential pattern for women in outlying areas than for men.

To the Degree That There Are Differences, Women Appear to Be More Woven into Non-Gay Neighborhoods

This dispersion of women at the edges of lesbian and gay clusters has important implications for the relation of women to their neighborhoods. In Birmingham, for example, where the core of lesbian and gay residential patterns remains on the south side of the city, there is some change. There is a clear movement of women toward the Crestwood area of the city, a blue-collar, single-family neighborhood. While men demonstrated the typical pattern of gays living in rental neighborhoods, there was no difference between women who rented and women who owned property. Against all the income and asset dimensions, the lesbian nareas demonstrate statistically significant correlations. These include per capita income, the income deciles, and median and average house valuation.[18]

The data from Atlanta show that neighborhoods with a comparatively strong lesbian presence are slightly less likely to be upscale,[19] and that lesbians are more likely to live in zip code–defined areas with a high number of female-headed households.[20] Since these latter two categories have been identified as near universal characteristics of "sexual-identity" space, the fact that women's presence does not correlate as strongly as men's reinforces the previous conclusions that women are less "ghetto-ized"—or, stated in a positive framework, though the peaks of concentration of gay men and women overlap, of the two, women are more likely to be woven into a broader range of neighborhoods in the city.

In the Bay Area, to the degree that there are differences between the sexes, women are slightly more likely to live in areas with married-couple households and with senior citizens, and with slightly lower income levels and housing valuation. Women in the Bay Area were also slightly more likely than men to live in neighborhoods integrated between Anglos and African Americans—clearly a reflection of the strength of lesbian presence in Oakland (correlation between the lesbian index and the percentage of blacks in the East Bay is $r = 0.2081$; $P = 0.032$). And a strong correlation of women with Latinos in San Francisco city is an obvious reflection of the overlap of Noe Valley and the Mission district.[21]

And in Baltimore, as noted earlier, analysis of the entire sample indicates that gay men and lesbians are much more likely to live in integrated neigh-borhoods regionally (at the zip code level) than are non-gays. This continued to be true by gender, though it was slightly more true for men. When the twenty-eight zip codes of Baltimore city alone were examined, the patterns persisted but were weaker. The presence of both gay men and lesbians corre-lated negatively with presence of whites (at over $r = -0.4495$), though the negative correlation for women was not as strong ($r = -0.3867$; P = .012). Men were more likely to overlap with African Americans, women with Asians, and both with Latinos. The presence of census bureau–defined "very poor" households can also be noted (as well as higher rates of unemploy-ment) in zip code areas that could be identified with a strong presence of lesbians.

Domains of Sexual Identity II:
Economic Correlates of Lesbian and Gay Neighborhoods

The economic standing of lesbian and gay communities has also fallen victim to excessive generalization. There is a perception that gay men and lesbians have high incomes—and if this were true,[22] it would be a natural corollary that gay neighborhoods would be more wealthy than others in standard met-ropolitan areas. But as in the case of race, there is in fact wide variation in the relative economic status of urban spaces in which lesbian and gay men tend to cluster. Again, it will not be the individual or household incomes of urban gay residents that is described, but the income and economic mea-sures of the kinds of urban space in which lesbians and gay men tend to live.

Household Income

In most of the forty metropolitan areas studied, there is little correlation between the dimensions of household income and the measures of gay and lesbian residential concentration. In fact, if there is an inkling of a general relationship it is a slight negative one. In metropolitan areas such as Bal-timore, Las Vegas, New Orleans, Chicago, Washington, Denver/Boulder, Mil-waukee, the Twin Cities, Detroit, St. Louis, Austin, and Boston, the house-hold incomes of zip code areas in which gay male and lesbian residents concentrate correlate positively with the lower to lower-moderate income brackets or negatively with the upper-income categories. In no MSA did the presence of lesbian and gay men correlate positively with the household income dimensions of $50,000 to $75,000, or the $75,000 to $99,000 cate-gories. Only in Atlanta, greater Los Angeles/Riverside, and Manhattan island (that is, not in the four "outer boroughs") did it correlate with household income over $100,000. In the aggregate then, except in these three locations, the notion that gay neighborhoods are relatively well-off neighborhoods is not true.

Measures of Community Economic Status

A slightly different picture emerges, however, when the income dimensions are switched from household to community income characteristics. When viewed through per capita income—a measure of community income that takes into account the size of households as well as the total household income—a different set of correlation coefficients emerges.

For the most part, among the nearly forty MSAs studied, there were no statistically significant relationships, either positive or negative, between per capita income and the presence of lesbian and gay residents. There were, however, some glaring exceptions to this rule. In greater Los Angeles, Seattle/ Tacoma, Birmingham, Houston, New York City, and Atlanta, the presence of gay men and lesbians in a zip code area correlated positively with per capita income within their respective urban regions. It was in Atlanta, however— not New York or Los Angeles—where the relationship was strongest.

Sexual Domains and Economic Distress

But there also are signs of economic distress in some communities in which gay men and lesbians tend to live. In Baltimore, for example, there was a negative relationship between gay presence and per capita income—the only MSA of the forty studied to display such a relationship. The percentage of census bureau–defined "poor" and "very poor" households correlated significantly with the concentration of lesbian and gay residents in the same general urban spaces of Baltimore. These areas were also below the median family income for the region, had a significantly higher percentage of the population unemployed and a high percentage of female-headed households with children. This is not the profile of an upscale community. Other cities demonstrated patterns like Baltimore's but were not as acute. These included Indianapolis, Denver, the Twin Cities, and Buffalo. While some of this may be a result of the method used—with zip codes covering a wide expanse that may include several smaller neighborhoods with differing economic profiles—that gay men and lesbians live in or near those neighborhoods belies any image of a sustained upper-middle-class lifestyle.

Economic Diversity within Metropolitan Sprawls

Within the largest metropolitan areas, which tend to have multiple centers of gay and/or residential concentrations, there again is wide variance. In New York City, indicators of relative economic prosperity of neighborhoods correlate with substantial lesbian and gay presence on balance. Citywide, there is a positive correlation with neighborhood per capita income and mean household income. When Manhattan is studied on its own, gay presence correlates with all the middle- and upper-income brackets and none of the lower-income brackets. The concentration of gay and lesbian residents in Brooklyn correlates with neighborhoods with even higher household incomes. Brooklyn, in fact, demonstrates strong correlations with per capita income and the higher household incomes. It seems the most bifurcated of the boroughs, with gay men and lesbians living in the more affluent sections of western Brooklyn, but also others in less affluent neighborhoods in north Brooklyn and elsewhere in the borough. In Queens, where there a strong gay presence is found in the Jackson Heights and Kew Gardens/Forest Hills sections of the borough, a third profile emerges for New York. Not surprisingly, the strongest correlation in Queens is in the middle-income bracket of $25,000 to $35,000 with negative correlations in regard to upper-income brackets.

In San Francisco city no significant correlation between lesbian and gay concentrations and indicators of household income or per capita income were found. Across the bay, however, lesbian and gay presence in the eighty zip codes of Contra Costa and Alameda counties correlated with the lower-income brackets ($10,000–$15,000 and $15,000–$25,000) as well as with the percent of census bureau–defined "very poor" residents. The economic status of Oakland and Berkeley's lesbian and gay residential concentrations appears less affluent than in San Francisco proper. And yet within the city of Oakland, "lesbian and gay space" is of a higher economic status than many other portions of the city.

Again, in greater Los Angeles, there are also differences among the several clusters of gay residential concentrations. The Los Angeles/Long Beach/Riverside MSA shows little correlation generally, but some specific relationships did emerge when separate regions of the Los Angeles basin are examined. Los Angeles County seems to resemble most gay neighborhood profiles in regard to income. While household income tends to correlate toward the middle- to lower-middle range categories, on per capita income the correlation with middle to high brackets is positive. Within Los Angeles city, as in Brooklyn, "gay neighborhoods" evidence two trends. There is both a correlation between the percent of the population designated as poor and very poor, and with the income bracket of $50,000–$75,000. Even within Los Angeles city there are several clusters of gay residents: the areas near West Hollywood, the Siverlake district, and the lower San Fernando Valley. Diversity can thus be found even within the city of Los Angeles.

In fact, the New York region (including Hudson and Bergen Counties, New Jersey), the San Francisco Bay Area, and the overall Los Angeles basin are so extensive geographically and economically that there are several or even many "gay spaces," each with slightly different racial, gender, and income profiles. There is no one economic profile nationally of urban spaces of sexual identity—or even one profile in specific cities.

Housing Stock, Gentrification, and Sexual "Enclaves"

Many of the references to gay men and lesbians in the literature on urban affairs concern their relation to the gentrification process;[23] and many of these references go back to initial work done by Castells and Murphy,[24] and to Castells himself. Their work was cited by others as a basis for the notion that all gay neighborhoods were gentrifying neighborhoods.[25] It is obvious that gay men and lesbians have been part of movements to take older sections of some cites and have rehabilitated them to the advantage of the city and the lesbian gay communities. South Beach in Miami, Capital Hill in Seattle, portions of northwest Washington, downtown Tampa, the Brownstone Belts of Brooklyn and Jersey City, and the Marigny district of New Orleans[26] are among the most cited examples.

Some other scholars ascribe the apparent co-emergence of gentrification and urban sexual domains not just to an economic rationale but also to (or instead of) changes in family structure and economics.[27] Lesbians and gay men were among a group of rapidly growing household forms—unmarried and attached cohabitants, young unmarried couples, roommates, single and coupled lesbians, and gay men—who were changing residential patterns in center cities.[28] The question is whether in doing so they have displaced other city residents.

The analysis of neighborhoods defined by zip code with strong gay and lesbian presence indicates at least two common factors in their housing markets.

LESBIAN AND GAY NEIGHBORHOODS ARE PREDOMINANTLY MULTIPLE-UNIT, RENTAL HOUSING

In all but the smallest cities (Des Moines and the Quad Cities) the presence of lesbians and gay men correlated strongly and significantly with multiple-unit housing. This was true of the more sprawling modern cities of the sun belt as well as the older industrial cities of the Northeast and Midwest. In addition, in nearly all cities (Honolulu and Des Moines were the only exceptions), the presence of gays and lesbians either correlated with the percentage of the population who were "renters," or negatively with the percentage who were "owners," or, more likely, both. Thus rental, multiple-unit housing dominates these sexual domains.

GAY NEIGHBORHOODS HAVE A HIGH PROPORTION OF OLDER HOUSING STOCK

There is also a consistency in that gay enclaves are typically in the older sections of cities. Throughout the cities of the Northeast and Midwest this is true, and would be expected. But it is also true in newer, rapidly growing cities of the sun belt, which is somewhat surprising. In Tampa/St. Petersburg, Houston, San Diego, Atlanta, and Miami/Ft. Lauderdale, gay presence tends to be in neighborhoods with a high percentage of housing units built before World War II. In only one county studied did the presence of lesbian and gay residents in zip code areas correlate positively with the percentage of housing units built since 1985: Hudson County, New Jersey, which contains three cities with observable gay and lesbian populations—North Bergen, and especially Hoboken and Jersey City.[29] These cities have shown substantial growth in the 1980s as housing prices in lower Manhattan pushed many younger professionals across the Hudson River into New Jersey.[30]

The Political Meaning of Urban Domains of Sexuality

It was in the context of urban transformation that these domains of sexual identity came to be noticed by students of urban affairs. No more were "gay spaces" limited to the Molly houses of London's East End, or boardinghouses in New York, San Francisco, or New Orleans. Rather, they came to be identified as an aspect of "urban transformation"—the reorganization of urban space from being arranged primarily by criteria of efficiency in production to efficiency in consumption that was associated with the emergence of the postindustrial urban form. To the degree that these new gay spaces were dealt with by scholars of urban transformation in the 1970s and 1980s, they were linked with the "back-to-the-city" and gentrification movements of urban transformation.

Castells implied this himself. He observed that male homosexuals were among the gentrifiers of the older ethnic neighborhoods of San Francisco, but others generalized this into broader themes—that these spaces were *inevitably* linked to gentrification. Intended or not, Castells's notion of gay territory as negative space, defensive space, a geography in which lesbians and gay men could protect their own sense of selfhood, is consistent with older ethnographic conceptualizations of ghettos. His new "gay ghetto" was bounded by symbols, set in juxtaposition against family space, as ethnic spaces had been set in opposition to each other generations before. Yet for most contemporary urbanists, the meanings of these spaces are not associated with either the traditions of the "ghetto" as seen by the older Chicago human ecology school (the city as a tapestry of ethnically associated spaces, inhabited by unassimilated workers, linked to rings of economic activity) or with more postmodern, human action perspectives that deny any transcendent meaning to urban space.

The more exacting picture of these contemporary urban spaces offered here adds nuance to this narrative by suggesting the primacy of the social over the economic in the construction of these urban domains of same-sex sexual identity. Six social and demographic characteristics of lesbian/gay urban spaces are near universal correlates among the cities studied. Lesbian and gay residential clusters tend to have: (1) smaller than average households; (2) a younger age profile; (3) a greater likelihood to be racially integrated than surrounding areas of the MSA (at least among Latinos and Asians and to some degree among African Americans); (4) predominantly multiple-unit, rental housing; (5) a higher proportion of older housing stock than other areas of their respective cities; and (6) a consistent presence of senior citizens, either living alone or otherwise. These unifying factors are all social and demographic.

But while there are defining social characteristics to these domains, there is wide variance in their economic status even to the point that in the larger metropolitan areas (New York, the Los Angeles basin, and the San Francisco Bay Area), differing socioeconomic classes can be identified among different clusters of lesbian and gay residents. When viewed across the nation, the cases of Indianapolis and Baltimore stand in stark contrast to Houston and Atlanta in terms of economic well-being. The clusters of lesbian and gay residents left in cities that had not as successfully maneuvered through the economic changes of the 1970s and 1980s were left unobserved. Only a portion of these merging neighborhoods were noticed: the lesbian and gay communities of New York, Atlanta, San Francisco, and Seattle were obvious to students of urban gentrification, but those of Baltimore, Hartford, Indianapolis, or Buffalo were not. The economic does not dominate here.

Instead, a narrative of these spaces different from the "back-to-the-city" movement, or of urban transformation, can be threaded together from recent work of historians and from what we have seen here. The beginnings of gay or lesbian spaces, gay neighborhoods, or networks of identity find their root less in economic development than in an assertion and self-conscious construction of identity in the context of economic change and social regulation. The traditional appropriation of a portion of urban space for sexual entertainment, "Bohemia," and "the Other" had also created spatial opportunities for a freer expression of same-sex affinity and identity: lower Broadway and the Front Street areas of early nineteenth-century New York; the Bowery, Harlem, and Greenwich Village and Brooklyn Heights in New York; the Tenderloin in San Francisco; the near north side in Chicago; and the French Quarter in New Orleans earlier this century. Some of the original works on gay and lesbian history and politics discussed these and other urban settings as "safe havens" for sexual minorities.[31]

While the locations of these spots surely were determined by the dynamics of the local urban landscape and—yes—its economy, their existence was not an expression of economic change effected by the emergence of the postindustrial urban complex. Instead their existence predated the economic (and spatial) restructuring of the postindustrial cities. Same-sex erotic identity spaces held sway through mercantile economic formations, industrial formations, and now postindustrial formations. But they were shaped within the social and economic structures of the time. That any of these spaces would become middle-class neighborhoods is what would surprise "gay" people of the nineteenth century; not their very existence.

The role of political economy in the growth of gay enclaves was given more appropriate attention by the early students of the gay rights movement. Dennis Altman and Barry Adam[32] were influenced by both the political-economy description of the reorganization of urban space for consumption rather than production and advocacy for lesbian and gay "rights." Altman came to see the open sexuality among men in New York and San Francisco's gay urban domains as not just a facet of identity and sexual experimentation, but also as a representation of American capitalist consumerism—filtered through a lens of sexual liberation and sexual identity.[33] He described the gay male bathhouse and backroom culture less as an arena of identity formation or political liberation than an isolated market of sexual exchange. For Altman, the isolated sexual market worked against the longer-term goal of making the public space of everyday life as visibly homosexual as it already was heterosexual. Compartmentalizing erotic symbols (in the broadest sense) and sexual activity to private commercial space detached public spaces and the business world from the gay movement's goals; this led to individuals being more dependent on business institutions and government for personal affirmation on a day-to-day basis.

This theme of Altman's early work brings together sexual identity politics with one of Ira Katznelson's important insights from his study of the history and political economy of northern Manhattan: that the separation of work and residence dramatically changed the nature of progressive politics.[34] The evolving specialization in use of urban space was accompanied by a fragmentation of the fundamental identities in urban politics. Industrial-era class politics, organized through union and other class-based activities, was centered at the workplace, while residential spaces were organized (if they were) around ethnic identity through various fraternal groupings, local political clubs, and church (especially Roman Catholic) and synagogue institutions that were embedded in ethnically defined social networks.

In a parallel analysis, Altman feared that the compartmentalization of sexual and affectional expression to residential or even commercial spaces would also compartmentalize sexual identity, separating the struggle to affirm identity-based rights only to residential neighborhoods or commercial sex establishments, neither of which would offer a serious political challenge to established heterosexist power. Though his understanding of identity was faulty, and his understanding of space negative, Castells also feared the loss of a transformative edge to lesbian and gay politics in San Francisco. His emphasis was on the spatialization of social and progressive movements within what contemporary postmodern geographers would call "Cartesian" space—space not defined by individual or group action, but by larger narratives or comprehensive frames of reference. For Castells, the context of urban social movements was the overall pattern of space utilization in contemporary social and economic processes; but the movements themselves were fueled by the intersection of class and other interests at specific sites within the urban setting.

While the transformative potential of San Francisco's gay rights movement never materialized in Castells's eyes, and Altman may have foreseen the anti-assimilationist themes of contemporary "queer" discourse in his own analysis, these urban domains do have political dimensions in terms of the practical politics of influence in urban governance as well more generally in identity formation (and reformation).

As a matter of the practical, to the degree that lesbians and gay men have achieved a role in electoral politics, it has almost always been in legislative districts in which these urban spaces serve as the focus of a political identity. The very concentration not only of residents but businesses and entertainment centers offers a convenience for mobilization to the polls that more dispersed minorities—Jews, middle-class Latinos, or Asians—might envy. It goes further, however. If we conceive of these identity spaces as open and diverse but with a defining character of same-sex affinity, it is not too much of a leap to understand that their polyglot nature also requires the building of coalitions with other group identities—ranging from racial and ethnic identities to what Richard DeLeon might call postmaterialist coalitions with environmentalists and religious minorities, among others.[35] It is a consistent theme of the politics of sexual identity at the urban level that coalitions with other identity groups is attractive and necessary.[36]

On a much grander stage, however, the role of these sexual domains in the formation of a political identity is critical. In the past, by emphasizing these domains as the bounded spaces of a closed-off gay ghetto, modeled on the older ethnographic analysis of ghettos, those few urban specialists who noted spaces of sexual identity missed several themes.

First, they underestimated the importance of such space in the construction of personal and collective political identities among those *who do not actually reside* in such physical spaces. One aspect of viewing these spaces as enclaves or defensive spaces was that it equated site with identity. Yet, Castro, Chelsea, Northampton, Provincetown, Montrose, etc., are open settings with no hard borders. If they are sites, they are open sites that serve as nodes in fields of identity. They are concentrations of individuals who possess vary-ing aspects of a collective identity and thus they influence many who only visit or who may only read of their histories. To some degree, the meanings of these spaces are derived from the identity, but the identity is not limited to the site. Second, as did Castells, both the ethnographic model of the "gay ghetto" and the spatial utilization themes of the urban transformation school focused attention on the expanse of such domains, not their internal identity transformations over time. If we take a theme from postmodern geogra-phers—that the meaning of space is in part at least derivative of human action—then we can immediately understand how urban spaces linked to a particular political identity will change as the identity changes. The history of the gay, gay/lesbian, queer, LGBT movement can be seen in the signs and symbols of each change and challenge to "gay" identity (-ies) left behind in the urban setting. Deep excavations are not needed to see that our identities are not stable. The changes in those identities also add nuance to the mean-ings of urban space. Finally, they interpreted characteristics that may only be transitory and descriptive as general themes—essentializing them if you will—and thus losing some of the diversity that exists within "gay" or "women's" space. Even in those "gay neighborhoods" that may have middle-class overtones, for example, some inhabitants have more economic options and others less.

What we need to take from this analysis are three overriding points. First, urban sexual domains are defined primarily in their social characteristics, not economic. The presence of male same-sex identity spaces existed well before the transformation of city economies from industrial to postindustrial, and from urban space being organized primarily around efficiency in production to efficiency in consumption. Second, these spaces are neither singular nor static. There are broad structures that influence the construction of these spaces, ranging from racial identities embedded in social and linguistic be-havior to the physical environments of each city. Nevertheless, there is also a broad variance evident in the differing accomplishments of each gay commu-nity. Finally, and in direct contrast to past interpretations, these sexual do-mains are not closed but open; they are less a location than a process and venue for politics but also a setting for identity formation and reformation.

Notes

1. Barbara Ponse, *Identities in the Lesbian World: The Social Construction of Self* (Westport, CT: Greenwood Press, 1978); Deborah Goleman Wolf, *The Lesbian Com-munity* (Berkeley: University of California Press, 1979); Dennis Altman, *The Homosex-ualization of America; the Americanization of the Homosexual* (New York: St. Martin's

Press, 1982); Stephen O. Murray, *Social Theory, Homosexual Realities* (New York: Gay Academic Union/Gai Saber Monographs, 1984).

2. Manuel Castells, *The City and the Grassroots* (Berkeley: University of California Press, 1985).

3. The measures were: (1) the presence of gay-/lesbian-owned businesses; (2) the presence of gay bars and entertainment centers; (3) areas including census tracts with dual male households, (4) census tracts containing election precincts that provided Harvey Milk with a majority or higher vote in the 1975 citywide board of supervisors race; and (5) reports of "knowledgeable residents" on the boundaries of the neighborhood.

4. The technique applied by Castells was the Spearman correlation of ranked variables (*City and the Grassroots*, 153).

5. Sy Adler and Joan Brenner, "Gender and Space: Lesbians and Gay Men in the City," *International Journal of Urban and Regional Research* 16 (1992): 24–34; Tamar Rothenberg, "And She Told Two Friends: Lesbians Creating Urban Social Space," in *Mapping Desire: Geographies of Sexualities*, ed. David Bell and Gill Valentine (London: Routledge, 1995), 165–80.

6. PUMS are data extracts issued by the census bureau. They are representative samples of census data from predetermined geographic areas.

7. The data was provided by Strubco, Inc./Quotient Research, a data-collection and direct-mailing firm based in New York City.

8. To further check the reliability of the instrument as an effective indicator of spaces, the indicators were checked against other methods of estimating lesbian and gay geographic concentrations in specific MSAs.

9. Austin, Las Vegas, Honolulu, New Orleans, St. Louis, Tampa/St. Petersburg, Des Moines, Albany, the Quad Cities, Miami, Omaha MSA, Phoenix, and Detroit are the exceptions. (Detroit includes greater Detroit but excludes the Ann Arbor area. Ann Arbor was excluded because its academic profile might skew the results.)

10. See Daphne Spain, "Gender Dualities and Urban Decline," unpublished paper delivered at the Urban Affairs Association, Cleveland, May 1992; Louise Jezierski, "Women Organizing Their Place in a Restructuring Economy," and Ibipo Johnston-Anumonwo and Sara McLafferty, "Gender, Race and Spatial Context of Women's Employment," in *Gender in Urban Research*, ed. Judith Garber and Robyne S. Turner, (Thousand Oaks, CA: Sage Publications, 1995).

11. One other finding should be noted. Except for Honolulu and cities on the West Coast, the continued presence of Asians in or near gay-defined neighborhoods was identified.

12. Gregory D. Squires, Larry Bennett, Kathleen McCourt, and Philip Nyden, *Chicago: Race, Class and the Response to Urban Decline* (Philadelphia: Temple University Press, 1987), chapter 4.

13. Sam Roberts, "In Middle Class Queens, Blacks Pass Whites in Household Income," *New York Times*, June 6, 1994, p. 1.

14. It also should be noted that most names/households on the list were *not* identified by gender (though in New York City and the San Francisco Bay Area they were) and thus the accuracy of the results must be seen in the broadest context. Still, despite these limitations, some patterns of residence between gay men and lesbians can be determined.

15. While most correlations in this analysis were assessed at two-tailed significance with .01 or .001 considered significant, for the analysis of gender, one-tailed significance and a 0.05 level was used.

16. George Chauncey, *Gay New York: Gender, Urban Culture, and the Making of the Gay Male World, 1890–1940* (New York: Basic Books, 1994).

17. There are two identifiable sites in Brooklyn that have additional concentrations of women in the sexual-identity sample used here: Bay Ridge, an older Italo-American, working-class neighborhood facing New York Harbor under the Verrazano-Narrows Bridge, and the residential areas just south of Prospect Park.

18. Nevertheless, not too much should be read from this since the number of households identified by gender is quite low for Birmingham.

19. For example, there is a no statistical relationship between per capita income and the presence of women by zip code, while for men there was a statistically significant and mildly positive one. The positive relationship with median house valuation was also weaker for women than men.

20. These neighborhoods are also slightly less likely to have a presence of Latinos, seniors, and residents in the 24–30-year-old category.

21. This is important because if men and women are not separated in the analysis, the relationship with Latinos residents would wash out and show no correlation between the sexual identity group and Latinos in San Francisco city.

22. Justice Antonin Scalia, in his dissent in *Evans v. Romer*, in fact assumed this to be true. There is considerable disagreement on this question, however. See M. V. Lee Badgett, *Income Inflation: The Myth of Affluence among Gay, Lesbian, and Bisexual Americans* (Washington, DC: Policy Institute, National Gay and Lesbian Task Force and the Institute for Gay and Lesbian Strategic Studies [IGLSS]), 1998.

23. John H. Mollenkopf, *The Contested City* (Princeton: Princeton University Press, 1983), 198; Susan S. Fainstein, Norman Fainstein, and J. Armistead, *Restructuring the City: The Political Economy of Urban Redevelopment* (New York: Longman, 1983) 215; Michael Peter Smith and Joe Feagin, "Urban Theory Reconsidered: Production, Reproduction and Collective Action," in *The Capitalist City: Global Restructuring and Community Action*, ed. Smith and Feagin (New York: Basil Blackwell, 1987), 98–99. The initial study was of the interaction of San Francisco's gay male population and the spatial and economic effect of the restructuring of the city. It was completed as Ms. Murphy's MCP thesis, "Urban Transformations: The Case of the Gay Community in San Francisco" (Department of City and Regional Planning, University of California, Berkeley, 1980).

24. Manuel Castells and Karen Murphy, "Cultural Identity and Urban Structure: The Spatial Organization of San Francisco's Gay Community," in *Urban Policy under Capitalism*, ed. Susan Fainstein and Norman Fainstein, (Beverley Hills, CA: Sage Publications, 1982).

25. See, for example, Robert Beauregard, "The Chaos and Complexity of Gentrification," in *Gentrification of the City*, ed. Neil Smith and Peter Williams (Boston: Allen and Unwin, 1986), 47–48. Beauregard's reference is to Gottlieb's article "Space Invaders: Land Grab on the Lower East Side," *Village Voice*, December 14, 1982, pp. 10–16, 50. To many students of urban affairs, the noticing of sexual identity as a factor in urban politics seems to be only important as a secondary aspect of gentrification. In Janet Adu-Lughod's otherwise masterful analysis of change in New York's

Lower East Side, she allots two sentences on the role of gay men (again not lesbians) to the recent history of the Lower East Side; but only in the gentrification of "Alphabet City." Her model is not Castells's San Francisco, however, but South Beach in Miami. That the area elected an openly gay man to the city council (Anthony Pagan) as well as to its local school board also seems important. Adu-Laghod, *From Urban Village to East Village* (New York: Blackwell, 1994), 185.

26. Lawrence Knopp, *Gentrification and Gay Community Development in a New Orleans Neighborhood* (Ph.D. diss., University of Iowa, 1989). An updated version can be found as Knopp, "Some Theoretical Implications of Gay Involvement in an Urban Land Market," *Political Geography Quarterly* 9, no. 4 (October 1990): 337–352.

27. Johnston-Anumonwo and Sara McLafferty, "Gender, Race and the Spatial Context of Women's Employment" Lynn Appleton, "The Gender Regimes of American Cities," in *Gender in Urban Research*, ed. Judith A. Garber and Robyn S. Turner, (Thousand Oaks, CA: Sage Publications, 1995).

28. Legets and Hartmen, "The Anatomy of Displacement in the United States," in *Gentrification of the City*, ed. Neil Smith and Peter Williams (Boston: Allen and Unwin, 1986), 1983.

29. In addition to the data shown here, see Joseph Downton-Wang, "On the Streets Where We Live: Gay and Lesbian Neighborhoods," *MetroSource*, Summer 1995, pp. 28–42, esp. 42.

30. Rachelle Garbarine, "Demand for Rent as Spurs Jersey City Waterfront Apartments," Real Estate Section, *New York Times*, June 23, 1995, p. B7.

31. For example, Murray's *Social Theory / Homosexual Realities* discusses some aspects of this issue here.

32. Altman, *The Homosexualization of America*, Barry D. Adam, *The Rise of a Gay and Lesbian Movement* (Boston: Twayne, 1987).

33. Altman, *The Homosexualization of America*, chapter 3.

34. Ira Katznelson, *City Trenches: Urban Politics and the Patterning of Class in the United States* (Chicago: University of Chicago Press, 1981).

35. Richard DeLeon, *Left Coast City* (Lawrence: University Press of Kansas, 1992).

36. Robert W. Bailey, *Gay Politics Urban Politics: Identity and Economics in the Urban Setting* (New York: Columbia University Press, 1999).

TEN

BEYOND GAY RIGHTS LITIGATION

USING A SYSTEMIC STRATEGY TO EFFECT POLITICAL

CHANGE IN THE UNITED STATES

Rebecca Mae Salokar

THE FRAMERS of the Constitution of the United States and the compound federal republican structure of this nation were strong advocates of democracy and the principle of majority rule. But, as evidenced in James Madison's exposition in *Federalist Paper* #10 (Rossiter 77–84), they also recognized that majority rule could jeopardize the civil rights and liberties of a minority. While Madison and his colleagues did their best to argue that the federal nature of the United States, combined with a system of divided yet shared powers at both the national and state levels, would prevent a majority faction from abusing the rights of a minority, the history of civil rights for African Americans in the United States is evidence to the contrary.

For over 150 years, people of color suffered discrimination under the rule of law. Despite a political system designed to protect individual rights by dividing power among the three branches of government and between the states and the national government, Madison's worst fears of majority tyranny seemed to come true. Following what was touted as the end of slavery and the initiation of full rights to former slaves with the passage of the Civil War Amendments (Thirteen, Fourteen, and Fifteen), states continued to withhold property rights and voting rights from African Americans. The U.S. Supreme Court declared in *Plessy v. Ferguson* (1896) that separate but equal facilities were well within the scope of law, and the U.S. Congress and a succession of presidents did little or nothing to revise existing discriminatory laws. It was not until the 1940s and 1950s, when the National Association for the Advancement of Colored People (NAACP) devised a national strategy of grassroots activity and a vigorous pattern of planned litigation that would ultimately reach the U.S. Supreme Court, that the issue of civil rights and liberties for African Americans became a viable and legitimate political agenda item for the nation.

The civil rights movement holds many lessons for other groups and minorities who lack political power in the United States. Women's organizations in the 1970s, for example, replicated the litigation strategies of the NAACP and won a series of cases before the Supreme Court that expanded women's legal, economic, and political rights (O'Connor). But times have changed and the ideological winds have shifted in the nation's capitol. Today, lesbians, gays, bisexuals, and transgendered (or LGBT) persons,[1] the historical successors to the rights movements of previous generations, face a very different political landscape. Eight years of the Reagan administration and four years of the Bush presidency meant that the doors to the U.S. Supreme Court were effectively closed to those who would argue for a broad interpretation of the Constitution, the application of civil rights and liberties to all persons, and a logical expansion of the right to privacy. The wave of conservatism that swept this nation, as seen by the election and subsequent reelections of a Republican majority in the U.S. Senate and House of Representatives in 1994, and a president in the White House who lacked the political will and/ or power to effectively end discrimination based on sexual orientation further thwarted any enhancement of rights at the national level through the end of the century.

But Madison's theory of governance can provide LGBT activists with a modicum of optimism. In this article, I present a dynamic model for understanding the role of litigation for civil rights issues within the American political system by examining the litigation efforts of LGBT organizations. Rather than simply measure success as winning on particular cases, political activity through litigation, I suggest, provides benefits "beyond the courtroom" that result in the enhanced political and social legitimation of LGBT issues, and simultaneously increases the potential for effective grassroots mobilization in other more majoritarian political arenas. There is a clear need to develop comprehensive, multifaceted strategies for political change that take advantage of both the federal nature and the multibranch organizational structure of the U.S. political system. Thus, the future leadership of the LGBT movement must be able to work at all levels of government—local, state, and national—and within each of the branches of government—judicial, executive and bureaucratic, and legislative—to direct the multiple tactics needed to effect political change.

In this chapter, I review the distinctions between movements and interest groups, discuss how best to characterize the LGBT activities of recent years, and review the scholarly research on litigation as a means for social change. I also briefly discuss the unsuccessful effort of LGBT organizations to replicate the civil rights tactics of earlier times as seen in the Supreme Court case of *Bowers v. Hardwick* (1986). The implicit message of *Bowers* was that national civil rights litigation on issues dealing with sexual orientation was a losing battle for the foreseeable future. With a Court dominated by conservative and moderate justices, the strategies employed by the African-American and women's civil rights movements are essentially ineffective for LGBT persons today. Activists should instead focus their litigation efforts at the state level and take advantage of the multiple access points that James Madison and the framers provided for in the drafting of the U.S. Constitution. While litigation ought not be the sole strategy for change, it can provide ancillary benefits for more traditional political activity in other arenas. And although this approach is clearly neither optimal nor efficient with respect to resources, incremental change may be the best possible outcome in a political arena that is increasingly conservative and resistant to a broadened interpretation of the nation's Constitution.

Interest Groups and the LGBT Movement

Studying and observing the ongoing political activities of the LGBT movement provide political scientists with an opportunity to replicate, reexamine, and reconceptualize their previous findings in what has been traditionally coined "interest group" litigation studies. Although the term "interest group" has been used by judicial scholars studying political change through litigation, its use in the context of LGBT litigation demands some preliminary examination and clarification. The definition of an interest group varies according to whether the representational aspects of such groups are emphasized or whether activity is the focus. However, political scientists generally agree that interest groups are "membership- or nonmembership-based organizations or institutions that engage in activities to seek specific policy or political goals from the state" (Petracca 7). This suggests that the key characteristics of interest groups are that they are purposive and political, while the degree of organization of an interest group may range from very formal structures with memberships to more informal associations of individuals. Interest-group activities may take place at any or all levels of the political system— local, state, or national (Thomas and Hrebenar 150–74). Furthermore, interest groups may attempt political and legal change by working through one or all of the branches of government—the legislature, the executive and bureaucracy, or the judiciary.

An interest group's political efforts may be narrow in scope, like the National Rifle Association's mission to curtail any form of gun control in the United States, or its goals may be more broad-based, as seen in the American Civil Liberties Union's agenda of protecting individuals' civil rights and liberties. An interest group may also be ad hoc and short-lived, formed for a single political purpose and disbanded once it has achieved its goal, but the propensity tends to be that interest groups evolve along with their agendas, thus extending the life of the organization beyond the duration of the initial rationale for its inception. Additionally, while influencing political outcomes is the primary direction of interest groups, their efforts are not necessarily constrained to the realm of institutional politics. More often than not, interest groups view public education as a critical activity that ultimately bolsters their political agendas. The National Rifle Association's sponsorship of classes on gun-handling safety is an example of an interest group's use of public education to enhance its political position.

To describe gay, lesbian, bisexual, and transgendered activities simply as "interest group" politics is a limited portrayal of the events of the past several decades. For one thing, LGBT persons are not formally organized or even informally associated. There is no one board of directors or recognizable leader, there is no national membership in a single organization, and the goals of some activists are clearly not directed at change through the body politic, but are focused, rather, on transforming the culture and social institutions of contemporary American society. Even attempting to fit LGBT politics into the rather loose definition of "interest groups" as an informal organization obscures the traditional characterization of interest groups simply because there is not one clear agenda that encompasses the many demands of LGBT activists. A more comprehensive description of LGBT activities must address not only the traditional political efforts of its participants working within the scheme of rights-based activities and constitutional structures, but should also include what is generally not cast in political science as "political," namely, the ongoing efforts of LGBT activists to change the distribution of power that serves as the broader context for social and economic relationships in American culture.

What we are witnessing when we examine LGBT activities transcends "interest group" politics and is probably better described by the social movement literature that has been traditionally couched in the discipline of sociology. And although political scientists have made contributions to that genre of scholarship, their focus has historically been on the role of interest groups within movements and the nature of the groups' work in the political venue of institutions and mobilization. These contributions have their limits. As Anne N. Costain notes, "Traditional measures of interest group influence frequently fail to capture the impact social movements have on legislation" (285), and, I would add, on politics in general.

Doug McAdams, a political scientist, has characterized social movements as attempts by "excluded groups to mobilize sufficient political leverage to advance collective interests through non-institutionalized means" (37). But this definition falls short when examined in light of the LGBT movement. First, LGBT activists are, in fact, employing traditional institutionalized means to advance their interests within the framework of the political system in addition to the noninstitutionalized activities that occur outside of the political structure (e.g., boycotts, public demonstrations, and civil disobedience). The movement's strategies include, for example, the noninstitutionalized work of groups like ACT-UP, as well as the traditional political lobbying of the Human Rights Campaign and the litigation work of Lambda Legal Defense and Education Fund.

But there is a larger, more endemic weakness to McAdam's definition and the work of interest-group researchers more generally that strikes at the heart of how we define and study "politics." The scholarly tendency has been to view politics narrowly through the lens of statism by focusing on the relationships between the individual or groups of individuals, on the one hand, and the various political institutions, on the other, within the context of constitutionalism and rights. What we have failed to incorporate into our studies of politics are the structures of power that are more socioculturally coded but that mediate relationships between individuals, and among individuals, social institutions, and political institutions set up by and legitimized through the Constitution.

To study the LGBT movement, scholars will need to move beyond a narrow definition of politics and entertain the notion of "political" as encompassing the social, cultural, ethical, and moral issues of society. What is sought by many LGBT activists is not simply political equality, equal protection of the laws, or the legal recognition of their relationships, but a wholesale examination and retooling of the most basic power relationships among individuals, social institutions (e.g., the family), and the regulatory capabilities of the state in order to shape a more just society. Ultimately, the LGBT movement is seeking broad-based change that is "political" in all senses of the word.

While the efforts of LGBT activists extend beyond what is commonly thought of as the political arena (read: the institutions of the state, narrowly defined), the movement infuses politics into what has generally been perceived as the domains of social relationships and cultural traditions. Contemporary political science should provide the starting point from which to study LGBT politics, but in turn, the discipline is also scrutinized and shaped by such an examination; as a result, our scholarly thinking can be further developed to include broader notions of politics even as LGBT activism can be informed by a systematic perspective. Bringing the interest-group research to bear on an examination of the LGBT movement is but one step in a new direction.

Within the larger LGBT movement, we have witnessed the development of a number of interest groups that fit the stricter classical sense of the term in that they are organized, have readily identifiable leaders and memberships, and are specifically seeking political change either through litigation, legislation, administrative policy change, or grassroots activity. Many of the well-known interest groups have taken on broad-based policy agendas—Lambda Legal Defense and Education Fund, the National Gay and Lesbian Task Force (NGLTF), or the Log Cabin Republicans—but there are other organizations that are more specific in their policy focus. The People With AIDS Coalition (PWAC), North American Man/Boy Love Association (NAMBLA), and the Gay and Lesbian Medical Association direct their political efforts at more narrow policy arenas, but are still part and parcel of the larger movement. In addition, there are innumerable state and local interest groups that are working for change within their cities and home states, like the Dade Action PAC (political action committee in Dade County, Florida), the Gay and Lesbian Advocates and Defenders in Boston, and the Texas Human Rights Foundation.

The multiplicity of interest groups within the LGBT movement is not unique. Both the gender- and race-based movements enjoyed the formation of a number of organized interest groups that directed litigation, mobilization, and strategies for policy change. And while there may be concomitant goals and overlapping efforts, the work of one group is not dependent upon the work of the others. The existence of a number of interest groups reflects the complexity of a movement's political agenda, the divergence of strategies designed for effecting change, and ultimately the diversity of a movement's population. Acknowledging this diversity is critical to understanding interest group development, strategies, and internal conflicts.

The diversity of the LGBT movement is nowhere better reflected than in the "Platform of the 1993 March on Washington for Lesbian, Gay and Bi Equal Rights and Liberation" (Blasius 175–78). The statement reflected the movement's call not only for political and social change for LGBT persons, but for an end to "discrimination and violent oppression based . . . on race, religion, identity, sex and gender expression, disability, age, class, AIDS/HIV infection." It called for the passage of the Equal Rights Amendment, for free substance abuse treatment on demand, for an increase in funding of medical research on diseases that are particular to women, for support of sex-reassignment surgeries as medical treatment . . . and the list goes on. By recognizing the diversity of the LGBT population and by including the demands of specific groups or populations within the movement's most formal statement of purpose to date, the 1993 March on Washington platform reflects the historical concerns of those who identify with the movement because of their sexuality, but whose identities overlap with those in other movements. Ultimately, the platform draws on the diversity of the LGBT population to expand the opportunities for coalition-building with other movements in American society.

The diversity of the LGBT movement can also be seen in the more internal debates over the future of rights and political/social change. Within the movement, there are arguments over goals and the means to achieve them. One strategy suggests that the LGBT movement is about simply obtaining the legal recognition of LGBT relationships and ending discrimination (see Sullivan for example) by employing traditional institutional politics and law with the ultimate goal of securing acceptance by the larger society through

mainstreaming and integration. These strategies refer to the civil rights movements of previous generations as models for change. Yet others call for more
progressive change that is culturally transformative in nature and that recognizes "gay civil rights . . . as part of a broader focus on human rights, sexual
and gender equality, social and economic justice, and faith in a multi-racial
society" (Vaid, *Virtual* 180). Those who advocate this direction for the movement seek wholesale change at the very roots of society, at the levels of
shared morals, personal ethics, culture, and social institutions. Those who
want to move beyond mainstreaming question the necessity of a simple declaration of gay rights through litigation or legislation, and even suggest that
such an exclusive focus would limit the movement's larger goals.

These arguments point to the limits of our scholarly understanding of
movement politics. It is clear that like the gender- and race-based civil rights
movements that strived to eliminate discriminatory practices rooted in law,
LGBT activists are working to remove similar barriers to effect political
change in the traditional sense and beyond. While the debate over strategy
and goals rages on, LGBT activists have continued to employ the more traditional civil rights strategies of previous generations. The findings of judicial
scholars in their work on interest-group litigation continue to have value in
understanding the civil rights aspects of the LGBT movement, and at the
same time the findings are expanded by an examination of this sexuality-
based movement for social justice.

Interest-Group Litigation: The State of Scholarship

Early works on interest-group litigation focused on the organizations that
managed the legal strategies for social change at the national level for the
women's and civil rights movements. And the strategies that have been employed by LGBT activists are similar to those seen in Clement Vose's study of
the NAACP (1959) and Karen O'Connor's work on women's organizations
(1980). By focusing on LGBT activity in the courts, however, we can expand
the levels of analysis to include not only a national strategy for change, but
also one that is state-based. Judicial scholars can now determine whether
earlier findings on interest-group litigation hold true for a state-focused litigation strategy, and as a result we can adapt models of civil rights litigation
and movement politics that encompass a more systemic view of American
politics.

Judicial scholars have long recognized the role of interest groups in litigation (Bentley; Truman). Studies over the past thirty-five years have focused
on the activities of groups concerned with specific policy areas such as sex
discrimination, racial discrimination, religious rights, the rights of the disabled, and free speech, as well as groups that have broader litigation agendas

(e.g., conservatives, the Legal Services Corporation, U.S. government). Most of the early research on interest-group litigation took the form of case studies of particular groups (i.e., Vose; O'Connor). A later vein of studies focuses on how interest groups utilize the amici curiae ("friends of the court") brief, a legal tool that allows nonlitigants to submit their views to the court.[2]

According to Epstein (9), research on the judicial activities of interest groups has basically taken four directions. First, scholars have tried to determine why groups turn to the courts and use litigation over other strategies for social change. Second, research has also focused on the different techniques used by interest groups when employing judicially directed tactics. A third vein of investigation has focused on the resources that organizations need in order to implement such a strategy, and finally, other scholars have attempted to measure the success of legal strategies for social change. Each of these has relevance for LGBT politics, which in turn can enrich the existing scholarship.

Early studies suggested that groups that employ litigation as a strategy for change turn to the courts because other political tools are either unavailable or beyond their resources.[3] Minorities, for example, who lack the votes and political base to effect change through electoral politics or organizations that have few fiscal resources to mount a major lobbying effort were believed to employ litigation as "a strategy to be used when all else fails or as a technique to be employed when goals are clearly unattainable in other political forums" (Epstein 10). The political disadvantage theory, however, has come into question in recent years; research has shown that litigation is used by a broad range of groups and is simply one of the tactics available to encourage political change.[4]

Lesbians, gays, bisexuals, and transgendered people have traditionally been thought of by the larger population and by many politicians who hold political office as a minority that does not have electoral power. However, this perception has changed rather dramatically in recent years as elected politicians of both parties have seen fit to court the "lavender vote," viewing it, in some instances, as a swing vote critical to their elections. While numerically the LGBT population continues to be a minority and from this perspective might fit the typology of a "politically disadvantaged" group, its political clout has increased and its issues are no longer ignored. Add to that the multifaceted activities of LGBT activists within the range of political arenas— at the national, state, and local levels, and through electoral as well as non-majoritarian politics—and it appears that the "politically disadvantaged" theory simply does not hold true for this movement and its interest groups. Litigation is but one aspect of the strategies for change employed by the LGBT movement.

In taking on litigation as a means to social change, interest groups rely most frequently on one of two strategies to gain access to the courts. Sponsorship of cases allows the organizations to direct the management of litigation and, in its purest form, to set up the conditions of a case by initiating the events that give rise to a legal action (test-case strategy) (Greenberg, "Litigation"; Hahn; Kluger; Vose). The interest group is either the named litigant (such as Planned Parenthood) or serves as the lead counsel to the litigant involved in the suit (a strategy frequently employed by the American Civil Liberties Union or NAACP, for example). Alternatively, interest groups may also choose to participate in cases already in the pipeline of litigation as an amicus curiae. This latter strategy limits the control that interest groups have over the issues and the effectiveness of this approach is questionable (Epstein).[5] Works by Bruer and Scheppele and Walker attempted to assess whether certain types of interest groups as classified by size, resources, and extralegal political activity are more likely to use one strategy over another.

This is an area that demands further research for the LGBT movement. While it is evident that the Lambda Legal Defense and Education Fund and other groups with litigation expertise have both used the amicus brief and sponsored their own litigation, the degree to which LGBT organizations rely on each tactic and the implications for control of the issues are areas that need systematic examination. What we do know, however, is that most of the scholarly work in this area has focused specifically on litigation by interest groups at the national level. Studies of LGBT litigation could build on these findings by moving the level of analysis to state courts, where much of the movement's litigation is currently taking place.

Research has also identified the resources necessary for effective interest-group litigation. Some of these are financial soundness, governmental support, repeated use of the courts by the group, access to legal expertise, publicity, and cooperation from like-minded groups (Epstein 12–13). Most studies suggest that interest groups have been largely successful in employing a litigation strategy to attain their goals. But Epstein found that the conservative organizations she studied were not as successful as their liberal cohorts, in part because of their relative inexperience in using this strategy and their lack of financial resources. The degree to which LGBT litigation has been successful has not been systematically measured and a much fuller study of the organizations that sponsor litigation on gay rights is necessary to determine whether or not LGBT litigation is following the patterns of previous interest groups. Such a comprehensive work would need to examine trends in success rates to assess the "learning curve" for LGBT litigators, the resource base of organizations both financially and with respect to the development of an in-house expertise, and the degree to which the interest groups can seek support from other organizations both within and outside of the movement.

For the most part, studies of interest-group litigation have been limited to analyzing the efforts of groups to effect change through litigation before the U.S. Supreme Court. Given the decisions of the Warren Court (1953–1969), and even its successor, the Burger Court (1969–1986), the nation's highest court provided liberal interest groups with both the access and the favorable outcomes they sought. Only recently have scholars shifted their attention to the activity of interest groups in lower courts, generally focusing on the lower federal courts.[6] But a significant amount of litigation by LGBT interest groups is taking place at the state level and a study of these organizations would allow us to test whether the previous findings at the national level hold true for state court litigation.

Bowers and LGBT Litigation

Knowing the history of the civil rights and women's rights movements, it is not surprising that LGBT activists placed their hopes for social change on the 1986 case of *Bowers v. Hardwick*. With the challenge of the Georgia sodomy statute going all the way to the U.S. Supreme Court, the potential existed for a high court decision that recognized the privacy rights of all people, but especially LGBT people, to engage in sexual conduct without government interference. Legal observers believed that a favorable decision on the narrowest of issues would open the doors to further litigation that could expand LGBT rights in other arenas. The more optimistic activists even hoped that the Court might use *Bowers* to go one step further by including LGBT persons under the umbrella of groups specifically afforded heightened protection through the equal protection clause of the Fourteenth Amendment. But all hopes were quashed when, on June 30, 1986, the Supreme Court announced its five-to-four decision upholding the right of a state to regulate sexual conduct between consenting adults.

The *Bowers* outcome was indicative of the changing mood of the U.S. Supreme Court. Since the early 1980s, federal courts have generally become less willing to expand the rights of traditional minorities. With the appointments by President Ronald Reagan of Justices Sandra Day O'Connor (1981), Antonin Scalia (1986), and Anthony Kennedy (1988), and President George Bush's successful nominations of David Souter (1990) and Clarence Thomas (1991) combined with the elevation of William Rehnquist to chief justice in 1986, the Supreme Court of the United States has been increasingly resistant to affirmative rights, expansion of national power vis-à-vis the states, and broad interpretations of the U.S. Constitution. And twelve years of Republican presidencies virtually assured a wholesale change in the personnel who sit on the lower federal courts. Thus, the 1995 decision of the Supreme Court in *Hurley v. Irish-American Gay, Lesbian and Bisexual Group of Boston* denying a LBG organization the right to march in a popular St. Patrick's Day parade should have come as no surprise to those who study the courts.

But it was the threat, real or perceived (Blasi; Wasby, *Continuity*), of a more conservative court under Chief Justice Warren Burger that sparked what is now known as "New Judicial Federalism." Anticipating that President Richard Nixon's appointments to the Court signaled a turn to the ideological right, potential litigants and interest groups began the tedious search through state constitutions for principles on which to base rights claims, and began to develop litigation strategies at the state level. In many cases, state supreme courts responded to legal arguments—that rights can be found in their own basic law—that complemented or went beyond that which the federal courts had established. In Florida, for example, the state supreme court overturned a parental consent statute that limited teenagers' access to abortion services on the basis of a right-to-privacy provision that had been added to the state constitution in 1980 (In re T.W., A Minor 1989). The same right to privacy had previously been used to protect the identity of blood donors in an AIDS-related civil action against a blood bank (Rasmussen v. South Florida Blood Services 1987).

In 1986, it was former Supreme Court Justice William Brennan who observed, "Rediscovery by state supreme courts of the broader protections afforded to their own citizens by their state constitutions . . . is probably the most important development in constitutional jurisprudence of our times" (see Note). And it is this "rediscovery" that has formed the crux of most LGBT litigation in the 1990s. Under the direction of the Lambda Legal Defense and Education Fund and through the Lesbian and Gay Rights Project of the American Civil Liberties Union (ACLU), litigation at the state level is being undertaken with the sole purpose of establishing a state-based judicial declaration of human rights. For example, state courts have been asked to rule on the right of marriage by same-sex couples in Hawaii (Baehr v. Miike 1999), Vermont (Baker v. Vermont 1999), and Alaska (Brause v. Alaska 1998). In 1992, the Kentucky Supreme Court sided with the arguments of LGBT activists in finding an implicit right to privacy in the Kentucky Constitution, and as a result, declared the state's sodomy laws unconstitutional (Kentucky v. Wasson 1992). The Georgia Supreme Court also nullified their consensual sodomy laws in 1998 (Powell v. State, 1998). And in Florida, litigation challenged that state's bans on adoptions and foster parenting by "homosexual" persons (Cox v. Fla. Dept. of HRS 1995, Amer v. Children's Home Society, 1997).

LGBT rights litigation has also followed a pattern of development evident in the earlier civil rights movement (Wasby, "Transformed" 568–69). Rather than using litigation solely as a proactive tool to gain new rights, LGBT activists have found themselves turning to the courts in a reactive mode to fight to maintain the few rights they succeeded in gaining through legislative enactments and municipal ordinances. In response to the efforts by the American Family Association and other conservative groups to put anti-gay state constitutional amendments on the electoral ballot, LGBT organizations have been forced to seek judicial remedies. In Colorado (*Evans v. Romer* 1994) and Cincinnati (*Equality Foundation of Greater Cincinnati v. City of Cincinnati* 1995), lawsuits were filed in response to the adoption of ordinances and state constitutional amendments that limit civil rights for LGBT persons. In Florida, successful litigation early in the constitutional amendment process prevented a proposed anti-gay amendment from even reaching the voters.

It is clear that since the *Bowers* decision, LGBT rights activists have used the principles of new judicial federalism as a means of effecting social change. While it would have been strategically easier and certainly more efficient to have had a Supreme Court decision that included LGBT rights under the equal protection umbrella, the reality of contemporary U.S. politics makes the possibility unlikely. So litigation at the state level continues. But while litigation can serve as an effective tool for policy change, LGBT activists need to develop a comprehensive strategy that involves the entire political system. Understanding that litigation is more than winning and losing on any one case in any single state can form the basis for developing such a strategy and can prove to be critical to the movement's long-term goals of social change.

Beyond Litigation

In "A Transformed Triangle: Court, Congress, and Presidency in Civil Rights," a retrospective article on the African-American civil rights movement, political scientist Stephen L. Wasby argues that the policy changes of that era were gained by utilizing the entire national political system. Although litigation provided an initial entrée into the political arena for African-American rights activists, their success was not based solely on litigation activities. Rather, litigation and favorable court decisions opened the policy doors to Congress and the White House, in essence legitimating their concerns and making civil rights policy part of the national agenda. Wasby suggests that we envision a triangular figure within which interest groups must work in order to effect policy change, with the three points of that diagram being the Supreme Court, the president, and Congress (see figure 10.1).

Wasby also notes, however, that the doors to each of these institutions, the courts, the presidency and administrative agencies, and the legislative branch do not necessarily remain open to the concerns of rights activists:

> Policy is not static. In some sense, it is like the weather: If you wait a bit, it will change. We have seen presidential administrations engage in such changes in the course of litigation. However, it is not only the substance of the policy that varies over time. Relations between principal policy making bodies also change. The relative access to interest groups provided by government institutions likewise

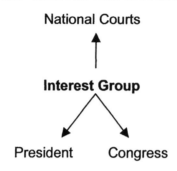

Figure 10.1. Traditional model of civil rights activity

varies, providing support for the proposition that "if one door is closed, there are two others that might be opened" for interest groups seeking entry (citing Rebecca Salokar to author, June 23, 1992). This provides confirmation that the existence of multiple access points assists the achievement of civil rights policies. (Perry, cited in Wasby, "Transformed")

In short, as the membership of the Supreme Court changes, as transitions in the White House take place, and as partisan control of Congress shifts or other issues become the focal point of the national political agenda, civil rights policy may be ignored or, even worse, abandoned altogether, by one or more of the national political institutions. At that point, groups must be willing to redirect the focus of their policymaking efforts between institutions. In a sense, the interest group must be willing to "shop around" for the institution that will provide them with the best "bargain."

While Wasby's model holds true for the earlier civil rights movements, it must be modified and expanded to take into account the current political climate for LGBT activists in their efforts to broaden civil rights. Given the current ideological stalemate between Congress and the presidency, as well as the conservative turn of the federal courts, shopping for the best institution to achieve policy change requires shifting efforts away from the federal arena and reshaping strategies for the state political systems or, alternatively, shopping in both markets simultaneously. Figure 10.2 depicts these enhancements to Wasby's model, employing a "New Federalism" perspective.

Generally, judicial scholars have only been concerned with interest group litigation as a tool for policy change through court decisions; their focus has been only on the legal outcomes and the decisions rendered. What Wasby's work adds to our thinking is that although legal change through judicial decisions may be the initial goal of interest groups, they may have to redirect their efforts to other institutions over time. Even with that caveat, however, the model may not be an entirely accurate depiction of policymaking. It is limited in that the model is unidirectional; interest groups target a political

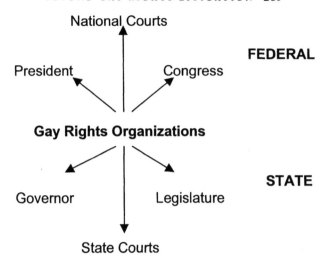

Figure 10.2. A "New Federalism" model of civil rights activity

institution, either at the state or national level, and change results only from the arena in which they are operating.

Early scholarship suggested that interest groups use the courts because other policymaking institutions are not available. For LGBT persons, this is probably a valid assessment in most states. Governors and legislators are generally not willing to take the lead in putting LGBT rights at the top of their policy agendas; even if sympathetic to the cause and interested in gaining the electoral support of LGBT citizens, their perception is often that advocating LGBT rights can mean political suicide on election day. Therefore, LGBT activists usually have no choice but to employ a litigation strategy to effect policy change in states. And success, according to the model described in Figure 10.2, is simply measured by winning and losing in court.

But there is more. Litigation can reap rewards in other forums. Consider, for example, LGBT activism in Florida. The state's recent governors, one a Republican (Bob Martinez) and two who fit the mold of traditional Southern Democrats (Bob Graham and Lawton Chiles), were unlikely candidates to promote civil rights for LGBT persons. Furthermore, the state legislative body became increasingly Republican in the late 1980s (not that this ideological transformation was particularly significant, considering that the legislature has traditionally been a stronghold for conservative Southern Democrats). With the legislative and executive branches virtually inaccessible, LGBT activists in Florida naturally turned to the courts to pursue a vigorous litigation agenda that invoked the state's constitutional right to privacy, battled over employment discrimination, and challenged Florida's ban on adoptions and foster parenting based on sexual orientation. Over time, their success in litigation has legitimized LGBT rights claims and complemented, as well as encouraged, the more traditional political strategies of establishing political action committees, public education programs, visible campaigning for candidates to both local and statewide office, and lobbying in support of or in opposition to municipal ordinances. On December 1, 1998, activists finally succeeded in convincing the Miami-Dade County Commission to include sexual orientation under its Human Rights Ordinance.

The Florida experience suggests that as interest groups win in the judicial arena, they may be able to shift their focus to other political branches and employ more traditional interest-group strategies such as lobbying to effect change. Favorable judicial outcomes can legitimate the cause, allowing elected officials to feel more at ease in addressing rights claims. Thus, interest group movement between institutions is not, as Wasby suggests, solely mandated by failure and the need to find alternative access points for political change.

But litigation in and of itself can legitimatize the interest group's concerns in the larger public arena by calling attention to the issues regardless of whether LGBT activists win or lose in the courts. The increased attention and public discourse have the potential to generate additional resources that can be used for future litigation or even legislative lobbying. While the literature addresses resources simply as tools for successful litigation, I suggest that these resources are not only essential in order to initiate a legal strategy, they are also a product of litigation and should be considered a measure of success for the interest group.[7] As we know from the research on interest-group activity in Congress, the size of the organization and its finances are two important factors for successful lobbying. The publicity from litigation can encourage new membership, spawn new organizations, and extend the network of organizations by attracting the support of like-minded groups and experts. In other words, our measure of "success" must include the benefits the interest group enjoys as a result of litigation, win or lose, that enable the group to mobilize more effectively and efficiently for future activity in all three political arenas—the judicial, legislative, and executive.

Over the past ten years, the number of LGBT-oriented organizations and their respective memberships has grown. And as group membership increases, the political power of LGBT organizations becomes more important to elected politicians. Gay lawyers' associations have formed in nearly every state; organizations of LGBT professionals meet regularly; political action committees have been established to influence local, state, and national elections; and every major city touts a multitude of LGBT social organizations. Unlike those established in the early to mid-1980s, these newer LGBT-oriented organizations were not founded in response to the AIDS crisis, although many lessons of group mobilization were learned from that era. Today, the "new" interest groups are a response to litigation and political successes, as well as to threats from conservative organizations. In south Florida, a private association of lawyers, the Gay and Lesbian Lawyers Association (GALLA), initially founded as a mentoring group for law students, began litigating on behalf of LGBT rights. In 1992, GALLA, with the Public Law Section of the Florida Bar, worked successfully within the formal framework of the state bar association to urge the Florida bar's board of governors to adopt an antidiscrimination policy that includes sexual orientation. Organizations originally designed to be support groups, whose membership rolls include gay men, lesbians, bisexuals, transgendered persons, and their supporters, like Parents and Friends of Lesbians and Gays (P-FLAG), have moved into the political arena by undertaking public education projects on teenage suicide and, in some instances, even presenting formal proposals for counseling services tailored for LGBT youth within the public school system. Yet other organizations have been founded specifically for the purpose of developing and directing strategies for political change. Safeguarding American Values for Everyone (SAVE) implemented a public education campaign designed to increase awareness of LGBT issues by taking out "One in Ten" advertisements on bus benches and county buses; when a proposed constitutional amendment surfaced in Florida that would have prevented cities and counties from protecting LGBT persons from discrimination, SAVE instituted letter-writing campaigns and petitions in opposition; and SAVE claimed success in persuading the governing body of the most populous county in the state, Miami-Dade to include sexual orientation in its antidiscrimination ordinance.

The success of litigation beyond winning and losing can also be seen by the fact that issues once relegated to the back pages of daily newspapers are slowly becoming important news and are now being brought to the public's attention. The "love that dare not speak its name" has moved from whispers behind closed doors to the center of public discourse, and in many instances it is litigation that has brought the attention. The *Baehr* case, for example, has been watched by every major newspaper in the country. *Romer v. Evans*, a case decided by the U.S. Supreme Court challenging the constitutionality of Colorado's constitutional amendment to limit LGBT rights, merited national media attention. And as LGBT issues gain attention, other interest groups outside the movement can find common ground and lend support. In the *Romer* case, the NAACP, the Episcopal Church, and the Association for Retarded Citizens filed briefs in opposition to the constitutional amendment. With respect to the *Baehr* case, the Japanese American Citizens League has put itself on record in support of same-sex marriages as a matter of civil rights; their position is a logical follow-up to their arguments against the antimiscegenation laws in *Loving v. Virginia* (1967).[8] Thus litigation can provide the opportunity for coalition-building and publicity, two resources that can assist in the legitimation of LGBT issues in the larger political arena and beyond the scope of politics conceived solely in institutional terms.

Another challenge to the traditional thinking about interest-group litigation as an insulated activity comes from the judicial impact studies of the 1970s (Becker and Feeley; Krislov, *Supreme*; Wasby, *Impact*) and from conventional wisdom. Quite simply, court decisions do not occur in a political vacuum. The results of litigation often dictate responses from legislatures and executive agencies by either requiring enforcement of the decision, urging adaptation of existing policies to conform with court orders, or forcing the development of new legislation. Imagine, for example, the impact of a decision striking down the traditional marriage laws of Hawaii in the *Baehr* case. Should the challenge by LGBT activists be upheld, a multitude of state laws in Hawaii would have to be amended simply to make the text of those laws gender-neutral; tax laws would have to be changed; estate and inheritance succession dictates would have to be revised; divorce laws would undergo major scrutiny and rewriting; and the list goes on. A single court decision like *Baehr* could keep the executive agencies of Hawaii and its legislature busy for years. Litigation, in other words, can force the elected branches to place LGBT rights and the larger social issues they implicate on their policy agendas.

But there is even more to this process. As legislatures and executive departments amend statutes, rules, and regulations, they simultaneously provide LGBT activists with further opportunities to test the new laws through additional litigation. In Florida, following the 1987 *Rasmussen* decision that established a right to privacy for blood donors, the state legislature drafted a comprehensive AIDS confidentiality statute and established HIV testing requirements including informed consent, the confidentiality of test results, and the parameters under which an individual's test results may be divulged to a third party. The state also instituted protections against discrimination in housing and employment for persons with AIDS and persons perceived as having AIDS. These new statutes must be interpreted and as a result they too have spawned new litigation over their implementation. In *Hummer v. Unemployment Appeals Commission* (1991), for example, an appellate court granted unemployment benefits to an HIV seropositive plaintiff even though he was fired for misconduct, namely lying and absenteeism. Because his absences were related to his medical treatments and his dishonesty stemmed from fear of reprisal should his health status have become known by his employer, the court found that the plaintiff's conduct was not "willful and wanton," but defensively related to his fear of legally unwarranted discrimination. What this case and others show is that litigation can spark a dynamic process of defining and redefining the limits of legal protections whereby court decisions necessitate policy action from the legislative and executive branches that, in turn, can serve as the basis for future litigation.[9]

These observations suggest that a comprehensive and systemic characterization of interest-group litigation must also include the dynamic interrela-

Figure 10.3. A dynamic model of interest-group activity based on litigation

tionships between political institutions and the benefits gained by the interest group through litigation activity. While litigation may continue to play a significant role for LGBT organizations seeking political change, consideration must be given to the effects of the political institutions on each other and on the interest group itself within the policy process. Unlike the traditional "iron triangle" model (legislative subcommittees, interest groups, and executive agencies) (Freeman; Hamm) employed to describe the policy process and found in nearly every American government textbook, the proposed model is not about mutual dependency based on a sharing of resources among the actors with concurrent benefits to each. Rather, it is an action/reaction model in which a decision or action by one player prompts a response by another (figure 10.3).

This model takes into account the federal nature of our political system as well as the interbranch relationships that result from an interest-group strategy based predominantly on litigation, and it reflects the impact and ancillary benefits that the interest group reaps from litigation. For LGBT activists, litigation can result in publicity of their issues, increased resources both within the political sphere as well as in group-related membership and financial resources, and the legitimation of LGBT issues on the agendas of the other branches of government.

One additional factor that is not addressed by figure 10.3 is the notion of horizontal judicial federalism or (to spell out what this rubric covers) the relationships that exist between states and their court systems. Horizontal judicial federalism suggests that the results of interest-group litigation in one state can directly or indirectly affect the outcomes of litigation in other states. There are two perspectives on this concept: first, "that state supreme courts typically look beyond their borders when confronting novel legal problems or when contemplating legal change" (Tarr and Porter 31–32, citing Harris), and second, that states may be obligated under the U.S. Constitution to recognize certain actions by other states.

While there has been some research on the diffusion of state court decisions across state lines, how frequently this occurs and the degree to which state courts rely on the legal rationales espoused by their sister courts remains largely unknown (Caldeira; Canon and Baum; Harris; Tarr and Porter). What we do know is that while the judges or justices of one state are not obligated to recognize or adopt the legal rationale employed by other states in similar cases if those decisions are grounded in state law, judges are usually aware of similar issues and decisions made in other states and can choose to adopt parallel arguments. For example, the Kentucky Supreme Court's decision striking down Kentucky's sodomy laws on the basis of a state constitutional right to privacy (*Kentucky v. Wasson* 1992) has been cited by other state courts either in passing or with a full discussion.[10]

The second aspect of horizontal judicial federalism invokes U.S. constitutional law. Article IV of the Constitution of the United States states that "Full Faith and Credit shall be given in each State to the public Acts, Records, and judicial Proceedings of every other State. And the Congress may by general Laws prescribe the Manner in which such Acts, Records, and Proceedings shall be proved, and the Effect thereof." Also relevant is the second clause of that same article: "The Citizens of each State shall be entitled to all Privileges and Immunities of Citizens in the several States." This second prong of horizontal federalism serves as the basis for the strategy Lambda Legal Defense and Education Fund publicly states it anticipates using in the matter of same-sex marriages (Link; Leiser).

If the Hawaii Supreme Court recognizes the right of same-sex marriage, and should they base their decision solely on state constitutional law as expected, the U.S. Supreme Court would have virtually no jurisdiction to review the matter immediately since federal law would not be at issue in the Hawaiian decision. What is anticipated, however, is that same-sex couples would travel to Hawaii to be married and then return to their home states where they would seek legal recognition of their marriage and lay claim to those benefits and rights that accrue from such recognition. This, of course, would spark a series of cases across the nation in state courts and eventually the U.S. Supreme Court would have to weigh in to settle the matter. While it is yet to be seen exactly how these constitutional provisions will affect matters of LGBT rights, representatives of the Lambda Legal Defense and Education Fund have stated that a favorable decision in the *Baehr* case could open the doors to a national right to same-sex marriages (Leiser; Link).[11]

The Hawaii case, however, illuminates one of the many liabilities of relying on a strategy based predominantly on litigation in a federal system. Anticipating the decision in Hawaii, more than half of the states took preemptive legislative action specifically to deny legal recognition of same-sex marriages in their states, forcing LGBT activists to divert their focus and energies from the case at hand and mount a defensive position even before the outcome of *Baehr* was announced. Just as LGBT activists can utilize the multiple access points of the American political system, so, too, can the conservative, anti-LGBT forces. In many respects, a state-based strategy may put LGBT activists into a "reactive" response mode with little control over shaping their own agenda, thereby limiting the potential for the movement to get beyond a legalistic strategy of change.

Another liability of state-focused litigation is the possibility that it can result in a patchwork of success wherein one state recognizes certain legal rights while others do not. As Urvashi Vaid describes the outcome, "By the 1990s, the legal rights of gay and lesbian people resembled a mottled map, with 'free' and 'unfree' territories, and wide disparities between states in their treatment of gay people" (*Virtual* 132). Already the patchwork of equality and inequality is visible when one considers the sodomy laws: seventeen states still maintain criminal sodomy laws. While this can be viewed as a negative outcome of state-based political work, a more optimistic spin would be that such inequalities can make good fodder for a future case that hinges on the principle of equality before the nation's highest court. It was exactly this issue, that rights for similarly situated persons were different between states, that prompted women to the litigation table over abortion rights in the 1970s.[12]

Additionally, duplicate efforts in several states may not be useful on some issues and could even complicate matters by either distracting from ongoing cases or by confounding the issues that are being addressed in litigation. For example, while Lambda Legal Defense initially focused its efforts on the Hawaiian marriage case and worked with what it believed to be an optimal factual scenario, the organization actively discouraged potential litigants in other states from initiating their own litigation. And for good reason: distinct from legislative activity on this matter, a negative ruling on same-sex marriage in New York, for instance, that anticipated and predated the finality of the Hawaiian case could have thwarted future litigation strategies in other states or, even worse, provided the justices and judges of Hawaii with the legal rationale to reject same-sex marriages in the *Baehr* case.

But the difficulties of a state-based political strategy go beyond legal concerns and decisional outcomes. By having to conduct legal and political activities at the state level, LGBT activists are forced to build a war chest of resources to support the costs of operating in each of the states. Besides the financial assets necessary to conduct such a comprehensive strategy, LGBT activists will need to garner a significant amount of human capital and political support for a decentralized campaign of this nature. Organizational leadership will have to be diversified and decentralized as well, and must include not only legal experts but also leaders who could work within the executive branch, in the legislative arena, and on grassroots mobilization strategies. Ultimately, the movement could suffer in that its energies and resources could be drained by the repetitive and duplicate strategies of operating in each of the states.

As important, managing such an effort demands intensive communication, organization, and cooperation among the various LGBT groups involved in litigation and political activity across the nation, as well as coordination within each state. At present, the movement suffers from the fact that each of a multitude of interest groups has carved out for itself its own niche of activity with little consultation or cooperation from like-minded groups within the movement (Vaid, *Virtual* 132–34). The litigation-directed organizations see the law as the optimal mechanism to effect change, and only recently have they recognized the need for grassroots campaigns of public education and support to minimize the public backlash to court decisions (Vaid, *Virtual* 134, noting LLDEF's Marriage Project). More important, the legalistic strategy subtracts from the resources that might be brought to bear on other more sweeping strategies for social and political change. Progressive strategists who view the movement's goals as more than just changes in the laws of the United States criticize those working within the legal arena for focusing only on short-term goals and on mainstreaming some participants in the LGBT movement who, except for their sexual orientation, would have little difficulty reaping the benefits of a society stratified by class, gender, and race. Further, casting LGBT issues solely within the framework of legal or rights-based language limits the horizon of the movement and its members in conceiving its political interests in broader sociocultural terms and pursuing them in coalition with others. In short, litigation can become a significant distraction. By levying this attack, however, the more progressive LGBT leaders can fail to understand the positive impacts a decision like *Baehr* may have on public discourse and the legitimation of LGBT issues in American society.

Information and technical expertise must also be shared. While several national organizations serve as clearinghouses for data, much as Lambda Legal Defense has done in its regular publications that review ongoing litigation in the states and at the national level, there is a need for a more comprehensive approach to information gathering, the sharing of technical expertise, and networking. Historically, lesbian and gay media have served as a decentralized clearinghouse monitoring not only litigation but all forms of political and social activity at the local, state, and national levels on the spectrum of LGBT issues. What would be optimal now is the development of a national "think tank" that would facilitate collaboration among LGBT activist organizations and siphon information from those organizations to the media (LGBT and straight). Once again, previous civil rights movements provide us with partial examples of two such organizations: the NAACP and the National Organization for Women. But a national organization for LGBT groups is even more necessary than for the women's and African-American movements. Given the resistance of the contemporary national government to address LGBT issues, much political work is by necessity decentralized at the state and local levels; this, combined with the fact the closet exists—permeable though it may be—even for those active in LGBT organizations, means that information about the range of ongoing activities is less readily collected and manageable. But a more important contrast with other movements derives from the nature of change LGBT organizations seek: when that kind of change is defined broadly to include the cultural values and norms as well as social institutions that are "politicized" when individuals "come out" in their contexts, organized LGBT efforts must be focused both within and beyond the traditionally conceived institutions of the political system. This suggests that information about the sociopolitical activities of the LGBT movement is one of the most valuable resources for political mobilization and merits widespread dissemination.

Beyond the need for intramovement cooperation between interest groups is intermovement cooperation, which is also an untapped resource for the LGBT movement. The effectiveness of any strategy for change, be it political, social, or cultural, will be doubly enhanced by the inclusion and support of like-minded groups. Through litigation, LGBT lawyers have been able to scratch the surface of intermovement coordination by gaining the amicus support of such interests as the Episcopal Church, the Association of Retarded Citizens, and the NAACP, as mentioned earlier, but much more needs to be done to find common ground with the women's movement, the environmental movement, and other social and political organizations with more limited policy goals (such as economic renewal, affirmative action, and immigration). By focusing on commonalities rather than differences, by sharing experiences, and by lending support to others, LGBT activists can build on political strategies to effect the broad-based social change that is implied by the diverse agendas of the movements' organizations.

One proposal to address the need for inter-movement cooperation that was suggested by Vaid at the 1996 Center for Lesbian and Gay Studies' "Identity/Space/Power" Conference is similar to the one I have made for intramovement collaboration: establishment of a "Center for Progressive Renewal" (CPR). Her proposal calls for an umbrella organization that would provide a link for the LGBT movement to progressive (with this term understood through its historical association with the U.S. Progressive movement) elements in other social movements like the women's movement, racial and ethnic movements, the peace movement, and the environmental movement. This organization's task would include developing strategies for, and presenting position papers on, ideology-, coalition-, electoral-, leadership-, and infrastructure-building. While such a concept has the appeal of making the broad connections between agendas of like-minded social movements, there is also the distinct possibility that the uniqueness of LGBT peoples' needs could be swallowed up and forgotten by such an approach.

Finally, litigation, in and of itself, has its limits. A Supreme Court decision tomorrow that includes LGBT people under the equal protection clause does no more to end homophobia than the Court's decision in *Brown v. Board of Education* did to end racial discrimination. Even major legislative initiatives like the 1964 Civil Rights Act and the Voting Rights Acts of 1957 and 1960 proved not to be quick-fix tools for racial equality, either politically or socially. And thus the critics are correct if we accept a narrow view of litigation and political activity as the remedy for the sociocultural and political domination LGBT people are subjected to. But what I have tried to suggest here is that we consider litigation and political activity through a more sophisticated lens.

Litigation, legislation, and policymaking are about much more than winning and losing in any one case, on any one issue, or in any one forum. Rather, political activity is a means to the larger social changes sought by the LGBT movement because it allows the movement to grow, to recognize and share its diversity, and, most important, to place LGBT issues squarely in the realm of public discourse. In turn, LGBT citizens can openly become full participants in the broader social and political currents of American life and can contribute as such to solving the array of problems confronting this society. What this goal requires is an understanding of politics, arising from our experience as LGBT citizens, that both encompasses and moves beyond the traditional notions of rights litigation, constitutional institutionalism, and electoral leadership.

Conclusion

In this chapter, I have suggested that LGBT organizations can learn much from the histories of previous civil rights movements and from the scholarly research on litigation, and can use this knowledge as a strategy for political change. But what I have also tried to point out is how the work for LGBT rights necessarily differs from earlier experiences. While activists for women and African Americans enjoyed a sympathetic national judiciary that was willing to entertain litigation on behalf of civil rights during the 1960s and

1970s, today's civil rights activists have found those doors more or less closed. As a result, the contemporary LGBT movement must employ a systemic approach to political and social change by taking advantage of the multiple access points our federal structure offers. States and local governments are much more important today than they were to the earlier movements, and given the contemporary political climate, a strategy based on decentralized political and legal activity is, perhaps, the only option open to LGBT activists. While litigation is significant in political change, and one of the major tactics adopted from previous civil rights movements, the more traditional political activities in the form of lobbying, influencing electoral outcomes by supporting sympathetic candidates, and developing openly LGBT candidacies must continue at both the state and federal levels.

The framers surely did not anticipate that sexual orientation would be an issue of policy concern when they drafted the Constitution over two hundred years ago. But they did recognize that those who lack the electoral power to influence and change the system will not fare well in a democratic system built upon majority rule. By establishing a dual system of government, providing for separate branches at each level of government, and establishing a judiciary that was not as dependent upon majoritarian principles, Madison and his colleagues ensured multiple access points to our political system that would allow interest groups, large or small, to influence government policy.

Those multiple access points are critically important to the diversity of the LGBT movement. It might be that certain issues like employment rights are better suited for litigation, while other goals such as the exercise of traditional political power through public policymaking are more likely to be reached by attaining office through local electoral politics. These are issues that need further consideration by both scholars in political science and activists within the LGBT movement. The nature of the federal system also demands that LGBT activists monitor the ideological winds in each of the fifty states, and then tailor their efforts and issues to those states and political branches that are most likely to be supportive. These are considerations that LGBT strategists need to mine when crafting future tactics for change.

I hope this writing will evoke a recognition by political scientists of the limits of our approaches in understanding and thinking about politics. Traditional political science is generally constrained to casting power relationships in the rather limited context of constitutionalism and the institutions derived from it. The study of LGBT politics expands our notions of the "political." It asks us to view social, cultural, and economic institutions and relationships with the same critical eye we bring to our study of constitutional politics. This means, for example, that we must examine the decision of the Disney Company to provide domestic-partner benefits to its employees as a political decision—as one in which those in power with particular ideas about how relationships ought to be structured are able to impose their values and expectations on others. While LGB persons enjoy the short-term economic benefits of domestic partnership recognition, the policies are, at their root, simply an extension of the heterosexual construct of marriage, a construct that is not fully reflective of LGB relationships and needs. Thus, domestic partnership policies are progressive in nature but are limited to the extent that they merely sanction replicas of heterosexual relationships.

Ultimately, the study of LGBT politics asks us to recognize that what has been traditionally cast as "private" and beyond the realm of political science—namely, sexuality—is imbued with power relationships that merit the systematic analysis of our discipline. In *Bowers*, a homophobic Court permitted the state to intrude on what had been traditionally thought of as private. Yet when LGBT activists and others concerned with the health of our youth attempt to encourage sex education in public schools, sexuality is secreted away to the private sphere of family and religion. The "politicalness" of this dichotomy comes to light, however, when a significant number of young adults in New York City contract sexually transmitted diseases and HIV infections; sexuality and sexual behavior are ultimately forced into the public arena despite the draconian efforts of homophobes to keep it "private." Political scientists need to revise their ideas about power and politics, particularly in the context of sexuality, as they bring them to bear on the range of issues raised by the LGBT movement.

The research of political scientists can also serve to enlighten those who are involved in the LGBT movement in that it can explicate the existing power relationships that LGBT activists confront in their ongoing agenda for change. The 220-year history of American constitutionalism and the entrenchment of its political structure means that LGBT activists must fully understand the dynamic relationships of policymaking and litigation if they are to be successful in pursuing change—regardless of whether that change is narrowly defined as political in the more traditional sense, or more expansively defined as political pertaining to power exercised through socioeconomic institutions and coded through cultural meanings in America. Such an understanding can provide LGBT activists with the insights necessary to mount an effective campaign for change and social justice in the United States.

Notes

An earlier version of this essay appeared in *GLQ: A Journal of Lesbian and Gay Studies* 3 (1997): 385–415. Copyright © 1997 OPA. Reprinted by permission.

I am indebted to Stephen L. Wasby for his comments on an earlier version of this chapter and to Mark Blasius for his wisdom, encouragement, and enormous patience.

1. Language often defines our own politics, and thus I have chosen to use the term "Lesbian, Gay, Bisexual, and Transgendered" (LGBT) throughout this article over other, perhaps more common, language to describe the gay rights movement. My own personal and political inclinations are to characterize the subject of this article more inclusively than restrictively, thereby explicitly recognizing the diversity of populations and interests that have found a niche in a movement based on sexuality. While I recognize that some members and organizations are resistant to this all-inclusive term, that it was employed by the organizers of the 1993 March on Washington seemingly reflects a decision of political significance.

2. For studies on sex discrimination, see Cowan; O'Connor; and O'Connor and Epstein, "Beyond Legislative Lobbying." On racial discrimination, see Barker; Cortner; Greenberg, *Judicial Process*; Kellogg; Kluger; Stewart and Heck, "Ensuring Access"; and Vose. Studies on religious rights include Manwaring; Morgan 1968; Pfeffer; and Sorauf. See Olson, "Political Evolution" and *Clients*, for work on the rights of the disabled, and Kobylka on free speech. For groups that have broader litigation agendas, see Epstein's work on conservatives, Lawrence's study of the Legal Services Corporation, and Salokar's research on the U.S. government. Studies that focus on the amici curiae brief include Bradley and Gardner; Caldeira and Wright, "Amici Curiae"; O'Connor and Epstein, "Amicus Curiae"; Puro; and Segal.

Interest groups that participate as an amicus curiae (friend of the court) are generally limited to submitting a written brief explaining their position in a case in which they have an interest that is pending before the Supreme Court. On rare occasions, the interest group may be permitted to participate in oral argument. In either case and with the exception of the attorney for the U.S. government, the solicitor general, permission of the litigants to the pending action must be obtained prior to any participation.

3. See Epstein, citing Barker; Berry; Greenberg; Jacob; Manwaring; O'Connor; Peltason; Sorauf; and Truman.

4. See Bradley and Gardner; Epstein; McIntosh and Parker; and Olson, "Interest-Group."

5. See Jacob; Krislov, "The Amicus Curiae"; O'Connor; Hakman; O'Connor and Epstein, Amicus Curiae"; Puro; and Sorauf.

6. See Epstein and Rowland; McIntosh and Parker; Olson, *Clients* and "Interest-Group"; Stewart and Heck, "Day to Day"; and Stewart and Sheffield.

7. Epstein hinted at this in her work on conservative organizations.

8. The Japanese American Citizens League not only filed an amicus brief in *Loving*, they were also permitted to participate in oral argument in that case by special leave of the Court.

9. Another example is *Doe v. An Unnamed Dental Office* (1992), where a dental assistant was fired from his job for refusing to take an HIV test. The Florida statute governing AIDS and employment instituted a two-pronged test (bona fida occupational qualification) for employee testing that mandates that the employer prove there are "no means of reasonable accommodation short of requiring that the individual be free" of HIV infection (Florida Statute §760.50). Again, this case challenged the implementation of legislation by seeking a definition of "reasonable accommodation."

10. For example, Florida: *State v. Cox and Jackman* (1993); Michigan: *State v. Lino*

(1994); Oklahoma: *Sawatsky v. City of Oklahoma City* (1995); and Texas: *City of Sherman v. Henry* (1995).

11. The marriage issue is further confounded by the passage of the federal Defense of Marriage Act (DOMA) in 1996. This legislation presents yet another litigation obstacle for LGBT activists who will be forced to challenge the constitutionality of the federal statute.

12. While the abortion issue was ultimately decided on the right to privacy, some scholars have suggested that the equality argument would have made for better law. Justice Ruth Bader Ginsburg, in particular, has been a vocal critic of the legal reasoning in *Roe v. Wade* (1973) and has argued that a decision based on equality would have ensured that abortion remained a protected right.

Works Cited

Barker, Lucius. "Third Parties in Litigation: A Systemic View of Judicial Function." *Journal of Politics* 29 (1967): 41–69.

Becker, Theodore L., and Malcolm M. Feeley, eds. *The Impact of Supreme Court Decisions.* 2d ed. New York: Oxford University Press, 1973.

Bentley, Arthur. *The Process of Governing.* Chicago: University of Chicago Press, 1908.

Berry, Jeffrey M. *Lobbying for the People.* Princeton: Princeton University Press, 1977.

Blasi, Vincent. *The Burger Court and the Counter-Revolution That Wasn't.* New Haven: Yale University Press, 1983.

Blasius, Mark. *Gay and Lesbian Politics.* Philadelphia: Temple University Press, 1994.

Bradley, Robert C., and Paul Gardner. "Underdogs, Upperdogs, and the Use of the Amicus Brief." *Justice System Journal* 10 (1985): 78–96.

Bruer, Patrick J. "Washington Interest Group Organizations and Modes of Legal Advocacy." Presented at the annual meeting of the American Political Science Association, Washington D.C., 1988.

Caldeira, Gregory A. "The Transmission of Legal Precedent: A Study of State Supreme Courts." *American Political Science Review* 79 (1985): 178–93.

Caldeira, Gregory A., and John R. Wright. "Organized Interests and Agenda-Setting in the Supreme Court." *American Political Science Review* 82 (1988): 1109–27.

———. "Amici Curiae before the Supreme Court: Who Participates, When, and How Much?" Presented at the annual meeting of the Midwest Political Science Association, 1988.

Canon, Bradley C., and Lawrence Baum. "Patterns of Adoption of Tort Law Innovations: An Application of Diffusion Theory to Judicial Doctrines." *American Political Science Review* 75 (1981): 975–87.

Cortner, Richard C. "Strategies and Tactics of Litigants in Constitutional Cases." *Journal of Public Law* 17 (1968): 287–307.

Costain, Anne N. "Social Movements as Interest Groups: The Case of the Women's Movement." In *The Politics of Interests: Interest Groups Transformed*, ed. Mark P. Petracca, 285–307. Boulder, CO: Westview Press, 1992.

Cowan, Ruth B. "Women's Rights through Litigation: An Examination of the American Civil Liberties Union Women's Right Project, 1971–1976." *Columbia Human Rights Law Review* 8 (1976): 373–412.

Dunlap, David W. "Ithaca Denies Gay Men a Marriage License." *New York Times*, December 4, 1995, p. B4.

Epstein, Lee. *Conservatives in Court*. Knoxville: University of Tennessee Press, 1985.

Epstein, Lee, and C. K. Rowland. "Interest Groups in the Courts: Do Groups Fare Better?" In *Interest Group Politics*, 2d ed, ed. Allan J. Cigler and Burdett A. Loomis, 275–88. Washington, DC: Congressional Quarterly, 1986.

———. "Interest Group Litigation in Federal District Courts." Presented at the annual meeting of the Law and Society Association, Vail, Colorado, 1988.

Freeman, J. Lieper. *The Political Process*. Rev. ed. New York: Random House, 1965.

Greenberg, Jack. "Litigation for Social Change: Methods, Limits, and Role in Democracy." *Records of the New York City Bar Association* 29 (1974): 9–23.

———. *Judicial Process and Social Change: Constitutional Litigation*. St. Paul: West, 1977.

Hahn, Jeanne. "The NAACP Legal Defense and Educational Fund: Its Judicial Strategy and Techniques." In *American Government and Politics*, ed. Stephen L. Wasby, 387–98. New York: Scribner, 1973.

Hakman, Nathan. "Lobbying the Supreme Court—An Appraisal of 'Political Science Folklore.'" *Fordham Law Review* 35 (1996): 15–50.

Hamm, Keith E. "Patterns of Influence among Committees, Agencies, and Interest Groups." *Legislative Studies Quarterly* 8 (1983): 379–426.

Harris, Peter. "Difficult Cases and the Display of Authority." *Journal of Law, Economics and Organization* 1 (1985): 209–21.

Jacob, Herbert. *Justice in America*. 3d ed. Boston: Little, Brown, 1978.

———. *Justice in America*. 4th ed. Boston: Little, Brown, 1984.

Kellogg, Charles. *NAACP: A History of the National Association for the Advancement of Colored People*. Baltimore: Johns Hopkins University Press, 1967.

Kluger, Richard. *Simple Justice: The History of* Brown v. Board of Education *and Black Americans' Struggle for Equality*. New York; Knopf, 1976.

Kobylka, Joseph F. "A Court-Created Context for Group Litigation: Libertarian Groups and Obscenity." *Journal of Politics* 49 (1987): 1061–78.

Krislov, Samuel. "The Amicus Curiae Brief: From Friendship to Advocacy." *Yale Law Journal* 72 (1963): 694–721.

———. *The Supreme Court in the Political Process*. New York: Macmillan, 1965.

Lawrence, Susan E. *The Poor in Court*. Princeton: Princeton University Press, 1990.

Leiser, Ken. "Panel Acts to Shun Same-Sex Marriages." *San Diego Union-Tribune*, January 25, 1996, p. A3.

Link, David. "Gay Rites." *Reason* 27 (January 1996): 28.

Manwaring, David. *Render unto Caesar: The Flag Salute Controversy*. Chicago: University of Chicago Press, 1962.

McAdams, Doug. *Political Process and the Development of Black Insurgency, 1930–1970*. Chicago: University of Chicago Press, 1982.

McIntosh, Wayne V. "And Now for Something Completely Different: Amicus Curiae Activity in Federal District Courts." Presented at the annual meeting of the Northeastern Political Science Association, Boston, 1984.

McIntosh, Wayne V., and Paul E. Parker. "Amici Curiae in the Courts of Appeals." Presented at the annual meeting of the Law and Society Association, Chicago, 1986.

Morgan, Richard E. *The Politics of Religious Conflict: Church and State in America*. New York: Pegasus, 1968.

———. *Disabling America: The Rights Industry*. New York: Basic Books, 1984.

Note. "Special Section." *National Law Journal*, September 29, 1986, p. S1.

O'Connor, Karen. *Women's Organizations' Use of the Courts*. Lexington, MA: Lexington, 1980.

O'Connor, Karen, and Lee Epstein. "Amicus Curiae Participation in U.S. Supreme Court Litigation: An Appraisal of Hakman's 'Folklore.'" *Law and Society Review* 16 (1981–82): 311–20.

———. "Beyond Legislative Lobbying: Women's Rights Groups and the Supreme Court." *Judicature* 67 (1983): 134–43.

———. "The Rise of Conservative Interest Group Litigation." *Journal of Politics* 45 (1983): 479–89.

Olson, Susan M. "The Political Evolution of Interest Group Litigation." In *Governing through Courts*, ed. Richard A. L. Gambitta, Marlynn May, and James C. Foster, 225–58. Beverly Hills: Sage, 1981.

———. *Clients and Lawyers: Securing the Rights of Disabled Persons*. Westport, CT: Greenwood, 1984.

———. "Interest-Group Litigation in Federal District Court: Beyond the Political Disadvantage Theory." *Journal of Politics* 52 (1990): 854–82.

"Panel Approves Gay Marriage." *National Law Journal*, December 25, 1995, p. A8.

Peltason, Jack. *Federal Courts in the Political Process*. New York: Random, 1955.

Perry, H. W., Jr. "Pluralist Theory and National Black Politics in the United States." *Polity* 23 (1991): 549–65.

Petracca, Mark P. "The Rediscovery of Interest Group Politics." In *The Politics of Interests: Interest Groups Transformed*, ed. Mark P. Petracca, 3–31. Boulder, CO: Westview Press, 1992.

Pfeffer, Leo. "Amici in Church-State Litigation." *Law and Contemporary Problems* 44 (1981): 81–110.

Puro, Steven. "The Role of the Amicus Curiae in the United States Supreme Court: 1920–1966." Ph.D. diss. University of New York at Buffalo, 1971.

Rossiter, Clinton, ed. *The Federalist Papers*. New York: Mentor, 1961.

Salokar, Rebecca Mae. *The Solicitor General: The Politics of Law*. Philadelphia: Temple University Press, 1992.

Scheppele, Kim Lane, and Jack L. Walker. "The Litigation Strategies of Interest Groups." Unpublished ms., University of Michigan, 1989.

Segal, Jeffrey A. "Amicus Curiae Briefs by the Solicitor General during the Warren and Burger Courts." *Western Political Quarterly* 41 (1988): 135–44.

Sorauf, Frank J. *The Wall of Separation: Constitutional Politics of Church and State*. Princeton: Princeton University Press, 1976.

Stewart, Joseph Jr., and Edward Heck. "Ensuring Access to Justice: The Role of Interest Group Lawyers in the 60s Campaign for Civil Rights." *Judicature* 66 (1982): 84–95.

———. "The Day to Day Activities of Interest Group Lawyers." *Social Science Quarterly* 64 (1983): 173–82.

Stewart, Joseph Jr., and James F. Sheffield, Jr. "Does Interest Group Litigation Matter? The Case of Black Political Mobilization in Mississippi." *Journal of Politics* 49 (1987): 780–98.

Sullivan, Andrew. "The Politics of Homosexuality." *The New Republic*, May 10, 1993, pp. 24–26, 32–37.

Tarr, G. Alan, and Mary Cornelia Porter. *State Supreme Courts in State and Nation*. New Haven: Yale University Press, 1988.

Thomas, Clive S., and Ronald J. Hrebenar. "Interest Groups in the States." In *Politics in the American States: A Comparative Analysis*, ed. Virginia Gray, Herbert Jacob, and Robert Albritton, 150–74. Glenview, IL: Scott, Foresman/Little Brown, 1992.

Truman, David B. *The Governmental Process*. New York: Knopf, 1951.

Vaid, Urvashi. *Virtual Equality*. New York: Anchor, 1995.

————. Oral presentation at the "Identity/Space/Power: Lesbian, Gay, Bisexual, and Transgender Politics" Conference. Center for Lesbian and Gay Studies of the Graduate School and University Center of the City University of New York. New York City (February 8, 1996).

Vose, Clement E. *Caucasians Only*. Berkeley: University of California Press, 1959.

Wasby, Stephen L. *The Impact of the United States Supreme Court*. Homewood, IL: Dorsey, 1970.

————. *Continuity and Change: From the Warren Court to the Burger Court*. Pacific Palisades, CA: Goodyear, 1976.

————. "How Planned Is 'Planned' Litigation?" *American Bar Association Research Journal* 1984 (1984): 83.

————. "A Transformed Triangle: Court, Congress, and Presidency in Civil Rights." *Policy Studies Journal* 21 (1993): 565–74.

Cases Cited

Amer v. Johnson, 17th Judicial Circuit in and for Broward County, Florida, No. 92-14370 (11) (unpublished opinion by Judge John A. Fruciante) (July 27, 1997)

Baehr v. Miike, Hawaii Supreme Court, No. 20371 (December 9, 1999)

Baker v. Vermont, Vermont Supreme Court, No. 98-032 (December 20, 1999)

Bowers v. Hardwick, 478 US 186 (1986)

Brause v. Alaska (Alaska Superior Court, Third District, 1999)

City of Sherman v. Henry, 910 SW2d 542 (1995)

Cox v. Florida Department of Health and Rehabilitative Services, 656 So2d 902 (1995)

Doe v. An Unnamed Dental Office, Florida Commission on Human Relations (1992)

Equality Foundation of Greater Cincinnati v. City of Cincinnati, 54 F3d 261 (1995)

Evans v. Romer, 882 P2d 1335 (1994) (cert. granted)

Hummer v. Unemployment Appeals Commission, 572 So2d (Fla. 5th DCA) 135 (1991)

Hurley v. Irish-American Gay, Lesbian and Bisexual Group of Boston, 115 S.Ct. 2338 (1995)

In re T.W., A Minor, 551 So2d 1186 (1989)

Kentucky v. Wasson, 842 SW2d 487 (1992)

Loving v. Virginia, 388 US 1 (1967)

Plessy v. Ferguson, 163 US 537 (1896)

Powell v. State (Georgia Sup Ct., #598A0755, Nov. 23, 1998)

Rasmussen v. South Florida Blood Service, 500 So2d 533 (1987)

Roe v. Wade, 410 US 113 (1973)

Romer v. Evans, No. 94-1039, 64 USLW 4353, Decided May 20, 1996

Sawatzky v. City of Oklahoma City, 906 P2d 785 (1995)

State v. Cox and Jackman, 627 So2d 1210 (1993)

State v. Lino, 527 NW2d 434 (1994)

ELEVEN

SPLITTING IMAGES

THE NIGHTLY NETWORK NEWS AND THE POLITICS OF

THE LESBIAN AND GAY MOVEMENT, 1969–1978

Timothy E. Cook

Bevin Hartnett

POLITICAL SCIENCE has long known that, in Michael Lipsky's famous coinage, protest could be a political resource for groups and social movements otherwise lacking in resources that make for power within politics.[1] Yet Lipsky recognized that such a benefit was difficult to attain. Protest leaders must direct their appeals not just to decision makers themselves, but also to their own followers, the news media, and "third parties" that could be brought in on their side. Most centrally, protest does not amount to much if it is not reported by the news media to reach a wider audience, set concerns and views on the political agenda, and put pressure on institutional political actors to do something.

That raises, in turn, the question: *can* social movements rely on the news media to broadcast their views? Or do social movements, instead, run the risk of having their message taken out of context and dramatically altered? Indeed, might social movements themselves be transformed by their search, successful or not, for favorable publicity?

Nowhere, it seems, would such coverage be as crucial as with lesbian and gay movements. After all, lesbians, gay men, and bisexuals do not grow up being socialized into that identity in the same way as is done in racial and ethnic communities. Instead, they are less dependent on immediate communities and more reliant on external cues, such as media coverage, for the information to construct their own self-image. As important, given the invisibility and consequent ability of lesbians, gay men, and bisexuals to "pass" in straight worlds, coming out—that is, openly declaring one's sexual orientation—has become a key political strategy to mobilize a community and demonstrate its breadth and depth to the larger society.

This essay examines the way in which one medium—television news— defined and helped construct the newly emerging lesbian and gay movement in the decade after the Stonewall riots in 1969 (the standard demarcation point for the contemporary gay movement), with a brief examination of the stories from late 1978 through 1981, just before the initial stories on AIDS moved us into a new era of news. Although there has been work on the coverage of newspapers and newsmagazines, there has been surprisingly little on television news. Yet the latter's mix of spontaneity and predictability, of direct sound bites and reporters' contexts, suggests that it could be exploited, whatever the intent of its creators, in freer ways than other media productions.

It also makes sense to start in 1968, not simply because that is the earliest date when television news broadcasts were routinely preserved, but because this allows us to chronicle how a relatively new phenomenon, the movement, was discovered and treated by the news. In broadcasting news about the lesbian and gay movement, television may have served to impose a particular frame on it that would channel, and possibly restrict, later political possibilities.

Many raise doubts about whether the news media can serve as a resource for sexual minorities. According to accepted wisdom, media reports of the movement are likely to be negatively stereotyped. Only unless and until segments of the movement itself monitor coverage and pressure newsrooms will news organizations, this argument goes, include openly lesbian, gay, or bisexual reporters and spend more time producing balanced, fair coverage.[2]

Let's take some representative examples. Simon Watney notices the British press's bias: "Homosexuality is constructed as an exemplary and admonitory sign of Otherness in the press, in order to unite sexual and national identifications amongst readers over and above all divisions and distinctions of class, race and gender."[3] Larry Gross concurs for the United States. After noting unpalatable choices between invisibility and negative stereotypes, Gross adds, "Lesbians and gay men are unusually vulnerable to mass media power, even more so than blacks, national minorities, and women. Of all social groups . . . we are probably the least permitted to speak for ourselves in the mass media."[4] An indispensable review by Fred Fejes and Kevin Petrich of many studies of lesbians and gay men in the American mass media concludes that while the bulk of images may no longer be overtly homophobic, "the situation has moved to a higher level of subordination and repression. Homophobia has been replaced by heterosexism . . . [which] denies an acknowledgment of gays and lesbians in their own distinct reality and diversity."[5] The news media, they find, resisted giving gay men and lesbians "the status . . . of a civil rights movement or an ethnic or racial community" and instead preferred to "define homosexuality as a 'lifestyle,' an ambiguous frame that lacked political or socially relevant content and implied that sexual orientation was a choice."[6]

Yet post–World War II American homosexuality reveals how the news media have long been targeted by activists who welcomed coverage as far back as the early 1950s.[7] This is a puzzle. How can we reconcile the scholarly consensus that the news media could not provide much of a resource for the movement with the evidence that activists from the earliest days of the movement saw news coverage as a benefit to them and acted accordingly?

For one, different parts of the movement were interested in news coverage for different reasons, often at the same time. The Mattachine Society in the 1950s found, in John D'Emilio's words, that "visibility, though a basic movement objective, was obviously a two-edged sword."[8] Even favorable publicity could and did strain the movement, parts of which feared public attention. But this approach would be challenged in the mid-1960s by more radical activists who favored public strategies to put forth a positive image of gay men and lesbians. These actors were in turn contested in the early 1970s by newer activists, particularly in the Gay Liberation Front (GLF) and then the Gay Activists' Alliance (GAA), who were less interested in combating prejudice than in mobilizing a movement and found news—almost regardless of the content—advantageous.[9] After all, whether the coverage was positive or negative might then be beside the point. Even anti-gay news could break the silence and indicate the presence and locations of alternative sexualities and sexual communities. D'Emilio has written about the mid-1960s: "Much of [media coverage] was exploitive and derogatory; some was sympathetic; occasionally one could even find celebrations of homosexual life. But the significance of the content paled in comparison with the importance of the sheer quantity of material that portrayed, dissected, and argued about the gay experience in America."[10]

Another possibility is that the news media were (and are) nowhere near as resistant to social movements on a routine basis than is usually assumed. Different modalities have varying notions of what is news. Reporters can deviate from political expectations for the news provided that they meet their superiors' production values for quality news. Unpredictable accidents can break the standard operating procedures of news organizations and introduce new topics for discussion. Under any of these conditions, there will be different openings for social movements at different locations at different times in different news outlets. Indeed, it may be that the news media are internally conflicted and ambivalent about how to cover homosexuality. Consider the "split image" in the first television news accounts on AIDS, with sympathetic portraits of the gay men with AIDS alongside a more critical view of homosexuals as a group and homosexuality as a practice.[11]

Social movements are not wholly shut out of the news. The finest account of the interactions of the news media and a social movement, Todd Gitlin's study of the New Left, suggests that different aspects of the movement may be covered at different times, with varying levels of positivity, neutrality, or denigration. Gitlin's theme is that this process blunts radical alternatives and preserves domination. Yet he also admits, "Some of what the movement wanted to broadcast, about the world and about its own purposes and its nature, *got broadcast.*"[12]

Gitlin implies a cycle of reporting about social movements:[13]

First the movement is *ignored*, not considered important or newsworthy—often because the movement itself pays little attention to such publicity.

Second, it is *discovered* and reported about in neutral or favorable terms as something intriguingly new.

Third, following the negative reaction of politically powerful authoritative sources, the movement is *denigrated*, usually by a greater emphasis on the viewpoints of its opponents, who are portrayed as more unified and powerful. Yet ironically, this new attention, even though it is negative, brings new participants to a movement, clarifies its importance, and serves to reenergize the movement.

Fourth, as the story becomes "old news" but the movement still craves publicity, the debate is *polarized* between two sides, each shown in increasingly militant, dramatic, and extreme ways, in order to defeat the "we've-covered-that" syndrome.

Finally, partly as the movement splits, and partly as the news needs of journalism shift, the portrayal of the movement becomes *bifurcated* between radical and more reformist wings—the former painted as illegitimate, the latter as not. Initially, Gitlin notes, the illegitimate side is seen as "penetrating and contaminating" the moderate wing—"a formula for ambivalence."[14] Eventually, however, the media help to *elevate a moderate alternative*, which is covered favorably and allowed to join the debate as an authoritative player.

Gitlin's model shows great promise in being applied to other social movements, too, particularly since he is careful to note how it results from the routine workings of journalism. Reporters' individual opinions and assessments are less important, given the rigorous attempts that reporters make to screen out their own viewpoints in favor of what they take (mistakenly) as objective indicators of newsworthiness. Instead, we would expect the coverage to be shaped by three factors: (1) the newsbeat of the reporter, which dictates the typical sources and events they routinely rely on for news; (2) the ways in which reporters may presume that the subject matter of sexuality has to be either avoided or euphemized, rather than sensationalized, for a mainstream audience; and (3) the reluctance of the news media to be seen as raising an agenda (and thereby exerting power) distinct from what is going on within governmental institutions and processes.

Methods

We examined the nightly news broadcasts of ABC, CBS, and NBC as archived by the Vanderbilt University Television News Archives. Their printed abstracts give a subject heading and story synopsis and are contemporaneously indexed by topic. Our initial search consisted of collecting those stories according to the annual and monthly indexes by subject matter. We complemented this approach with an electronic search, via the archives' website. Through this engine, we used the following keywords (and their variants): homosexual, gay, lesbian, queer, bisexual, transvestite, transgender, and transsexual. The results left us with hundreds of stories from 1969 through 1981 that contained some reference to one of the keywords. Combining these two lists (which overlapped greatly), we then restricted our attention to those stories containing out-of-studio film, under the assumption that the combination of audio and visual makes for the particular power of television news stories. This search left us with approximately ten hours total of compiled footage, which Vanderbilt collected, copied, and lent to us.

We concentrated further on film stories centrally about lesbian and gay issues. Many stories touched only slightly on such issues. For instance, amid stories covering political conventions and elections, a gay candidate, issue, or platform would be one of many subjects discussed. Each of us independently viewed the stories and put them into one of three categories: if the lesbian/gay content was central to the story (it would not have been a newsworthy story in the absence of the lesbian/gay content); marginal stories (the stories would have been newsworthy without that content); and questionable stories (difficult to say one way or the other). We agreed, without consultation, on over 90 percent of these stories; we then discussed the remaining cases and reached consensus on their categorization. About half of our stories fell into the second category of marginal gay content. Fewer than twenty stories fell into the "questionable" category, so we folded those into the "marginal" category.

We focus here on the eighty-four stories from 1969 through 1981 that fell into the category of "central gay content" (see appendix for a complete list), as these seem to us the ones most strongly "about" homosexuality. Next we coded the sources in these stories that were quoted in order to find out who was allowed to speak. We relied on the "super" on the screen identifying the source in the report, the verbal labeling by the reporter, or the source's own self-identification. In addition to categorizing the source as gay/lesbian/bisexual/transgender or straight based on the information provided, and as male or female, we also coded their position.[15]

Finally, we examined each of the stories to see if they could fall into one of the categories suggested by Gitlin's analysis: (1) a discovery story where lesbians, gay men, and/or bisexuals were respectfully presented, with little or no representation of the viewpoints of their opponents or detractors; (2) a denigration story where the opponents of lesbians, gay men, and/or bisexuals are given greater control over the framing of the story; (3) a polarization story, which is distinguished from denigration stories by the portrayal of one or both sides as extreme; and (4) a bifurcation story, where the movement itself is shown to be divided between radicals and reformists, with the latter receiving more favorable coverage.

The Contours of Coverage, 1969–81

The number of stories on the nightly network news having any reference to homosexuality is small and fluctuates from year to year. Figures 11.1 and 11.2 present the variation over time and by network in stories with, respectively, central and marginal gay content.

Note the time line. No story with clear gay content was covered simultaneously by more than one network until May 1975, when Technical Sergeant Leonard Matlovich appealed his discharge from the Air Force for having declared his homosexuality. Such stories were relegated to at least the second half of the news—more often in the final third—far away from the pressing stories of the day. Stories that did get covered on more than one network were longer-length pieces detailing the political conventions and platforms in 1972. In clips of five-plus minutes in length, gay issues were given less than ten seconds of air time. In short, gay news seemed to be of little importance.

Upswings in coverage invariably were in the context of governmental institutions and processes: in 1975, with Matlovich's case in military court; in 1977 and 1978, with the numerous referenda seeking to repeal gay rights ordinances; in 1978 and 1979, with the murder of San Francisco's gay supervisor Harvey Milk by his former colleague Dan White, White's trial for murder and conviction on a lesser charge of voluntary manslaughter, and the apparently gay-led "White Night" riots that ensued at city hall. We can also see a spillover effect: the designation of gay men and lesbians as worthy of news stories was associated with an increase in the number of stories that had marginal gay content. If—and perhaps only if—homosexuality was considered an appropriate focus for the news did reporters seem more willing to mention it even in stories that were news for other reasons.

Homosexuality was not considered to be much of a story, then, though NBC was usually more likely to run stories than either CBS or ABC. This result is surprising, given the well-established similarity of the subject matter of news (if not in the precise interpretation or slant of that news) across all three networks, at least for agreed-upon stories such as the Iran hostage crisis or presidential election campaigns.[16] With less frequently covered, more "optional" news, there may be greater variation from one network to the next.

Who was allowed to speak? Figure 11.3 presents the count of sources from 1969 through 1981 of all persons quoted on film in a story with clear

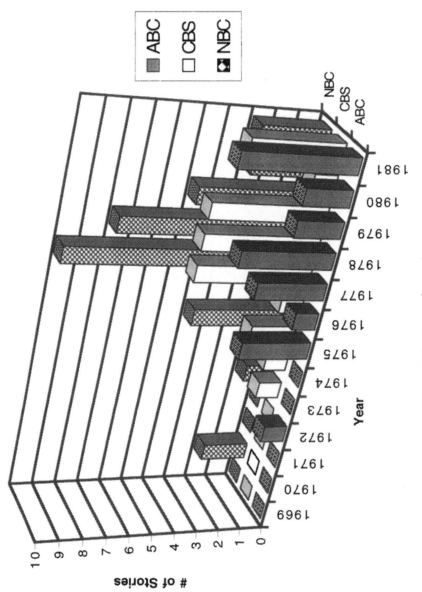

Figure 11.1. Stories of central gay content

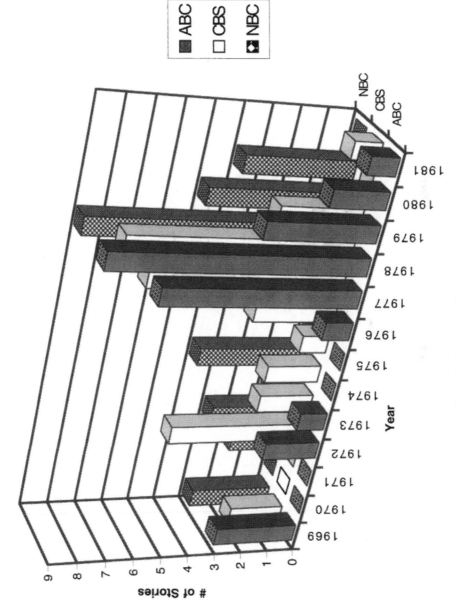

Figure 11.2. Stories of marginal gay content

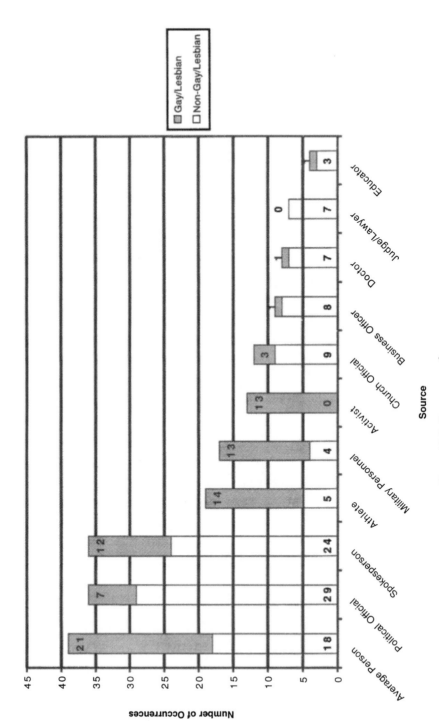

Figure 11.3. Frequency of source occurrences

gay content. What is striking about the figure is that within some categories, there was a genuine balance between identifiably gay or lesbian sources and those that were not; in particular, although gay men and lesbians were outnumbered among spokespersons, the number of activist sources almost makes that up, and "persons-in-the-street" tended to be more often lesbian/gay than not. By contrast, gay men and lesbians were strongly underrepresented among elites: political officials, church and business leaders, and physicians.

Gay men are quoted far more than lesbians, however, generally by a ratio of three-to-one throughout this time period, even when the movement was most newsworthy, 1977 through 1979. (We should also underscore that, at least as far as we can identify, all the gay/lesbian sources were white, which was not the case with other sources quoted.) Gay men were quoted 65 times in comparison with lesbians' 23. Television, like other news media, tended to define homosexuality as a largely male phenomenon.

Discovering a Movement, 1969–75

So gay men and (to a far lesser extent) lesbians are allowed to speak, but the authoritative elites quoted are largely presented as straight. What happens when we look inside the reports that did get broadcast? At this stage, we turn away from quantitative coding and attempt a more qualitative analysis—at the very least to generate categories that can be used for more rigorous testing.[17]

The movement itself made little news, only by demonstrating at already newsworthy events like party conventions (NBC, 7/5/72) or working within the system with gay rights bills (CBS, 5/6/74). The Stonewall riots of 1969 went unnoticed. Footage from the annual commemorations of Stonewall that became gay pride marches was never aired until the CBS story of gay rights bills in 1974 and was not considered newsworthy enough to receive film stories in their own right until 1979. Most surprisingly for this time period, the movement's possibly most significant achievement—successfully provoking the American Psychological Association (APA) to repeal its categorization of homosexuality as a mental illness—never received a network news film story, even for the APA's final vote. The foibles of the gay movement in the 1970s were epitomized by how one demonstrator from "the Gay Raiders" had to invade the CBS studios, shouting and waving a sign in front of anchor Walter Cronkite's impassive gaze, before the screen momentarily went blank and the demonstrator was hustled out of camera range (CBS, 12/11/73).

The few early reports, however, are illuminating. Footage appeared that would be endlessly replicated in later coverage. One key visual was of gay men and/or lesbians dancing—in part to relieve the bland visual focus on "talking heads," in part because of the difficulty of visualizing how gay men or how lesbians act physically toward each other, and in part because of the easy availability of dance floors (whether at universities[18] or in gay bars[19]) to camera crews.

Yet, almost all of these were "discovery" stories. With one salient exception, they gave sympathetic depictions and/or allowed at least equal access to gay people and their opponents to present their views with little commentary or editing. This was presumably easy to do, because none of these stories—unlike contemporary newsmagazines—tried to characterize the overall state of American homosexuality. These stories expressly covered isolated phenomena: the rumored gay takeover of Alpine County, California (NBC, 10/22/70 and 11/13/70); gay student organizations on campus (NBC, 4/13/73); a sailor accused of being gay appealing his discharge from the Navy (ABC, 3/23/72); and gay rights bills in selected cities (CBS, 5/6/74). These new subjects drew their newsworthiness from old narratives—continuing concern with the "sexual revolution," civil rights battles, and television's fascination with California as source of offbeat social developments.[20] Television news freed itself from having to generalize about homosexuality, discovered a previously uncovered but intriguing lone incident, and covered it respectfully.

The one exception proves the rule, when one "discovery" story touched off a counterreaction, a "denigration" story. The paired stories on NBC on Alpine County reveal the pitfalls of covering the gay movement, both for gay rights activists and for reporters themselves.

Alpine County was the least populous county in California. Members of the GLF in Berkeley and Los Angeles conceived the idea (probably only half-seriously) of moving en masse to the county, voting themselves into the government, and establishing a "gay mecca." On October 22, 1970, after the story appeared on the front pages of California newspapers, NBC anchor John Chancellor introduced the final story, known in the news business as the "kicker":

> There are 384 citizens of Alpine County, California, and usually they take their politics with tolerance and good humor. But something extraordinary is happening to the people of Alpine County, something political which the founding fathers never thought of. Watch.

The report began with film of three men in Los Angeles in psychedelic surroundings (the standard visual symbol of the counterculture). The camera rapidly zoomed in on one with long hair, a Fu Manchu mustache and a bandanna, identified as Lee Heflin of the GLF, who said:

> Primarily, what we are after with this is a place in this country where we can live as freely as the majority do. We are like all minorities in this country, oppressed

by the Establishment. We are hoping to set up a counterculture within this county where we can develop our own life style as freely as we choose.

The scene cut to correspondent Ray Cullin in Alpine County on an isolated ranch, which he said the GLF proposed to make a "gay liberation colony." After explaining just how the GLF could legally take over the county, Cullin cited county officials as "deeply concerned." He ended by interviewing some locals (shot in close human-interest range) who, he said, were "stunned by the possibility of a gay takeover." The report ended with an elderly woman who asked, "Now, I don't know why they should want to take over the government of the county. What's wrong with the way it's run now?" Cullin asked, "What about their presence? Does the fact that they want to move in bother you?" and got back, "Well, if they don't come too close, it wouldn't worry me," to end the report (and the newscast).

The overall tone was wonder and bemusement. It allowed Heflin's liberationist viewpoint to be broadcast fairly complete. But the quick zooms, the up-close-and-personal framings, the lack of a final line by the reporter at the close, and its status as the kicker all set this apart from hard news stories.

On November 13, NBC returned to Alpine County with a story earlier in the broadcast—thereby certifying its status as hard news. The county government's stern official reaction in a public meeting produced a denigrating story. This piece neither referred to nor quoted any gay movement spokespersons.[21] Instead, reporter Don Oliver's language of homosexuals "forcing their way in," "invading" and "controlling" society, culminated in a line about the feared unrecognizable other: "Newcomers in Alpine County are eyed with suspicion. Each stranger could be an advance scout for the Gay Liberation Front." Compared to the earlier, more benign report, the emigration was portrayed as a threat (in a county supervisor's words) to the "public as a whole." This interpretation gained credence not only by the avalanche of various county groups—from mothers' clubs to American Indians—but by a San Francisco social worker who said, "You don't have any idea of what will happen when a homosexual group moves into your county or even moves into your neighborhood." Before one gets to Oliver's close that the chances of a gay takeover have gone from a thousand to one to a million to one, the report condensed into a few minutes a wealth of fears of homosexuals—especially the invasion by "them," the unseen enemies, threatening the fabric of "us," the varied public.

Oliver's report demonstrated how easily the news media *could have* approached the story: a polarized conflict of gay men and lesbians with the rest of "respectable" society. Yet what is most striking is its uniqueness. It neglected to portray both sides of the issue, interviewing only the opponents of the GLF and expressing only the fears that the community had of this newly visible gay minority. In contrast, the remaining stories from 1969 through

1975 were at least evenly balanced, and in some, the opponents of homosexuality were not represented at all. Most fully, Betty Rollin's report on homosexuality on campus (NBC, 4/13/73)—presaged by Jack Perkins's story on the sexual revolution at various universities (NBC, December 31, 1969)—painted a respectful portrait of gay men and lesbians, allowing a sympathetic interpretation of their lives and culture.

"Remember Joe College?" Rollin began, against film of football players. After granting that "he is still grunting on the football field at the University of Iowa," she switched to a campus gay dance, the faces again clearly visible. Rollin's voiceover narrated: "But everything has been so shaken up in the last decade, there's been so much moral and sexual change and confusion in this country." This opposition is a hallmark of television news: establish a tension to catch the viewer's attention.

The dichotomy of Joe College (outside, in the light, on public display, "clean-cut," masculine) versus gay and lesbian students dancing (inside, semi-shadowy, in private, long-haired, androgynous) could have been resolved in several ways.[22] Instead, after musing on change and confusion, Rollin started to address the contrast by concluding "there's no longer one kind of hero or one way to be on campus or anywhere else. Now, on campus, there are many acceptable ways to be. And one of them is homosexual."

How would we know what is "acceptable"? First, Rollin visually resolved the contrast. In the open air, she showed students walking to class, in a distant shot presenting "students" as a unitary group, stressing commonalities. Rollin added a message of continuity over time that verbally answers the apparent disruption: "The theory is that there are no more homosexuals on campus than there used to be, only that more of them are admitting what they are and organizing." Having established this visual and verbal resolution between Joe College and the gay student, it is an easy segue to an authoritative source—the university administrator framed in the at-arm's-length shot commonly used for people in power. With his benediction that the student group had met all criteria for official recognition, the report moved to a discussion in a dorm living room with Rollin and five others while she approvingly intoned, "Before 1970 when the group was founded, campus homosexuals had to resort to the bar scene. Now they say they have a decent place to meet."

Two gay men now spoke, male students identified by name and shown within "touching distance" of the viewer. In Gaye Tuchman's interpretation, this not only personalizes and individualizes the interviewee at the same time that it makes subjects into a symbol or representation of their group, it also establishes intimacy between subject and viewer.[23] One mentioned coming out to his parents, saying that "we're the best of pals," and indicating how neither he nor they discussed their sex life to each other. The other answered Rollin's question, "What do you want?" by saying, "Well, I think more than anything, we'd like people to know that we too are people, we have feelings as they have feelings, we are capable of love and desires as they are."

The frame of the story stresses equality between students, gay and straight. Yet was this acceptance conditional? Aspects of urban gay life, such as the gay bar (the traditional and "pre-political" center of lesbian and gay communities), were implicitly decried as not "decent"; the gay men's similarity to the rest of the world was underscored. Above all, Rollin's construction of sexuality was relentlessly essentialist. Note the words to her final stand-up:

> The question is, do homosexual organizations encourage homosexuality? Psychiatrists we spoke to think not. They point out that in this society nobody wants to be a homosexual who isn't one and that if a kid goes as far as joining a homosexual club, he is a homosexual. All that the club does is make him feel less alone and less terrible about sexual feelings he has and can't help having.

Discovery stories during this period also extended to the civil rights of lesbians and gay men. The news briefly mentioned gay rights when covering the two parties' 1972 nominating conventions. Then CBS aired a long outtake on gay rights in New York, Boulder, and San Francisco (CBS, 5/6/74). It was, to be sure, a kicker, but it lasted five minutes—an eternity on television.

Cronkite began by neutrally intoning, "Part of the new morality of the sixties and seventies is a new attitude toward homosexuality. The homosexual men and women have organized to fight for acceptance and respectability." Gay rights legislation had already been enacted in several cities.[24] Those laws gave the story a national cachet. CBS showed a map of the United States with black dots, the cities where laws had already passed, then increasing numbers of white dots, where they were under consideration. The national scope was also reflected by melding a story from Bob McNamara on New York and Boulder on efforts to pass gay rights bills with a report from Richard Threlkeld about gay presence and power in San Francisco.

McNamara showed little evidence of an organized gay movement in New York. Only brief film footage of a New York gay pride march hinted otherwise. He counterposed a sound bite from a lone presumably gay activist against his opponents: a member of the New York firemen's union, an outraged young white male observer, and a spokesperson for New York's Catholic archdiocese. The visuals also depicted broad opposition to gay rights: both men and women and both whites and blacks are shown signing the petitions. Though these sources voiced anti-gay sentiments and stereotypes, the opposition had yet to form an organization that the news media could reliably turn to as an authoritative voice for anti-gay forces. Moreover, when McNamara turned to Boulder, the opposition was nowhere to be found. He closed with John Muth, shot outside on campus, who discussed the aims of the movement (mentioned in the super only as "gay activist"). His last line predicted, "And I think this eventually will come." Threlkeld's report from San Francisco could and did present a new, unchallenged future.

Threlkeld presented not only external shots of the gay Polk Street neighborhood but the first nightly news images of the "dozens of nightclubs and bars that cater to gays." Threlkeld was matter-of-fact: "Here more than in any other city in America, gays have come closest to their goal: acceptance as just another minority group." Threlkeld turned to indications of officials "[trying] hard to make gay liberation not a demand but a real fact," and concluded as the footage returned to the bar, "The consensus of the consenting adults we talked to is that homosexuals, like other minorities, have come a long way down the road toward full equality in the last decade."

The discovery phase reached a climax with the first news event to be recognized by all three networks: Leonard Matlovich disputing his discharge from the Air Force after having come out to his commanding officer.[25] Matlovich's tale matched the production values of the news perfectly. The clarity and drama of his public declaration of being gay made the story supremely easy to explain.[26] In addition, instead of getting caught by superiors, Matlovich brought his homosexuality to them, along with an exemplary service record that included commendations for his effort in Vietnam. Ready to propel the story by being its protagonist and by stating both humility for his homosexuality alongside principles of equality, Matlovich chose to speak to the media and for the movement. Finally, by leading up to the military hearings, the news was able to have a predictable, continuing story within a government process, the most standard form of hard news imaginable.

Far from posing a threat to the social fabric or to legitimized institutions, Matlovich's portrayal was respectful and frequently sympathetic. ABC (9/16/75) presented Matlovich, within touching distance, saying, "There is [sic] no medical grounds whatsoever that the armed forces can discriminate against us . . . If there are no medical grounds, then what are there? What have I done to prove myself incompetent?" CBS's first report (5/26/75) was shot in a backyard, with Matlovich filmed authoritatively, saying he came out in order to stop "never coming to the protection of my fellow minority group." On all three networks, Matlovich was quoted as saying that lesbians and gay men constituted a minority group deserving protection from discrimination.

But Matlovich's favorable coverage seems to have been conditional. First, Matlovich's legal case urged not overturning the regulation but making an exception. This strategy could appeal to the media's penchant for individualism. Kenley Jones finished his initial report for NBC (9/16/75), "If Matlovich gets a favorable ruling here, it will mean that homosexuals cannot be separated from military service merely for being homosexuals. They will have to be judged as individuals, not as a group—which is what gay liberationists have been seeking in civilian life all along." Second, Matlovich was able to profess that he was not out to prove a point but only to not be "afraid of losing my job all the time, that's all." Third, Matlovich said he had no choice being gay. All three networks prominently featured his testimony, "I cried a lot. And I prayed a lot. I prayed to become like everyone else. I did not want to become gay, but I have no choice."[27] To questions as to whether as an Air Force instructor "he would try to persuade his students to become gay," Matlovich replied, "If you can persuade a student who is not gay to become homosexual, I would have persuaded myself to be heterosexual long ago" (ABC, 9/17/75).

The components that made for respectful coverage of Matlovich can best be seen by a contrasting story. Taking place between Matlovich's initial discharge and the trial that fall, NBC (6/12/75) covered the discharge of two members of the Women's Army Corps (WACs) because of their lesbian relationship. Though contributed by the previously sympathetic Betty Rollin, this story was more negative than any about Matlovich. After the opening interview with both of the women together (and in uniform) protesting their discharge, a sound bite with a fellow WAC insisted "the Army's no place for queers." After noting unnamed army officials' characterization of lesbians in the WACs as "corruptive and disruptive," Rollin claimed that psychiatrists doubted that gay people would be a problematic presence in the military. Part of the difference, then, was Matlovich's proactive control over the story, with interviews with him at his home or his own testimony as the key content. By contrast, these two women seem to have been unluckily discovered, caught, and spotlighted on a military base where, free from the strictures of a trial, opposing sources could be easily found.

In sum, what coverage through 1975 did exist struck an ambivalent, even matter-of-fact tone of discovery about homosexuals, and even about gay rights. Up to and including the one agreed-upon news item about homosexuality, the nightly network news was respectful and rarely resorted to denigration. Individual gay men (and, to a far lesser extent, lesbians) could describe themselves—or even be described by the reporter—as members of another minority group striving for civil rights. Yet the approval was conditional: these lone homosexuals were presented as individuals and reporters noted how their sexual orientation was a matter of predestination, not choice.

Denigration: Anita Bryant Legitimates the Gay Rights Struggle as News

With Matlovich's hearing over, television stories on lesbian and gay issues initially fell back into oblivion, and 1976 only saw coverage of gay rights among many other concerns in the discussion of the party platforms. However, in June 1977, public disputes over cities' gay rights ordinances began to attract news attention, starting with the ultimately successful referendum campaign to repeal the gay rights ordinance in Dade County, Florida, followed by other referenda in a seemingly national campaign about (and against) lesbians and gay men.

If we were to gauge this coverage simply by its tone, much was indeed denigrating of homosexuality in general and the lives of gay men and lesbians. Yet at the same time, this fight brought a chance for the gay and lesbian movement as a whole, rather than a lone individual such as Matlovich, to become a player in a hard news story. In effect, the tone may have worked against the movement but the framing did not: gay news was now understood in terms of civil rights.

The repeal campaigns were well suited for the production needs of the news. Reporters gravitated to the referenda not as single events but as episodes in an ongoing saga of the progress or retreat of gay rights legislation. In effect, the city ordinances all stood for individual instances of a national process, with each city referendum potentially swaying the tide of the debate one way or the other. The clarity of the up-or-down vote reduced the complexity of the issue and let the reporters keep score.

The anti-gay side also had a celebrity who initiated the campaign, singer and orange-juice spokesperson Anita Bryant, who founded an organization called Save Our Children. Matlovich's proactivity made him the protagonist of the 1975 coverage; Bryant's efforts made her the center of the 1977 stories. Each network ran a story on the repeal effort (NBC, 6/2/77; CBS, 6/3/77; ABC, 6/6/77) that started "cold"—not with the reporter but with Bryant herself. In addition, in all three, Bryant was pictured singing "Jesus Loves Me" before kindergartners graduating from her church school. Unlike the Matlovich story, presented as a question of civil rights alone, television audiences were given a contrast—both visually and verbally—between the sacred and the profane, the religious and the political, in a "vicious" (NBC, 6/2/77), "emotional" (ABC, 6/6/77) drama.

With Bryant as the centerpiece, gay rights forces were relegated to second place. All three networks' initial reports balanced Bryant's accusations with sound bites from gay activists, but there was no consistent spokesperson opposed to Bryant.[28] All three reports excerpted the pro-repeal side's ads. NBC and ABC broadcast deprecating images of a gay pride parade with the ad's voiceover, "The same people who turned San Francisco into a hotbed of homosexuality want to do the same thing to Dade County." Only CBS showed both pro- and anti-repeal ads.

Denigration was not wholly in place until after the election and the clear two-to-one defeat of the ordinance, perhaps representing to reporters the first empirical demonstration of voters' disdain for gay rights. The first NBC story was casual and conversational, including a lengthy sound bite from one activist (never identified as gay) that threats to gay rights were a threat to all civil rights. But much of this report focused on the "bizarre moments" of the campaign, reflecting "paranoia on both sides," and reporter Fred Francis concluded in puzzlement over the logistics of voting "yes" to repeal. CBS focused largely on elites, contrasting two opposing campaigns at their headquarters. Only ABC's report (6/6/77) gave a preview of what all three networks would present later: polarization between God-fearing churchgoers fearing supposed dangers to their children versus pleasure-loving gay men concerned about restrictions of newly won liberty. Thus, reporter Bill Wortham began (against the backdrop of the "Jesus Loves Me" clip), "When Anita Bryant is singing in her church, many feel there is a particular poignancy to her words. Miss Bryant and thousands of others in Miami believe their children are endangered by a local law granting new freedoms to homosexuals." This reference to "new freedoms" shifted the frame. Gay rights no longer was focused on egalitarianism in Wortham's report but on special privileges for gay people, seen as selfish if not sybaritic. Shots of workers at Save Our Children headquarters preceded a clip from their ad that, in Wortham's own words, "contrast[ed] the all-American look of the Miami Orange Bowl parade with a gay demonstration in San Francisco, an implied threat of things to come."

Wortham's consideration of the pro-ordinance side provided only minimal balance. Anti-repeal leader Jack Campbell, shot close-up, gave a lengthy sound bite describing gay professionals and decrying Bryant's emphasis on perversion. But then, Wortham pointed out that Campbell was a "successful businessman who makes his money running a string of gay bathhouses," along with footage showing a half-naked man in a hot tub, implicitly depicting those "new freedoms" to which Wortham alluded. After more presentation of the pro-repeal side, Wortham wrapped up his story, uncomfortably perched in a gay dance club. The camera showed gay men dancing with each other behind him, ignoring the camera's attention. Wortham contrasted the two sides. One he termed fearful about "corruption" in the classroom; on the other hand, homosexuals sought "the right to go into those classrooms every bit as strongly as the opposition is demanding the right to keep them out."

Denigration appeared elsewhere in subtler ways. Reporters implied that no one who was not gay or lesbian would favor gay rights. On election day (NBC, 6/7/77) Francis profiled Rich Ely, a man who both came out as bisexual and registered to vote for the first time. The moral of the tale? "Gay activists are hoping that there are others who have registered their sexual preferences in the voting booth to defeat Anita Bryant's campaign." Cronkite, the day after the vote (6/8/77), introduced the film report: "Gays, vowing not to give up, staged night-time demonstrations" versus "Anita Bryant, *who led the straights of Miami* [emphasis added], talked of taking her cause to other cities."

Militancy and Polarization

This polarized conflict gave reporters ways to keep the saga going as a national, not regional, story, once the returns were in. In part, they were cued into this by both sides in Miami presenting this as a national fight, and the rhetoric presented had become more militant. Francis said the "national gay community" defiantly thanked Bryant for mobilizing attention (NBC, 6/8/77). Bernard Goldberg's follow-up on CBS (6/8/77) showed a demonstration in San Francisco and closed with a militant warning from David Whitman, identified as a "gay activist":

> We're going to let them know that Anita Bryant and any other Christian bigots have stepped on the wrong minority, because we will fight back. We won't go back into the closets any more.

Reports a month later (ABC, 7/19/77; NBC, 7/20/77) of a debate over Bryant's retaining her job as orange-juice spokesperson showed angry demonstrations against her. Bryant was still the key protagonist. The accounts focused on the threat to her livelihood posed by her crusade against gay rights, yet these stories also provided access to the movement, now portrayed as almost exclusively militant.

This polarization frame was still available when the next efforts to repeal gay rights ordinances occurred, starting with St. Paul (Minnesota), Wichita (Kansas), and Eugene (Oregon) in April and May 1978. Bryant had now retreated from the political stage. Viewers saw new anti-gay leaders, usually local ministers surrounded by their congregations and churchgoing families. On the other side were gay men, usually presented as half-clothed, loud and out to disturb the social order. Now, however, there was a moderate group in between the two—though not yet a moderate *gay/lesbian* presence—apparently discomfited with both sides, instead of the gay/straight divide that had predominated after the Dade County defeat. The first of these reports, from St. Paul the week before the vote, on NBC (4/20/78), cataloged several near-simultaneous events. Reporter Jim Lovell first showed a peaceful anti-repeal rally before the state capitol of a "coalition of homosexuals and liberals." Next, inside a quiet church, families and citizens were shown meeting "by the thousands to denounce homosexuality as a sin." Then, half-clothed gay men danced in a noisy theater, members of a "third faction . . . who openly flaunt their beliefs and equate conservatism with fascism." After quoting the city council President that the election outcome would hinge on turnout, Lovell showed a shot of two men embracing in the theatre, and wrapped up his report: "Some observers feel that the repeal of the ordinance would be the fault of these, the flamboyant gays, whose behavior antagonizes not only these [the footage now showed people leaving church], the churchgoing conservatives, but also many voters who would otherwise be neutral."

Polarization increased after the laws were repealed in St. Paul and especially Wichita, where the competition for the middle foreshadowed by Lovell seemed to have failed. NBC's (4/26/78) reporter in St. Paul claimed, "Voters did reject the lifestyle of homosexuals like Jerry Ferguson," but quoted Ferguson's defiant claim, "I think people who thought they could vote us away and vote us back into the closet are going to be in for a surprise." CBS (4/26/78) spliced together a point/counterpoint between a local minister (listed as "anti-gay rights") and a political scientist about civil rights. Yet this apparent balance was undercut when CBS gave the minister the last word, zooming dramatically closer to his face as he said, "It is a message from the liberal north to the conservative south that people aren't willing to accept this as a human rights issue. They feel strongly that it is a moral issue." His stance seemed to be endorsed by the reporter's closing line, "The high turnout was a sign of how strongly people feel on this issue."

Reporters depicted momentum against gay rights. ABC's (5/8/78) anchor Harry Reasoner introduced a Wichita preview with, "There seems to be a snowballing movement across the country against legal protection for homosexuals." Other intros (NBC 5/21/78; ABC 5/22/78) showed a map of the United States depicting, one by one, the jurisdictions that had repealed gay rights laws—the reverse dynamic of the CBS graphic four years before that had illustrated the gradual progress of such legislation.

The Wichita stories were especially polarized. On ABC (5/8/78), even gay people agreed that they were not equal citizens; gay activist Robert Lewis defended the ordinance by saying, "We still have a sodomy law in the state of Kansas which will be enforced," and adding that it "certainly doesn't condone homosexuality." To be sure, the correspondent did note that "heterosexual men and women are also campaigning for the law as a guarantee for civil rights for all citizens," quoting Mayor Connie Peters's warning about votes for "civil rights for blacks, for women, for Chicanos, for Indians, for handicapped people, for aged people."

Yet the resounding repeal made such a moderate alternative hard to present. CBS (5/10/78) presented a minister demanding Peters's apology. Most notably, Al Johnson's NBC (5/10/78) report cataloged the entire community's opposition to gay rights. Johnson said that Reverend Ron Adrian's "supporters called it an overwhelming victory for the right to protect their children," amidt shots of beaming, applauding nuclear families. Citing exit polls on how various groups voted, Johnson sampled the opposition of a black woman ("It doesn't bother me, being, me because I'm grown, but I don't want my children exposed to this"), a middle-aged white man ("I just feel that it's wrong to be gay"), and a blue-collar worker ("I think, I think, homosexual and all that stuff, it's just, I think it's going too far"). As the film took us back to a gay bar, where half-clothed men danced and sipped drinks, Johnson noted, "The gays here say they will not go into hiding, that they will not change their lifestyle because of the repeal," but finished by saying, "Thirty-eight other cities have gay rights laws, and now there is concern among those in favor of equal rights for homosexuals that what happened in Wichita could happen there too."

This sense of doom for the gay movement dominated stories in the immediate aftermath of the Wichita vote. Francis in Miami (NBC, 5/21/78) gave us the network news's first documented look into a drag show ("This extravagance is evidence that gays here have not gone back into the closet"), but noted how "homosexuals . . . share in the paranoia about repression. Gay leaders here say the current backlash is reminiscent of Nazi Germany." As with other reports (ABC, 5/8/78; NBC, 5/10/78), he closed by saying that "the future looks bleak for the gay rights movement."

The Rise of the Moderate Alternative

Even while this polarization was emphasized by the news media, however, reporters had already begun to display some discomfort with the extremeness of the two sides. As has often been the case with other social movements, the production values that spotlit militancy were in tension with the news media's longstanding preference for moderatism and order. Thus, although news reports continued to reveal what it openly labeled two extremes, they also began to distinguish between apparently acceptable and unacceptable homosexuals. This attempt to seek a middle ground could and did eventually become the base for what Gitlin would have predicted: the elevation of a moderate alternative that encompassed parts of the lesbian and gay movement.

The first indication of this search for a middle ground can be found in Betty Rollin's extraordinary three-part "Segment 3" series that aired on NBC on September 12, 13, and 14, 1977. "Segment 3" had been created earlier that year to make NBC's broadcast distinctive; the time between the second and third sets of commercials was devoted to a single in-depth report.[29] In the first part, Rollin surveyed the question of homosexuality; on the next two evenings, she presented lengthy profiles, one of a gay man (Jerry Schiff), one of a lesbian (Erica Bell). These are landmark stories that we will analyze in much greater detail in further work. For our purposes here, Rollin's stories underscore her return to conditional egalitarianism. For instance, each profile of Schiff and Bell stressed how each of them came out as gay or lesbian only after years of struggling against their feelings, even to the point of becoming engaged or married before they saw the light. Homosexuality, it seems, was an acceptable option but only if and when heterosexuality has failed.

The first report explicitly revealed a search for a moderate solution.

Searching for consensus in history, among psychiatrists, in religious practice, Rollin came up empty-handed. Instead, her inconclusive contrasts needed resolution. Rollin launched into her final summary, which deserves to be quoted at length. Not only does it stress the strength of opinion toward the moderate approach to homosexuality by society at large, it also clearly indicates that most gay men and lesbians, too, belonged within that group:

> So the controversy is bound to continue: some people saying that homosexuality is abnormal, even sinful; others saying that it is perfectly normal; and a large in-between group which feels slightly queasy about homosexuals but also feels queasy about discriminating against them. In the long run, it is probably that group which will decide how welcome homosexuals will really be in our society. In the meantime, while a showy minority of homosexuals march, the silent majority still hides.

The moderate alternative appeared in hard news stories, too. After the Dade County, St. Paul, and Wichita referenda, it is impressive to see how the Eugene referendum was handled in a less denigrating and polarizing way by all three networks (ABC, CBS, 5/22/78; NBC, 5/24/78). The conflict was presented with respect. For the first time in the context of a gay rights referendum, gay men and lesbians were shown not simply in bars and theaters, but more sedately—discussing the issues in their own home (ABC), appearing in coat and tie to engage in a one-on-one televised debate or campaigning door-to-door (CBS), or participating in a candlelight march (NBC). The rhetoric the reporters took from the gay activists quoted no longer referred to sexual freedom but egalitarianism and individualism:

> There's a lot of people out there who think I'm sick and perverted and don't think I deserve a job or think I can do the kind of work they can do. And I want to be judged according to my ability. I want the chance to do a job because I can do it well, and not because of what my sexuality is. (Kent Newby, filmed on his couch at home next to a man termed as his gay "roommate," ABC)

> There really is no such thing as a homosexual lifestyle, any more than there's such a thing as a heterosexual lifestyle. If you could be a fly in one of our houses, you wouldn't see anything unusual. (Robert Monical, voiceover to two women going door-to-door campaigning, CBS)

To be sure, anti-gay sentiments were elicited from campaigners, commercials, and one woman-in-the-street. Yet the prevailing tone of these reports was one of respect for gay people; ABC even gently spoofed the pro-repeal side for its willingness to overlook "heterosexual hanky-panky." Polarization could still be in the background but used by movement activists to their own benefit. In particular, Don Kladstrup's report on CBS closed with an interview with gay San Francisco county supervisor Harvey Milk, looking ahead to other possible defeats and even violence, with Milk's sound bite, "Look what happened to the black movement. When they felt they were being shoved in the corner, they broke out. And it was only then that all of a sudden the nation said, hey, we are human beings. And if you keep on chipping away at the rights of sixteen million Americans, well, what other choice do they have?" Even after the Eugene ordinance was repealed, the man interviewed on behalf of the gay community in NBC's story from San Francisco was a minister, labeled as a "gay rights advocate," but a reputable figure for the homosexuals.

Why this shift into a less polarized, more moderate frame? First, journalists portrayed the campaign to be duller than its predecessors—"low-key" (CBS) with Anita Bryant pointedly uninvited (NBC). Second, these repeal stories, like the others, were handled by network correspondents at regional bureaus, with consequently different patterns of storylines and authoritative sources. The variation among those based in the South, the Midwest, and the West—particularly if they hailed from San Francisco[30]— could account for much. And there's a third possibility: after Wichita, the polarization of gay men and lesbians against the rest of the world was both old news and uncomfortable for reporters whose unspoken values, reinforced in their day-to-day choice of storylines, encompassed individualism and moderatism.

The moderate frame would reemerge even more strongly in the fall with California's Proposition 6, the Briggs Initiative. The defeat of this proposition (which would have allowed school boards to bar known homosexuals or advocates of homosexuality from teaching in California public schools), along with the much less noticed defeat of a repeal move in Seattle, signaled the end of the continuing story. The tables were now turned, as State Senator John Briggs's anti-gay campaign was now denigrated more than the side of gay men and lesbians.

To be sure, the Briggs Initiative's danger was often noted to be its free speech restrictions against straight people. The first network report, Ken Kashiwahara's on ABC (10/11/78), began with a profile of a high school French teacher, who "is not a homosexual but . . . could still be fired if Proposition 6 passes because she supports gay rights." Barry Peterson (CBS, 10/26/78) termed the proposition "as confusing as it is emotional." Heidi Schulman (NBC, 11/5/78) warned that "unlike earlier gay rights questions in other parts of the country, it would not apply just to homosexuals."

Reporters also took cues from the elites opposing Briggs and the poll numbers that followed suit. Versus earlier polar opposition, "the controversial initiative has united both gay and straight organizations who are trying to defeat it by such activities as fundraising discos and informational tables," said Kashiwahara. Briggs's "one-man-campaign" was against the range of his opponents, "everyone from the California superintendent of schools and the governor [Jerry Brown] to Ronald Reagan and the Episcopal bishop."[31] Kashiwahara implied that Briggs was trying to manipulate the emotions of California voters, allowing Harvey Milk to forcefully rebut Briggs in a debate:

BRIGGS: You normal people who have children and take the burden of having children, raising children, do you want a sexually disoriented person teaching your child?

MILK: The child molester is heterosexual. The rapist is heterosexual. Most murderers are heterosexual. Do you want those people teaching your children? You keep turning it around, Senator, and you're lying through your teeth and you know it.

Finally, the human-interest angle that was so strong in the early 1970s reappeared here. CBS profiled a second-grade teacher in Healdsburg ("a small, sleepy town," CBS, 10/26/78) named Larry Berner. The local school board had tried to fire Berner when they learned he was gay. The newsworthy angle focused on the small town and the lone individual gay man. Peterson's first report (10/26/78) juxtaposed visuals of a gay pride march, Briggs speaking, shots of children in schools, and a Hollywood fundraising dinner against shots of Berner in a sunny school playground, while Peterson pointed out the support Berner had received in Healdsburg. Next, Peterson showed a debate between Briggs and Berner. Briggs warned darkly that "Somebody one time said, give me, just give me a generation of teaching children, and I will have that country." But Berner got the last word:

You would have any teacher dismissed because that teacher stated the truth, that many gay people live productive and fulfilled lives. That is why I and tens of thousands of other lesbians and gay men are risking our careers, our social standing and our personal relationships to expose your campaign of hate and contempt for our lives.

In Peterson's report, this battle was apparently won by Berner, who hugged various people while Briggs was heckled by someone shouting, "You can be gay and Christian!"[32] Peterson's final voiceover: "Berner was congratulated by his supporters, while some of those same people jeered Briggs. Polls which once showed the anti-homosexual measure doing well suggest it may now be slipping out of favor."

When Proposition 6 was defeated, the news presented it as a victory for "gays and others opposed to Proposition 6" (NBC, 11/8/78). Peterson's follow-up (CBS, 11/8/78) quoted Berner, who interpreted the outcome in a way that hearkened back again to egalitarianism:

There's a real message for gay people to come out of their closet because that's how we won that election. We talked to our neighbors and friends and they accepted us as human beings.

Peterson's closing line quoted what he called "one cheering celebrant: 'It's clear that gays have a lot of friends in California.'"

Conclusion

With the defeat of Proposition 6, then, the news media had presented all of the stories that Gitlin might have predicted from his study of the New Left. As was the case there, the news media initially discovered the lesbian and gay movement and largely reported on it in respectful ways, sometimes even without any reference to its opponents. When the anti-gay forces led by Anita Bryant responded to these developments, though, the news shifted into a more denigrating tone, with further and further polarization as the votes from referenda to repeal gay rights legislation mounted. Yet, in part because of shifts in political elites' cues on the issue, in part because of the shift from one set of reporters to the next as the referenda moved from the South and the Midwest to the more traditionally pro-gay West Coast, and in part because of reporters' own preference for reporting moderatism rather than extremism, the denigration and polarization of the first referendum stories was succeeded by an emphasis not only on the conflicted state of public opinion at large but on the more mainstream individuals within the lesbian and gay movement itself.

At the same time, though, the process had produced a plethora of frames readily available to and availed by reporters to interpret lesbians and gay men—angry militancy, moderate leadership, personal pleasure-seeking, individual human interest. All of those frames would reappear in 1979, with the "White Night" riots and their aftermath, showing militancy and outrage alongside efforts, not always successful, by reporters to emphasize how the rioters represented only an illegitimate fraction of San Francisco's gay community. Harvey Milk's murder, in retrospect, was not a large event for the news, which focused instead on the killing of Mayor George Moscone, and where both Milk's being gay and the response of the gay community gradually disappeared in the days after the deaths.

In short, having gone through an entire cycle of coverage, most concertedly with the coverage of the various anti-gay referenda of 1977 and 1978, the news media still had not decided what homosexuality was all about. Though all three networks converged on San Francisco's Gay Freedom Day in 1979 apparently because of their stated concern about a possible repeat of the violence of White Night, the profusion of frames sometimes led to confusion and incoherence from one network to the next. At other times, those frames might be internally contrasted, as in the protests over the filming of the movie Cruising, where CBS's (7/28/79) reporter noted, "The gays feel the picture focuses on the seamiest side of homosexuality and ignores the way most gay people live." In general, journalists were not confronted with having to resolve these contradictory impulses, because homosexuality was rarely considered to be newsworthy in the absence of some sort of preexisting political or legal controversy, such as was presented by the cavalcade of referenda in 1977–78. This spotty coverage again made it more difficult for lesbian and gay movements to raise their profiles and get into the news on their own terms at moments of their own choosing.

In short, television news and its construction of homosexuality cannot be easily categorized as wholly positive or wholly negative, wholly anti-gay or wholly gay-affirming. This alone would tend to refute the expectations raised by Watney, Gross, Fejes and Petrich, and others. Indeed, our conclusions are the exact opposite of Fejes and Petrich's argument that the media would be unwilling to frame the lesbian and gay movement as a "civil rights movement or an ethnic . . . community" and would present homosexuality as a (presumably reprehensible) choice.

Yet, both in the mid-1970s when the lesbian and gay movement first attracted widespread attention and then again in the early 1980s when reporting on gay subjects was dominated by the discovery of the AIDS epidemic, the network news offered a split image of lesbians and gay men.

On the one hand, television news has a long record of respectful portrayals of and interviews with gay men and, less frequently, lesbians—all judged less as homosexuals and more as individuals. Television's tendency to personalize and individualize a story—and to turn the microphone over, however briefly, to their interviewees—enabled gay men and lesbians to add pro-gay, even liberationist viewpoints. Although often these individuals were rebutted by their opponents, often they were not, providing an opportunity to defend a viewpoint and build a constituency.

However, television news was less favorable when it came to homosexuals as a group, the movement as a whole, and perhaps even homosexuality as a collective phenomenon—especially when presented visually as a half-clothed, pleasure-seeking set of dancers and paraders more interested in altering sexual norms than in equal treatment under the law. Sometimes that split would emanate from different stories; at other times the contradiction would be contained within a given story itself, resulting in a contrast between the mainstream of lesbians and gay men and an unruly subculture (presented as "flaunting," "showy," "seamy," "violent," etc.).

Why does this matter? One answer is that this split image can create different results when applied to cases when the movement seeks or needs to make news. The most striking example of this is the early AIDS coverage, which could stigmatize gay men as a group even while respectfully profiling gay men with AIDS. Similarly, a cursory recollection of the news coverage of the controversy over President Clinton's attempt to lift the ban on lesbians and gay men in the military would suggest that when individual military personnel could appeal to the human-interest, up-close-and-personal bias of television news, the coverage could be quite positive toward the aims of the movement, providing a case for the inclusion of "yet another minority group" into societal institutions. However, when authoritative sources such as Senator Sam Nunn or General Colin Powell could reframe the issue around homosexuals as a group threatening the armed forces, that coverage could become dramatically different.

Such framing is particularly important because public opinion about homosexuality is also split, characterized by complexity, ambivalence, and inconsistency. Majorities of those polled from the 1970s through the 1990s consistently agreed that "sexual relations between two adults of the same sex is always wrong," and that "homosexual relationships between consenting adults are morally wrong."[33] Surveys starting in the 1980s showed that "gay men and lesbians, i.e., homosexuals" as a group are rated on average lower than any other group, rivaled only by illegal aliens and Palestinians.[34] Yet at the same time, substantial and growing majorities since the 1970s have agreed that "homosexuals should . . . have equal rights in terms of job opportunities."[35] Perhaps Betty Rollin appears to have been right in 1977 (and maybe even today) when she described "a large in-between group which feels slightly queasy about homosexuals but also feels queasy about discriminating against them."

Yet the split image shows how the lesbian and gay movement could use the news media, even in the 1970s, to get a message across—admittedly not the most radical message, and not always one that went unanswered, but one that, in the context of its time, was occasionally remarkably progressive. Recall Gitlin's important reading:

> Because the idea of "objectivity" and the standards of "newsworthiness" are loose, . . . routines of news coverage are vulnerable to the demands of oppositional and deviant groups. Through the everyday workings of journalism, large-scale social conflict is imported into the news institution and reproduced there . . . but muffled, softened, blurred, fragmented, domesticated at the same time.[36]

The generalizations about lesbians, gay men, and the media then are only partially valid when it comes to network news broadcasts. Contrary to expectations, television was as willing to cover the movement in civil rights terms as to emphasize the homosexual "lifestyle"; television tended to focus on lesbians and gay men with a presumption that their sexual orientation was not a choice; gay men and, to a lesser extent, lesbians were also allowed to speak for themselves and for the movement, even if not as frequently as presumed heterosexual elites; and, above all, homosexuality has not been, to recall Watney's generalizations for the British press, "an exemplary and admonitory sign of Otherness."

Why were these expectations off-base? In part, that is because the generalizations for fiction, such as films or television series, can only partially carry over to the news, whose attraction and authority is based on its ability to claim it reflects something current about the real world. In that sense, much as with the tabloid talk shows that Joshua Gamson has recently studied,[37] the emphasis in television news on the new and the spontaneous, and its willingness to focus on the individuals it covers and directly include their voices, provides an opening for a lesbian and gay movement.

Appendix:
News Stories Coded with Central Gay/Lesbian Content

10/22/70	NBC	Alpine County
11/13/70	NBC	Alpine County
3/23/72	ABC	Martin Navy discharge
4/13/73	NBC	Gay college students (University of Iowa)
12/11/73	CBS	Gay Raiders zap Walter Cronkite
5/6/74	CBS	Gay rights (NYC/SF/Boulder)
5/26/75	CBS	Matlovich
5/27/75	ABC	Matlovich
6/12/75	NBC	Discharge of WACs at Fort Devens
9/8/75	NBC	Homosexuals and Presbyterians
9/16/75	ABC	Matlovich trial
	CBS	
	NBC	
9/17/75	ABC	Matlovich trial
	CBS	
	NBC	
8/18/76	CBS	Renée Richards at U.S. Open
	NBC	
11/12/76	ABC	Closeup: Prison rape
6/2/77	NBC	Gay rights referendum, Dade County, FL
6/3/77	CBS	Gay rights referendum, Dade County, FL
6/6/77	ABC	Gay rights referendum, Dade County, FL
6/7/77	NBC	Gay rights referendum, Dade County, FL
6/8/77	ABC	Gay rights referendum, Dade County, FL
	CBS	
	NBC	
6/9/77	NBC	Gay rights referendum, Dade County, FL
6/19/77	CBS	Anita Bryant
6/24/77	NBC	Army/Sode/transsexuals
7/19/77	ABC	Anita Bryant and orange juice promotion

7/20/77	NBC	Anita Bryant and orange juice promotion
8/18/77	ABC	Renée Richards/transsexualism
9/12/77	NBC	Segment 3 (homosexuality)
9/13/77	NBC	Segment 3 (homosexuality: portrait of gay man)
9/14/77	NBC	Segment 3 (homosexuality: portrait of lesbian)
10/25/77	NBC	Segment 3 (boy prostitution)
11/2/77	CBS	Anita Bryant, anti-gay campaigns
12/16/77	CBS	Transsexualism in Oklahoma
3/27/78	CBS	Gay rights/San Francisco
4/20/78	NBC	St. Paul/gay rights referendum
4/26/78	CBS	St. Paul/gay rights referendum
	NBC	
5/8/78	ABC	Wichita/gay rights referendum
5/10/78	CBS	Wichita/gay rights referendum
	NBC	
5/21/78	NBC	Homosexuals and Presbyterians
5/22/78	ABC	Eugene/gay rights referendum
	CBS	
5/23/78	NBC	Homosexuals and Presbyterians
5/24/78	NBC	Eugene/gay rights referendum
6/25/78	NBC	Gay demonstration in San Francisco
10/11/78	ABC	California/Proposition 6
10/26/78	CBS	California/Proposition 6
11/21/78	ABC	Jeremy Thorpe accused of conspiracy to murder
11/23/78	NBC	Jeremy Thorpe accused of conspiracy to murder
4/2/79	CBS	San Francisco recruits gay police officers
	NBC	
4/20/79	NBC	Segment 3 (homosexuality)
5/22/79	ABC	Dan White verdict, "White Night"
	CBS	
	NBC	
6/24/79	ABC	Gay pride
	CBS	
	NBC	
7/28/79	CBS	Filming of Cruising
9/15/79	CBS	Homosexuals and Episcopals
10/14/79	NBC	DC Gay Rights March
7/9/80	NBC	Campaign 1980/gay rights in platforms
9/9/80	ABC	Matlovich reinstated
10/8/80	CBS	Bauman scandal/campaign for reelection
	NBC	
10/25/80	NBC	Bauman scandal/campaign for reelection
11/24/80	ABC	Matlovich reinstated

2/5/81	ABC	Hinson scandal
2/20/81	CBS	Homosexuals in San Francisco
5/1/81	ABC	Billie Jean King
	CBS	
	NBC	
5/7/81	ABC	Billie Jean King
5/10/81	ABC	Commentary on homosexuals
11/24/81	NBC	Special: Spies and Callboys
12/10/81	ABC	Billie Jean King
	CBS	
12/11/81	CBS	Billie Jean King
	NBC	

Notes

This paper has gone through numerous iterations and has been presented many places, from a seminar at the Center for the Humanities and Social Sciences at Williams College in 1988 and the 1989 Yale gay studies conference through the 1999 International Communication Association. Our thanks to all of our interlocutors for their comments, suggestions, and encouragements. Particular thanks go to the Dean of the Faculty's office at Williams College, whose support, through the program to encourage collaborative research of faculty and students, funded the research of Bevin Hartnett for one summer and allowed us to acquire the complete set of Vanderbilt tapes.

1. Michael Lipsky, "Protest as a Political Resource," *American Political Science Review* 62 (1968): 1144–58.

2. The fullest enunciation of this point of view is Edward Alwood, *Straight News: Lesbians, Gays, and the News Media* (New York: Columbia University Press, 1996).

3. Simon Watney, *Policing Desire: Pornography, AIDS and the Media* (Minneapolis: University of Minnesota Press, 1987), 98.

4. Larry Gross, "Out of the Mainstream: Sexual Minorities and the Mass Media," *Journal of Homosexuality* 21 (1991): 19–46, quote on 26.

5. Fred Fejes and Kevin Petrich, "Invisibility, Homophobia and Heterosexism: Lesbians, Gays and the Media," *Critical Studies in Mass Communication* 10 (December 1993): 396–422, quote on 412. Both this and Gross's article handle all mass media, but both are explicit in including the news media in their literature review and critique.

6. Fejes and Petrich, "Invisibility," 403.

7. In general, see John D'Emilio, *Sexual Politics, Sexual Communities: The Making of a Homosexual Minority in the United States, 1940–1970* (Chicago: University of Chicago Press, 1983); Toby Marotta, *The Politics of Homosexuality* (Boston: Houghton Mifflin, 1981); and Alwood, *Straight News*.

8. D'Emilio, *Sexual Politics, Sexual Communities*, 122.

9. On radical homophiles' pursuit of news, see D'Emilio, *Sexual Politics, Sexual Communities*, chapter 9. On the GLF and GAA and the news, see Marotta, *Politics of Homosexuality*, chapters 5–6. The GAA would eventually change its tune: "During GAA's first six months of activity, when the goal had been simply to reach nonpolitical homosexuals, any press coverage of gay political activity was welcomed. But when it became clear that GAA actually could exercise political influence . . . the precise sort of news coverage given became important." Marotta, *Politics of Homosexuality*, 180.

10. D'Emilio, *Sexual Politics, Sexual Communities*, 134–35.

11. Timothy E. Cook and David C. Colby, "The Mass-Mediated Epidemic," in *AIDS: The Making of a Chronic Disease*, ed. Elizabeth Fee and Daniel Fox (Berkeley: University of California Press, 1991), 84–122.

12. Todd Gitlin, *The Whole World Is Watching: Mass Media and the Making and Unmaking of the New Left* (Berkeley: University of California Press, 1980), 242.

13. Gitlin, *Whole World Is Watching*, esp. 25–31. Gitlin himself does not argue that such a cycle occurs, given that these phases empirically overlap considerably. Nevertheless, as a general model of the interactions of social movements and the media, it holds considerable promise and the evidence to date from other social movements seems to fit this model as well; e.g., cf. Gaye Tuchman's analysis of the women's movement in her *Making News* (New York: Free Press, 1978), chapter 7.

14. Gitlin, *Whole World Is Watching*, 109.

15. These categories were: doctor, political activist, political spokesperson, athlete, average person, military personnel, political official, educator, church official, judge/lawyer, and business officer. Some clarifications here are in order. The category of doctor included physicians, psychologists, and psychiatrists. Activists were distinguished from spokespersons as follows: to be considered a spokesperson, the source had to be explicitly speaking on behalf of an organization or recognized in the report as a leader of one side or another (e.g., Anita Bryant or Leonard Matlovich). By contrast, activists were not directly attributed to an organization but would be a participant in a political activity (e.g., canvassing, demonstrating). The term "average person" refers to the person-on-the-street (or within a bar, club, or university campus) that the reporter chose to interview but is not identified with any affiliation. The category of military personnel included all ranks within the military, including lesbian and gay soldiers prior to their discharges. Political officials included both elected and appointed ones; educators included teachers and professors at all levels. Church officials were coded as such unless they spoke for a political organization.

16. See the various studies examined and cited in Timothy E. Cook, *Governing with the News: The News Media as a Political Institution* (Chicago: University of Chicago Press, 1998), 76–84.

17. This logic is best captured by Gitlin, *Whole World Is Watching*, appendix.

18. NBC, 12/31/69; NBC, 4/13/73.

19. CBS, 5/6/74.

20. Edward Jay Epstein, who studied NBC in the late 1960s noted, "Almost all stories about California during this period were depicted as taking place in curious, eccentric and highly unpredictable circumstances." Epstein, *News from Nowhere: Television and the News* (New York: Random House, 1973), 244. This angle was encouraged by the expense of sending breaking stories to New York by cable from California and the necessity of maintaining a veneer of coast-to-coast reporting—resulting in a welter of feature stories that could be sent by air and banked for later use.

21. None of them were in Alpine County at the time, and indeed, an "election" in the Berkeley chapter of GLF had rejected the idea of the Alpine County takeover several days before.

22. The most subversive would have been to say: Joe College is gay.

23. Tuchman, *Making News*, chapter 6.

24. The news missed these stories presumably because most of the initial laws were passed with little opposition. See James Button, Barbara Rienzo, and Kenneth Wald, *Private Lives, Public Conflicts: Gay Rights and American Communities* (Washington, DC: CQ Press, 1998), 67–68.

25. For more general information about the case, and about Matlovich, see Mike Hippler's biography, *Matlovich: The Good Soldier* (Boston: Alyson, 1989).

26. By contrast, in the lone previous case to gain television attention, ABC's (3/23/72) respectful coverage of the appeal of the dismissal of Navy Radioman Robert Martin, the dispute centered on the admissibility of evidence, notably what that report termed "so-called love letters to an ex-sailor." Martin himself never spoke. Only through his lawyer did we hear Martin's side—that he was not even gay.

27. The precise wording varies from one network to the next; this version is taken from NBC (9/17/75).

28. ABC quoted Jack Campbell, a Miami bathhouse owner who emerged as a leader of the antirepeal campaign; CBS used one soundbite from Campbell but focused primarily on activist Robert Kunst; and, in the weird way that one news story bleeds into another, NBC used Leonard Matlovich, a recent arrival in Miami. Matlovich would later move to San Francisco and be featured in the stories in 1978 on the Briggs Initiative. His case is probably the leading example of someone who used media attention to gain prominence in the lesbian and gay movement despite virtually no base of support within the movement itself beyond his celebrity. See Hippler, *Matlovich*, passim.

29. Herbert J. Gans, *Deciding What's News: A Study of CBS Evening News, NBC Nightly News, Time and Newsweek* (New York: Vintage, 1979), 165.

30. Indeed, Kladstrup had already contributed a story on CBS (3/27/78) on the passage of San Francisco's gay rights ordinance. Kladstrup bridged the conflict between Supervisors Harvey Milk and Dan White—the latter, who would assassinate Milk later that year, in what we must now recognize as a chilling premonition of his smoldering anger—by turning to the business community to note its lack of opposition to the measure.

31. Schulman made a similar statement about "most California political leaders, from Governor Jerry Brown, to former Governor Ronald Reagan" on NBC (11/5/78).

32. This scene was also shown on NBC.

33. Alan S. Yang, "The Polls—Trends: Attitudes toward Homosexuality," *Public Opinion Quarterly* 61 (1997): 477–507, questions 2 (NORC), 3 (Yankelovich).

34. Yang, "Polls," question 24 (NES). See also Kenneth Sherrill, "On Gay People as a Politically Powerless Group," in *Gays and the Military: Joseph Steffan versus the United States*, ed. Marc Wolinsky and Kenneth Sherrill (Princeton: Princeton University Press, 1993), 84–120, at 95–100.

35. Yang, "Polls," question 44 (Gallup).

36. Gitlin, *Whole World Is Watching*, 270.

37. Joshua Gamson, *Freaks Talk Back: Sexual Nonconformity and Tabloid Talk Shows* (Chicago: University of Chicago Press, 1998).

PART FOUR

SEXUALITY AND THE POLITICS

OF KNOWLEDGE

TWELVE

"OUTING" ALAIN L. LOCKE

EMPOWERING THE SILENCED

Leonard Harris

OPEN SECRETS are a way of keeping sexuality silent, closeted, hidden, sheltered, closed, and powerless. That is why everyone says it—he is a homosexual—and then promptly remains silent. The open secret: Alain L. Locke, 1884–1954, has the name Arthur Locke on his birth certificate, informally renamed Allen LeRoy by his mother, renamed himself the more urbane and (for his time and sensibility) homoerotic name, Alain, in his high school years, and remained a homosexual throughout his life.

At best, prevailing scholars tell us that Locke was a homosexual but that his Herculean labors focused on race relations. Nearly every Locke scholar holds this view, including Michael Winston, Jeffrey C. Stewart, Johnny Washington, Russell J. Linnemann, David Levering Lewis, and Houston A. Baker, Jr.[1] Not one historian, whether homosexual, bisexual, heterosexual, African American, or European, not one member of the Baha'i faith of which he was deeply enamored, nor any pragmatist or noted cultural pluralists—for all of their earnest or self-effacing propaganda about tolerance and inclusion of difference—have offered an alternative view. George Hutchinson's *The Harlem Renaissance in Black and White*, for example, dedicated to uncovering the deep common bonds, cultural influences, and practical relationships between blacks and whites, leaves completely unaddressed any substantive relationship between black and white homosexuals.[2] If a reader were confined to reading only Hutchinson's book he would believe that all of Locke's ideas were completely shaped by his early education under the Felix Adler Ethical Society, teachers at Harvard, and associates such as Horace Kallen. Never is Locke assumed the creator of complex idea nor is a single role he played within the black and white homosexual communities relevant to describing American culture. We are misled by prevailing scholarship to believe that Locke's sexuality was irrelevant to his intellectual and personal history.

The open secret is also used to allow Locke to be a representative of group-transcendent norms, which are principles, beliefs, arguments, and practices that should be, or are, followed by all persons across lines of specificity. Principles or norms that should be followed by everyone, independent of their membership in any group, are principles or norms that should be compelling. Even if, for example, a given group believes that slavery is justified as a matter of its religious traditions, the right of individuals to freedom transcends and supervenes on such a particular group norm.

I have spoken to three persons who attended courses taught by Locke, all of whom knew that Locke was gay. Each responded as if I had asked a dumb question because the answer was obvious; the answer was readily known. And each wondered why it mattered. My interviewees would then discuss Locke's ideas, his manners, and his influence on their lives. Locke represented for them group-transcendent norms. My interviewees could be Lockean *and* a host of other identities such as Jewish, women, heterosexual, black, elderly, Washingtonian, and a Locke student. Locke was a representative of group-transcendent norms for my interviewees, each in possession of the open secret and thus ostensibly unaffected by the taint of homosexuality.

In 1983 I completed an anthology titled *Philosophy Born of Struggle*.[3] The anthology was such a draining experience because historians of American philosophy, all of them, had failed to publish a single page about the history of any African-American philosopher or why they were often absent from the literature. I was emotionally devastated because American philosophers, whether pragmatist, Marxist, or vitalist, remained almost completely silent about the terrible reality of American racism.[4] For all of their discourse on the nature of democracy, individual freedom, or rights, they left the exclusion, imprisonment, and subjugation of racial groups outside their discussions.

Again, this constructs silence—absolute, total, and complete silence. Everywhere racial conflict was present—at every university, every conference, and within everyone's experience. Yet, even the philosophy of pragmatism, which emphasizes discussing human experiences, natural surroundings, and our interactions with our environment, was relatively silent about race.

What must be true for the only black and homosexual classical American pragmatist to be ignored in the works of pragmatists? How is it possible for pragmatists, deeply committed to seeing themselves as uniquely "American" *and* inclusive of diverse experiences, to fail to explore the intersection of race and sexuality so closely married in Locke's work? What is the character of the incongruity between honoring Locke as an aesthete, friend, philosopher, pragmatist, African American, American, and homosexual?

Silence about sexuality is a different silence than the silence about race. No one expresses pride that Locke was gay. Yet, Locke's unbelievable accomplishments have been a source of pride and have provided tremendous encouragement for all sorts of persons. There is, for example the Alain Locke Elementary School in Philadelphia; the Alain Locke Building at Howard University; the Alain Locke Prize at Harvard University, founded in 1993 by Henry L. Gates, Jr., for the highest grade-point average in African-American studies; an Alain Locke room in the Humanities Building at Harvard University; a Phi Beta Sigma Presidential Futures—Alain Locke Scholarship Program for a high grade-point average and sincere interest in the corporate environment; an honorary republication of Locke's articles concerned with education in *The Crescent* of Phi Beta Sigma; the Alain L. Locke Society that publishes the Alain L. Locke *Newsletter* at Purdue University; and an Alain L. Locke web page.[5] African Americans have been very proud of Locke's accomplishments, knowing his secret.

Locke was born in Philadelphia, the only child of Pliny Ishmael Locke, a Howard University–educated lawyer, and Mary Hawkins Locke, a teacher and member of the Felix Adler Ethical Society. Locke was raised an Episcopalian, but later was attracted to the Baha'i faith. He was the first African-American Rhodes Scholar at Oxford in 1907. He also attended lectures at the University of Berlin from 1910 to 1911, before returning to the United States and joining the Howard University faculty in 1912. As a student, Locke was associated with other students who would also become luminaries, such as Horace M. Kallen, noted author of the concept cultural pluralism; H. E. Alaily, president of the Egyptian Society of England; Pa Ka Isaka Seme, black South African law student and founder of the African National Congress; and Har Dayal, a nationalist and Marxist from India. Locke received his doctorate in philosophy from Harvard in 1918 and by 1925 was a major force in creating and directing the Harlem Renaissance.

Locke's sentinel book, *The New Negro* (1925), announced the Harlem Renaissance and entailed Locke's promotion of cultural pluralism.[6] *The New Negro* was a collage of works attesting to the vibrancy of culture and standing as a defeat of stereotypes. The anthology included photos of the art of Winold Reiss and Aaron Douglas, and pictures of African artifacts portrayed as art. It included articles by such authors as J. A. Rogers, E. Franklin Frazier, Charles S. Johnson, Melville J. Herskovits, and W.E.B. Du Bois; it included the poetry by Countee Cullen, Langston Hughes, Arna Bontemps, and Angela Grimke. The book also included the texts of spirituals and short biographies. Thus, the Harlem Renaissance, under Locke's influence, represented the integration of the aesthetic into the arena of public consciousness as a political force.

When Peoples Meet (1942), edited by Locke with Bernhard J. Stern, was intended as a way of forcing recognition of cultural diversity as a worldwide reality, a diversity that compels us to consider the importance of tolerance, respect, and the need for reciprocity.[7] *When Peoples Meet* was Locke's last major anthology and effort to bring out of the closet the reality of diversity.

Locke's accomplishments and the honors created in his name have all occurred in a world of silence. This silence is coterminous with a certain absence of discussions about Locke.

I have become accustomed to talking in the dark, speaking openly but unseen and unheard. I am usually alone in presenting the history of African and African-American philosophers to philosophers who believe "philosophy" has nothing to do with particularities. I am often the only speaker arguing for the view that philosophies born of struggles to overcome oppression are of merit. Locke's philosophy and its commitment to the liberation of particularities too often beget curiosity rather than earnest evaluation.

The absence of Locke in the places where he should be can be disquieting. There was, for example, a tremendous difference between presenting a paper on Locke and community at the Personalist Conference at Oxford University in 1995 and presenting a paper on Locke and community at the Black Nations/Queer Nations Conference of the Center for Lesbian and Gay Studies at the City University of New York in 1995. Other than my presentation, Locke was absent in Oxford and New York, but there is an existential difference associated with his presence in only one voice in New York. The difference is that the entwining bond of Locke's homosexuality and his philosophy has more than abstract, tangential, or minor importance to the lived experiences of homosexuals. There is something especially wrong with the absence of Locke in anthologies on black gay identity and homosexual philosophers. There should be a special attachment, a common ethnological appreciation, a bond of recognition for having similar experiences, closeted or not, by members of a community constantly faced with prejudice. Thus the homosexual community should embrace Locke in a more earnest way than communities with less common sources for bonding. Perhaps if Locke were so embraced his absence in other communities would not be so disquieting.

Read this, then, as an outing, necessarily speculative due to the absence of historical research and debate. This outing is also frightening, tentative, and uncertain because I recognize that it relies on my own subjective limitations, fears, and lack of information. However, if subjects are to become self-conscious agents that form ontological entities demanding community, power, and freedom, outings are necessary. "The ontological possibility of a lesbian and gay community is limited by the extent to which lesbians and gay men come out into it."[8] Formed social entities, peopled by open and self-conscious subjects, engaged in institution-building and connections, are crucial for the possibility of collective agency.

Outing I

If Locke speaks—that is, if we rely on his published works about homosexuality—he does not speak of himself as a representative of the homosexual community. If Locke is spoken for—that is, if his published works are understood as the consequence of his homosexuality—then Locke is silent and interpreters speak. If I rely on available archival letters, notes, and pictures,

Locke does not speak as a homosexual burdened by a sense of lack, inade-quacy, perversion, shame, or fear. If I try and interpret the archival record as if Locke is speaking as a homosexual struggling to overcome insecurities or the burden of being closeted, but does not know it, I must lie constantly. Locke's sexuality is, I believe, normality. "Normality" is that which is taken for granted; that which is not seen as an aberration but as endemic to the everyday.[9]

When I speak of Locke as a philosopher, I am copping out of speaking of Locke as a homosexual. When I speak of Locke as a homosexual, I am copping out of speaking of Locke as a representative of African people. Locke's representation of African people inclines me to avoid Locke the elitist in favor of Locke the champion of the oppressed, silenced, absent, excluded, closeted, and veiled. When I speak of Locke the elitist, I also hide the Locke committed to promoting popular, folk, and lower-class culture.

The reality of multiple places, including its transgressions, and the place of "polymorphic, varied, individually modulated" emotion, as Foucault partially defines homosexuality, makes it difficult to capture full personhood.[10] The difficulty is similar to the difficulty of trying to capture ethnic identity: "As a culture, we call ourselves Spanish when referring to ourselves as a linguistic group and when copping out. It is then that we forget our predominant Indian genes. . . . We call ourselves Hispanic or Spanish-American or Latin American or Latin when linking ourselves to other Spanish-speaking peoples of the Western hemisphere and when copping out. We call ourselves Mexi-can-American to signify we are neither Mexican nor American, but more the noun 'American' than the adjective 'Mexican' (and when copping out)."[11] Mestizo identity often affirms Indian and Spanish heritage, *raza* may refer to Chicanos' racial identity, *tejanos* may be Chicanos from Texas, and *metis* or *metissage* may be the racial base of Euro-Asians. Letting Locke speak or speaking for Locke invariably seems to be a cop-out—that is, a way of avoid-ing important features of his person.

Locke, it seems, is silent unless I try and appreciate him in his multiple being, whether he speaks or I speak for him. Countee Cullen and Bruce Nugent, both gay Harlem Renaissance intellectuals, provide excellent exam-ples of the difficulty of letting Locke speak and speaking for Locke while trying to center and capture his homosexuality. It should be noted, however, that Locke was a homosexual long before the Harlem Renaissance. When he went to Harvard in 1904, he joined other homosexuals he knew, such as C. H. Dickerman, from his Central High School years in Philadelphia. He remained in correspondence with Dickerman and others while in Europe and found his personal life in some regards easier to manage in, for example, Berlin of 1911. Locke, then, had a long history of managing multiple worlds at the beginning of the Harlem Renaissance.

Locke was a friend to more than one Harlem Renaissance homosexual, and he consoled and provided guidance. Cullen wrote Locke first in 1922 to inquire about Rhodes scholarships.[12] Both Cullen and Locke expressed an interest in Langston Hughes as a potential lover. This interest has been discussed elsewhere.[13] Primarily, it involved an effort by Cullen to encourage Locke to pursue Hughes and Hughes's initial reluctance. Cullen and Locke shared information and advice about other lovers; for example, a young man named Ralph Loeb. Cullen, in addition, wrote Locke to frankly discuss issues of moral and social conduct, such as how to manage a potential gay partner's rejection. In one important exchange, Locke advises the younger Cullen when asked for advice: "I think I may assure you of but one standard of judgment—and that is the law of a man's own temperament and personality. But one cannot often discover this, especially if there are convention-complexes except through confessional self-analysis."[14] Alden Reimonenq suggests that Cullen's androcentric poetry's self-absorbing analysis derives from such recommendations.[15] At the very least, Locke helped provide Cullen with resources to negotiate his homosexuality and poetry. "Young Cullen, troubled by his gayness, had to struggle with mostly Locke's nurturing. Given the fundamentalists' exhortations against sex, in general, and homosexuality, in particular, Cullen could not turn to his father (an African Methodist Episcopal minister)."[16]

Countee Cullen, like all African-American homosexuals, was doubly oppressed by race and sexuality. It is reasonable to suppose that Cullen was able to "express himself openly only in reference to race, but that he may be assumed to have invested in this expression the frustration and anger generated at the other source, his sexuality."[17] If we can offer a reading of texts that extrapolates the racial elements we can also offer a reading that extrapolates the sexual elements. In addition, on Gregory Woods's account, we should be able to read Claude McKay's poem "If We Must Die" as if "referable to homosexual oppression" just as this work can be read in association the way Winston Churchill read it "when he used it to represent the situation of Britain forced into a corner by Nazi Germany."[18]

Numerous authors have warned against undue associated readings, particularly assuming that every ethnic or racial experience is the same and that the world of every sexually oppressed population provides insight into the oppression of others.[19] Moreover, the experiences of racial and sexual oppression have numerous differences. However, respecting uniqueness in no way prevents venturing associations, analogies, derivations, or similarities with due caution.

Reimonenq has a similar approach as Woods to Cullen when he interprets Cullen's poem "Tableau," dedicated to a white lover, Donald Duff: "The poem announces Cullen's awareness of the impending discrimination for those who dared to secede from the ranks of 'normalcy.'" Under the poetic veil of speaking out against racism, Cullen achieves a larger purpose by also criticizing antihomosexual bigotry. In the last amazing stanza, the speaker imagines the black and white lovers—who have been described walking "Locked arm in arm"—as oblivious to look and word:

> They pass, and see no wonder
> That lighting brilliant as a sword
> Should blaze the path of thunder.
>   *Color* 14[20]

Cullen's discourse on race is thus treated as a veil. The discourse presages hidden messages or it is motivated by hidden forces. The world of veiled and hidden messages exists in a world of veiled and hidden personal relations; and the world of veiled and hidden personal relations never escapes the world of racist social constructions.

Wallace Thurman, noted Harlem Renaissance author and editor of the journal *Fire!!*, authored the short story in the journal titled "Cordelia the Crude." This story has a "New Negro protagonist whose myopic compassion for a child prostitute turns out to have confirmed her in the profession."[21] The New Negro protagonist intentionally satirized the elitism of older intellectuals, in particular, Benjamin Brawley, but it also arguably encloses Locke—well known to have performed this role in confirming and midwifing. Thurman became noted for his emphasis on the importance of presenting folk culture without moralizing.

Thurman was critical of the African-American traditional use of literature as veiled propaganda for promoting social equality and presenting the race in laudatory roles rather than the demeaning stereotypes of self-deprecators, erotic buffoons, or intellectual inferiors with no interest in sophisticated pursuits. *Fire!!* was intended as a revolt against such publications as *Opportunity* and *Crisis* as well as the controlling influence of Locke. The emphasis in *Fire!!* was the warrant of the folk—the unmediated presentation of raw life. This presentation would occur without the filter of at least three concerns: presenting stories and poems that would be palatable to whites; presenting stories and poems that would help further the cause of racial equality; and presenting stories and poems in ways that elevate folk art from its crude expressions to a universalized polished form. The editors at *Fire!!*, such as Zora Neal Hurston and Bruce Nugent, have been seen as young artists who did not want to be limited by the dictatorial actions of older, more conservative and well-established black leaders.

David Levering Lewis, I suspect, was right when he contended that "Thurman [et al.] had meant to shock. The 'decadent,' 'primitive' influence of Van Vechten's *Nigger Heaven* was defiantly acknowledged by the editor, who called for the erection of a statue in Van Vechten's honor at the same corner of 135th Street and Seventh Avenue where the author [Van Vechten] had been so recently hanged in effigy."[22] Van Vechten's *Nigger Heaven* was seen by numerous groups as an example of a white person seeing Negroes as emotional, irrational, and inferior beings; a people driven by base emotions and lacking any intellectual interests. It was a systemically degrading work because the characters were reduced to concerns with nothing but stereotypical enjoyment. A guiding theme of *Nigger Heaven* was an afterlife where "niggers" would release their true wild, frantic, unabashed emotions and live according to their eternally primitive conceptual schemes. *Nigger Heaven* legitimized segregation by presenting a racially segregated vision of life after death; a vision that presented all African Americans as sensually determined irrational beings.

The vicious racism of Van Vechten's stereotypes is not excusable. The presentation in George Chauncey's *Gay New York* of Van Vechten as just another supportive intellectual judging gay fashion shows in Harlem hides the racism deeply embedded in the relationships between blacks and whites.[23] There were radically different potential futures of black and white gays because the variables affecting their lives often differed. Blacks, for example, almost never inherited assets and could not trade in precious metals, fine arts, artifacts, or dangerous goods such as weapons or explosives. When blacks and whites were lovers, too often their almost always closeted relations were tremendously hard to maintain because of the burden of race. Consequently, foregrounding the community of homosexuality in this instance submerges the reality of race. Chauncey in *Gay New York* does not take as determinant as he might the obvious: every encounter between blacks and whites was already an encounter between unequally empowered agents, even if they were trying to overcome the reality of their socially inherited positions.

The general truth that *Fire!!* exemplifies a revolt against the older New Negro approach avoids the specificity of the Harlem Renaissance gay community. That is, foregrounding the intricacies of the racial community submerges the reality of sexuality. Lewis does not take seriously the obvious: nearly one-quarter of the authors of *Fire!!* were bisexual and known to one another to be so.[24]

Assuming the editors of *Fire!!* were enamored with the primitivism portrayed in *Nigger Heaven*, it is arguable that they were also reacting against the modernist moment of the Harlem Renaissance. The modernist moment was the forced, and willed, change of African-American folk culture into high culture; the rejection of emotional expression for the controlling metaphor of science; and the subjugation of folk idioms to more polished and sophisticated forms attractive to a cosmopolitan culture. The modernist moment might have been seen as a veiled form of oppression, especially the oppression of folkways within which free expressivity occurred. Concern with applauding freedom, emotive excess, and romantic flings and simultaneously upholding a picture of the folk as full persons was a difficult balancing act. Modernity, particularly its standardization of culture, was everywhere being imposed. Moreover, freedom for homosexuals often meant rejecting personal family traditions—folk traditions—yet relatively highly educated artists romanticized the unlettered and often crude community. Complicating the intersection of race, class, and sexual agendas were personal relations. Some of the editors of *Fire!!* had serious disagreements with Locke about how to represent the black community as well as their own sexuality. However, they all engaged in intellectual exchange with one another throughout the renaissance.

Nugent was the most open homosexual among the younger Harlem Renaissance authors. Nugent wrote Locke before and after the publication of *Fire!!* He appreciated Locke's efforts to promote black artists and sought his suggestions on where to publish. Thurman was deeply troubled by his own bisexuality. Zora Neal Hurston and Locke never reconciled their intellectual differences. Hurston, for example, emphasized the merit of folk expressions and Locke emphasized the value of using folk art as the source of sophisticated art and literature. The ever vigilant guardian, Locke, advised nearly everyone on how to veil his or her sexuality.

Locke's choice of veiling during and prior to the renaissance was one among several reasonable options in a homophobic and racist world. Locke's mother once advised him to be careful because the "vice patrol," Howard University's administration, fired Montgomery Gregory from Howard's theatre teaching staff because he was seen leaving a "lurid" establishment frequented by homosexuals. Arguably, the lesson was not lost on Locke: veil or lose a complete intellectual and social world, not to mention invite the possibility of torture, lynching, or death. Locke included Gregory's work in *The New Negro*. Nugent selected a different option to live out his sexuality.

Nugent was openly gay, to Locke's disapproval. "Locke had decided," says Nugent, "that he had his finger on the pulse of every black person who was doing anything. Almost everybody listened to his dictates, except Wally [Wallace Thurman] and me."[25] In relationship to his poem, "Smoke, Lilies, and Jade," in *Fire!!*, often considered an early African-American presentation of homoerotic love, Nugent contends, "How could you write anything gay in 1926?" His reply is "I didn't know *it was gay* when I wrote it."[26] Nugent wrote the poem as a love poem.

Nugent saw himself as expressing an idea and not representing or being caused to create his poem as a function of his homosexuality. It is tempting to approach Nugent's poem as "really" initiated as a function of his homosexuality. Nugent, consequently, would not then be speaking properly for himself. He would be interpreted in a way that makes his poetry a necessary function of his sexuality. Nugent would not be able to escape particularity, or, rather, his particularity would not be a source of universality—that is, love across lines of sexual forms expressed through a particular form of which he is a conscious agent of its creation.

If Nugent is seen as concerned with the aesthetic dimensions of his work and comfortable with his homosexuality, he may not easily function as a hero. It may not be enough that his works are intertwined with his homosexuality. We may need a stronger claim to satisfy the need for heroes who represent the struggles of a social kind—whether the kind is a race, gender, or sexuality. If Nugent is not constantly struggling to accept his homosexuality as a normal form of life, troubled because society has not accepted him as a person, or if he is not fighting to be open and out of the closet, then Nugent may not provide an appropriate model because he would not be confronting some of the most difficult features of homosexual life. Possibly, this is why Nugent is rarely lauded as an estimable representative of the gay community no matter how often he has been interviewed and has explained his multiple motivations—as an artist, an African American, and a homosexual.

Locke did not have high regard for folk culture as such; he was consistent in trying to have folk culture transformed into high culture. This was a source of theoretical disagreement between Locke and numerous persons, including Cullen, Nugent, Thurman, and Hurston. However, Locke was tireless in his efforts to expand human freedoms. Even if Locke was misguided in his effort to control how African-American folk culture should be reformed and presented as embodying universal aesthetic norms, he was not misguided in trying to bring it out of the closet. Moving from the closet into normality—whether the closet was that hiding racial and culturally reality or, by association, the closet of hiding homosexuality—Locke struggled to elevate, transform, and create universality in a way that allowed for diverse sexuality and cultural diversity respected in everyday life. The effort to promote and respect diversity, however, is not always equally promoted by Lockean scholars.

Outing II

The speech of interpreters, the control of documents, and the effort to shape Locke's image has too often proffered nothing short of moral terror. The terror of speaking for is a conscious act. The interpreters know they are empowered to speak on behalf of, in the name of, in the place of, and as the representative of the silent.

African Americans in charge of Locke's legacy have consciously worked to speak for Locke—and speak they have—to keep the open secret a closeted phenomenon while promoting "acceptable" pictures of decidedly "Negro" gentility. "Negro" gentility is formed by the cultural traits that a conservative heterosexual middle class, black and white, dictate as acceptable. Such traits are assumed embodied in any normal person, but especially in highly accomplished and honored Negroes. They would be heterosexual, dedicated to racial uplift, and committed to racial unity.

It is possible that the desire to keep Locke eligible for honor motivated efforts to control the Locke image. The following information I learned through interviews. The names of the persons I interviewed will not be revealed here. Like any coming out, it often occurs in stages, especially when careers would certainly be adversely influenced.

It is alleged that Dorothy Porter, formerly responsible for the Locke papers at Howard University, destroyed prophylactics that Locke had saved with names attached. The rumor is that Locke once saved prophylactics he used for anal or oral sex. I have the word of two persons who were told this.[27]

Michael R. Winston, the head of the Moorland-Spingarn Library shortly after Dorothy Porter, removed from scholarly access letters that explicitly discussed or alluded to Locke's sexual life. He told a curator, on her first day of work, to remove from the Locke papers all letters that discussed or alluded to homosexuality and give them to him. It is rumored that such letters were progressively returned to the archives.

Race Contacts, edited by Jeffrey C. Stewart, is a series of lectures Locke presented in 1916, having been denied the opportunity to teach a class on the subject by Howard University. The series provides insight into Locke's rejection of the idea of race—an extremely radical approach for his time. Going further even than Franz Boas, the most progressive anthropologist of the time, Locke declared race a social construction. Racial categories were not rooted in biological categories in the sense that biological race categories could in any way be said to parallel the way we identify races socially. Locke was not trapped, consequently, in accepting the categories that society had so conveniently made seen normal and natural.

I noted every unpublished work in the Locke papers in 1982 and offered, at that time, the most comprehensive list of unpublished works relevant to philosophy.[28] If my recollection serves me well, there was only a reading list in the folder marked "Syllabus" for a course that Locke hoped to teach. There were no notes for the lectures Locke presented in 1915 that became Race Contacts. No one made reference to Race Contacts material from the archives until it was published by Stewart, a very close associate of Winston.

It is rumored that a white former English instructor at Howard University submitted a proposal to republish Race Contacts in the mid-1970s. She was turned down and thereafter the notes were removed from obvious access in the archives. In addition, although Stewart wrote his dissertation on Locke in 1979 and has received numerous forms of support work on various features of Locke's life, he has not completed a Locke biography because, according to one scholar associated with Stewart, he does not want to be identified as the biographer of a homosexual.[29] I do not believe that this true, but still no biography exists.

The foreword of *Race Contacts* was written by Winston.[30] Stewart provides a brilliant introduction, covering the major themes in the book, their import for historians and sociologists, as well as how those themes are explored by such authors as Henry L. Gates, Jr., Houston Baker, and Russell Powell. However, at least two categories of persons are completely absent: black philosophers and gays of that period. Neither group is particularly popular among conservative black intellectuals nor much of the black community. Although all of the major conferences on Locke except for a session at the African Americans and Europe Conference (Centre d'Etudes Afro-americaines de la Sorbonne Nouvelle, February 1992) have been sponsored by philosophers, black philosophers nowhere appear in Stewart's introduction. Yet, Stewart must be credited with providing pioneering work on Locke. Without his Herculean efforts, Locke's work might be lost forever. Without Stewart's reconstruction of Locke's notes and close reading of his works and influences, we would not be able to see how Locke differs from Franz Boas, nor how Locke, like Marx, sees race as a vortex of social reality. Nor would we be able to see Locke's critique of race and his pragmatist approach to race as a tool, nor his conceptions of instincts, values, and social constructions.

It matters not at all to the warrant of Locke's ideas whether he cruised the waterfronts of New York looking for sailors, saved prophylactics with the names of lovers, or felt betrayed by a lover. No one should be thereby deterred from seeing herself as Lockean and Jewish, a woman, heterosexual, black, elderly, Washingtonian, or a Locke student. It is in no way disparaging of Locke's image to know Locke lived a fairly settled love life in his older years with Arthur Fauset in Washington D.C., having had a fairly diverse array of lovers in his earlier years. The private Locke should be uncovered without the fear that his homoeroticism means "defective" because all forms of eroticism by gays reflect defect, disease, and corruption. If Locke went cruising the waterfronts of New York for women, persons intent on perpetuating an acceptable image of middle-class America would probably lionize him as a lover. I suspect that the Howard University–associated guardians of Locke's image believed that homosexual behavior was, or would be understood as, abnormal, deviant, decadent, and reflective of a troubled African-American failure.

The effort to present a palatable image is beneficial to the perpetuation of homophobia by making the homosexual abnormal—always in need of special protection because he or she is always lacking, always defective. The effort to keep Locke's image safe, allowing it to be appropriated by middle-class officialdom, is simultaneously the perpetuation of a composite lie—the lie that Locke's homosexuality was irrelevant to his project; the lie that we need the protection of guardians and "speakers for" to keep us safe from his untoward disease; the lie that pitifully thin financial support for such a great scholar is secured by a failed homophobic effort to perpetuate an appropriate image.

When Reimonenq, Woods, Bean, or Chauncey speak of Locke it is with flavor, tracing desire, suppressed energies, poems of love, intellectual debates enlivened by personal conflicts, veiled meanings, and contests over ways to express. When they speak, we hear the veiled intentions, hidden influences, and gender- or sexually specific efforts to achieve freedom. When Hutchinson, Stewart, or Winston speak of Locke, it is as though Locke was a disembodied Cartesian moving through space, influencing and being influenced by other minds—bodies are suspended in separate, static, mechanical housing.

There are two worlds—each speaking for—neither capturing Locke appropriately. Each world is entrapped by background assumptions about what counts as appropriate, what meanings are veiled, and, at the worst, what ideas are caused by the "gay mind" or the "Negro mind"—those mental elixirs, humors, and essences that are the real sources of dementia, defect, disease, inferiority, and perversion.

In a 1935 article titled "Values and Imperatives," Locke provides a broad view of community.[31] According to Locke, "All philosophies, it seems to me, are in ultimate derivation philosophies of life and not of abstract, disembodied 'objective' reality; products of time, place and situation, and thus systems of timed history rather than timeless eternity."[32] Locke knows the lie that philosophies have nothing to do with life; that life has nothing to do with philosophies.

Outing III

If Locke is understood as normal—and homosexuality understood as normal—Locke arguably fails to satisfy some important features of how honored representatives are constructed. Honored representatives, whether they are representatives of classes, races, ethnic groups, or sexual minorities, are always exalted persons who embody important group traits. So long as a group has some standing in the moral community—that is, its members are considered worthy human beings—then an individual can be an honored representative. That is, the possibility of an individual's being honored as a representative of a group is contingent on the group's having inclusion in the moral community.[33] Locke, however, fails to overcome deep-seated insecurity about his homosexuality. Locke overcomes disadvantages of segregation, academic competition, publishing exclusions, and overt racial hatred. Exalting persons who overcome such disadvantages is a major feature of African-American history just as overcoming insecurity about being a homosexual is an important feature in the history of homosexual communities.

Locke's homoeroticism is, like Nugent's, self-consciously normal. The archival resources do not provide a picture of overcoming; his homoeroticism is just that, homoeroticism. Locke displays the courage, confidence, and loyalty needed to perform the tremendous task of midwifery arguably because his homosexuality is normality.

It is normal for individuals to represent social kinds—for example, workers, capitalists, bankers, Arabs, Jews, or Chinese. Such individuals thereby tend to try to exhibit kind-specific traits. Persons accepted as normal can convince others that they are the source of, or have knowledge of, group-transcendent norms. Persons completely entrapped in their specificity, or persons with ideas and practices solely accountable for, or reducible to, their specificity offer persons outside that specificity no form of a model, nor ideas and practices that can be usurped, taken on, or adopted without implicitly making their position corrupt. If our representatives must evince important traits of the kind—for example, being a homosexual to represent the homosexual community—it is false that our representatives must be abnormal, defective, insecure, ashamed, or bereft of the courage, loyalty, and confidence needed to midwife.

If I am mistaken that (a) one reason Locke has not been appropriated as a representative of the homosexual community is because he treats himself and his friends as normal, and (b) that honored representatives of groups embody important traits indicative of the group, then I am not mistaken about the following: Locke was a philosopher who offered group-transcendent norms amid contested options—options contested by beloved and highly respected black and white homosexuals—and this requires seeing Locke as creative, authentic, independent, and a worthy representative of multiple identities that are polymorphically intersecting. What is always attributed to persons as due respect—the power to choose, decide, create, shape, and author goods we all need—are attributes of persons across lines of race, class, gender, or sex.

It is a demented homophobic world that makes it difficult to imagine honoring—that is, showing deference to and exalting—homosexuals. Such a world, deathly afraid of its own sexual imaginations, makes it hard to conceive of a homosexual as having intrinsic integrity, integrity of character. Such a world makes it difficult, but not impossible.

Outing IV

Locke helps make it possible to esteem without silencing, to appreciate empowerment through homosexuality as normality without closeting, shame, or suppressing the specificity of homosexual experiences.

Locke developed a radical version of pragmatism—critical pragmatism.

Locke's version of pragmatism differs from James's and Dewey's approach (both traditionally married heterosexuals) in its emphasis on the need to constantly revalue our choices, in its arguments for the import of aesthetics as a source of group-transcendent values, and in his suspicion of instrumental reasoning and warnings against "science" as a source for reasoning models. Moreover, Locke's insistence on imperatives such as tolerance and reciprocity distinguishes his moral interests.

Locke's value theory offers a rich approach to same-sex communities because his approach entails (a) seeing social categories as constructed and not necessarily reflective of underlying biological or ontological essences, and (b) seeing particularities as the source of universality. I address features of Locke's approach in the following tentative way.

I have been unable to determine whether Locke thought that homosexuality was caused by choice or biology. To my knowledge, there is no sustained argument or research on this issue by Locke. However, he rejects the idea of using biological categories to explain cultural or social categories, particularly biological race categories. Moreover, he holds that psychological categories such as repose or excitement are heuristic descriptions. Such categories pick out general inclinations but we should avoid using them as picking out stable values entrapped in those categories. Values are always subject to transvaluation, transposition, and revaluation. Thus values are always subject to revaluation, and traits or desires can move from one value field to another. Logic, for example, can be beautiful for one person and sterile for another; a source of excitement for a period of time and a source of anxiety for another period; nothing makes logic inherently entrapped in only one category or field of valuation. Arguably, then, gender and sexual reality entail modes of transition, transposition, and transvaluation. There is, by implication, nothing peculiar about homosexuality or bisexuality; nothing peculiar about persons finding their home in one or more forms of erotica. What is misguided is to treat a value field as if it represents, embodies, or causes some set of stable norms. The ethnology of essentialism—that a social or biological construction inherently defines, causes, or is correlated to character traits that embody virtues—is incompatible with a Lockean view of values. Thus, I speculate that Locke would find compatible works on homosexuality as a social construction, such as Edward Stein's *Forms of Desire* or David F. Greenberg's *The Construction of Homosexuality*.[34]

Locke's constructivist approach to groups allows us to see that the boundaries of groups, inclusive of sex- and gender-based groups, are always contested; they are never naturally given nor historically stable. Who counts as woman, man, gay, lesbian, or transsexual is always contestable, rendering the search for the "authentic" kind dubious. The "Negro," for example, in Locke's account, does not exist as an undifferentiated, culturally static, biologically caused, historically stable social entity.[35] The "Negro" for Locke is, however, ontologically real. What counts as peculiarly "Negro" are idioms and styles. What counts as its ontology are constantly evolving, shifting boundaries of idioms and styles. By analogy, what counts as homosexuality may gain from a focus on multiple styles and norms rather than fixed boundaries and character traits assumed embedded invariably across the kind. Capturing the uniqueness of various same-sex and queer experiences and yet keeping open transgressions and differences is a Lockean conceptual move.

Locke treats groups as if they are transient sources of values.[36] Yet, a group can be relatively stable and function to advance the betterment of society. Locke thought at one point in his career, for example, that the proletariat might function to help destroy prejudice and exploitation. He also thought that African Americans might function to help Americans change their ideas of Negroes' culture as the source of group transcendent norms. Moreover, he thought that dedication to African-American uplift was dedication to a particularity, itself contributory to human liberation. Representing the interest of a particularity was thus representing the interest of humanity; promoting the unique features of Negro culture was a contribution to universal civilization—*tout court*, for the homosexual community.

One possible reason for the absence of work on Locke by homosexual authors and the silencing of his homosexuality by heterosexual authors is because we have failed to appreciate Locke's conception of groups and rely on a fairly common form of fallacious reasoning: classification of ideal types is fallaciously used to explain group behavior.[37] If a person is homosexual we fallaciously assume that that explains her or his beliefs, values, and behaviors as if they were an instantiation of the group. Homosexuals in general have been forced to hide their sexuality, but it is fallacious to assume that each and every gay person has hidden his or her sexuality.

Authors dependent on an ideal of the African-American community as heterosexual, dedicated to racial uplift, and committed to racial unity must offer a special explanation for why a highly accomplished African American dedicated to racial uplift and committed to racial unity was a homosexual. That is, his abnormality must be explained because it is a feature of an individual member of a kind such that the kind ideally would not produce such a trait in an individual member.

The bond of common experiences and desire should, from the standpoint of an image of the African-American community as authentic when members representing that community are heterosexual, give legitimacy only to representatives that fit the ideal. Deviants from the norm, consequently, must be explained as a special, accidental case because individual members and representatives of a kind ideally would not have deviant traits.

Contrary to the approach of authors who explain black life depending on an image of the black community as authentic only when its members are heterosexual, being black does not explain attitudes toward homoeroticism any more than same-sex love explains attitudes toward race. Prevailing scholarship too often has no way of appreciating the power conflicts, lines, moments, styles, or traces of homosexual forms of desire embedded in Locke's work because looking for them has meant looking for deviance, lack, corruption, disease, and abnormality. And too often progressive gay scholarship has failed to appreciate the deep influence of race, thereby belittling Locke's primary focus, because seeing race entails giving voice to a feature that, ideally, should not exist. We can be suspicious of romanticizing groups while living, fighting, and struggling through group unity to create the reality of transcendent norms—the sort of norms that respect particularity, specificity, and all of our uniqueness.

Outing V

It will be a battle to keep the buildings, schools, and scholarships named for Locke; to secure support for any project in Locke's name; to keep Locke a hero for the universal and universalizable features of his philosophy—to keep him, and get him loved, respected, honored, and believed by persons of radically different valuations of homosexuality.

It will be a battle to prevent every word, every deed, every book, every friend, and every battle interpreted as caused by, explained by, a manifestation of, or a reflection of an erotic nature, invirtuous character, a misguided desire, and a gay (read diseased) mind (read idiot). It will be a battle because there is always a tendency to reduce the thought of persons considered deviant to a simplistic stereotypical image, one that fits the traits compatible to what the deviant social kind is assumed to manifest. Thus, blacks may be reduced to persons motivated only by stereotypical traits. There should be a rereading of Locke in light of his own belief that all philosophies are philosophies of life, and in light of the relationship of his homoeroticism to his philosophy of cultural diversity, tolerance, and reciprocity. Following from this, there should also be readings that foreground the principles, arguments, distinctions, and claims that he intended as describing group-transcendent norms, but which for him were grounded in value fields including erotic feelings, and the relation of feelings to the creation of values and their revaluation or transvaluation from one value field to another (between, for example, homoeroticism and attributes of persons across race, class, gender, and cultural categories). The complexity of rereadings is, I believe, a continual project especially for authors who have struggled diligently to fight on behalf of outings.

Locke faced the dual oppression of race and sexuality—one does not exist, separate and apart from the other. The reality of multiple oppression was not peculiar to Locke:

The homosexual community always faces multiple oppressions—as worker and gay, racialized minority and gay or lesbian, as woman and lesbian, as revolutionary and bisexual, as transsexual, etc. We can heuristically treat each social entity as separate. We can, for example, perceive the homosexual community as a composite ontological entity struggling for the liberation from exclusion and suppression within radically diverse nations, religions, and ethnic groups; the working class as a separate social entity acting historically toward the completion of a teleology; or the scientific community as a social entity enlivened by a mission to uncover the hidden truth behind appearances. The reality of our multiple, polymorphic being is nonetheless salient.

There will be ways that the misery suffered by sexism cannot be explained, described, or appreciated by using the epistemic categories associated with racism. Locke consistently rejecting having his beliefs reduced or explained by one feature of his personality. He expressed his opinion, for example, on numerous issues besides race relations and never made his sexuality a public matter. If, however, outing allows us to speak it should not allow us to reduce each person to a stereotypical kind nor totalize the experience of race, sex, gender, or national location as if one location supplies us with all the knowledge we need to appreciate others. And if homoeroticism is understood as polymorphic, rather than as an undifferentiated experience causing all homosexuals to have the same belief, then organizing to fight for the end of homophobia can occur without an organization pretending to be the sole legitimate authority or representative. Our polymorphic being and multiple identities, given Locke's way of understanding valuation, recommends tolerance, reciprocity, and appreciation of uniqueness between various locations of our experiences.

Locke described himself, in a letter dated October 1, 1949, in the following way: "Three minorities—Had I been born in ancient Greece I would have escaped the first [homophobia]; In Europe I would have been spared the second [anti-black legal segregation]; In Japan I would have been above rather than below average [height]." In considering whole persons we should not deny that they are a composite of all of their uniqueness, giving voice to each as best we can. In one sense we may attempt to speak, and speak for, persons suffering exclusion because of homophobia with a sense of our own fallibility, yet try with a sense of courage to cross boundaries. We may treat Locke (and possibly ourselves) the way Houston Baker, Jr., treats him in Modernism and the Harlem Renaissance—as a maroon, a runaway slave living outside of plantation society, violating oppressive categories of society while attempting to change the very society out of which he came.[38]

How is it possible to honor Locke, that is, exalt him because of his intrinsic qualities, virtues of character—his courage? How can we love and respect him as an aesthete, friend, philosopher, pragmatist, American, African American, and homosexual?

One way it is possible, I believe, to progressively surmount the vagaries of prejudice is through philosophies born of struggle to overcome oppression. Such philosophies take seriously the struggles, whether closeted or open, private or public, of populations besmirched with images of inferiority, disease, and pathology. Such populations, I believe, are populations out of which the most worthy group-transcendent norms arise. Locke's philosophy is a living philosophy: Locke's approach allows us to see that group-transcendent norms are already embedded in particular communities; that transvaluation is a normal feature of persons; that value fields are fields of desire, want, exaltation, and tension. Group-transcendent norms are already embedded in homosexual communities; specific norms are already the lines around which ontological unity is possible—never absolute, never completely stable, never static—yet a source of universality and empowerment, unsilenced, *When Peoples Meet*.

Notes

1. See Jeffrey C. Stewart, *Race Contacts and Interracial Relations* (Washington, D.C.: Howard University Press, 1992); Johnny Washington, *A Journey into the Philosophy of Alain Locke* (Westport, CT: Greenwood Press, 1994); Russell J. Linnemann, ed., *Alain Locke: Reflections on a Modern Renaissance Man* (Baton Rouge: Louisiana State University Press, 1982); David Levering Lewis, *When Harlem Was in Vogue* (New York: Knopf, 1981); Houston A. Baker, Jr., *Modernism and the Harlem Renaissance* (Chicago: University of Chicago Press, 1987).

2. George Hutchinson, *The Harlem Renaissance in Black and White* (Cambridge, MA: The Belknap Press of Harvard University Press, 1995).

3. See Leonard Harris, *Philosophy Born of Struggle* (Dubuque, IA: Kendall Hunt, 1983.

4. See Leonard Harris, "What, Then, Is Racism?" in *Racism* (New York: Humanity Press, 1999), 437–50.

5. *The Crescent*, Phi Beta Sigma Fraternity, Washington DC.

6. Arnold Rampersad, introduction to *The New Negro*, ed. Alain L. Locke (New York: Macmillan, 1992).

7. Alain L. Locke and Bernhard J. Stern, *When Peoples Meet* (New York: Progressive Education Association, 1942).

8. Mark Blasius, *Gay and Lesbian Politics: Sexuality and the Emergence of a New Ethic* (Philadelphia: Temple University Press, 1994), 218.

9. I reject the idea that being "normal" is inherently oppressive because it bespeaks conformity because normalcy also bespeaks acceptance. I hope one day that everyone will conform to relations that disallow homophobic and racially motivated hate, rape, and murder. Normalcy is also indicative of accepting one's self and others. Contrary to

Michael Warner's view in *Fear of a Queer Planet* (Minneapolis: University of Minnesota Press, 1993), normalcy as well as antisocial behavior can be oppressive, depending on the character of the behavior and associated meanings; the regime of the normal is no more inherently oppressive than the regime of the abnormal or different.

10. Michel Foucault, "Friendship as a Way of Life," in *Foucault Live*, ed. Sylvere Lotringer (New York: Seminotext(E), 1989), 311–12.

11. G. Anzaldua, *Borderlands/La Frontera* (San Francisco: Spinsters/Aunt Lute, 1987), 63.

12. Cullen to Locke, September 24, 1922, Alain L. Locke Papers, Moorland-Spingarn Research Center, Howard University.

13. See Faith Berry, *Langston Hughes* (Westport, CT: Lawrence Hill, 1983), 36–45.

14. Locke to Cullen, February 3, 192(3), Countee Cullen Papers, Archives Research Center, Tulane.

15. Alden Reimonenq, "Countee Cullen's Uranian 'Soul Windows'," *Journal of Homosexuality* 26, nos. 2/3 (1993): 149–53.

16. Ibid., 151.

17. Gregory Woods, "Gay Re-Readings of the Harlem Renaissance Poets," *Journal of Homosexuality*, 27, nos. 3/4 (1994): 133.

18. Ibid.

19. Joseph Bean, *In the Life: A Black Gay Anthology* (Boston: Alyson, 1986). Also see Eric Garber, "A Spectacle in Color: The Lesbian and Gay Subculture of Jazz Age Harlem," in *Hidden from History: Reclaiming the Gay and Lesbian Past*, ed. Martin B. Duberman, Martha Vicinus, and George Chauncey, Jr. (Middlesex: Penguin, 1991), 318–33.

20. Reimonenq, "Countee Cullen's Uranian 'Soul Windows'," 150.

21. Lewis, *When Harlem Was in Vogue*, 196. Also see Wallace Thurman, ed., *Fire!!* 1, no.1 (1926).

22. Lewis, *When Harlem Was in Vogue*, 196.

23. George Chauncey, *Gay New York* (New York: Basic Books, 1994).

24. Lewis, to his credit, admitted that his earlier work did not pay sufficient attention to the homosexual world. (Discussion with author, Purdue University, 1996.)

25. Quoted in Lewis, *When Harlem Was in Vogue*, 216.

26. Quoted in Charles M. Smith, "Bruce Nugent: Bohemian of the Harlem Renaissance," in *In the Life: A Black Gay Anthology*, ed. Joseph Beam, (Boston: Alyson, 1986), 214. Also see Nugent's short story, "Sahdji," in Locke's *The New Negro*.

27. The two people were James Spady and Esme Bhan.

28. Harris, *Philosophy of Alain Locke*, 319. Based on the ten-page "List of Unpublished Manuscripts in the Alain Locke Collection," 1982. The current list of the Alain Locke Papers, 1993, consists of 218 pages. Magic!

29. Jeffrey C. Stewart, "A Biography of Alain Locke: Philosopher of the Harlem Renaissance" (Ph.D. diss., Yale University, 1979).

30. I wrote Michael Winston requesting information on works regarding Locke's homosexuality, including information on any actions that involved the removal of sexually sensitive material from public access in the archives. I have not received a response.

31. Alain Locke, "Values and Imperatives," in *The Philosophy of Alain Locke: Harlem*

Renaissance and Beyond, ed. Leonard Harris (Philadelphia: Temple University Press), 31–50.

32. Ibid., 34.

33. See J. K. Campbell, *Honour, Family and Patronage* (Oxford: Oxford University Press, 1964); J. Pitt-Rivers and J. G. Peristiany, *Honor and Grace in Anthropology* (Cambridge: Cambridge University Press, 1992); Orlando Patterson, *Slavery and Social Death* (Cambridge, MA: Harvard University Press, 1982); Leonard Harris, "Honor, Eunuchs, and the Postcolonial Subject," in *Postcolonial African Philosophy*, ed. Emmanuel C. Eze (New York: Blackwell, 1997), 252–59, and "Honor: Empowerment and Emasculation," in *Rethinking Masculinity*, ed. Larry May and Robert A. Strinkwerda (New York: Rowman and Littlefield, 1992), 191–208.

34. Edward Stein, ed., *Forms of Desire: Sexual Orientation and the Social Constructivist Controversy* (New York: Routledge, 1992); David F. Greenberg, *The Construction of Homosexuality* (Chicago: University of Chicago Press, 1988).

35. See Alain Locke, "Who and What Is 'Negro'?" in *Philosophy of Alain Locke: Harlem Renaissance and Beyond*, ed. Leonard Harris (Philadelphia: Temple University Press, 1983), 207–28.

36. See Leonard Harris, "Rendering the Subtext: Subterranean Deconstruction Project," in *The Philosophy of Alain Locke: Harlem Renaissance and Beyond*, (Philadelphia: Temple University Press, 1989), 279–89.

37. See John D. Greenwood, "The Social Constitution of Action, Objectivity and Explanation," *Philosophy of Social Science* 20, no.2 (June 1990): 195–207; Frederick Suppe, "Explaining Homosexuality: Philosophical Issues, and Who Cares Anyhow?" in *Gay Ethics: Controversies in Outing, Civil Rights, and Sexual Science*, ed. Timothy F. Murphy (New York: Haworth Press, 1994), 223–68.

38. See Baker, *Modernism and the Harlem Renaissance.*

THIRTEEN

LESBIANS AND GAYS AND

THE POLITICS OF KNOWLEDGE

RETHINKING GENERAL MODELS

OF MASS OPINION CHANGE

Alan S. Yang

Introduction

SINCE THE 1960S, the United States has undergone an increasing pluralization of social life that has been cut through by different social divisions and antagonisms. During this period, a number of social movements emerged that had the potential to mobilize group members along these newly salient (as distinct from more traditional class-based) social divisions, resulting in a variety of different subject positions for individuals. The emergence of these movements (e.g., sexuality-, gender-, race-based) poses an important question for theories of public opinion change: What is the role of these social movements and group members who act as collective actors in shaping public opinion about them and issues of concern to them?

This paper will examine an important general model of mass opinion change as applied to the case of lesbians and gays described in the epilogue of John Zaller's *The Nature and Origins of Mass Opinion*. Zaller uses the case of the American Psychiatric Association's reversal of its stance toward homosexuality and its effect on mass media coverage of homosexuality to illustrate a "top-down" model of opinion change that assigns priority to the role of experts and elites. I will argue that Zaller's own example is not, in fact, a good illustration of an elitist "top-down" model of opinion change. If anything, this example suggests that experts themselves may be susceptible to influence on the part of the very social actors about whom they are supposed to be experts. The prospect of expertise being a function of decidedly political struggle with social actors "on the ground" suggests that elitist models of mass opinion change must incorporate an analysis of the politics of knowledge that is central to social movements such as the gay and lesbian movement. Such an analysis will allow a more complex understanding of the relationship among experts, the mass media, and the mass public (public opinion) in the process of public opinion change.

Beyond an Elitist, "Top-Down" Model
of Opinion Change toward Homosexuality

Mass opinion change, according to Zaller, is a function of the elite environment that provides information and cues to ordinary citizens through the mass media. Elites, here defined as both partisan elites as well as credentialed "experts" possessing technical expertise presumed to be "value-neutral," act as sources of reliable and accurate information (truth claims) and provide frames and cues to ordinary citizens who lack the resources and interest to keep highly informed. This, in turn, structures how ordinary citizens evaluate social and political issues.

The relationship between expertise and "the truth," though taken for granted in this model of mass opinion change (credentialed experts discern and report "the truth"), needs to be further queried, particularly when the very objects of truth claims (e.g., gays and lesbians) are themselves engaged in contesting the content of the truth claims, by which I mean, following Michel Foucault, the "rules according to which the true and the false are separated and specific effects of power attached to the true."[1] Then, analyzing and questioning (1) why a particular area of social life (e.g., homosexuality) becomes an object for truth claims (e.g., designation as psychiatric disorder), (2) how truth claims are institutionalized as a tradition or discipline of knowledge (e.g., scientific conventions and methods), and (3) who can exercise power based on these truth claims (e.g., American psychiatry, mental health clinicians) is what I call, following Mark Blasius, the "politics of knowledge."[2] I will argue that the relationship between expertise and truth claims, on the one hand, and politics, on the other, is a central problematic that scholars of mass opinion change must contend with, particularly when the role of expert(ise) is such a critical variable in models of mass opinion formation and change.

The general "elitist" (top-down) model of opinion change discussed above assigns very clear roles to the mass public (who receive, process, and likely accept elite communications) and elites (as legitimate producers of information and frames for interpreting it) (Zaller, 1992, 1996; Key, 1961). The key mediating variable is the mass media, which convey elite communications to the mass public. This general model of mass opinion change may be schematized as follows:

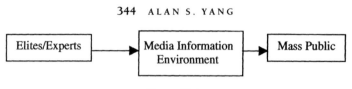

Figure 13.1.

In the epilogue to *The Nature and Origins of Mass Opinion*, Zaller demonstrates the importance of expertise in how the mass media frames its coverage of homosexuality. Zaller asserts that the decision of the American Psychiatric Association (APA) in 1973 that homosexuality was not a psychiatric disorder was the impetus behind the mainstream media's shift in coverage from framing homosexuals as deviant or ill to a framing of homosexuals as a minority group fighting for their civil rights (Zaller 1992). He cites the APA as the "most authoritative source of secular understanding" of homosexuality as a disease. The media, relying on an expert community (American psychiatrists), were partial to this view so long as it remained the official expert view. Once the APA officially changed its stance toward homosexuality in 1973, the media markedly changed the way it framed stories about homosexuality, according to Zaller, moving toward a civil rights paradigm and away from a "disease and deviance" framing. Zaller's evidence of the marked change in the decade surrounding the 1973 decision[3] underscores just how dependent the media is on subject-matter specialists and experts in the framing and reporting of news.

The relationship between the media and experts is consistent with Zaller's broader theory that conceives of an idealized system of public information where political ideas and perspectives develop among policy specialists and diffuse downward to the public via the mass media. This elitist model, while notable for its parsimony, leaves important questions unexamined by treating elites as a relatively insulated set of actors that merely produce truth claims and frames based on more or less autonomous decision-making procedures. Rather than treat elites as exogenous to a model of mass opinion change (see figure 13.1), we need to query what leads to changes in the elite information environment in the first place. An important step in this endeavor is to acknowledge the agency of collective actors fighting for social change—in this case, lesbian and gay activists.

Largely absent from Zaller's rendering of the APA decision is the role of homosexuals themselves. I want to suggest that collective actors target elites in an effort to persuade and educate them to formulate positions favorable to the interests of the group. Through a process of negotiation and confrontation, collective actors are instrumental in the reformulation of knowledge claims, frames, and interpretations provided by elites (experts, in particular), thus altering the elite information environment. Changes in this environment are reflected in the mass media and are ultimately received by the mass public. This supports the view that the objects of elite discourses may also be the conscious agents of change of these same elite discourses, altering the media information environment and, ultimately, public opinion.

Further, collective actors also engage in political interventions (direct action, press conferences, creation of autonomous community-based institutions, etc.) that may be represented in the mass media, achieving visibility and thereby challenging dominant, or proffering their own, constructions of social life (e.g., the "truth" about homosexuality). Targeting cultural norms in a symbolic struggle over meanings and interpretations (Gamson 1992), group members contribute to the universe of political discourse through a process of "conceptual revision" (Connolly 1993) by sponsoring ideological packages and frames that challenge hegemonic understandings. Of course, these endeavors may be transmitted by the mass media with bias and be subject to interpretation and (mis)representation by elites (Gitlin 1980; Hallin 1986). Nevertheless, representation of these political interventions in the first place could not occur without an active politics of resistance on the part of collective actors pursuing one strategy and not another; utilizing one set of ideological packages (frames) and not another.

By using the case of homosexuality and American psychiatry, Zaller illustrates both the elegance as well as the limits of a general model of opinion change that treats elites and experts as exogenous to the model. A model of mass opinion change toward socially marginalized groups (e.g., lesbians and gays) and issues of concern to them would be well served by treating these elites as endogenous to the model and would further address the role of collective actors (in this case, lesbians and gay men) in this process. Below is a model that reflects discussion up to this point:

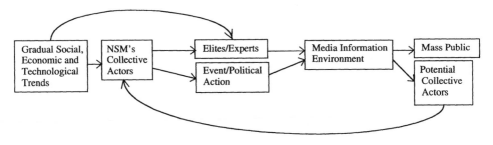

Figure 13.2.

Such a model acknowledges that collective actors from marginalized groups recognize that in order to change public perceptions of themselves and issues of concern to them, in addition to influencing public opinion more directly, elites must also change the way they represent their group. Part of the strategy in changing group representation within the context of the media information environment, then, is to change the universe of elite discourses. A critical aspect of this also includes changing who gets to become an "expert" in the first place. The expansion of exactly who is an expert on a particular area of social and political life is reflected in the battles of lesbian and gay activists to become their own experts on questions of homosexuality.

Just as important as challenging expertise (or transforming what expertise is and where it may come from), collective actors facilitate public interventions in the form of political initiatives that may be represented in a less mediated fashion in the mass media. Media representations of political initiatives provide the mass public with frames and information that, over time, challenge dominant constructions of socially marginalized groups (e.g., lesbians and gays). The media information environment will therefore reflect the combined effect of both indirect (through elites) and more direct (staging of political interventions) collective action. This altered media information environment will be received by the mass public and will eventually lead to changes in mass opinion.

Finally, an important subset of the general public is the "issue public" of potential collective actors in the form of group members who may not yet possess a strong sense of group identification. They will be affected by changes in the media information environment at the level of altered consciousness, moving, perhaps, toward politicized group consciousness. The increasing visibility or "recognition" (as distinct from "respect," or positive representation[4]) in the mass media, irrespective of its character, will alter the consciousness of group members, creating a potential bloc of future collective actors.

Public Opinion Change and the Role of Lesbian and Gay Collective Actors

During the period after World War II, the mass media were mostly silent on the issue of homosexuality. When homosexuality was represented at all, homosexuals were primarily cast as the objects of a constellation of three sets of elite discourses: (1) partisan elites (politicians), (2) administrative elites (law enforcement officials), and (3) medical experts (psychiatrists). By this period, homosexuality had been effectively transformed into a clinical entity as a result of prior work in the fields of sexology, psychoanalysis, and psychiatry. The "medical model" of homosexuality had by mid-century branded homosexuality with pathology within American psychiatry. This was made official in the 1952 DSM-I, the official diagnostic reference for clinicians treating psychiatric disorders, which listed homosexuality as a "sociopathic personality disturbance" (Bayer 1987).

During this period, "sexual perversion" was grounds for arrest on newly passed sexual psychopath laws (augmenting the impact of largely unenforced but symbolically powerful sodomy laws), which officially recognized homosexuality as a socially threatening disease, as well as exclusion from government employment, military purges, FBI surveillance, and urban police harassment (D'Emilio 1983)

In terms of representation in the media information environment during this period, there is an absence of lesbians and gays speaking on their own behalf. While homophile organizations had been around since the early 1950s, the stance toward psychiatrists had generally been one of quiet cultivation of the profession's practitioners and respectful dialogue. Medical experts who could speak about the "social problem" of homosexuality from a position of scientific neutrality, it was reasoned, could be allies in educating the broader public and perhaps ameliorate anti-gay persecution at the hands of the police and law, arguing that homosexuals afflicted with a medical condition should be pitied and treated rather than prosecuted by the state (D'Emilio 1983).

By the mid-1960s, important social changes would intervene to alter the media information environment around homosexuality. First, within psychiatry, the more or less unchallenged status of the medical model of homosexuality began to be more widely questioned, though it continued to represent the mainstream view. Indeed, in 1968, the DSM-II listed, with little fanfare, homosexuality as a "non-psychiatric mental disorder." Further, the culture of protest that characterized this period legitimized direct action and other forms of protest as instruments of discontent. Both of these changes were seized on by increasingly radical homophile activists. Homosexuals no longer would continue to simply function as objects of elite discourses, but increasingly became subjects capable of speaking on their own behalf (Bayer 1987; D'Emilio 1983).

There was a decisive shift on the part of radical homophile activists who refused to cede to psychiatrists the right to remain the unquestioned experts on homosexuality. The Stonewall riots of 1969 also ushered in an increase in highly visible direct-action protest strategies on the part of gay liberationists as well as the establishment of increasingly visible community institutions (e.g., lesbian and gay bars, bookstores, community centers), especially in large urban areas. The rise of gay liberation and the proliferation of publicly identifiable community formations coincided with an attendant increase in lesbians and gays willing to "come out." The work of community building and activist interventions occurring "on the ground" during the period of the late 1960s and early 1970s ushered in an era of movement politics that would have an important impact on the media information environment. This activist work by lesbian and gay collective actors was, I argue, a critical mediating variable in public opinion formation and change (D'Emilio 1983; Adam 1987; Marotta 1981).

The APA and the Politics of Knowledge

One critical intervention pursued by gay activists of the period was an all-out assault on the medical model as epitomized in the DSM-I classification of homosexuality. Ronald Bayer's analysis of the politics behind this reversal suggests that the challenge by lesbian and gay activists was central to the decision by the expert body to reverse course.

Bayer meticulously details the change in the homophile movement's stance toward American psychiatry's designation of homosexuality as a psychiatric disorder during the 1960s. The Mattachine Society, for example, had been initially receptive to psychiatric experts who, though arguing that homosexuality was a disease, could also state that homosexuality was not a willful choice representing a decision to reject the moral values of society, thus challenging the received notion that homosexuality ought to be the target of legal prosecution. By the 1960s, homophile activists began to insist that homosexuals not cede to scientific experts the right to speak on the question of homosexuality. According to early gay activist Frank Kameny, the so-called experts had forfeited the right to speak because they lacked the capacity to withstand the distorting value-laden assumptions of broader society. This rupture in the historical alliance between scientists and the homophile movement marked a critical juncture in American psychiatry's unchallenged expertise on homosexuality (Bayer 1987).

By the late 1960s, the culture of political protest that had legitimated direct action as an instrument for the expression of discontent had given the radical homophile movement (and later, the gay liberation movement) the means for an assault on American psychiatry. Gay activists utilized a variety of strategies (e.g., demonstrations, disruptions of professional conventions and meetings, zaps⁵) to make their demand for the deletion of homosexuality from the DSM clear. By the 1971 APA annual convention, homosexual activists entered into the first direct discussion with those in the APA leadership responsible for classification of psychiatric disorders. This recognition was seen as a result of gay activists' strategy of social protest. By 1973, gay activists (and allies, straight and gay, within the profession) had successfully forced the APA to confront the extent to which social values had framed the most basic elements of their professional work. Gay activists and their allies argued that psychiatry's diagnostic standpoint had become a major prop for social repression and that stigmatization brought on by psychiatric classification had become a source of suffering. By 1973, the board of trustees of the APA decided to remove homosexuality from the DSM and though dissident psychiatrists, outraged by their perception that the board had bowed to political pressure by gay liberationists, forced the board to submit its decision to a referendum of the entire membership, the decision held (Bayer 1987).

This particular case study illustrates how a deeply political struggle on the part of the very objects of science's "objective" expertise permeated the supposedly autonomous and ideologically neutral functioning of an organization of scientists.

The case of homosexuality and American psychiatry suggests that students of mass opinion change revisit general elitist top-down models of opinion change. If the truth of, for example, medical science, is susceptible to interventions by activists who possess, by and large, no formal credentials or authority to speak as practitioners in the name of expertise[6], one must reconsider the directional arrow of causality. Do experts simply autonomously make pronouncements on an issue, framing and giving content to media coverage and, ultimately, reception on the part of the mass public? Or must we consider that expertise itself is shaped by social movements and might these interventions on the part of activists reflect a broader shift in cultural norms that exist in society? In this scenario, experts can hardly stand outside a model of mass opinion change; expertise is continually challenged both in its substance and how it gets constituted.

The Case of the Military

Although the decline of the medical model of homosexuality has had an important long-term impact on the media information environment and, thus, mass opinion, the past twenty-five years since the APA decision have brought a host of new challenges for the lesbian and gay movement. Public attitudes toward homosexuality, lesbians, and gays have come to encompass a wide range of different dimensions: attitudes toward general principles of equality, specific civil rights issues, the moral rightness or wrongness of homosexuality, the social standing of lesbians and gays, etc. (Yang 1997). Given the plurality of issue areas that encompass what Americans think about homosexuality, we might expect to see particular dimensions of attitudes toward homosexuality conform better than others to a general elitist model of opinion change. That is, certain issues will lend themselves more readily to challenges to established expertise and elite interpretations on the part of lesbian and gay collective actors or the ourtright inclusion of lesbians and gays as "credible"[7] experts in the media information environment.

One particular issue where an elitist top-down model of opinion change conforms most closely to the Zallerian model is the issue of public support for allowing lesbians and gays to serve in the U.S. military. Here, elite opinion, as transmitted by the mass media, was able to produce abrupt, though short-term, changes in public opinion in a manner remarkably close to what would be predicted by a general elitist model of opinion change.

It is the issue itself (internal military policy) that renders a top-down model relevant. The issue of whether openly gay men and lesbians would impede "combat readiness" or "unit morale" was perhaps quite naturally a matter in which the mass media relied on expert sources. The expert sources in this instance, however, were predominantly culled from the military establishment itself and its key congressional patrons. That this set of elites was almost completely united in the view that unit morale and combat readiness would suffer under the proposed Clinton plan ensured a policy consensus from perhaps the most important expert body on military policy: the military establishment itself.

The distinctive requirements of military life were, not surprisingly, left largely to "the experts" to articulate. Given the traditional deference to the military establishment on the issue of its own internal rules and organization by both the political branches of government and the courts, the impregnable consensus among experts on the U.S. military was inevitably reflected in media coverage of the gays in the military controversy.

An effective "counterpoint" to a united military establishment's "point" would have best come from other military establishment figures or political elites with acknowledged experience in military policy, as opposed to spokespersons from lesbian and gay organizations, who, after years of struggle and organization building, could be dismissed as keenly particular and self-interested advocacy groups.[8] On the issue of internal military rules, then, "the experts" were able to effectively dominate the framing of the controversy in the mass media.

Thus, the terms of debate revolved around the issue of combat readiness and unit morale as opposed to "equal citizenship" or "civil rights," this latter framing favored by lesbian and gay groups and relevant allies.[9] The military establishment and its congressional patrons, acting as experts on this policy matter, were able to advocate for their particular framing of the issue in media representations and, thus, effectively exclude other possible "experts" who might have a stake in the outcome of the policy debate. The issue of combat readiness and unit morale became merely a technical question that demanded expertise borne of deep involvement with military norms, routines, and organization.

In June 1992, the gradual increase in public support over time for hiring gays and lesbians for the armed forces had reached clear majority levels (Yang 1997). Majority support for allowing lesbians and gays in the military was evident among voters for all candidates in the 1992 presidential election, including Bush supporters (Hugick 1992). By the middle of 1993, however, public support had fallen at an abrupt rate. This significant though short-term decline in the public's support for gays in the military is anomalous when seen in the context of overall trends in public attitudes toward homosexuality, which have evinced gradual change over time (Yang 1997). This abrupt drop in public support can be attributed to a dramatic change in the media information environment: the sudden salience of the controversy as a central issue on the national agenda.

While Clinton had come out in favor of lifting the ban during the campaign, the Bush team, in the aftermath of the Houston convention of 1992, was wary of highlighting Clinton's unprecedented pledge to lesbian and gay groups to end the ban. Bush strategists felt that tackling "family values" issues after the convention, where strident attacks on Democrats as anti-family drew poor reviews, even among some Republican political operatives, would be politically dangerous. Thus, by the time of Clinton's election, he was "solidly on record in support of a controversial policy that had not been seriously tested in the political arena" (Towell July 24, 1993:1971). Suddenly, the issue exploded with startling force.

During the transition, senior military officials began to express unusually vehement opposition to Clinton's proposal. The issue gained media prominence when a memo by Les Aspin was leaked, warning that a repeal of the ban faced strong opposition on Capitol Hill and would have the support of only thirty-nine senators. The memo stated that after consulting with military leaders during a six-month suspension of disciplinary actions against suspected homosexual servicepersons, Aspin would draft an executive order on how, but not whether, to lift the ban. On the morning of January 25, 1993, supporters of the ban deluged congressional offices and the White House switchboard with calls opposing Clinton's planned move (Towell January 30, 1993). What for Clinton had been a little-remarked-upon campaign promise to yet another interest group had become an issue that inflamed the passions of those in the military establishment, as well as their supporters in the public.

Colin Powell, chairman of the Joint Chiefs of Staff, came out in "unusually frank and energetic public opposition" to Clinton's stand on gays in the military. He sounded the military's profound concern about what effects such a move might have on morale and combat readiness. Given candidate Clinton's well-publicized troubles during the election campaign with his lack of military service, publicly opposing Powell, who was both head of the Joint Chiefs and a Desert Storm hero, made Clinton's position tenuous from the start. Powell's status as an expert on military matters could not be questioned. Clinton's political vulnerability on military issues, particularly in the face of opposition by his own Joint Chiefs, was underscored by a statement by Senator Dan Coats (R-IN), who remarked in a January 26 Senate speech that "you would think that someone who has not served a day in uniform would be particularly careful to consult his military chiefs" (Towell January 30, 1993: 228–29).

The chair of the Senate Armed Services Committee, Senator Sam Nunn (D-GA), also came out in opposition to the Clinton plan. Nunn had built a reputation as an expert on defense issues and had the support of many in the military establishment, as well as the respect of both Republicans and Democrats in the Senate on defense-related issues. Nunn represented another source of expertise on national security matters, at least within the Senate, and his opposition to the Clinton plan cannot be underestimated in terms of its effect on other Democratic senators (Doherty and Towell 1993). In supporting the ban, he cited the contention of military personnel that the presence of openly gay members in the often confined quarters of a combat unit would corrode unit morale (*CQ Weekly Report*, March 27, 1993).

Typically, the House and Senate Armed Services Committee had marched lockstep with the military, especially since the cold war, as evidenced by the consistently ample Pentagon budgets. Lawrence Korb, a former assistant secretary of defense, observed that Clinton erred in not realizing that Nunn and Powell were not just two Washington bureaucrats: "Nunn is Mr. Defense on the Hill. Democrats and Republicans alike take their cues on defense issues from the Georgia legislator because of his expertise, independence and long involvement with national security. Similarly, Powell is the most charismatic and well connected military leader since Douglas MacArthur . . . since he had served as President Reagan's assistant for National Security, he was wise in the ways of the media and the Congress" (Korb 1994: 225).

While Clinton tried to frame the lifting of the ban as a civil rights issue, the Joint Chiefs saw it as a military readiness issue. This is not to say that the expertise offered by the military establishment was rooted in sober appraisal, borne of reason. In fact, the military leadership ignored systematic research and analysis on this controversial issue. They chose to ignore, and effectively suppressed, for example, a Pentagon-commissioned RAND Corporation report,[10] which concluded that military commanders should not consider sexual orientation by itself germane to determining who can serve. Earlier research and analysis, in the Crittenden and the Department of Defense's Personnel Security Research and Education Center (PERSEREC)[11] reports (1957 and 1988, respectively) had reached similar conclusions, but the military establishment chose not to consider, let alone reference, these reports (Korb 1994). Despite findings to the contrary that came from reports commissioned by the military itself, the military establishment was able, at the very least, to obscure dissenting findings from serious media scrutiny. The military establishment's success in suppressing findings that contravened its own view should be seen in the context of its unique position vis-à-vis the media of virtual monopoly control of information about its own workings.

During the months leading up to July 15, the date of Clinton's scheduled decision, congressional hearings were held to consider the matter. These hearings provided a podium for prominent members of the military establishment to give expert testimony, providing further ammunition for the opponents of lifting the ban. The relative saturation of the media information environment provides an opportunity to assess the effect on attitudes toward support for gays in the military.

The following table provides an example of the abrupt short-term change in attitudes toward gays in the military during the period of the controversy. These data show that by February 1993, the previously even division of opinion had clearly shifted to majority disapproval of "allowing homosexual men and women to serve in the armed forces of the United States." This clear majority disapproval prevailed as late as June 1993.[12]

TABLE 1
Do you approve or disapprove of allowing openly homosexual men and women to serve in the armed forces of the United States?

	LAT 10/92 (%)	LAT 1/93 (%)	LAT 2/93 (%)	LAT 6/93 (%)
Approve	48	45	40	41
Disapprove	44	47	54	52
Not Sure/DK	6	8	5	5
Refused	2	—	1	2
N	1833	1733	1273	1474

The next table shows that opposition increased to clear majority opposition to "Bill Clinton's plan to allow gays and lesbians to serve in the United States military" between January and May 1993.

TABLE 2
Do you favor or oppose Bill Clinton's plan to allow gays and lesbians to serve in the United States military?

	YP 1/93 (%)	YP 5/93 (%)
Favor	43	36
Oppose	48	55
Not Sure	9	9
N	1800	1000

Finally, disapproval of Clinton's handling of the issue of gays in the military increased dramatically (a fourteen-point increase) between January and July 1993 from plurality approval to clear majority disapproval.

TABLE 3

Do you approve or disapprove of the way Bill Clinton has handled the issue
of gays in the military?

	ABC/WP 1/93 (%)	PSRA 7/93 (%)
Approve	44	37
Disapprove	42	56
Don't Know	14	7
N	549	725

The above data show that public opinion on the question of allowing gays to serve in the military changed abruptly and moved toward increasing opposition during the first half of 1993. The data reflect the cumulative effect of expert opposition to lifting the ban and media coverage and interpretations that legitimized this expertise. The military case seems to follow a general top-down model of opinion change, where particular elites (a united military establishment) provided political information and frames (combat readiness, unit morale) to the mass public through the mass media. These frames, in turn, served as the primary basis upon which the mass public could evaluate the controversy. What distinguishes the military case from other issues of concern to lesbians and gays is the particular nature of the policy area; that is, military experts were here assumed to have the strongest claim to expertise on internal military organization and the rights of lesbians and gays to serve openly therein once the issue had been successfully framed in the mass media as a matter of combat readiness and unit effectiveness.

The virtual monopoly of expertise by the military establishment precluded the emergence of other credible experts who might have offered alternative viewpoints. This monopoly also extended to control over information that *might* have provided an effective counterpoint in the form of commissioned reports whose conclusions ran counter to those of the military establishment.

Conclusions

The analysis of the policy debate over gays in the military suggests that certain facets of public attitudes toward homosexuality lend themselves to elite leadership in a manner conceived by a general top-down model of opinion change. Here, a matter of internal military policy determined a set of credible experts on the part of the mass media. That this set of experts was largely culled from a military establishment and sympathetic political elites who happened to be united in opposition to the Clinton proposal virtually guaranteed that the primary framing became one of combat readiness and unit morale. Under such a framing, other possible credible experts became either irrelevant or unintelligible; alternative frames that appealed to fairness, equal citizenship, and civil rights were lost once the more technical questions offered by the military's framing became accepted doctrine.

Further, the inherently undemocratic character of the U.S. military virtually ensured that lesbians and gays would have little opportunity to effectively challenge what came to be accepted as truth about the military by policymakers, the media, and the mass public, as reflected in opinion polls. This may be a strong case of an expert community's being relatively autonomous in its ability to determine what knowledge is relevant for policy ("the facts" about combat readiness) and what the content of "truth claims" of this knowledge will be, thus shaping public opinion.

When one considers the whole range of issues of concern to lesbians and gays, however, questions of expertise become more complicated, in part because issues that can be intelligibly framed as matters of rightness or wrongness, health and sickness, equality, respect for difference, and civil rights, for example, invite a plurality of possible "credible experts." Some issues may require lesbian and gay "expert" voices; others require experts who may be susceptible to challenge by or to being informed by lesbian and gay collective actors (or both simultaneously). In these cases, expert opinion and elite decision making derived from it would not be virtually autonomous, but a function of decidedly political struggles.

The military controversy, far better than the APA reversal, adheres to an elitist model of opinion change. In the case of the military, the relevant experts were (1) practically unchallenged in their role as legitimate sources of expertise for the making of public policy (especially once the framing of unit morale and combat readiness had been established as what was relevant for policy), and (2) not informed by or susceptible to influence from the social actors they were supposedly experts about—lesbian and gay servicepersons and their advocates.

The relationship among experts, lesbian and gay collective actors, the mass media, and public opinion will vary on an issue-by-issue basis. Zaller's own use of the APA example demonstrates that the relationship among expertise, the mass media, and public opinion is not necessarily one way (top-down), especially when one considers the role of social movements in this process. To have a general top-down model across all possible issues one would need to universalize the conditions of expertise that existed in the military example. I would argue that this is neither methodologically tenable nor empirically warranted.

A model of public opinion change toward socially marginalized groups and issues of concern to them requires that we query the nature of expertise, its relation to the lived experience of individuals and collective goals of the social actors it is ostensibly about, and the interaction between the two that is played out as the politics of knowledge.

Notes

1. "Truth and Power" in Foucault 1980: 132.

2. Blasius 1994: 43–49. As distinct from and historically as a source of resistance to psychiatric expertise in the politics of knowledge, Blasius writes of a "lesbian and gay ethos." "An ethos of lesbian and gay existence is a source for the production of truth. By 'truth,' I mean . . . procedures for producing statements to the effect (following Wittgenstein) [that] 'this is how things are' and for institutionalizing both of them as knowledge and people who 'tell the truth.' In this case, it is procedures for producing, regulating, distributing, and circulating statements about homoeroticism historically and about the experience of it as lesbian or gay today" (212).

3. Based on a content analysis, Zaller finds that media coverage of homosexuality prior to the 1973 reversal framed stories of homosexuals as a minority group fighting for their rights for a total of fourteen minutes in the five years prior to 1973, while it employed this civil rights paradigm to the framing of homosexuality for 135 minutes in the five years following the decision. He uses these findings to illustrate how the expert opinion of the APA served as deep background for the press (Zaller 1992: 318). While the APA reversal may have played an important role in the change in framing (from disease to civil rights), the actions of lesbian and gay collective actors were central to providing content to the civil rights framing in the first place. A narrative locating lesbians and gays as agents of social change is glossed over.

4. Here, "recognition" refers to any coverage at all of certain social groups irrespective of the actual content of coverage, whereas "respect" denotes positive representation of a social group and its members. Liebert and Sprafkin (1988: 198–207) trace the development of media representation of social groups (e.g., African Americans, women) through the prism of "recognition" and "respect."

5 A zap is a strategy of publicly confronting prominent elected officials or political leaders, especially in public forums, forcing them to respond to questions on gay issues, thus increasing visibility on gay issues via the media.

6. This is not to underestimate the important contributions of lesbian and gay psychiatric professionals (e.g., Charles Silverstein) or sympathetic straight practitioners (e.g., Evelyn Hooker), whose work was crucial in influencing the pace and very character of change within the psychiatric profession.

7. By "credible," I refer to the judgment of those in the mass media (e.g., editors, reporters, producers) charged with seeking out elites to frame, interpret, and provide information on particular "newsworthy" topics.

8. Page, Shapiro, and Dempsey 1987 demonstrate that particularistic interest and advocacy groups generally have, if anything, a "negative effect" on public opinion; that is, opinion moves in the direct opposite to that it is trying to lead.

9. For example, the Campaign for Military Service, a Washington, D.C.–based umbrella organization of advocates of lifting the ban on lesbians and gays, attempted to influence the debate on behalf of lesbian and gay servicepersons in response to May

10 congressional hearings that were framed around the questions of combat readiness and unit morale. They included testimony by service members speaking about the effects of the discriminatory policy. None of the news outlets, however, picked it up. This lack of a competing center of information from the lesbian and gay side, which was framing the question as one of discrimination and equal citizenship rights, made it even more likely that the mass public would accept the military establishment's perspective in the absence of a competing framing and interpretation.

10. The RAND Corporation study, costing $1.3 million, concluded that the ban could be lifted without adversely affecting the "order, discipline and individual behavior necessary to maintain cohesion and performance." The RAND study was completed in the spring of 1993 but was withheld by the Pentagon; Democratic senators forced its release, which did not occur until August 1993. The timing of the release seemed calculated to ensure the least amount of publicity. See Lehring 1996: 272–74.

11. The Crittenden Report, named after the chair, Captain S. H. Crittenden, Jr., U.S.N., released in 1957, concluded that "no factual data exist to support the contention that homosexuals are a greater risk than heterosexuals." This study was suppressed by the Navy for twenty years until a court order forced its release. In 1988, a second study financed and overseen by the Department of Defense found that homosexuality was "unrelated to job performance in the same way as is being left or right handed." Like the Crittenden Report before it, the PERSEREC report was suppressed by the Pentagon. Pentagon memos were shown to have directed PERSEREC to fundamentally rewrite the report to remove all claims that homosexuals were suitable for military service (Lehring 1996).

12. The ten-point increase in disapproval between 10/92 and 2/93 is a real change in opinion levels, following Page and Shapiro's six-percentage-point criterion to denote statistically significant opinion changes between two time points. This criterion substitutes, in a rough fashion, for macrotests that confirm with roughly 95 percent certainty that a given change was not produced by sampling error. "There is no way to avoid uncertainty about the exact number and identity of genuine opinion changes; faced with inevitable sampling error in surveys, one must either count some random deviations as significant changes, or else dismiss some real (but small) cases of opinion change as insignificant. The important point is that any real changes we missed were very small" (Page and Shapiro 1992: 423–24).

Works Cited

Adam, Barry. *The Rise of the Gay and Lesbian Movement*. Boston: Twayne, 1987.

Bayer, Ronald. *Homosexuality and American Psychiatry: The Politics of Diagnosis*. Princeton: Princeton University Press, 1987.

Blasius, Mark. *Gay and Lesbian Politics: Sexuality and the Emergence of a New Ethic*. Philadelphia: Temple University Press, 1994.

"Clinton Rekindles Debate over Gays in the Military." *Congressional Quarterly Weekly Report*, March 27, 1993, p. 772.

Connolly, William. *The Terms of Political Discourse*. 3rd ed. Cambridge, MA: Blackwell, 1993.

D'Emilio, John. *Sexual Politics, Sexual Communities: The Making of a Homosexual Minority in the United States, 1940–1970*. Chicago: University of Chicago Press, 1983.

Doherty, Caroll J., and Pat Towell. "Fireworks over Ban on Gays Temporarily Snuffed Out." *Congressional Quarterly Weekly Report*, February 6, 1993, pp. 272–74.

Epstein, Steven. "Democratic Science? AIDS Activism and the Contested Construction of Knowledge." *Socialist Review* 21, no. 2 (1991): 35–64.

Foucault, Michel. *Power/Knowledge: Selected Interviews and Other Writings, 1972–1997*. Ed. Colin Gordon. New York: Pantheon Books, 1980.

Gamson, William A. "The Social Psychology of Collective Action." In *Frontiers in Social Movement Theory*, ed. Aldon D. Morris and Carol McClurg Mueller, 53–76). New Haven: Yale University Press, 1992.

Gitlin, Todd. *The Whole World Is Watching: Mass Media and the Unmaking of the New Left*. Berkeley: University of California Press, 1980.

Hallin, Daniel C. *The "Uncensored War": The Media and Vietnam*. New York: Oxford University Press, 1986.

Hugick, Larry. "Public Opinion Divided on Gay Rights." *Gallup Poll Monthly*, June 1992, pp. 2–6.

Key, V. O. *Public Opinion and American Democracy*. New York: Knopf, 1961.

Klandermans, Bert. "The Social Construction of Protest and Multiorganizational Fields." In *Frontiers in Social Movement Theory*, ed. Aldon D. Morris and Carol McClurg Mueller, pp. 77–103. New Haven: Yale University Press, 1992.

Korb, Lawrence. "Evolving Perspective on the Military's Policy on Homosexuals." In *Gays and Lesbians in the Military: Issues, Concerns and Contrasts*, ed. Wilbur J. Scott and Sandra Carson Stanley, 219–29. New York: Aldine de Gruyter, 1994.

Lehring, Gary L. "Constructing the 'Other' Soldier: Gay Identity's Military Threat." In *Gay Rights, Military Wrongs: Political Perspectives on Lesbians and Gays in the Military*, ed. Craig A. Rimmerman, 269–94. New York: Garland, 1996.

Liebert, Robert M., and Joyce Sprafkin. *The Early Window: The Effects of Television on Children and Youth*. 3rd ed. New York: Pergamon Press, 1988.

Marotta, Toby. *The Politics of Homosexuality*. Boston: Houghton Mifflin, 1981.

Page, Benjamin, and Robert Y. Shapiro. *The Rational Public: Fifty Years of Trends in Americans' Policy Preferences*. Chicago: University of Chicago Press, 1992.

Page, Benjamin, Robert Y. Shapiro, and Glenn R. Dempsey. "What Moves Public Opinion?" *American Political Science Review* 81, no. 1 (1987): 22–43.

Towell, Pat. "Campaign Promise, Social Debate Collide on Military Battlefield." *Congressional Quarterly Weekly Review*, January 30, 1993, pp. 226–29.

———. "Months of Hope, Anger, Anguish Produce Policy Few Admire." *Congressional Quarterly Weekly Review*, July 24, 1993, pp. 1966–71.

Yang, Alan. "Trends: Attitudes towards Homosexuality." *Public Opinion Quarterly* 61, no. 3 (1997): 477–507.

Zaller, John. "The Myth of Massive Media Impact Revived: New Support for a Discredited Idea." In *Political Persuasion and Attitude Change*, ed. Diana C. Mutz, Paul M. Sniderman, and Richard A. Brody, 17–78. Ann Arbor: University of Michigan Press, 1996.

———. *The Nature and Origins of Mass Opinion*. Cambridge: Cambridge University Press, 1992.

FOURTEEN

LESBIAN AND GAY THINK TANKS

THINKING FOR SUCCESS

M. V. Lee Badgett

"I would prefer that we think our way to success."
—John D'Emilio

Introduction

IN THE CONTEXT of issues related to lesbian, gay, bisexual, and transgender (LGBT) people, political and judicial processes increasingly involve the testimony of academic "experts," who are often pitted against one another. The 1990s witnessed the following debates in courtrooms and legislative hearing rooms across the United States:

- Philosophers John Finnis of Oxford and Martha Nussbaum of Harvard duel over interpretations of Plato and whether a secular basis for the condemnation of homosexuality exists in Western culture. Far from the seminar rooms where such debates typically take place, this argument was played out in a Colorado courtroom as a court heard arguments related to a state constitutional amendment forbidding laws that would protect gay, lesbian, and bisexual people from discrimination.[1]

- Four psychologists, two sociologists, a psychiatrist, and a pediatrician argue whether male-female married couples provide the best environment in which to raise children. This debate took place as cross-examination in the courtroom of Judge Kevin Chang in Hawaii, as he considered whether Hawaii's refusal to allow same-sex couples to marry violated the state's ban on sex discrimination. Judge Chang ultimately ruled that the state "has not proved that allowing same-sex marriage will probably result in significant differences in the development or outcomes of children raised by gay or lesbian parents and same-sex couples, as compared to children raised by different-sex couples or their biological parents."[2]

- The Family Research Council (FRC), an anti-gay lobbying and research group, distributes analyses to members of Congress condemning the Employment Nondiscrimination Act, a bill that would outlaw employment discrimination based on sexual orientation. The FRC's analysts argue, "Homosexuals are among the most advantaged people in our country."[3] Other publications, such as those I have written for the Institute for Gay and Lesbian Strategic Studies (an organization that I direct), present a very different picture of the workplace status of gay people—a picture of vulnerability and disadvantage rather than privilege.[4]

While these events are relatively recent, the debate over what constitutes knowledge about gay, lesbian, and bisexual (and sometimes transgendered and transsexual) people is not. LGBT political movements have been engaged in a war of facts, figures, and ideas for over a century. Activists have had to contradict many assertions of "facts" about gay people and their role in society: gay people are mentally ill; sexual orientation can be changed through psychiatric treatment (or prayer); gay people are more likely to molest children; gay men and lesbians die at much younger ages than do heterosexuals; the tolerance of homosexuality always leads to the downfall of civilizations. One or more of these claims are still hauled out in almost any public debate about an issue related to gay people, despite the best efforts of activists to counteract or deflect such claims. These examples show how the politics of knowledge takes on concrete meaning in the lives and struggles of LGBT people, and the institutions that create and disseminate knowledge assume important roles in the political process. This paper examines the role of one particular kind of institution—the think tank—with a focus on the possible contributions to political outcomes from several emerging gay-oriented think tanks. In this institutional context, the particular form of knowledge that is both created and contested is expert knowledge.

Beginning in the late nineteenth century, gay intellectuals and their allies organized scholarly societies to fight back against the mountain of misinformation blocking political and social progress for LGBT people. These early efforts to increase the engagement among academic researchers, policymakers, and the general public appear, in retrospect, to have been largely ineffective in directly changing the legal status of LGBT people, as the next section of this paper will show.

Recent developments suggest that more fruitful engagement might now be possible. First, a growing awareness has emerged within the rapidly expanding LGBT political movement of the enormous potential for involving academic researchers in attacking those old canards. Second, within the academy, interest in studying the lives of LGBT people and in theorizing about sexuality has blossomed into several academic programs or departments, research funds, lecture series, book series, and research centers. While these two separate developments seem destined to come together—the rapid development of a new cohort of experts alongside a new political role for expert knowledge about LGBT people—tensions and difficulties between academics and activists have become apparent. Those tensions have inspired a new set of institutions that also arise out of a third historical development—the rise of think tanks, "the private, nonprofit research groups that operate on the margins of this nation's formal political processes . . . [and are] situated between academic social science and higher education, on the one hand, and government and partisan politics, on the other hand."[5]

Think tanks, of course, are a common feature of the broader political landscape, particularly in Washington, D.C. A brief discussion and historical overview of such institutions in the third section reveals that they may provide useful institutional models and strategies for bridging the academic-public divide on gay issues. Although they are conceived of as producers of research, often by highly credentialed researchers, think tanks produce research quite different from typical university-based research. From the conceptualization of research questions, to an interdisciplinary outlook, and especially to the packaging and dissemination of findings, policy research in think tanks constitutes a very different enterprise from its academic cousins, even when the policy researchers and academic researchers use similar research methods and data. Think-tank research is intended to answer more directly the questions that arise in the daily debate of policy proposals and in the discussion and development of future policy options.

The climate of increasing ideological involvement by think tanks creates a political space for institutions conducting research on politically charged topics. But the tension between ideological commitment and institutional credibility that think tanks must face also means that the emerging LGBT think tanks need to develop alternative strategies for maintaining credibility and developing influence. As the final section of the paper will show, these tensions might push LGBT think tanks toward a more hybrid model.

The Forerunners of LGBT Think Tanks

R. Kent Weaver has noted that think tanks have a greater presence and influence in the United States than in most other countries,[6] but today's new LGBT think tanks can trace their ancestry to several European efforts. Often out of their own concern with social policy issues, European intellectuals organized research societies and institutes that studied various issues related to sexuality, including homosexuality.

In the late nineteenth century, the medical profession and the early sexologists busied themselves with classifying various forms of nonprocreative sexual behavior.[7] This effort was at least partly motivated by the needs of public policy, since criminal codes against such behavior required professionals to identify miscreants and to decide if they should be held responsible for their acts. Out of this effort came the medical model of homosexuality, which classified homosexuality as a disease, a departure from the prior approach of defining certain sexual acts as immoral. Scholarly resistance to the disease model came from several sources.

In Germany, gay activist and scholar Magnus Hirschfeld was active in the late nineteenth century in the Scientific-Humanitarian Committee's efforts to abolish Paragraph 175, which criminalized homosexual activity between men.[8] Hirschfeld brought various forms of scientific evidence to bear on the issue, concluding that "Paragraph 175 is contrary to progressive scientific knowledge."[9] In 1919, he founded the Institute for Sexual Science (ISS), which had a number of concerns in addition to homosexuality. The institute offered psychiatric, marital, and career counseling, treated sexually transmitted diseases, and distributed information on family planning and sex education programs. The building included a library and sex museum.

Hirschfeld's slogan, *Per Scientiam ad Justitiam* ("Through Knowledge to Justice"), suggests his own sense of the relationship of knowledge and research to gay political movements. Both Hirschfeld and the institute were active in policy issues. In addition to activism against Paragraph 175, Hirschfeld also served as an expert witness in court cases, and the center's legal department advised and represented men accused of sex crimes. Hirschfeld could even grant them asylum at the institute until their cases were heard in court. Christopher Isherwood, who rented a room from Hirschfeld's sister next to the institute, noted that the ISS was important for Hirschfeld's education efforts with the police, lawmakers, and the public because the institute "was a visible guarantee of his scientific respectability which reassured the timid and the conservative."[10] Hirschfeld's respectability was also the key to getting the leading psychopathologist of the day, Richard Von Krafft-Ebing, to temper his position on homosexuality in revised editions of his influential *Psychopathia Sexualis*.

But the rise of the Nazis led to the institute's downfall in 1933, when Nazi students stormed and vandalized the center and burned books and other materials. Hirschfeld was out of the country but died a few years later.

In England, scholars such as Havelock Ellis (whose wife was a lesbian) and Edward Carpenter (who was homosexual) argued that homosexuality was in fact a harmless variation of human sexuality and not a disease at all, although perhaps a congenital anomaly. Inspired by Hirschfeld's example, Ellis, Carpenter, and others formed the British Society for the Study of Sex Psychology in 1914. The society's clearest purpose was to promote scientific inquiry into sexuality, quite broadly defined.[11] Recognizing that the creation of better knowledge alone would not lead to the social change envisioned by the founders, their further goal was to

organise understanding in the lay mind on a larger scale, to make people more receptive to scientific proof, and more conscious of their social responsibility; so that, at the back of the experts, when they pronounce judgment, will be a greater weight of public opinion—more available for organised expression—ready and willing to move others in the direction pointed by science.[12]

The society's educational work, mostly lectures and pamphlets, took on many issues, including women's suffrage and birth control, and public education on homosexuality was a major theme. Jeffrey Weeks concludes that the society had little influence on government policy, contributing to the education of a "relatively small layer of people."[13]

The United States first saw a gay-positive research organization at Indiana University when Alfred Kinsey incorporated the Institute for Sex Research in 1947.[14] Kinsey was a zoologist and expert on the gall wasp. When he was assigned to teach a course on marriage in 1938, he responded to an absence of nonclinical information about sexuality by taking histories of his students. This effort led to the famous Kinsey studies of men's and women's sexuality, which are still cited as a source of information about variation in human sexual practices. It is also, of course, the misquoted source for the famous—and famously flawed—claim that 10 percent of Americans are gay.[15]

Kinsey, whose policy-related activities involved advising legislators, law enforcement officials, judges, and education officials, certainly saw his work as important for public education about homosexuality as a step toward legal reform. John D'Emilio's discussion of the Kinsey reports suggests that Kinsey's research had several implications for public policy related to homosexuality, both good and bad.[16] On the one hand, the high frequency of homosexual behavior suggested that punishment was socially destructive. And within the gay and lesbian communities, Kinsey's studies helped to overcome a sense of isolation and provided "ideological ammunition" in political fights. On the other hand, according to D'Emilio, such large numbers fueled public hysteria about the dangers of homosexuals in, for instance, public employment.[17]

The institute received funding in its early years from the Rockefeller Foundation, but the support was cut off in 1954 in the midst of religious and political controversy about the center's findings.[18] The National Institute for Mental Health provided support after the Rockefeller money was cut off. Other financial support for the institute's work came from speaking fees, royalties from publications, and the university. The organization exists today as the Kinsey Institute for Sex, Gender, and Reproduction.[19] The Kinsey Institute's mission has expanded beyond Kinsey's original focus on research to include clinics for men's sexual health and women's menstrual problems, information services for lawyers and others, and collections of books and pictures that are open to scholars.

All three gay think-tank forerunners shared an interest in broad concerns related to sexuality, a tolerant understanding of homosexuality, and a desire to link their scientific understanding to social policy. But facing overwhelming opposition from unsympathetic governments and with inadequate backing from small nascent gay political movements, none of them appear to have had much direct influence on the legal and social position of LGBT people.

In 1956 a new kind of organization emerged, as the ONE Institute of Homophile Studies was founded to address scholarly concerns specific to lesbians and gay men. ONE Institute was an adjunct of ONE Inc., a Los Angeles–based homophile organization founded in 1952. (The term "homophile" was used as a more positive term than the more clinical "homosexual" to express love for someone of the same sex.) The institute's mission was premised on homophiles' need to learn more about themselves and other homophiles in the world. The founders asked key questions about the politics of knowledge: "Why are clearly documented records concerning homophile behavior throughout history and world societies not given due notice? Can scholarship which ignores the lives and the presence of millions of men and women claim legitimacy?"[20] To address these inadequacies in conventional educational institutions, ONE Institute offered community-college-level classes in a variety of disciplines, including biology, history, psychology, sociology, law, religion, literature, and philosophy, and ONE was authorized to give M.A.'s and Ph.D.'s in homophile studies. Funding came primarily from student tuition, benefits, individual donations, and occasional foundation grants.[21] (And as will be discussed in a later section, ONE Institute continues to operate in a rather different form.)

The efforts of ONE Institute did not generally include direct research on policy issues, other than discussions of policy issues in courses and public lectures. Two exceptions to the institutional focus on more academic matters are worth noting. The agenda for ONE's 1961 Midwinter Institute was the development of a homosexual bill of rights. Discussions at the meeting were contentious, however, and led to the fragmentation of the group and the departure of lesbians from ONE.[22] A second more auspicious exception was the development in 1957 of a grant proposal (which was never funded) to study the civil rights status of homosexuals.[23] This proposal laid out an ambitious and sophisticated study concerned with violations of civil liberties and the existence of sex laws. The project included a study of the definitions of and distinctions between acts and the class of individuals known as homosexuals. The authors also proposed a statistical analysis of demographic and social characteristics of homosexuals and of their legal treatment. In the tradition of ONE Institute's course offerings, the proposal argued for an analysis of how various disciplines, including religion, politics, sociology, psychology, biology, and anthropology, were thought to support American sex laws.

ONE Institute also provided a forum for the discussion of the role and relevance of research in the lives and political efforts of lesbians and gay men. Some gay activists mistrusted psychologists, in particular, for their efforts to treat homosexuality with brutal methods, such as shock treatment. Others believed that research was not a particularly pressing concern for a gay movement that required more militance rather than endless discussions rooted in "the comfortingly detached respectability of research."[24] Early gay activist Frank Kameny argued that, in general, even supportive research was "not of the vital importance which could properly lead many of our homophile groups to characterize themselves as research organizations . . . or to divert into research resources better expended elsewhere."[25] An example of ONE Institute's role in this debate concerns its association with Dr. Evelyn Hooker. Her research compared the psychological adjustment of nonclinical samples of gay men to heterosexual men and provided evidence against the prevailing view that homosexuals were mentally ill, findings that were influential in the American Psychiatric Association's decision to remove homosexuality from the list of mental disorders in 1973.[26] Hooker attended conferences at ONE, and at a very early stage of her research she spoke at ONE and answered many questions about her research and her intentions, helping to overcome at least some of the suspicions of the gay people in her audience about psychology and research.[27]

ONE Institute was a departure from the general public education model used by the earlier sexuality research organizations and is, therefore, a more direct precursor to the modern LGBT think tanks. ONE made education a priority within the lesbian and gay communities and encouraged the reinterpretation of many disciplines. And although new research was not a primary purpose of the organization, ONE Institute leaders recognized that academic research was connected with public attitudes toward homosexuals and homosexuality and supported the kind of modern empirical research—such as testing hypotheses and using an appropriate sample—found in Hooker's work, for instance. In these ways, ONE reflected a new kind of organization.

The Existence and Evolution of Think Tanks

Scholars of think tanks would recognize some similarities between the Institute for Sexual Science, Kinsey's Institute for Sex Research, and even ONE Institute and the various non-gay contemporary research institutions found in the history of think tanks. Understanding the rise of recent LGBT think tanks, which are quite different from their ancestors, requires an understanding of the development of think tanks within the larger context of the politics of knowledge. The evolution of the think tank in U.S. political culture created the conditions for a new kind of gay-related think tank to emerge.

James Smith outlines several stages in the historical development of think tanks in the United States.[28] Early research organizations making up Smith's first generation of think tanks, such as the Russell Sage Foundation and what is now the Brookings Institution, arose out of Progressive Era reforms and the scientific management movement. In the late nineteenth century, medical metaphors of cure and diagnosis predominated, guiding research organizations that sought not just to alleviate symptoms but to seek out root causes as a means to solve social ills. In the early twentieth century, efficiency of government and business operations became a popular metaphor guiding researchers. For instance, Brookings researchers developed accounting, evaluation, and cost-benefit tools to use in making budgetary decisions. An emphasis on rationality and efficiency pulled policy research more firmly into the realm of trained social scientists.

Smith's second generation of think tanks dates from after World War II through the 1970s. After the Great Depression shook public confidence in social science, the war restored some faith in social scientific progress. Smith characterizes this era as one of "broad agreement on the ends of policy," particularly agreement over the need to sustain employment and fight communism. The role of experts was primarily to analyze and recommend the best means to those ends, using social science skills and analytical methods to study public policy. New think tanks emerged as the result of contract-research arrangements with the federal government, with the most notable organizations being the RAND Corporation for defense-related research and the Urban Institute for social policy research related to War on Poverty programs.

Smith identifies a third stage of think tank development arising from increasing ideological and intellectual conflict among "experts." With this stage, Smith notes the rise of a new "metaphor of the market and its corollaries of promotion, advocacy, and intellectual combat" that guided new or redesigned think tanks.[29] New conservative think tanks had roots in the failure of Barry Goldwater's 1964 campaign for U.S. president, a failure that convinced conservatives of the need for building their own intellectual institutions to support broader political efforts. In this era, extensive funding from wealthy conservative donors and many smaller donations facilitated the rise of conservative think tanks. One recent study documents the ongoing support for conservative think tanks from twelve of the largest conservative foundations, finding that from 1992 to 1994 those foundations gave $79 million to think tanks and advocacy groups.[30]

Several rather different conservative institutions have emerged in this third generation. The American Enterprise Institute has been operating since 1943, but was revitalized in the 1960s and 1970s by "policy entrepreneur" William J. Baroody, who emphasized academic respectability while recognizing the importance of marketing research findings. The Heritage Foundation, which was organized by former congressional staffers in 1973 with money from Joseph Coors, is more of an advocacy organization than research factory. The

Family Research Council, an organization founded in 1983 by former Ronald Reagan appointee and Republican presidential candidate Gary Bauer, was part of Focus on the Family from 1988 to 1992. The Family Research Council publishes regular anti-gay position papers and analyses of pro-gay policy proposals and is now defined as a nonprofit educational institution by the IRS.[31]

The marketing efforts by right-wing think tanks characterize those institutions as much as their ideas do, according to Smith and Sally Covington. Researchers spin research and analysis into multiple formats—briefing papers, handbooks for Congress, books, policy reports, and op-ed pieces—with the help of extensive public relations departments. In addition to distributing research products to policymakers, think tanks extend their influence to the court of public opinion through their media contacts, with appearances on radio, television, the Internet, magazines, and newspapers.

The battle over facts, figures, and ideas has also spawned left-of-center think tanks, but the leaders in the institutional battle over knowledge in the policy-setting context are clearly the conservative organizations. Think tanks on the left end of the spectrum, such as the Institute for Policy Studies or the Economic Policy Institute, are much smaller and garner less foundation support. Covington compares the budgets of eight multi-issue, left-of-center, domestically oriented research organizations, which totaled $18.6 million in 1995, to budgets of the top five right-wing think tanks, which exceeded $77 million.[32] Covington and others lay at least some of the blame for the market power over ideas currently wielded by the conservative organizations on the funding strategies of more mainstream foundations, which did little to create strong research institutions to counterbalance the conservative organizations or to connect more moderate or liberal research institutions with grassroots and more formal political organizations.

Although scholarship related to think tanks has tried to classify and distinguish between different kinds of think tanks, other scholars have argued that think tanks across the ideological spectrum face similar issues in their quest for attention and influence, whether in Washington or beyond the beltway. Political scientist Andrew Rich argues that all think tanks share a striving for credibility of conclusions and recommendations, access to decision makers, public visibility, and organizational independence. Credibility is the most important characteristic possessed by think tanks, distinguishing their work from, for instance, reports issued by advocacy organizations. Credibility buys think tanks the "benefit of the doubt" when promoting potentially questionable research findings. Achieving credibility is related to independence, as "journalists and policy makers consistently cite the unpredictability of think tank findings as a distinctive sign of their credibility and independence—from government and specific interests—in the policy-making process."[33] And yet, Rich points out, seeking out visibility and access can work to undermine credibility by highlighting the need for think-tank findings to have both promotional and ideological value, characteristics not always compatible with social scientific standards for credibility.

Heightened competition for funding and the contradictions inherent within think tanks' quest for success in an ideologically combative political environment suggest that think tanks may not always have the institutional clout that they now appear to wield in the battles over knowledge. But they have been useful institutions for the conservative creation and re-creation of self-serving "facts" about LGBT people, particularly in the 1990s, judging from the voluminous reports on gay-related topics from the FRC and the smaller output from the Heritage Foundation. More important, though, this latest stage in the history of think-tank development, placed in the context of the larger LGBT political movements, has created room for new institutions to emerge to meet older needs for research to counteract stereotypes as well as to provide newer opportunities for more proactive research.

The Rise of New LGBT-Related Research Organizations

New organizations in various forms have emerged in Europe to carry on the research efforts begun by Hirschfeld and his contemporaries. Many of these research organizations consist largely of archives and research libraries for scholars, such as Homodok in the Netherlands or the Archive for Sexuality and Schwules Museum in Berlin. In other countries, such as the United Kingdom, political advocacy organizations such as Stonewall have taken on research responsibilities. Stonewall has conducted national surveys on discrimination and anti-gay violence and distributes a series of fact sheets summarizing research on its topics of interest.[34]

The think tank–oriented political culture of the United States has produced three different kinds of research-related efforts in the 1990s, all of which share an interest in developing and disseminating research about the lives and needs of LGBT people, and all of which lay some claim to the role of "think tank." The Center for Lesbian and Gay Studies (CLAGS) and the modern version of ONE Institute have clearer ties to past efforts to connect academics with the larger world, as both are based in universities and concerned primarily with promoting more traditional academic programs and publications. Recently, another kind of research group has popped up as national political organizations have organized research or education departments. In the third kind, two other organizations—the Institute for Gay and Lesbian Strategic Studies (IGLSS) and the Policy Institute of the National Gay and Lesbian Task Force (NGLTF)—have developed that better fit the definition of think tanks used by students of think tanks.

Two organizations specializing in research related to LGBT people have explicit ties to universities. In 1994, ONE Institute merged with the International Gay and Lesbian Archives and found a home at the University of Southern California. Using the world's largest library and archival collection devoted to lesbian and gay studies as a base, ONE Institute is becoming an international research center. ONE's Center for Advanced Studies, under the leadership of anthropologist Walter L. Williams, has offered grants to researchers from Russia, Brazil, Canada, Australia, and other nations, as well as to graduate students at USC. Researchers have focused on a variety of topics, including the legal status of same-sex relationships, workplace discrimination, and strategies to reduce heterosexism, as well as more theoretical work on gender transitivity and the heteronormativity of political philosophy.[35]

On the other side of the country, CLAGS, at the Graduate School of the City University of New York, also continues the tradition of gay-focused and gay-founded research organizations. Founded in 1991 by a group of lesbian and gay scholars led by historian Martin Duberman, CLAGS has become an important meeting place for the growing number of academics engaged in lesbian and gay studies. CLAGS has held a number of public conferences and colloquia covering a wide range of academic disciplines in the humanities and social sciences, with titles such as "Identity/Space/Power: Lesbian, Gay, Bisexual and Transgender Politics," "Lesbian and Gay History: Defining a Field," "Homosexuality and Hollywood," "Homo Economics: Market and Community in Lesbian and Gay Life," and "Black Nations/Queer Nations: Lesbian and Gay Sexualities in the African Diaspora." CLAGS also provides over $85,000 per year in financial support to scholars.[36] While CLAGS seeks to bring activists and academics together in order to make scholarship available to the larger community, the content of programs and publications tends toward the scholarly end of the spectrum without the kind of direct outreach to the public on specific, timely topics that characterizes policy think tanks.

The second kind of LGBT-related research effort takes place within advocacy organizations. At least two large U.S. national organizations, the Human Rights Campaign (HRC) and the Gay and Lesbian Alliance Against Defamation (GLAAD) have recently established research or education departments. HRC's primary research activity has involved commissioning public opinion polls, which are then used to develop the organization's strategies, and the education department has coordinated some efforts to collect and disseminate information relevant to HRC projects.[37] GLAAD has recently developed an interest in research and analysis related to cultural and media issues, but this interest has not yet (as of this writing) produced academic-related research.

The third kind of research organization, that defined by IGLSS and the NGLTF Policy Institute, fits the definition of think tank offered by Smith more directly: "the private, nonprofit research groups that operate on the margins of this nation's formal political processes. [They are] situated between academic social science and higher education, on the one hand, and

government and partisan politics, on the other hand."[38] These two organizations represent the clearest attempts to engage in the battle over the politics
of knowledge on the same institutional and strategic terrain as the right-wing
think tanks.

IGLSS was founded in Washington, D.C., in 1993 by a group of activists
and academics, including military and AIDS activists Greg Scott, J. B. Collier,
Gill Sperlein, and Ann Northrop. IGLSS is the only new research organization that is independent of both political organizations and universities. With
a research office in Amherst, Massachusetts, the IGLSS mission is to conduct
research, analysis, and education efforts on policy issues important to LGBT
people. IGLSS research products have included short fact sheets, briefing
papers (the *Angles* series), technical reports, a website (www.iglss.org), and
longer reports on research projects, and those products have been distributed
widely to policymakers, the news media, and activists. Past and ongoing
research and analysis projects cover several timely topics, such as employment discrimination, earnings of gay people, the economics of marriage, conversion therapies, education issues for LGBT youth, domestic partner benefits, and giving and volunteering in the LGBT communities. Like their
counterparts in (much larger) right-wing think tanks, IGLSS-affiliated researchers give briefings and workshops, testify before legislative committees,
and are quoted widely in the press.

In 1995 the NGLTF in the United States created a think tank within it—
the Policy Institute. Under the leadership of historian John D'Emilio and
later of activist Urvashi Vaid, the Policy Institute has undertaken a variety of
activities to promote thinking and research about LGBT issues. The Policy
Institute has held several series of roundtable sessions to bring together activists and scholars, LGBT leaders of communities of faith, and leaders of different
LGBT political organizations. Published research reports have documented
state legislative issues and policies, have analyzed the ex-gay movement, attitudes toward LGBT people, and GLB voting patterns, and have debunked the
myth of gay affluence (a joint Policy Institute–IGLSS publication). A recent
expansion of the Policy Institute includes a Leadership Training Institute, in
which Dave Fleischer will help prepare state and local LGBT organizations to
defeat anti-gay electoral and legislative efforts.

The diversity of efforts to institutionalize research on LGBT-related issues
suggests that the political importance of contests over knowledge is now
increasingly apparent to organizations and activists. The growing demand for
gay-centered knowledge and the growing supply of professional researchers
interested in gay-related topics have created the necessary conditions for an
explosion of research effort and influence on the public's understanding of
LGBT life. The institutions mediating the research effort matter, as the history of think tanks tells us, so the growth and character of these LGBT
institutions will also help shape the struggle over knowledge.

Challenges and Opportunities for LGBT Think Tanks and Related Research Efforts

The ability of these new entities and research efforts to influence the politics of knowledge around LGBT issues will depend on their ability to meet several challenges and to create new opportunities. As Andrew Rich points out, the big challenges for modern think tanks in their efforts to influence the course of public policy are related to credibility, access, visibility, and independence.

The most essential element for long-term influence in political struggles over knowledge is surely credibility. Unless the claims of accuracy are accepted by the public or by policymakers, research findings produced or released by any LGBT-related research organization have little value, even if everyone knows about them. As Rich's analysis suggests, advocacy organizations such as HRC or GLAAD (and perhaps NGLTF) are likely to have the hardest time establishing credibility, since they are suspected of having a vested interest in having particular conclusions drawn from research. Organizations independent of advocacy groups should have some advantage in this regard, although any effort undertaken by (or perceived to be undertaken by) an LGBT person or by an organization with gay, lesbian, bisexual, or transgender in its name is likely to be suspect.

Developing and implementing strategies for credibility, then, will be essential for the university-based organizations and for think tanks like IGLSS or the Policy Institute. One strategy suggested by Rich's research into think tanks is that organizations be "unpredictable" in their findings. In other words, if research findings appear to fit into gay organizations' political strategies too neatly, the findings will be suspect. What this might mean for LGBT-related research is unclear, but confirming right-wing claims about gay people should not be necessary to be "unpredictable" and credible. More likely unpredictability in this context would mean going against conventional LGBT political wisdom, which appears to exist on issues such as public opinion or domestic partner benefits, for instance, or going against the perceived interests of particular gay organizations. That sort of unpredictability will help to establish the independence of researchers from political agendas in the eyes of journalists and policymakers.

Another perspective on the need to avoid clearly self-serving findings is that lack of agreement among LGBT people and organizations on political strategies and goals means that the "right answer" would not obviously exist for many research questions related to controversial goals and strategies. Furthermore, both LGBT and non-LGBT organizations have sophisticated public relations departments that can "spin" research findings to suit any political agenda, a situation that could either reduce concerns about biased research or could increase cynicism and doubt about *all* policy-related research.

One credibility-enhancing move by IGLSS and the Policy Institute, as well as by the university-based organizations, has been to publish and support research by scholars with standard academic credentials, mostly university professors with doctorates. HRC contracts with independent pollsters to add to the credibility of their polling data.

A further alternative strategy being pursued by IGLSS starts with the observation that conservative think tank publications do not adhere to usual scholarly standards, particularly with regard to documentation of sources and submission of studies to peer-reviewed journals. Reading the footnotes of a FRC report shows that their sources are telephone conversations or their so-called experts' own publications in obscure presses, or even unpublished legal briefs or affidavits.[39] IGLSS researchers draw on research published in peer-reviewed journals and submit their own original research to the scrutiny of peers. While this bucks the trend among think tanks, which have moved away from promoting more scholarly products and projects, the intense scrutiny that LGBT-related products will likely face argues for a more rigorously academic approach.[40]

Achieving access and visibility to further the influence of research might depend on giving up some independence, since grassroots and lobbying organizations have better activist distribution networks and access to policymakers than do most researchers. Building distribution networks and publicity networks that are separate from advocacy organizations is one possible route for LGBT research organizations, which is the path taken by non-LGBT think tanks.

Another serious institutional challenge faced by research organizations, related to visibility, is in obtaining funding for the support of research and for institution-building. The proliferation of research efforts could have two different effects. If organizations compete for funding from a relatively limited pool of donors and foundations, the ensuing competition could leave funding too scattered to support strong, lasting, and effective institutions. If more organizations encourage new funding sources to support research, on the other hand, then the size of the pie could grow substantially, increasing each organization's funding slice even as more slices of it are being taken. To date, the kind of massive funding commitment made by wealthy conservative donors and foundations in creating today's set of right-wing think tanks has not occurred for LGBT organizations.

Given the resources necessary to create and maintain these new organizations, one might well ask whether support for those institutions and their research truly matters. As mentioned earlier, Frank Kameny's argument three decades ago was that research was not as important as political organizing and a more militant presence. And since research on LGBT-related topics has increased independently of research organizations, what value do think tanks add? This challenge to LGBT research organizations is a challenge to their very existence.

Since Kameny's writing, a larger, more demanding, and more successful political movement has emerged within the LGBT communities, and many different kinds of nonprofit organizations have emerged to meet varying needs. The larger political and institutional context has changed as well, with the rise in importance of think tanks in the political process. Those institutions provide a model for LGBT think tanks and other organizations to focus resources on questions of immediate importance, to bridge the gap between academics' long time lines and activists' pressing needs, to provide accessible publications free of academic jargon, and to market products widely. In other words, think tanks can do things that neither universities nor political organizations do particularly well in the battle over knowledge. And to the extent that conservative think tanks contributed to the rise of conservative policymaking in the 1990s, LGBT-related think tanks could contribute to the further success of the LGBT movement.

Research organizations can play other strategic roles within the LGBT movements as well. Smith identified two important roles for think tanks, first as brokers of ideas and as settings for consideration of ideas, and second as a place to build consensus among political leaders. Related to the first role, think tanks could become sites of more democratic public education and debate outside the academy, promoting panels, workshops, and writings on ideas relevant to LGBT life and politics. CLAGS, ONE Institute, the Policy Institute, and IGLSS have all made efforts to this end. NGLTF's Policy Institute roundtables have served the second purpose well, bringing together religious leaders and political leaders to discuss common interests and to coordinate actions.

Well-publicized, credible research provided by think tanks and other organizations can also help define the middle ground in debates.[41] Even if this research serves mainly to neutralize or cast doubt on alleged "findings" offered by conservative researchers, it helps to cut out the secular support for extremely anti-gay positions that is rooted in claims of unhealthy behavior by LGBT people.

Think tanks also provide another institutional level on which the LGBT political movement can form alliances and build bridges to other groups and issues. Other progressive and liberal think tanks in the United States, such as the Institute for Women's Policy Research (IWPR), the Economic Policy Institute, or the Joint Center for Political and Economic Studies (traditionally focused on African-American policy issues), might work on social and economic policy issues also of interest to LGBT people, but rarely (if ever) do those think tanks add a sexual orientation dimension to their research and analysis. But cross-cutting interests on research on civil rights policies should prompt a *combined* research effort by IWPR, the Joint Center, and IGLSS, for example, to address issues of concern to many groups. Similarly, the International Gay and Lesbian Human Rights Commission could collaborate with Amnesty International or Human Rights Watch to conduct research on LGBT people around the world. Many other issues, whether related to immigration, welfare reform, social security reform, foreign policy, or health-care policy, could also be taken up by groups of researchers with expertise on the LGBT perspective, joining with researchers with expertise on women, people of color, or low income populations, for instance.

Think tanks will not be the answer to every problem the LGBT political movements face, but research institutions can be powerful tools in the larger battle over knowledge. Without a political movement, think tanks might be unnecessary and would certainly be less effective. But it is equally likely that without a lot of thinking and research, the LGBT political movement would be far less effective and less likely to achieve its goals. That research matters and that credible research can support efforts to obtain LGBT equality is clear from examples such as the same-sex marriage case in Hawaii: the plaintiffs' experts convinced the judge that no evidence supported the state's claim that marriages by same-sex couples would undermine children's well-being. The impact of research in the larger realm of public opinion and in legislative action is more difficult to evaluate, but the media and some policymakers seek out information and appear to appreciate its importance.

The politics of knowledge and research is inextricably bound to the debate on LGBT political issues. The discredited and discreditable research that has supported the opposition to legal equality for LGBT people suggests that those interested in LGBT equality have little choice but to engage in debate over what counts as knowledge. The more recent involvement of scholars with prestigious credentials on both sides of gay issues suggests that future battles will be even more heated than past ones. In the United States, think tanks have been institutions mediating the relationship between researchers and their nonacademic audiences. The emergence of LGBT-related think tanks in the United States and other research-related organizations around the world suggest that future skirmishes over knowledge may be played out on a more even playing field, where increased resources devoted to research and the marketing of research by LGBT-based organizations lead to more and better research on LGBT people and their lives.

Notes

The author would like to thank Mark Blasius, Andrew Rich, Walter L. Williams, and participants at the CLAGS conference "Identity/Space/Power: Lesbian, Gay, Bisexual, and Transgender Politics" for helpful suggestions and comments.

1. John Finnis, "Is Homosexual Conduct Wrong? A Philosophical Exchange: Disintegrity," *The New Republic*, November 15, 1993, pp. 12–13; Martha Nussbaum, "Is Homosexual Conduct Wrong? A Philosophical Exchange: Integrity," *The New Republic*, November 15, 1993, p. 13.

2. *Baehr v. Miike*, First Circuit Court, State of Hawaii, 91–1394 (1996).

3. Robert H. Knight, Daniel S. Garcia, and Paul T. Mero, "'Gay Jobs Bill' Tyranny, Not 'Tolerance,'" *Insight* (Family Research Council, 1994).

4. See M. V. Lee Badgett, "Vulnerability in the Workplace: Evidence of Anti-Gay Discrimination," *Angles* 20, no.1 (September 1997): 1–4; and Badgett, "Income Inflation: The Myth of Affluence among Gay, Lesbian, and Bisexual Americans" (New York: Policy Institute of the National Gay and Lesbian Task Force and the Institute for Gay and Lesbian Strategic Studies, 1998).

5. James A. Smith, *The Idea Brokers: Think Tanks and the Rise of the New Policy Elite*, (New York: Free Press, 1991), xiii.

6. R. Kent Weaver, "The Changing World of Think Tanks," *PS: Political Science and Politics* 22, no. 3 (September 1989); 570.

7. Jeffrey Weeks, *Coming Out* (London: Quartet Books, 1977), 25–26.

8. Barry D. Adam, *The Rise of a Gay and Lesbian Movement* (New York: Twayne, 1995), 19–28.

9. See "Petition to the Reichstag," reproduced in *We Are Everywhere: A Historical Sourcebook of Gay and Lesbian Politics*, ed. Mark Blasius and Shane Phelan, (New York: Routledge, 1997), 136.

10. Christopher Isherwood, *Christopher and His Kind*, (New York: Avon Books, 1976), 18.

11. See "The British Society for the Study of Sex Psychology," in *We Are Everywhere: A Historical Sourcebook of Gay and Lesbian Politics*, ed. Mark Blasius and Shane Phelan (New York: Routledge, 1997), 181.

12. Ibid., 182.

13. Weeks, *Coming Out*, 137.

14. This section draws heavily on Wardell B. Pomeroy, *Dr. Kinsey and the Institute for Sex Research* (New Haven: Yale University Press, 1982).

15. See Edward O. Laumann, John H. Gagnon, Robert T. Michael, and Stuart Michaels, *The Social Organization of Sexuality* (Chicago: University of Chicago Press, 1994).

16. John D'Emilio, *Sexual Politics, Sexual Communities* (Chicago: University of Chicago Press, 1983), 37.

17. Also, see documents in Jonathan Katz, *Gay American History: Lesbians and Gay Men in the U.S.A.* (New York: Crowell, 1976), 139–55, for evidence of how the fear of large numbers of homosexuals drove anti-gay hysteria in government employment.

18. Pomeroy, *Dr. Kinsey*, 379.

19. Dick Kaukas, "Prurient Interests: Kinsey Institute's New Director Faces Daunting Problems," *The Courier-Journal*, November 19, 1995, p. 1H.

20. W. Dorr, Legg, ed., David G. Cameron, and Walter L. Williams, *Homophile Studies in Theory and Practice* (San Francisco: ONE Institute Press, 1994), 37.

21. Ibid., 331.

22. Ibid., 187; D'Emilio, *Sexual Politics*, 123.

23. See Legg, *Homophile Studies*, appendix 8.

24. Frank Kameny, "Does Research into Homosexuality Matter?" in *We Are Everywhere: A Historical Sourcebook of Gay and Lesbian Politics*, ed. Mark Blasius and Shane Phelan (New York: Routledge, 1997), 335–39.

25. Ibid., 339.

26. Ronald Bayer, *Homosexuality and American Psychiatry: The Politics of Diagnosis* (New York: Basic Books, 1981).

27. Legg, *Homophile Studies*, 157.

28. Smith, *The Idea Brokers*.

29. Ibid., 194.

30. Sally Covington, *Moving a Public Policy Agenda: The Strategic Philanthropy of Conservative Foundations* (Washington, DC: National Committee for Responsive Philanthropy, 1997).

31. Data on the American Enterprise Institute and the Heritage Foundation is from Smith, *The Idea Brokers*. The information on the Family Research Council is from its website: www.frc.org.

32. Covington, *Moving a Public Policy Agenda*, 37.

33. Andrew Rich, "The Origins and Proliferation of Contemporary American Think Tanks: From the Progressive Era to the Eve of the 21st Century," presented at 26th Annual Conference of the Association for Research on Nonprofit Organizations and Voluntary Action, 1997.

34. See the Stonewall website, http://www.stonewall.org.uk/general/.

35. Information from Prof. Walter L. Williams and http://www.usc.edu/isd/archives/oneigla/index.html.

36. Information on CLAGS from http://web.gc.cuny.edu/clags.

37. Andre Alexander, *Human Rights Campaign Annual Report*, 1997–98, published on http://www.hrc.org.

38. Smith, *The Idea Brokers*, xiii.

39. For instance, see Robert H. Knight, and Daniel S. Garcia, "Homosexual Adoption: Bad for Children, Bad for Society," *Insight* (Family Research Council, 1994). nn. 3–7, 11–14, 20–22.

40. I thank Andrew Rich for making this point.

41. Smith, *The Idea Brokers*, 213.

LIST OF CONTRIBUTORS AND AFFILIATIONS

Dennis Altman, La Trobe University, Melbourne, Australia

M. V. Lee Badgett, University of Massachusetts, Amherst, and Institute for Gay and Lesbian Strategic Studies

Robert Bailey, Rutgers University (Camden)

Mark Blasius, City University of New York, LaGuardia and Graduate School

Cathy J. Cohen, Yale University

Timothy E. Cook, Williams College

Paisley Currah, City University of New York, Brooklyn

Juanita Díaz-Cotto, State University of New York at Binghamton

Jan-Willem Duyvendak, Erasmus University, Rotterdam, and Verwey-Jonker Institute, Utrecht, The Netherlands

Leonard Harris, Purdue University

Bevin Hartnett, Smith College

Rosalind Pollack Petchesky, City University of New York, Hunter and Graduate School

David Rayside, University of Toronto

Rebecca Mae Salokar, Florida International University

Alan S. Yang, Columbia University

NOTES ON THE CONTRIBUTORS

DENNIS ALTMAN is Professor of Politics at La Trobe University, Melbourne, and author of nine books including *Homosexual: Oppression and Liberation* and *Power and Community: Organisational and Cultural Responses to AIDS*. He has had a long involvement in international AIDS work and is co-chair of the 2001 AIDS in Asia and the Pacific Conference, to be held in Melbourne. His next book, *Global Sex*, will be published by the University of Chicago Press in 2001.

M. V. LEE BADGETT is Assistant Professor of economics at the University of Massachusetts, Amherst, where she also teaches courses related to public policy. She is the research director of the Institute for Gay and Lesbian Strategic Studies, a national think tank. Her research focuses primarily on race, gender, and sexual orientation in labor markets, and on public policies that address discrimination. Her book on the economic lives of lesbians and gay men will be published by the University of Chicago Press in 2001. Her work has appeared in many academic journals, including *Industrial and Labor Relations Review, Feminist Economics, Industrial Relations, International Labour Review, Review of Black Political Economy*, and *Feminist Studies*, and as chapters in many books.

ROBERT W. BAILEY is Associate Professor, Graduate Faculty of Public Policy and Administration, Rutgers University, Campus at Camden, where he teaches public policy, urban politics, and management. In addition, he has held senior policy positions in New York City and State government. His most recent book is *Gay Politics, Urban Politics: Identity and Economics in the Urban Setting*. Bailey is currently working on a book-length manuscript on postmodern policy analysis.

MARK BLASIUS is Professor of Political Science at the City University of New York (Graduate School and LaGuardia), where he teaches political philosophy and the politics of sexuality, has served as Deputy Executive Officer of the Ph.D./M.A. Program in Political Science, and serves as a member of the Board of Directors of the Center for Lesbian and Gay Studies. He has worked on behalf of the Lesbian, Gay, and Bisexual Caucus for Political Science as its co-chair, and within the American Political Association as the first chairperson of its Committee on the Status of Lesbians and Gays in the Profession. His books include *Gay and Lesbian Politics: Sexuality and the Emergence of a New Ethic* and *We Are Everywhere: A Historical Sourcebook of Gay and Lesbian Politics* (co-editor with Shane Phelan). He is currently working on a monograph in political theory about the political economy of sexuality, sexuality and ethics, and their relation to social justice. He has also published in *Political Theory*, *The American Political Science Review*, *GLQ*, the *Journal of the History of Sexuality*, *Alternatives: A Journal of World Policy*, and has published or reprinted in other places.

CATHY J. COHEN is Professor of Political Science and African-American Studies at Yale University. She also serves as the co-director with Roger Smith of the Center for the Study of Race, Inequality and Politics at Yale. Cohen is the author of *The Boundaries of Blackness: AIDS and the Breakdown of Black Politics* and co-editor with Kathleen Jones and Joan Tronto of *Women Transforming Politics: An Alternative Reader*. She has published articles in numerous journals and selected edited volumes including the *American Political Science Review*, *GLQ*, and *NOMOS*. Her field of specialization is American politics, although her research interests include African-American politics, women and politics, lesbian and gay politics, social movements, and urban politics. Most recently, she was awarded a Robert Wood Johnson Health Policy Fellowship.

TIMOTHY E. COOK is the Fairleigh Dickinson, Jr., Professor of Political Science at Williams College, and Adjunct Professor of Public Policy at the Kennedy School of Government at Harvard University. He is the author of numerous articles and several books: *Making Laws and Making News: Media Strategies in the U.S. House of Representatives*; *Crosstalk: Citizens, Candidates, and Media in a Presidential Campaign*; and *Governing with the News: The News Media as a Political Institution*.

PAISLEY CURRAH is Associate Professor of Political Science at Brooklyn College of the City University of New York. She is the Director of the Women's Studies Program at Brooklyn College and a member of the Board of Directors of the Center for Lesbian and Gay Studies. Her recent work focuses on the inclusion of gender identity and gender expression in nondiscrimination laws and on related transgender policy issues. She is the co-author, with Shannon Minter, of *Transgender Equality: A Handbook for Activists and Policymakers*. Her book *Legislating Genders* is forthcoming with Temple University Press.

JUANITA DÍAZ-COTTO is Associate Professor of Sociology, Women's Studies, and Latin American and Caribbean Area Studies at the State University of New York at Binghamton. She is the editor (under the pseudonym of Juanita Ramos) of *Compañeras: Latina Lesbians (An Anthology)* and author of *Gender Ethnicity and the State: Latina and Latino Prison Politics*.

JAN-WILLEM DUYVENDAK is Professor of Community Organization at the Erasmus University of Rotterdam and director of the Verwey-Jonker Institute, a social research institute in Utrecht, The Netherlands. Duyvendak is author of

The Power of Politics: New Social Movements in France; *The Pillarization of the Gay Movement* (in Dutch); co-author with H. Kriesi, R. Koopmans, and M. Giugni of *New Social Movements in Western Europe*; and co-editor, with B. D. Adam and A. Krouwel, of *The Global Emergence of Gay and Lesbian Politics: National Imprints of a Worldwide Movement*. Duyvendak is a former assistant professor of gay studies at the University of Nijmegen, The Netherlands. His fields of specialization are social movements, urban politics, political history, political theory, and social policy.

LEONARD HARRIS is Professor of Philosophy at Purdue University and former Director of African American Studies at Purdue. He is the editor of *Racism*; *The Critical Pragmatism of Alain Locke*; *Children in Chaos: A Philosophy for Children Experience*; *The Philosophy of Alain Locke: Harlem Renaissance and Beyond*; and *Philosophy Born of Struggle: Anthology of Afro-American Philosophy from 1917*. He is the co-editor with A. Zegeye and J. Maxted of *Exploitation and Exclusion: Race and Class* as well as the editor of the *Newsletter on Philosophy and the Black Experience*. He promotes the Alain L. Locke Society and the Philosophy Born of Struggle Association. He has published in such journals as the *International Philosophical Quarterly, Presence Africaine*, and *Transactions of the Charles S. Peirce Society Journal*.

BEVIN HARTNETT received her M.S. in sports and exercise studies in 2000 from Smith College. She graduated from Williams College in 1998 with a B.A. in political science. Her work was made possible by an initiative by the Dean of the Faculty's Office at Williams for collaborative research between faculty and students.

ROSALIND POLLACK PETCHESKY is Professor of Political Science and Women's Studies at Hunter College of the City University of New York and founder and former international coordinator of the International Reproductive Rights Research Action Group (IRRRAG). She is the author of *Abortion and Woman's Choice: The State, Sexuality and Reproductive Freedom*, which won the American Historical Association's Joan Kelly Prize, and co-editor of *Negotiating Reproductive Rights: Women's Perspectives Across Countries and Cultures*. In 1995 Professor Petchesky was awarded a MacArthur Fellowship.

DAVID RAYSIDE is Professor of Political Science at the University of Toronto, and from 1993 to 1997 was Vice-Principal of University College at that University. He has an activist as well as an academic interest in sexual diversity issues, having written on such topics as antidiscrimination legislation in Ontario, public opinion and gay rights, homophobia in Britain, AIDS politics in Canada, and the U.S. military. His book *On the Fringe: Gays and Lesbians in Politics* examined the complexities of activist entry into mainstream politics in Britain, Canada, and the United States, and is still the subject of his comparative research.

REBECCA MAE SALOKAR is Associate Professor of Political Science at Florida International University in Miami. She is the author of *The Solicitor General: The Politics of Law* and co-editor of *Women in Law: A Bio-Bibliographical Sourcebook*. Her current research focuses on the variations in privacy rights imbedded in state constitutional law.

ALAN S. YANG recently completed his Ph.D. in the Department of Political Science at Columbia University and is currently a Lecturer at the School of International and Public Affairs, Columbia University. He has published in *Public Opinion Quarterly* and *Public Perspective*; his report "From Wrongs to Rights: Public Opinion on Gay and Lesbian Americans Moves toward Equality" was released by the Policy Institute of the National Gay and Lesbian Task Force. His current research interest is the role played by social activism in mass opinion change.